Graham Sutherland

Landscapes, War Scenes, Portraits 1924–1950

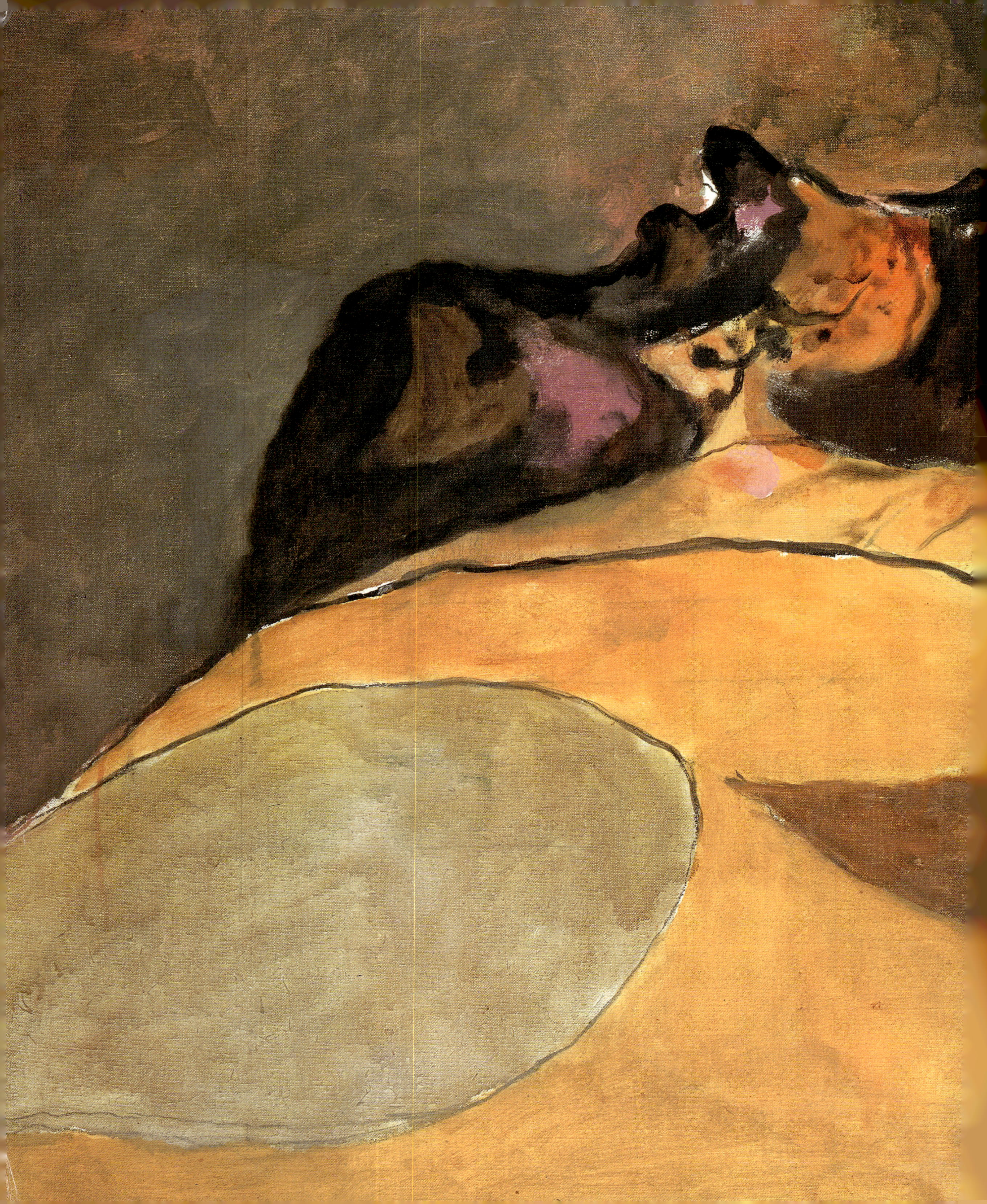

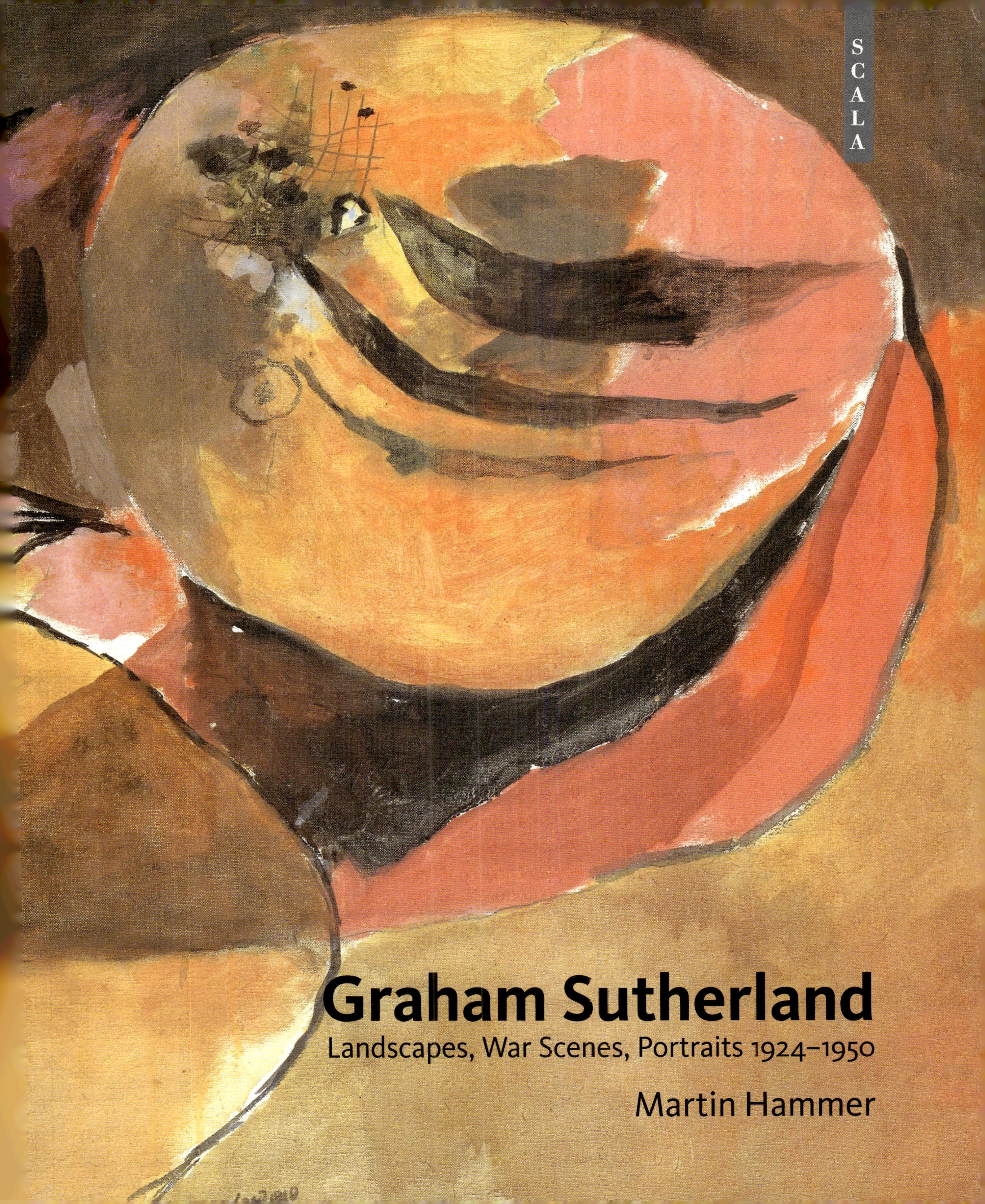

SCALA

Graham Sutherland

Landscapes, War Scenes, Portraits 1924–1950

Martin Hammer

For all copyright credit information relating to other artists featured in this catalogue please see the Picture Credits on page 176.

First published in 2005 by
Scala Publishers Ltd
Northburgh House
10 Northburgh Street
London EC1V 0AT
www.scalapublishers.com

ISBN 1 85759 404 5

British Library Cataloguing in Publication Data. A catalogue record for this book is available from the British Library.

Design: Nigel Soper
Project Editor: Oliver Craske
Copy Editor: Christine Davis
Production Director: Tim Clarke
Printed in Italy.
10 9 8 7 6 5 4 3 2 1

Published on the occasion of the exhibition 'Graham Sutherland: Landscapes, War Scenes, Portraits 1924–1950', organised by Dulwich Picture Gallery.

Exhibition itinerary:
Dulwich Picture Gallery, London
15 June – 25 September 2005

Djanogly Art Gallery, Nottingham
8 October – 11 December 2005

The exhibition at Dulwich Picture Gallery has been generously supported by:
Jonathan Clark Fine Art
Paul and Louise Cooke Endowment Ltd
Robinson Bequest
Stanley Scott Bequest
The Friends of Dulwich Picture Gallery

Pages 2–3: Graham Sutherland, *Mountain Road with Boulder* (Cat. 37, detail)

Contents

Foreword by Ian Dejardin 6

Introduction
A Precarious Tension of Opposites 8
Notes 45

Catalogue and Documentary Texts
1. Early Prints 1924–1932 46
A Trend in English Draughtsmanship by Graham Sutherland, 1936 48

2. Landscapes 1936–1942 62
An English Stone Landmark by Graham Sutherland, 1937 64
Welsh Sketch Book by Graham Sutherland, 1942 68
Graham Sutherland by Kenneth Clark, 1938 78

3. War Artist 1940–1944 100
Images Wrought From Destruction by Graham Sutherland, 1971 102

4. New Departures 1943–1950 140
Thoughts on Painting by Graham Sutherland, 1951 142
About My Thorn Pictures by Graham Sutherland, 1946 156
English Painting by Graham Sutherland, 1947 161
Graham Sutherland by Robert Melville, 1952 170

Index of Works 173
Further Reading 175
Credits 176

Foreword

Ian Dejardin
Director, Dulwich Picture Gallery

This exhibition is the third in a series held at Dulwich Picture Gallery revisiting and reassessing some of the 'titans' of twentieth-century British art. Following shows dedicated to John Piper and Henry Moore, it is fitting that we consider the art of Graham Sutherland, once every bit as famous as they, but now fallen slightly out of sight. He was born in 1903, a rich year for artists – both Piper and Barbara Hepworth were born in that year. One of that extraordinary generation dominated by Paul Nash, Ben Nicholson and Moore, he, like them, lived through two World Wars and grappled with the trauma and self-searching that these cataclysms provoked, while at the same time engaging with the electric current of new artistic ideas flowing from Europe. Like Piper, he found particular inspiration in nineteenth-century English Romanticism, reconnecting with the art of a hundred years before. In Sutherland's case, the galvanizing inspiration proved to be Samuel Palmer, in whose idiosyncratic vision he detected a kinship with that of Vincent van Gogh. But equally, no one of that period, and certainly not Sutherland, could remain unaffected by an awareness of the overwhelming presence of Picasso. Again like Piper, Sutherland wrote cogently about his own art, and this catalogue contains several fascinating pieces written by him.

Sutherland found early recognition, and rightly so – the landscapes, war paintings and early portraits on display here attest to his brilliance and individuality; but there is a general sense that his later career ultimately disappointed, as his early, spiky and uncompromising work gave way to something more formulaic. Like Dulwich's exhibitions dedicated to Piper ('John Piper in the 1930s: Abstraction on the Beach', 2003) and Moore ('Henry Moore', 2004), it is the early forging of a unique style, the reassessment of a hugely creative talent searching for a voice, that has provided the focus of this show.

We have been exceptionally fortunate in our Curator for this exhibition, Martin Hammer, who has selected the show, which promises to restore Sutherland's reputation. Martin is a Senior Lecturer in twentieth-century British and American art at Edinburgh University, with many publications to his credit, including a major study of the artistic relationship between Sutherland and Bacon that is also appearing this summer. He conceived the present catalogue, which features an illuminating introductory essay, a series of texts from the period by Sutherland and others, and illustrations of works that in several cases have not been reproduced in colour before and indeed some that may well have never been illustrated. It will prove an invaluable resource to students of this period of British art as well as those wishing to rediscover this vital modern British artist. In addition, Martin was closely involved with the hang of the exhibition and the design of the catalogue, and many thanks are due to him for his exceptional energy and enthusiasm.

At Dulwich, organization of the show fell predominantly to Eloise Stewart, Exhibitions Officer. She and the rest of the exhibitions team, led by the Head of Exhibitions, Victoria Norton, and including James

Hall and Mel Shaw, are to be congratulated for their hard work and customary professionalism. Elsewhere, Kate Knowles and Dida Tait have done sterling work in the fields of marketing and development. Our thanks are also due to Scala, publishers of the catalogue, and their project manager, Oliver Craske, for another enjoyable and successful collaboration; to Christine Davis, for her careful editing; and to Nigel Soper, for his excellent design.

We never forget that for every exciting loan to an exhibition such as this, there is a lender left with a blank space on their wall – our deepest thanks therefore go to all of those owners without whose selfless generosity the exhibition could not have been realised at all. Martin Hammer joins us in this, and would particularly like to thank James Kirkman, formerly the artist's friend and dealer; Robin Light of the Crane Kalman Gallery; and Angus Stewart, organizer of the centenary Olympia show, for their invaluable help in locating works in private collections. We must also thank James Rawlin, Head of Sotheby's Modern British Painting department for his assistance in valuations, and the executors of Sutherland's estate for their generous copyright permission. As always we must not forget to thank the Museums, Libraries and Archives Council (MLA) and HM Government for the cover granted through the Government Indemnity Scheme, in particular the expertise and support of Gregory Eades and Maxyne McDonald.

The other essential for any successful exhibition venture is of course sponsorship. We have benefited from a generous grant from the Stanley Scott Bequest, and another from the Robinson Bequest. Our sincere thanks go to those who administer these funds. I would also like to extend our warmest thanks to Jonathan Clark Fine Art, one of the leading dealers in twentieth-century British art, for most generously putting his money where his heart is in our support; and to Paul and Louise Cooke Endowment Ltd for a similar act of largesse. The Friends of Dulwich Picture Gallery, without whose support so many of the Gallery's achievements would be inconceivable, have again rallied round in the most generous manner.

Finally: this exhibition, like all the others held at Dulwich Picture Gallery over the past nine years, has been championed throughout with characteristic enthusiasm and determination by Desmond Shawe-Taylor the gallery's departing Director. I wish him all the best in his future career. He will be very much missed.

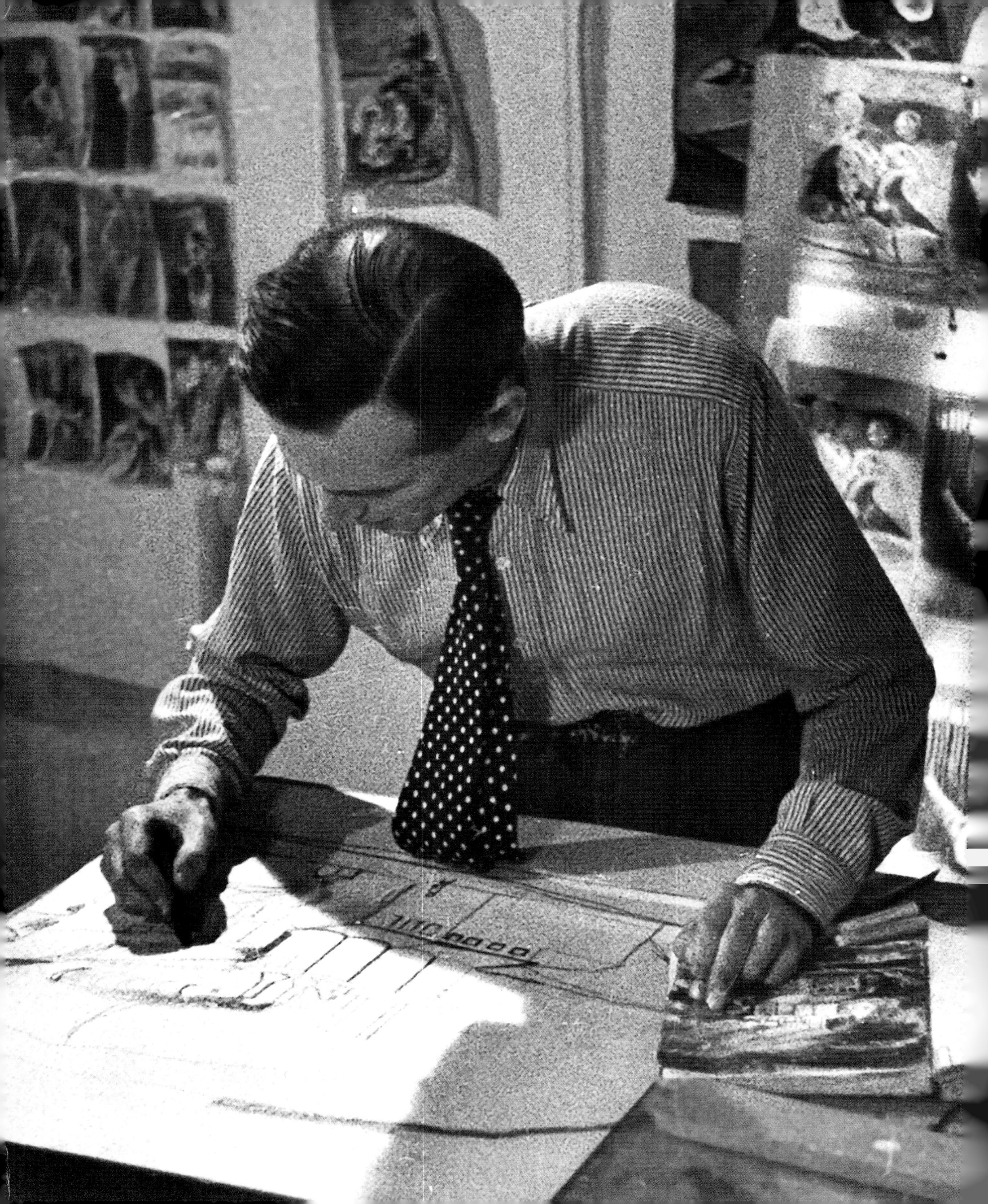

A Precarious Tension of Opposites

The year 2005 is an apposite moment to reconsider the art of Graham Sutherland (1903–1980). First of all, it marks the sixtieth anniversary of the end of the Second World War, and Sutherland's pictures of devastated buildings, and of the processing of raw materials for manufacturing armaments, have always seemed amongst the most compelling artistic products of that time. A desire to contribute to the process of commemoration and reflection, as the events themselves fade into history, underlies the strong representation of Sutherland's official war art in this exhibition.

In addition, it is now 25 years since Sutherland's death, and there is an old adage that such a period needs to elapse before the test of time can deliver its verdict. Thus far, it has to be said, Sutherland has not fared too well. After an exhaustive memorial exhibition at the Tate Gallery in 1982, he somewhat disappeared from view, and only those vehemently opposed to postmodernist tendencies (notably the critic Peter Fuller) were inclined to express much admiration for his work.[1] The centenary of Sutherland's birth in 2003 produced some modest displays but no great fanfare. More attention might have been expected given that, between the one-man show that launched his career as a painter in 1938 and the first retrospectives devoted to his art in the early 1950s, Sutherland was almost universally regarded as the most significant and influential contemporary British painter. Aside from its pictorial virtues, his work clearly struck a chord with the dark mood that prevailed during these years. Thereafter, Sutherland's career continued to prosper by all the conventional yardsticks, but a gradual slump in his critical reputation coincided not only with wider shifts in taste and outlook but also with a falling off in his own work. It is hard to dispute the general consensus that the later religious commissions, landscapes, prints, and portraits of the great and the good, tend all too often to look overblown and formulaic.

In order to make a case for the continuing interest of Sutherland, in artistic as well as historical terms, the selection of the current exhibition concentrates on the first half of his career, especially the decade from 1936 to 1946, and on the categories of imagery that, arguably, yielded his most effective and inventive achievements, namely the landscapes, war pictures and early portraiture. This deliberately partial account leaves out the explicitly religious pictures of the 1940s, and also Sutherland's extensive work as a designer. The catalogue allows us to take account of the artist's writings, which provide an articulate commentary on the conscious attitudes and motivations that informed his work. The illustrations that follow are interwoven with a sequence of texts by the artist himself, as well as a pair of early essays by Kenneth Clark and Robert Melville, who were at the forefront of the critical promotion of Sutherland's art.

Finally, both exhibition and catalogue incorporate a small selection of works by other artists, past and present. We shall see in due course why particular artists and images have been chosen, but the general point is that comparative juxtapositions may help us to situate Sutherland's work art-historically. They open

Fig. 1
William MacQuitty
(1905–2004)
c. 1944
Photograph from the set of
Out of Chaos
MacQuitty International
Photographic Collection.

up affinities and possible points of departure, but they also, of course, highlight differences and, by extension, those impulses that remained constant within Sutherland's art. The most cursory inspection of his work reveals variations on a repertoire of shapes and conjunctions of colour, and a tendency to rework and revise images, as in the versions of *Red Tree* (Cats 17–18), *Green Tree Form* (Cats 33–34) and *Entrance to a Lane* (see Cats 74–75). These are merely the most obvious symptoms of an underlying coherence to his production, which later on perhaps shades into limitation and repetition.

In this introduction my aim is to describe, however schematically, an artist's discovery, refinement and elaboration of his distinctive pictorial idiom. Analysis of any particular departure in Sutherland's work needs to navigate the interplay between direct observation, external inspiration and internal momentum. It is quite true that his pictures were always rooted in an initial observation of particular places, scenes or configurations in the natural world. These would be recorded at first hand in sketchbook studies that the artist would then use as a starting point for making adjustments and transformations, in a sequence of further sketches, and the entire procedure might eventually lead to a finished composition. 'Paraphrase' was Sutherland's own term for the process involved. But what conditioned his choices of motif, for example, and his decisions about the formal language that could best convey the meanings, associations and feelings that a particular subject encapsulated? I intend to explore how his creative processes were informed by a continuing responsiveness to the artistic resources that were available to him, including specific images or texts that he almost certainly knew. One resource that was always available was Sutherland's own previous work, and we need to consider how decisions in any given instance might also have been conditioned by concerns and conventions rooted in the existing fabric of his art.

Graham Sutherland (1903–1980) was born in south London into a respectable middle-class family. His father worked as a barrister, then a civil servant. Around 1910 the family moved to Sutton in Surrey. After attending Epsom College, Sutherland became an engineering apprentice at the Midland Railway Works at Derby (1920–21). His inclination to be an artist finally overcame parental resistance, and he studied at Goldsmith's School of Art in London between 1921 and 1926. There he specialized in the fashionable medium of etching, befriending like-minded students such as Paul Drury. Sutherland was seen as a precocious talent. In 1924 he had his first one-man show of prints and drawings at the Twenty-One Gallery, London, and he swiftly became an Associate of the Royal Society of Painter-Etchers and Engravers. In 1927 Sutherland was invited to teach part-time at Chelsea School of Art, where his colleagues later included Henry Moore, a friend and continuing inspiration. He continued to teach until the outbreak of the Second World War, transferring around 1934 from etching to composition and book illustration. Sutherland's romantic relationship with fellow student Kathleen Barry led to his conversion to Catholicism in 1926, in preparation for their marriage the following year. The couple lived in various parts of Kent, settling in 1937 in Trottiscliffe. The death in 1929 of their only child, at the age of three months, is sometimes seen as an element in the darker tone that overtook Sutherland's work from *Pastoral* (1930; Cat. 10) onwards, though this only becomes predominant in the second half of the 1930s when there were plenty of additional reasons for projecting a mood of despondency, given unfolding events in the wider world.

In seeking patterns of continuity in his work, we should take account of this first decade of Sutherland's production, even though the artist himself came to view his 1920s etchings as something of a false start. Like several of his artist friends, he soon came to identify his point of departure in art

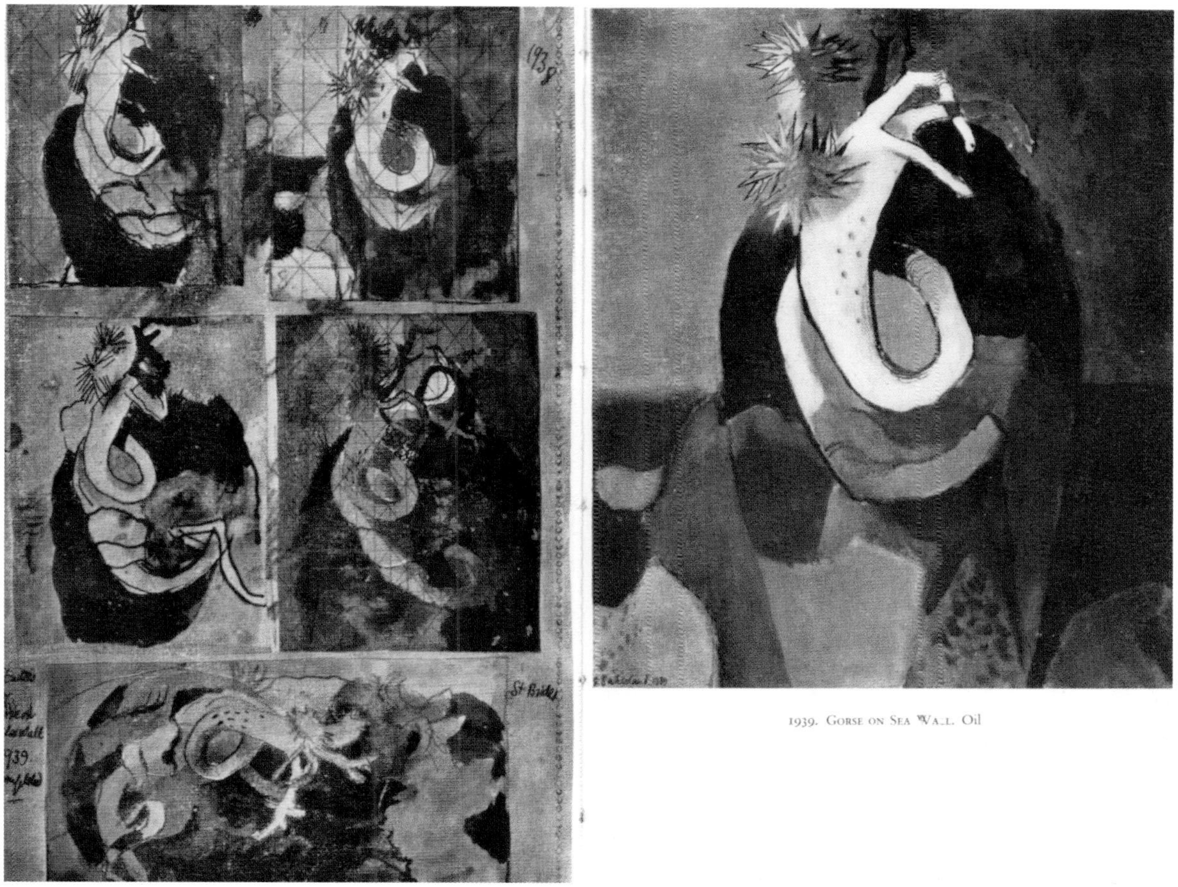

Fig. 2
Graham Sutherland
Double-page spread from *Horizon*, Vol. V, No. 28, April 1942, accompanying Sutherland's essay 'Welsh Sketch Book' (see pp. 68–70). It illustrates *Gorse on a Sea Wall* (Cat. 24) and preparatory sketches.

produced in Britain around a hundred years earlier, especially the prints of Samuel Palmer. Three Palmers that Sutherland himself eventually owned are included in the present show, as a gauge of what he assimilated (Cats 2–4). Generally, Palmer was a major rediscovery of the 1920s, as reflected in a substantial showing of his work at the Victoria and Albert Museum in 1926. The vision of rural harmony, piety and tranquillity that his art conveyed, with such poetic intensity, doubtless acquired its resonance from the widespread yearning for psychic reparation following the brutal horrors of the First World War. In artistic terms, Sutherland's early etchings should not be written off as merely nostalgic or provincial, but as symptomatic of a wider displacement and tempering of the modernist impulses that had strongly come to the fore in Britain just before the war. He later recalled that he knew about Cézanne, and even Matisse and Picasso, but was nevertheless too immersed in Palmer to be able to derive any lessons from their example.[2] Yet on another occasion, Sutherland remembered seeing Palmer as the 'English Van Gogh', invoking another of the pioneering moderns who, one has to remember, had only been known about in Britain since Roger Fry's groundbreaking Post-Impressionism exhibitions of 1910 and 1912.[3] For Sutherland, Palmer and Van Gogh may have converged in the emotional charge that they channelled into an idealized landscape imagery; in their preferences for rhythmic accumulation of detail, evoking the profusion and vitality of the natural world; and in their assertions of light as an almost palpable presence. These, at any rate, are the qualities present in the earliest etchings in which Sutherland's own artistic personality comes through, such as *Village* (Cat. 7) and *Cray Fields* (Cat. 8), both works of 1925, where we already encounter a strong disposition to subordinate description to the expression of mood.

The thing he remembered finding 'wonderful' about Palmer was that 'strong *emotion* ... could change and transform the appearance of things'.[4]

Sutherland carried on producing etchings until the early 1930s. With hindsight, his repertoire of motifs can often be seen to anticipate the more abstracted imagery of later paintings. In *Number Forty-nine* (1924; Cat. 6), for instance, an early work executed before Palmer's inspiration had taken hold, the intricate description of the lattice-like structure of the roof, in areas where the thatching had disappeared, strikingly anticipates Sutherland's record of the remains of an East End pub battered during a German bombing raid (Cat. 41). The conspicuous form of the setting sun in *Cray Fields* finds numerous echoes in Sutherland's later production, while the high panoramic viewpoint of *Village* is recapitulated in pictures such as *Welsh Landscape with Roads* (1936; Cat. 14). The nocturnal lighting of these and other prints becomes a pervasive feature of landscapes and wartime scenes, where descriptive detail is at times barely visible amidst the prevailing gloom. In *Wood Interior* (1929–30; Cat. 9) one may discern Sutherland's savouring of mysterious pockets of space, with trees and dense foliage blocking off the light, which re-emerges in the sequence of *Entrance to a Lane* pictures. It has frequently been observed that the writhing, somewhat anthropomorphic tree form to the right of *Pastoral* is the forerunner of a whole sequence of pictures involving the metamorphosis of tree roots, which take on human or animal attributes (e.g. Cats 29–36). Equally, there is a certain continuity between *The Garden* (1931; Cat. 11), where a rose bush is positioned centrally within a shallow frontal space, and the far more ambiguous and monumental *Standing Form against a Hedge* (1950; Cat. 83) from two decades later, an emphatically modernist picture which retains nevertheless an overtone of garden imagery.

Sutherland's later etchings open up the sustained dialogue that he was to engage in with advanced British contemporaries over the next two decades. In particular, their stylized, simplified treatment of form and space reflects the inspiration of Paul Nash, whose own work had been powerfully affected by a viewing in 1928 of the early 'metaphysical' cityscapes of Giorgio de Chirico. As in Nash, the human figure now largely disappears from the landscape in Sutherland's art, scarcely to re-emerge until the war work, and natural elements themselves become surrogates for bodily imagery, as well as vehicles for arousing an emotional response in the viewer. Over the next few years, Nash, along with Henry Moore, Barbara Hepworth, Ben Nicholson and others, set about bringing British art into line with the current experimental climate in continental Europe.[5] This development forms the necessary backdrop to Sutherland's own conversion to the cause. In more practical terms, he was thrown off course by the

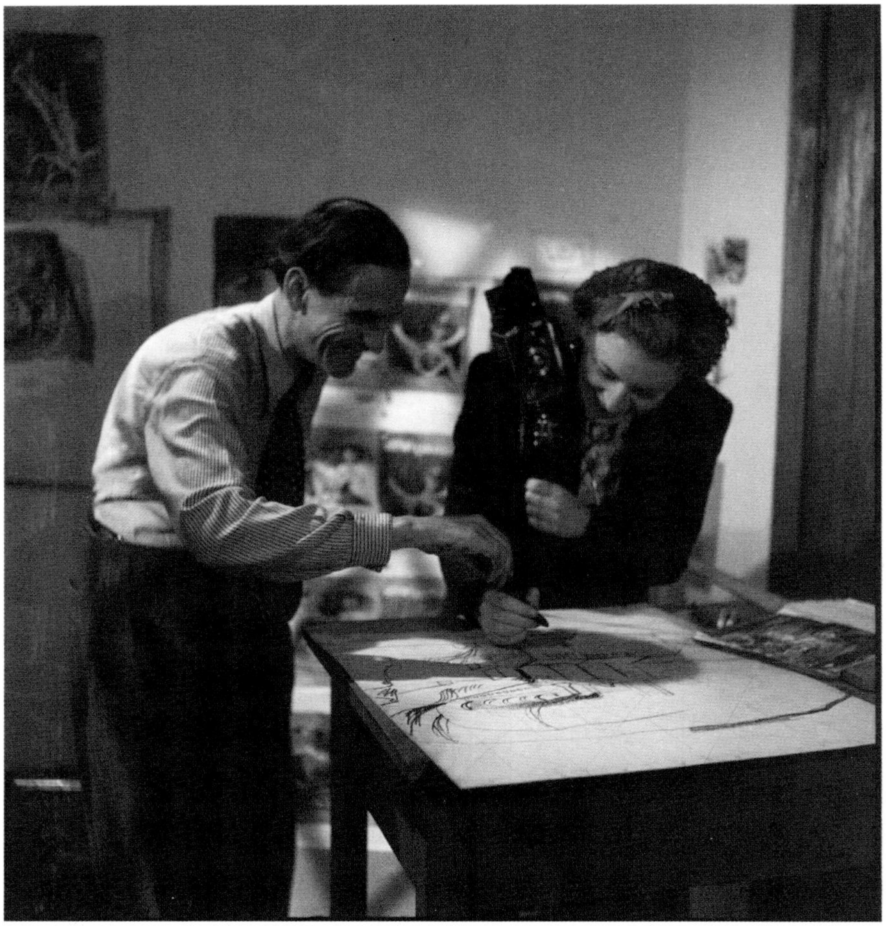

Fig. 3
William MacQuitty
(1905–2004)
Graham Vivian Sutherland; Lee Miller
1943
Bromide fibre print
National Portrait Gallery, London.

depression in the world economy, which brought about a crash in the hitherto buoyant market for contemporary prints. The destabilizing of his career made it easier to assume a more experimental approach to his work.

The 1930s marked a crucial turning point. Sutherland recast his ambitions entirely, and began to turn himself into a modern painter. The fact that so little survives from the first half of the decade suggests that the transition was not an easy one, and that he probably destroyed a quantity of unresolved experiments in watercolour, gouache and oil. Aside from his teaching, Sutherland was reliant financially upon a steady stream of commissions to design china, fabrics, glass, book jackets and illustrations, and posters for the London Transport Board and the Shell-Mex oil company, all tasks at which he proved highly adept.[6] In both his posters and his independent pictures, landscape imagery remained Sutherland's core preoccupation. He travelled regularly in search of motifs, initially to Dorset and then, from 1934 onwards, to Pembrokeshire, which he visited at least twice a year.

By the mid-1930s Sutherland was starting to be taken seriously within progressive artistic circles in London. After a period of relative obscurity, his pictures on Welsh landscape themes began to appear in commercial exhibitions and to find buyers. Thanks to his friendship with Oliver Simon, his essays 'A Trend in English Draughtsmanship' (1936; see pp. 48–50) and the more recondite 'Graven Images: Line Engraving and the Illustrated Book' (1937) appeared in *Signature*, a magazine focusing on typography, the graphic arts and fine book production. 'An English Stone Landmark' was published in *The Painter's Object* (1937; see pp. 64–65), the anthology of texts on contemporary art devised by Myfanwy Evans, wife of John Piper and also editor of the avant-garde magazine *Axis* (1935–37). This was a period of rapid transition in English art, and the impression is that Sutherland identified with, and was valued within, a specific grouping which took its primary bearings from Paul Nash, and increasingly asserted its distance from doctrinaire Social Realism, Surrealism and abstraction. This faction combined a wide-ranging curiosity about European Modernism with an unashamed interest in distinctively English artistic and vernacular traditions, as well as the native scene.

Most importantly, Sutherland was taken up by Kenneth Clark, an exact contemporary who in 1934 had become a remarkably youthful director of the National Gallery, intent upon including figures like Cézanne in the company of the Old Masters. Clark befriended Sutherland and took the artist under his wing. Over the years Clark built up a vast collection of his work, which seemed perhaps to extend and synthesize the legacy of past artists he revered, notably Cézanne and Samuel Palmer. Clark owned several Palmers, and one might even read a symbolic passing on of the torch into his gesture of giving Sutherland a small Palmer drawing of *The Valley Farm* (Cat. 2).[7] It was also Clark who contrived for Sutherland to have a one-man show in late 1938 at London's prestigious Rosenberg and Helft Gallery, and in a preface for the catalogue he celebrated Sutherland's independence from current avant-garde tendencies, and the English, specifically Romantic, dimension of his art (see p. 78).

Sutherland established his fundamental artistic identity with the two versions of *Red Tree* (Cats 17 and 18) and *Welsh Landscape with Roads* (Cat. 14), all made in 1936. These images were triggered by observations recorded in Pembrokeshire, before and during a trip in September of that year, which were then transmuted into pictures over the succeeding months. Indeed, commentators have tended to follow the lead of the artist, who attached great significance for the development of his art to his discovery of the landscape of the two headlands projecting on either side of St Bride's Bay. The literature often includes maps of where he worked and photographs of areas or motifs that he painted. Sutherland himself evoked what this very particular countryside meant to him in the essay 'Welsh Sketch Book' (1942; see pp. 68–70), where the set-piece descriptions of places and sensations read as direct equivalents to the vision projected in his paintings. In the informal context of letters from Pembrokeshire to friends such as Clark, his enthusiasm comes across more directly:

> The country here is tremendously impressive: for variety, size, poetry and colour I had no idea that these islands contained anything like it. I believe one could do really great work with such a stimulus. I have been working every day & have found some electrifying motifs. It is not easy country, and perhaps needs a closer familiarity than most. I believe that I may have enough material for 8 new pictures. Yesterday we were spellbound at sunset by the effect of the sun coming though holes in the clouds and making orange red patches in the blue black mountains.[8]

Sutherland's sense of the character of Pembrokeshire was in tune with wider perceptions. The region was still extremely difficult to reach, except by means of slow country roads, and retained a wild and 'unspoilt' character. In a 1937 book about Wales, aimed at a popular readership, we are told that 'a man wandering among the cromlechs and stone circles of the windy Pembrokeshire hills may warm his imagination with many glowing visions' of ancient civilizations and religious rituals.[9] The evocation of the western coastal area strikingly brings to mind the kinds of pictorial imagery that Sutherland extracted from his visits: '... these are the oldest lands of Wales, the ancient ribs and earliest rocks of geologic time, cut only by little streams which drain these plateaux. These streams have worn steep watercourses down to the creeks of the coast, so that you will find in Pembrokeshire the roads full of sudden descents, the hills turning sharply downward from the plain, sloping to a bridge, and mounting the other side again.'[10]

Sutherland always emphasized that first-hand observations of places and things, akin to Wordsworthian 'moments of vision', provided the essential starting point:

> Even though most of my work is done in the studio, I have to start with something that exists ... I go for walks with no particular preconceived ideas. I have a very small note-book and I look right and left as I am walking, and suddenly I see something that interests me and make a note of it. Then later I come back and make a more complete note of it. These notes are extremely important as they are the basis of the final painting, and in addition they have the virtue of speed; the moment of seeing is often fleeting ... It is a thing that you see suddenly and it can't be recaptured. It is the element of the accident and the accidental encounter which is important.[11]

Such accidental encounters were, however, cultivated and identified within a framework of prior expectations. Consciously or otherwise, artists tend to respond to places or motifs because they seem compatible with preconceived ideals. This is implicit in Sutherland's account in 'Welsh Sketch Book' of the process of interpretation and stylistic transformation he evolved in order to convey the essential impact of sensations observed at first hand in Pembrokeshire:

> It was in this country that I began to learn painting. It seemed impossible here for me to sit down and make finished paintings 'from nature'. Indeed, there were no 'ready-made' subjects to paint. The spaces and concentrations of this clearly constructed land were stuff for storing in the mind. Their essence was

> intellectual and emotional … I found that I could express what I felt only by paraphrasing what I saw. … I felt as much part of the earth as my features were part of me. I did not feel that my imagination was in conflict with the real, but that reality was a dispersed and disintegrated form of imagination.

He acknowledged that he had been working with a necessary 'singleness of purpose' and that for the last few years he had been 'preoccupied with a particular aspect of landscape'. Indeed, the attentive reader may notice exact, doubtless unwitting, verbal repetitions between 'Welsh Sketch Book' and the shorter 'An English Stone Landmark', in which, five years earlier, Sutherland had described his visit to Brimham Rocks in Yorkshire in connection with a Shell poster commission (see pp. 64–65). It is also indicative that virtually all the titles he gave to his pictures make general reference, at most, to the Welsh origins of his motifs – only the 1938 etching *Clegyr-Boia* (Cat. 21) provides topographical particulars.

Sutherland's general conception of the meaning and psychological charge of landscape had strong cultural roots. The association between stylistic abstraction and motifs of unspoilt landscape imagery was a well-established theme in modernist art by the 1930s, extending back from recent pictures of Cumberland by Ben and Winifred Nicholson to Gauguin's response to Brittany and Tahiti, or to Van Gogh's images of the countryside around Arles, the cornfield imagery and swirling rhythms of which seem to be echoed in Sutherland's description of *Brimham Rock* (1937; Cat. 12). I suspect that Sutherland was inspired too, as were so many of his contemporaries, by D. H. Lawrence's primitivist vision of the natural world, as an antidote to modernity: 'The spirit of place is a strange thing. Our mechanical age tries to override it. But it does not succeed. In the end, the strange, sinister spirit of the place, so diverse and adverse in differing places, will smash our mechanical oneness into smithereens …'.[12] Likewise, Paul Nash's recent arguments for the sense of *genius loci* as a component of the English sensibility doubtless conditioned Sutherland's fixation on Pembrokeshire, which took on a similar role and status in his imagination as New Mexico or Sardinia, say, had assumed for Lawrence, or Avebury with its great stone circle for Nash himself.[13] With hindsight, though, we should be sceptical with regard to the notion, which was certainly current in the period, that engaging with landscape imagery was a peculiarly English preoccupation.[14] As a corrective, one might think, for example, of Sutherland's American contemporaries such as the photographer Edward Weston, and his anthropomorphic presentation of found natural objects, or the painter Georgia O'Keeffe, whose primordial New Mexico landscapes, informed by emphatic bodily suggestions, offer at times such a close and fascinating parallel to Sutherland.

A more direct pictorial determinant of the 1936 landscapes was Sutherland's engagement with Surrealism and its English offshoots. There was plenty of opportunity in London to look at contemporary European art in the original, notably at the great 'International Surrealist Exhibition' that summer, in which Sutherland showed two untypical, self-consciously modern pictures, at the invitation of Roland Penrose. He later acknowledged: 'The one field in which the surrealists helped me to widen my range was in their propagation of the idea that there was worthy subject matter for painting, in objects the painter would never have looked at before … Surrealism helped me to realise that forms which interested me existed already in nature …'.[15] Illustrated magazines were another significant means of transmission: 'I became aware, after I had started work in Pembrokeshire, that unconsciously some of my forms – to me at least – started to look a little bit like the kind of things I had been seeing at the time as reproductions in *Cahiers d'Art*. My feelings then were, not that I was trying to be un-English, but that for the first time in my life I was aware that there was something going on beyond the English tradition.'[16] For Sutherland, then, contemporary European art served to stimulate a process of observing and transmuting landscape imagery, rather than to open up an engagement with, say, the theoretical or ideological concerns that informed the creation of Surrealist art proper.

There is a particularly telling affinity between Sutherland's work and the contemporary paintings of André Masson. For instance, a juxtaposition of *Welsh Landscape with Roads* and Masson's *Ibdes in Aragon* (1935; Cat. 16) reveals parallels in the fluid handling of paint, the vivid use of colour, the rhythmical organization of the design, and the juxtaposition of sharply defined foreground elements – the skull in the Sutherland and the cock in the Masson – against a deep landscape backdrop. At some level, one might speculate, Masson's images of an arid and barren landscape, charged with emotional and psychological energies, may well have made their mark on Sutherland's work. He could in fact have seen a one-man Masson exhibition at the Wildenstein Gallery in London in early 1936, which focused on the artist's work since his move to Spain in 1934.[17] The catalogue's characterization of Masson, who was temporarily estranged from the Surrealist group, would have struck a chord: 'The Surrealists claimed him [Masson] for a time, but again he escaped from the restrictions of an organised school of painting. He turned to Nature and his own imagination for his inspiration.' We can in fact assume Sutherland's interest from the documented enthusiasm of Kenneth Clark, who bought a picture from the Wildenstein show and met Masson in London.[18] As it happens, Sutherland is unlikely to have known *Ibdes in Aragon* in advance of creating *Welsh Landscape with Roads*; Clark evidently bought this further Masson in February 1937 during a visit to Paris. Perhaps, in this instance, Clark was in some sense responding to a Masson because it reminded him of the work of his favourite modern English painter.

The Surrealists generally were obsessed in the mid-1930s with the idea of the 'found object', meaning the chance encounter with, and appropriation of, some item from the everyday world that had the capacity to spark off unconscious fantasies and feelings in the artist and, in turn, suitably receptive viewers. In this context we should note that, from 1936 onwards, many of Sutherland's major pictures are dominated by some particular object, or small-scale natural configuration, which the artist encountered, drew and perhaps literally removed to his studio, to serve as a point of departure. These sources remain legible in their own terms, but the process of artistic transformation frequently invested the original material with additional layers of reference. In *Red Tree*, for instance, especially the more stylized version (Cat. 18), there are already suggestions of a reclining human figure, conveyed through Sutherland's use of fleshy colour as well as the organic stylizations to which he subjected the piece of wood. The fusion of landscape and figure connotations in the recent work of Henry Moore may well have been a stimulus, as indeed might Moore's recurrent use of found natural forms as the starting point for drawings or sculptures. Generally, from Pembrokeshire and later the Midi area of France, Sutherland extracted a kind of landscape imagery that he saw as the opposite of 'scenic' – a term that signified something akin to picturesque, whereby the elements in a vista lent themselves to the creation of a harmonious, balanced spatial construction. In more irregular, rugged places, Sutherland found himself drawn, he recalled, to particular natural elements that had 'a kind of presence': 'I won't go further than that, and say it was a human presence ... Shadow had a presence; certain configurations of rock seemed to go beyond just being rock, they were emanations of some kind of personality.'[19] This process of focusing in and extracting the particular from a wider panorama often yielded a form of pictorial organization more comparable to figure than landscape painting:

Green Tree Form: Interior of Woods
1940
(Cat. 34, detail).

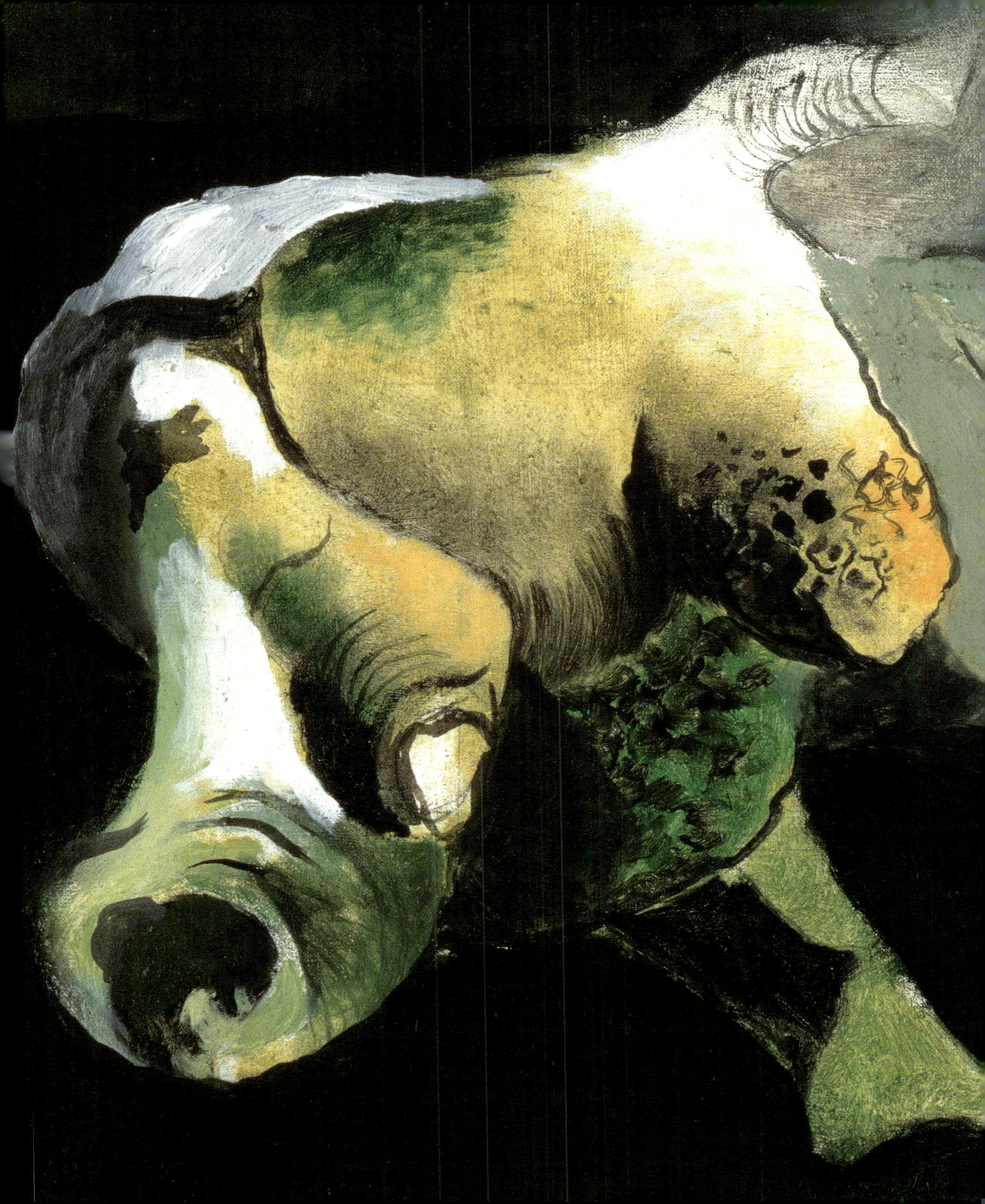

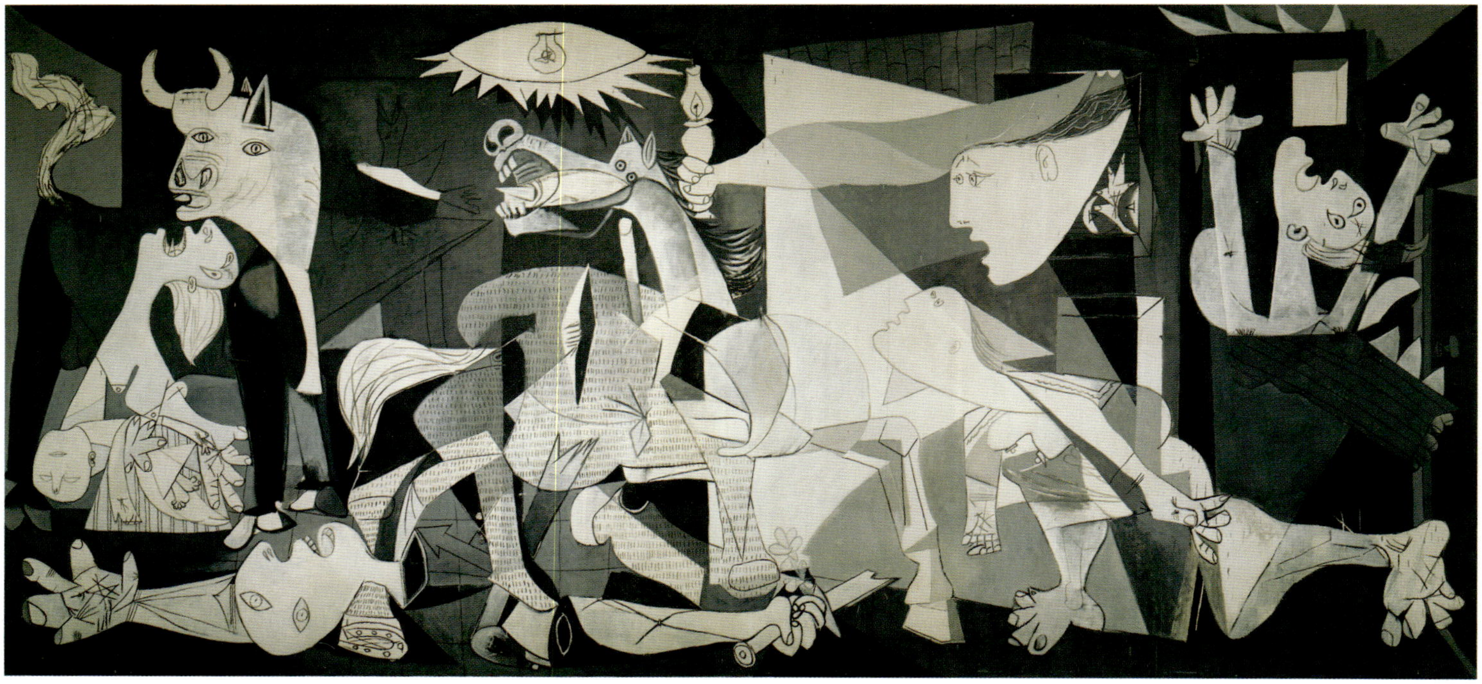

I have never liked this idea, in looking at a landscape for pictorial purposes, that something is going on outside the canvas: that a hill, for instance, continues right and left. I rather like the idea that that the thing is self-contained, exactly as a figure would be self-contained if you were to draw it ... there was a need for me at the time, perhaps, to make landscapes into a thing which, as far as possible, could be got within the four walls of the canvas.[20]

The projection of anthropomorphic or bestial connotations pervades the menacing pictures Sutherland made around the beginning of the war, such as *Gorse on Sea Wall* (1939; Cat. 24), *Green Tree Form: Interior of Woods* (1940; Cat. 34) and *Association of Oaks* (1940; Cat. 29). In fact, specific images of figures and animals were a crucial point of reference in their genesis. Sutherland's work bore the profound imprint of Picasso's recent phase of work, encapsulated by the great *Guernica* mural which had been produced for the 'International Exhibition' in Paris in summer 1937, as a gesture of Picasso's sympathy with the republican opposition to General Franco (Fig. 4). The following October, just after the Munich crisis which so nearly led to war, Picasso's painting and its preparatory drawings were exhibited at the New Burlington Galleries in central London. An image prompted by outrage at a specific event during the Spanish Civil War had by now come to assume a far wider significance, for the present age, as Herbert Read remarked, of 'disillusion, despair and destruction': 'Not only Guernica, but Spain; not only Spain, but Europe, is symbolised in this allegory'. Guernica was a surrogate altarpiece for an age without communal religious faith: 'It is the modern Calvary, the agony in the bomb shattered ruins of human tenderness and frailty. It is a religious picture, painted, not with the same kind, but with the same degree of fervour that inspired Grünewald and the Master of the Avignon Pieta, Van Eyck and Bellini.'[21] For Sutherland, too, one suspects, Picasso now seemed to have become a different kind of modern artist, who had turned away from self-engrossment and was driven by a compulsion to capture the historical moment, to express in contemporary artistic terms what it felt like to be living through the gathering European crisis, which was

Fig. 4
Pablo Picasso (1881–1973)
Guernica
1937
Oil on canvas
Museo Nacional Centro de Arte Reina Sofia, Madrid, Spain.

Gorse on Sea Wall
1939
(Cat. 24, detail).

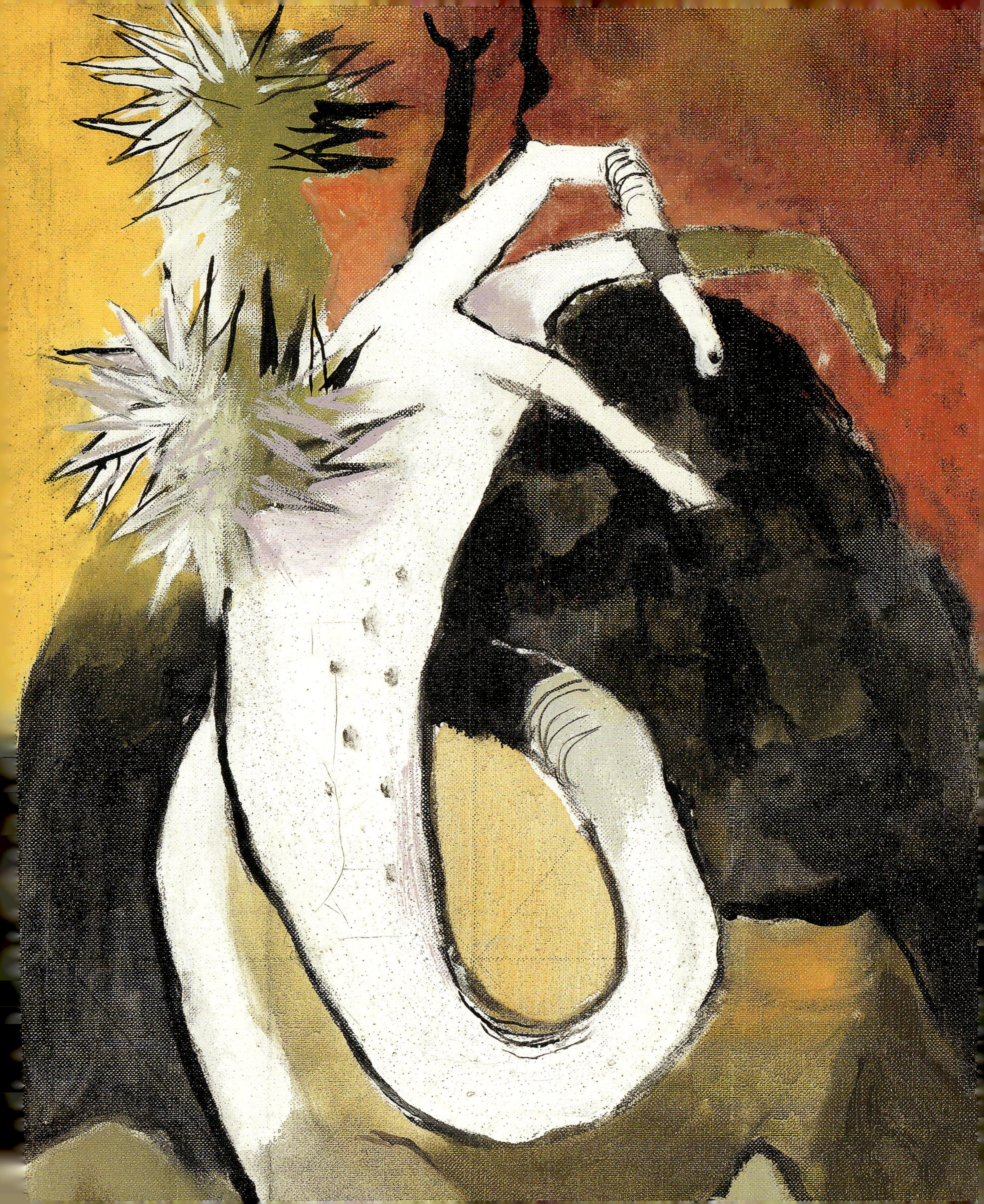

inexorably leading to a war to stop Fascism. Hence the effect Picasso had on an artist like Sutherland:

> Picasso's Guernica drawings seemed to open up a philosophy and to point a way whereby – by a kind of paraphrase of appearances – things could be made to look more vital and real. The forms I saw in this series pointed to a passionate involvement in the character of the subject, whereby the feeling for it was trapped and made concrete. Like the subject and yet unlike ... Everything I saw at this time exhorted me to a greater freedom. Only Picasso however seemed to have the true idea of metamorphosis, whereby things found a new form through feeling.[22]

The impact of these Picassos is everywhere apparent in Sutherland's work during the period of the descent into war. In *Gorse on Sea Wall* the spiral unwinding of the root was elaborated not just from the agonized hands of Christ in Grünewald's Isenheim Altarpiece but also from details such as the twisting, screaming head of the dying horse in *Guernica*. The writhing form of a tree root in Sutherland's *Midsummer Landscape* (1940; Cat. 32) is a direct descendant of Picasso's horse, as portrayed in some of the early studies where it subsides to the ground mortally wounded, rather than rearing and screaming in agony. The lumbering, monstrous form in *Green Tree Form: Interior of Woods* might equally be seen as transmuted from Picasso's studies of the distraught mother clutching her dead infant. The 'leg' of the uprooted tree trunk matches the arm with which the mother supports her convulsed body, while the strong diagonal line defining its upper edge recalls the angled leg with which Picasso's figure seeks to propel herself forward.

Moreover, *Guernica* reinforced Sutherland's interest in nocturnal lighting as a way of projecting mood and heightening the pictorial drama. Edward Sackville-West aptly noted how at a certain point, 'Sutherland's obsession with darkness resulted in a bass octave of so fuliginous an obscurity that some of his finest inventions ... can only be properly distinguished in very bright daylight and cannot be reproduced satisfactorily at all ... these pictures have a quality unique in modern landscape painting – an expression of doom and foreboding.'[23] In this sense, Sutherland's work reflected the pessimism that prevailed in Britain around 1939/40: 'Kenneth Clark, who was then in the Ministry of Information, knew just how serious the situation was becoming ... how near to capitulation we were. The blackness of the atmosphere of war was like the prospect of death and more and more funereal. We lived from day to day.'[24] Equally, the critical responses to his second one-man show, at the Leicester Galleries, in May 1940, where many of these found object pictures were shown, indicated a growing perception that Sutherland's pictures distilled the essential mood of wartime; for one critic they were 'intensely romantic and full of a spiritual agony which make them the finest tragic expression I know ... of the suffering of a society at war'.[25] Remarkably, in spite of the wartime economic climate, 22 of the 30 works in the exhibition were sold to public or private collections.

Sutherland's dialogue with what was 'going on beyond the English tradition' was clearly crucial for the development of his work. But we should also bear in mind the artist's qualification that he was not 'trying to be un-English'. His attitudes towards the apparent dichotomy of national and international were in fact very much a product of their period. In England, Surrealism was widely perceived from the start, by critics such as David Gascoyne and Herbert Read, as well as artists like Nash and Moore, less as a revolutionary subversion of artistic traditions and accepted values, and more as a continuation in new terms of a tendency to celebrate the powers and insights of the imagination which had deep roots in

English culture, especially in nineteenth-century Romanticism. According to Read, his English artist friends, the descendants of William Blake, were 'to the manner born'.[26] Sutherland took a similar line in his 1936 essay 'A Trend in English Draughtsmanship' (see pp. 48–50). He asserted here his commitment to an essentially 'subjective' kind of art, whereby observed scenes or objects 'become absorbed in the reservoir of the subconscious mind out of which emerge the reconstructed and re-created images'. This approach 'has derived an immense stimulus from abroad', he conceded, yet 'the best English work, whilst retaining its essential universality, shows definite native characteristics'. The indigenous tradition with which he clearly identified ran from Blake, Palmer and Turner through to Moore and Nash, with the last recently responsible, in Sutherland's view, for a 'series of paintings of extraordinary significance and power'.

If Masson was one possible stimulus, Nash too contributed to Sutherland's initial renditions of the landscape of the imagination that he had located in Pembrokeshire. The Surrealist preoccupation with sensations of the marvellous and mysterious had already encouraged Nash to revive a Romantic interest in remote landscape scenery bearing the traces of ancient human occupancy.[27] *Brimham Rock* (1937; Cat. 12) is one of several Sutherland studies focusing on prehistoric forms, in the manner of Nash's abstracted interpretations of the prehistoric megaliths at Avebury, which the artist had first visited in 1933. Equally, Sutherland's *Welsh Landscape with Roads* (1936; Cat. 14) might be compared with Nash's *Landscape of the Megaliths* (1934; Cat. 15) as an image of a 'mysterious', primordial landscape, far from urban civilization, which metaphorically evokes regions of the mind existing at a deeper level than the surface clutter of consciousness. Both pictures feature a simplification of natural features, the use of a high horizon to articulate the space, and a dramatic interplay between distant panorama and incongruous foreground elements, respectively the abstracted megaliths and the cow's skull. However, the differences are also revealing. Here, as in Sutherland's work generally over the next few years, 'primitive' landscape imagery serves more overtly than it does in Nash's work as a vehicle for transmitting mood and evoking a highly charged atmosphere of pathos and melancholy. Eric Newton was struck by the 'primaeval, elemental, at times almost brutal' character of the pictures in the 1938 show: 'Mr Sutherland's world is an unfinished thing, as though it had been abandoned half-way through the fifth day of creation. His shapes, for all their subtlety, are clumsy. They suggest dinosaurs and mammoths. His hills heave themselves grimly against the sky. They are stark uncomfortable monsters made of raw earth and rock.'[28]

The notion that English Romantic art remained a compelling resource for the contemporary artist provided the basis for neo-romanticism. This was not so much a coherent movement as an artistic outlook, pioneered by Nash, which gathered momentum during the second half of the 1930s and came to fruition, understandably enough, in the patriotic atmosphere of the war years. Sutherland was clearly steeped in Romantic art during the second half of the 1930s and beyond, and to that extent he is rightly seen as a central figure in neo-romanticism, alongside figures like John Piper and Ivon Hitchens. The label went back to 1942, when a critic responded enthusiastically to the conjunction of work by Sutherland, Hitchens, Frances Hodgkins and Henry Moore in a survey of current trends in British art. The approach of these 'neo-romantics' now seemed far more compelling and relevant than the self-engrossed alternatives presented by abstraction or Surrealism.[29] That same year saw the publication of Piper's *British Romantic Artists*, a manifesto-like book that surveyed the rich legacy of the great nineteenth-century landscape artists and concluded with a discussion of their successors, who provide a welcome antidote to arid

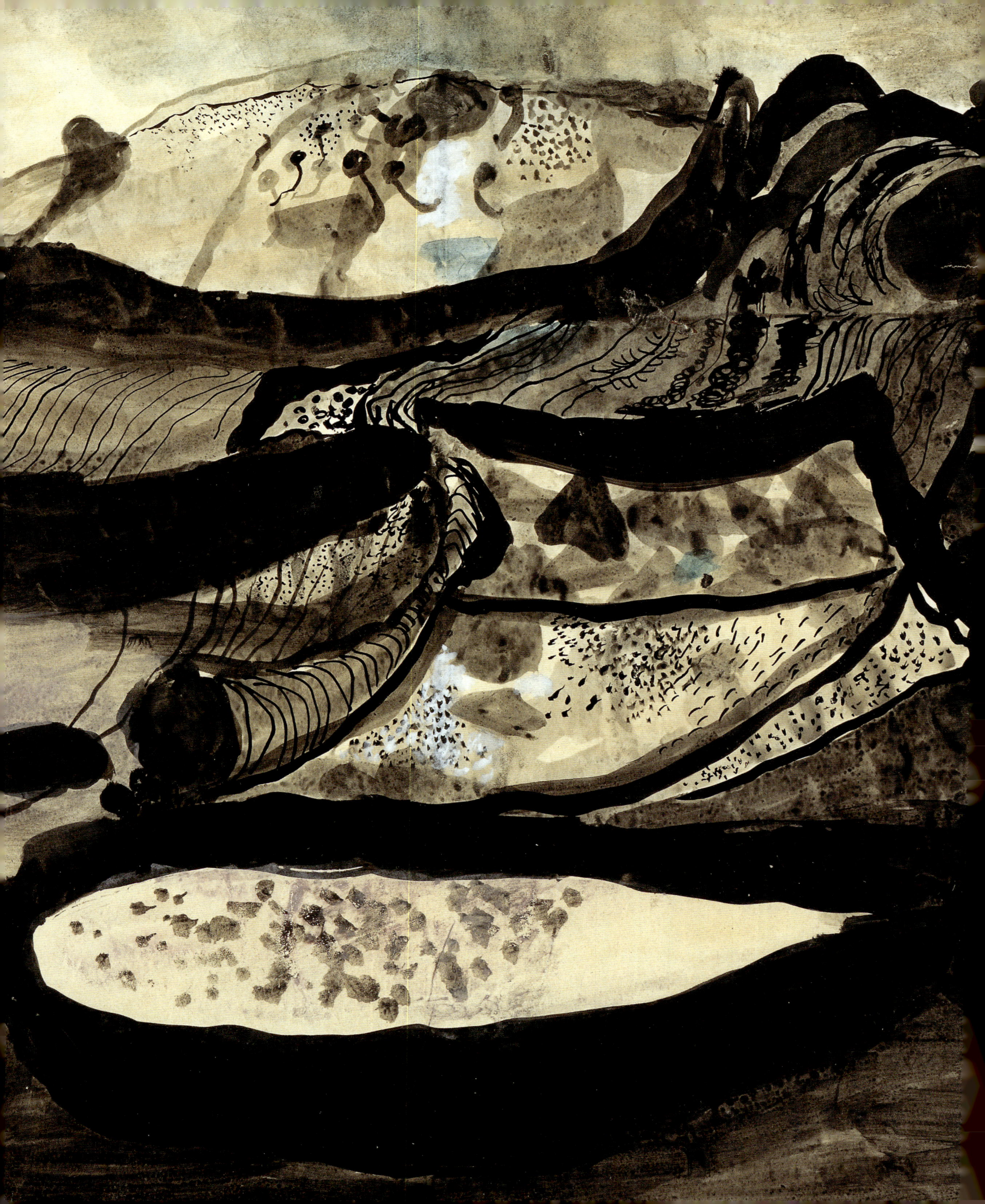

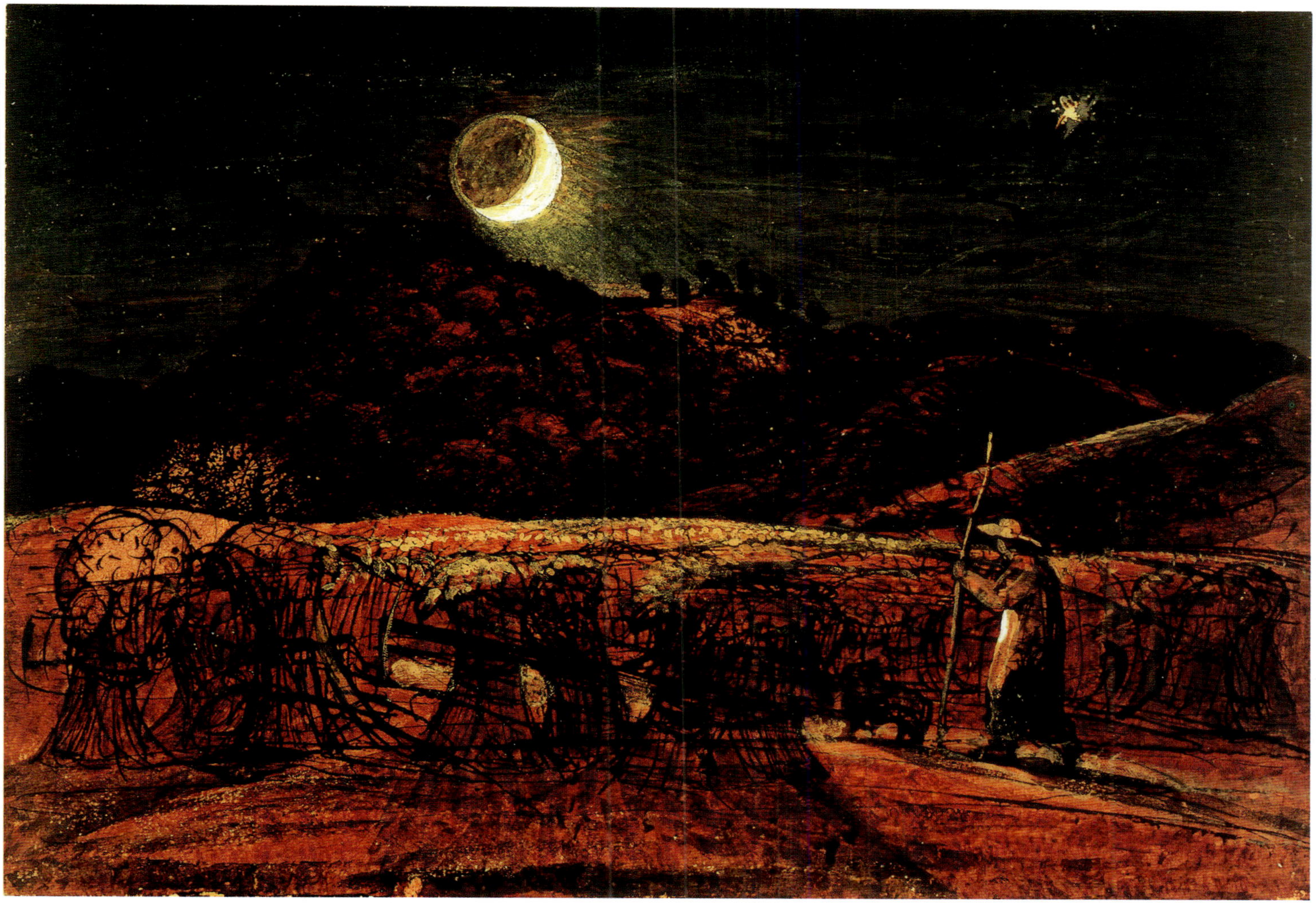

Fig. 5
Samuel Palmer (1805–1881)
A Cornfield by Moonlight
1826–32
British Museum.
(1985-5-4-1)

Dark Hill
1940
(Cat. 28, detail).

Bloomsbury formalism. The final sentences of the book are devoted to Sutherland, with the obligatory reference to Wordsworth:

> Graham Sutherland paints the elements, and the more elemental natural forms: tumbled rocks, organic tangles of gorse on sea walls, and sun falling behind a volcanic pile of mountains. But these are the occasions rather than the subjects for his pictures. He is the most subjective of the younger painters, and has said that he wants his pictures to have 'a certain strangeness'. To become absorbed by one of them is to know the meaning of Wordsworth's
>
> '... Rolled round in earth's diurnal course
> With rocks, and stones, and trees.'[30]

According to Edward Sackville-West, who wrote the first monograph on Sutherland for the 'Penguin Modern Masters' series, working in close collaboration with the artist, it was Blake and Palmer who constituted 'most obviously perhaps the focus of Sutherland's deepest admiration', and 'the pointers to the emotion behind Sutherland's painting'.[31] The evidence of the pictures confirms that Sutherland seems now to have been mainly looking at the late wood engravings of William Blake, and at the early paintings of Samuel Palmer rather than the more conventional later etchings. For Sutherland, and indeed for several contemporaries, the visionary intensity and stylistic abstraction of such work made it more accessible to

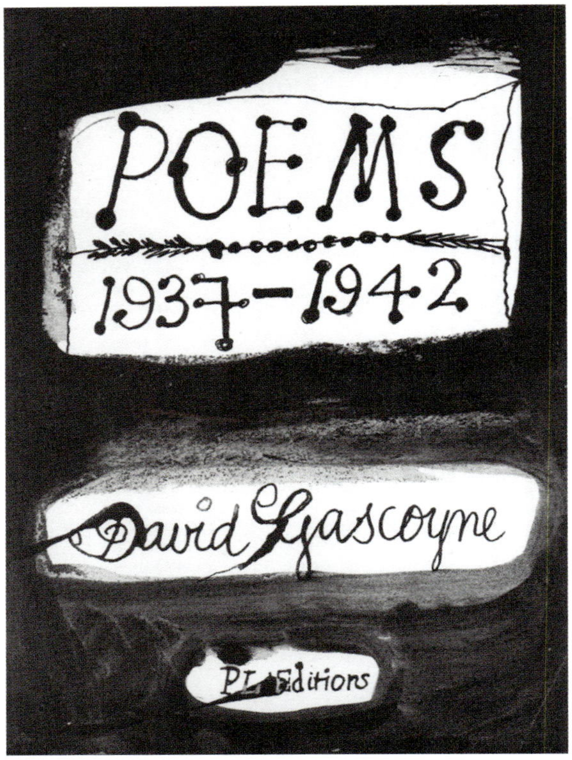

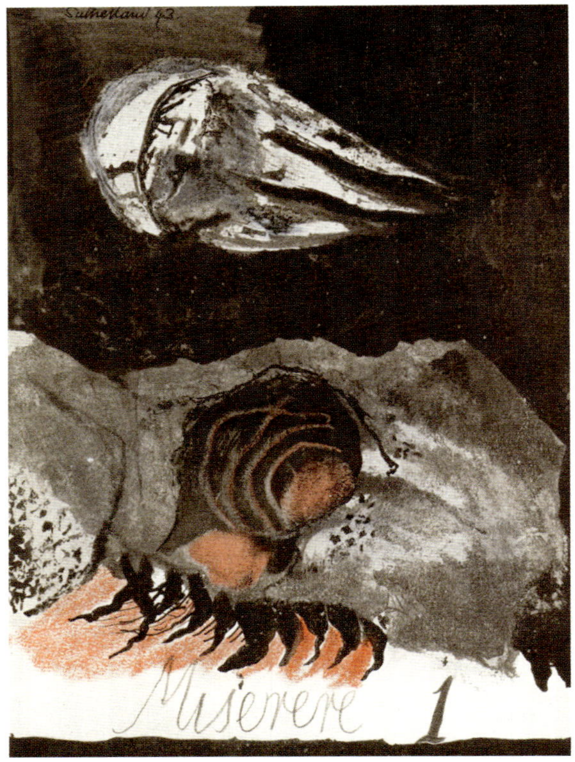

Fig. 6
Title page and preface to 'Miserere' section from David Gascoyne, *Poems 1937–42*, 1943 (with illustrations by Sutherland).

contemporary sensibilities than the more naturalistic strands in Romanticism. Palmer's youthful paintings had been included in a major 'Exhibition of British Art' held in 1934 at the Royal Academy.[32] Moreover, a love for the work of Palmer was common ground, as we have seen, between Sutherland and Kenneth Clark. More perhaps than any other work by Palmer, the painting *A Cornfield by Moonlight* (1826–32), owned by Clark, served as a talisman, informing not just Sutherland's approach to imagery and style but also his techniques of combining pen drawing with body colour and building up repeated touches of black to describe foliage (Fig. 5). Many Sutherlands drew sustenance from the way Palmer constructed enclosed spaces, using pathways, mounds, trees and the contours of distant hills to create a rhythmical articulation of the design, and to generate strongly defined shapes that could contain a dense accumulation of descriptive detail. Palmer also remained a model for Sutherland's interest in the effects of sunset and nocturnal lighting, endowing the natural landscape with mystery and an emotional charge. Yet, while the etchings of a decade earlier had inherited a mood of benign tranquillity from Palmer, Sutherland's mature paintings subverted their pastoral vision, projecting a darkness that is emotional as well as visual.

In this respect, a more relevant model was provided by the late work of William Blake, with which Sutherland seems to have been particularly engaged during the war years. The apocalyptic Dante illustrations seem to have been at the back of his mind when conceiving his gloomy, hellish vision of the looming interiors of Welsh steelworks, the figures dwarfed by machinery (e.g. Cats 55–57). In April 1942, Sutherland remarked in a letter: 'Don't you think the new Tate Gallery Blakes are the most exciting artistic event for years?'[33] He was responding to the exhibition at the National Gallery of the Tate's wartime acquisitions, which included his own *Green Tree Form*, shown alongside the group of Blake colour prints presented by W. Graham Robertson, featuring such major masterpieces as *Elohim Creating Adam*, *Nebuchadnezzar* and *Newton*.[34] That same month saw the appearance of 'Welsh

Sketch Book', where Sutherland noted that the 'form and scale of the rocks here [Pembrokeshire], and the minutiae on them' bore a striking similarity to Blake's treatment of the background in the Newton drawing. Equally, his illustrations to David Gascoyne's *Poems 1937–1942* (Fig. 6) reveal an immersion in Blake's illustrated books, and Sutherland remarked that he had conceived the volume 'as something to be read and carried about in the pocket ... slightly reminiscent of the "knockabout" quality of the original editions of Blake's *Songs of Innocence*'.[35] Edward Sackville-West remarked perceptively that Sutherland had also absorbed from Blake a 'colour scale imposed by the English climate on the stuff of our island – the egg yellows, the veiled pinks, the sudden blacks'.[36]

The argument for Sutherland's Romantic affinities can be extended beyond Palmer and Blake. On the one hand, we might at times note compositional debts to the work of naturalistic artists such as Constable and John Cotman. On the other hand, the fiery apocalyptic aspect of his work brings to mind Wright of Derby, Turner or even John Martin, whose vision of an infernal subterranean world in his *Paradise Lost* illustrations finds an echo in Sutherland's fixation on the tunnels he witnessed at first hand in Cornish tin mines. However, the general point is that, like Paul Nash and Herbert Read, but unlike some younger artists and critics influenced by the prevailing patriotic mentality, Sutherland continued to view national and international, modern and traditional, as entirely compatible points of reference. One can well understand his irritation at attempts to claim his art, in the mid-1940s, for what had now become a far more insular, nostalgic version of the neo-romantic aesthetic. Sutherland went so far as to write cross letters to magazines where such appropriations of his work had appeared (see p. 161). He conceded only that he had received 'great adolescent stimulus from Palmer and Blake', and later went even further, claiming that 'between, say, 1935 and the war, I was not really conscious at all of being specifically English in tradition'.[37] Such remarks tell us more about Sutherland's post-war sense of himself as an international modernist than they do about the roots of his art during the first decade of his mature production.

European Modernism and British Romanticism provide the most obvious contexts for understanding the roots of Sutherland's work. But it may also sharpen our grasp of the sensibility articulated in his pictures to introduce parallels with the treatment of landscape imagery in contemporary literature, where we also encounter subversions of received pastoral conventions and expectations. There is no reason to think that he knew Jean-Paul Sartre's *Nausea* (published in France in 1938, and in English translation in 1949), but one might profitably consider Sutherland's *Tree Form* (1941; Cat. 36), a gloomy picture in every sense, in conjunction with the episode in the novel where Sartre's narrator describes what happened to him one day in the park:

> The root of the chestnut tree plunged into the ground just underneath my bench. I no longer remembered that it was a root ... Words had disappeared, and with them the meaning of things, the methods of using them, the feeble landmarks which men have traced on their surface. I was sitting, slightly bent, my head bowed, alone in front of that black, knotty mass, which was utterly crude and frightened me. And then I had this revelation ...[38]

The revelation was a metaphysical sense of the absolute Absurdity or contingency of things, which provided 'the key to Existence, the key to my Nausea, to my own life'.[39] By fictional means, Sartre was attempting to convey a fresh perspective on human consciousness that would subsequently be dubbed existentialism. Thus Roquentin's experience of the root dramatized the gulf between physical existence in the raw, and the conceptualizations that we seek to project or impose on experience:

> Faced with that big, rugged paw, neither ignorance nor knowledge had any importance; the world of explanations and reasons is not that of existence. A circle is not absurd, it is clearly explicable by the rotation of a segment of a straight line around one of its extremities. But a circle doesn't exist either. That root, on the other hand, existed in so far that I could not explain it. Knotty, inert, nameless, it fascinated me, filled my eyes, repeatedly brought me back to my own existence … I saw clearly that you could not pass from its function as a root, as a suction-pump, to that, to that hard, compact sea-lion skin, to that oily, horny, stubborn look …[40]

Equally, for a more pervasive affinity with Sutherland's imagery, we might turn to the work of T. S. Eliot, especially in the light of an observation by the writer Kathleen Raine that 'For my generation T. S. Eliot's early poetry, more than the work of any other poet, has enabled us to know our world imaginatively.'[41] Sutherland's found object pictures, from *Red Tree* (1936; Cats 17–18) to *Midsummer Landscape* (1940; Cat. 32) and *Horned Forms* (1944; Cat. 72), present a close visual and conceptual equivalent to Eliot's morbid imagery in poems such as 'Rhapsody on a Windy Night':

> The memory throws up high and dry
> A crowd of twisted things;
> A twisted branch upon the beach
> Eaten smooth, and polished
> As if the world gave up its skeleton.[42]

Likewise, we might contemplate *Gorse on Sea Wall* (1939; Cat. 24) as well as the variants on an arid natural scene in *Mountain Road with Boulder* (1940; Cat. 37) or *Red Landscape* (1942; Cat. 38), in relation to a celebrated passage from 'The Burial of the Dead', Eliot's opening movement of *The Waste Land*:

> What are the roots that clutch,
> what branches grow
> Out of this stony rubbish? Son of man,
> You cannot say, or guess, for you only know
> A heap of broken images,
> where the sun beats,
> And the dead tree gives no shelter,
> the cricket no relief,
> And the dry stone no sound of water. Only
> There is shadow under this red rock,
> (Come under this shadow of this red rock),
> And I will show you something different
> from either
> Your shadow at morning striding behind you
> Or your shadow at evening rising
> to meet you;
> I will show you fear in a handful of dust.[43]

Sutherland's work as an official war artist did much to reinforce the view that his art was especially in tune with the wider mood. It was thanks to Kenneth Clark, once again, that he was able to participate in the War Artists Advisory Committee (WAAC). Clark chaired this government-sponsored scheme, which was modelled on that developed in the First World War, when artists had been commissioned to depict the events and experiences of the conflict. The invitation reached Sutherland in June 1940, just as his part-time teaching at Chelsea was coming to an end and he was about to embark on training as a munition gauge maker. In August, he was told to stand by to make pictures of debris and damage caused by air raids, imagery that was soon available in abundance after the Blitz began in September 1940. From late 1940 onwards, he was working under the terms of a series of six-month contracts issued by the Ministry of Information. In return for the actual works he

Dwarf Oaks
1941
(Cat. 35, detail).

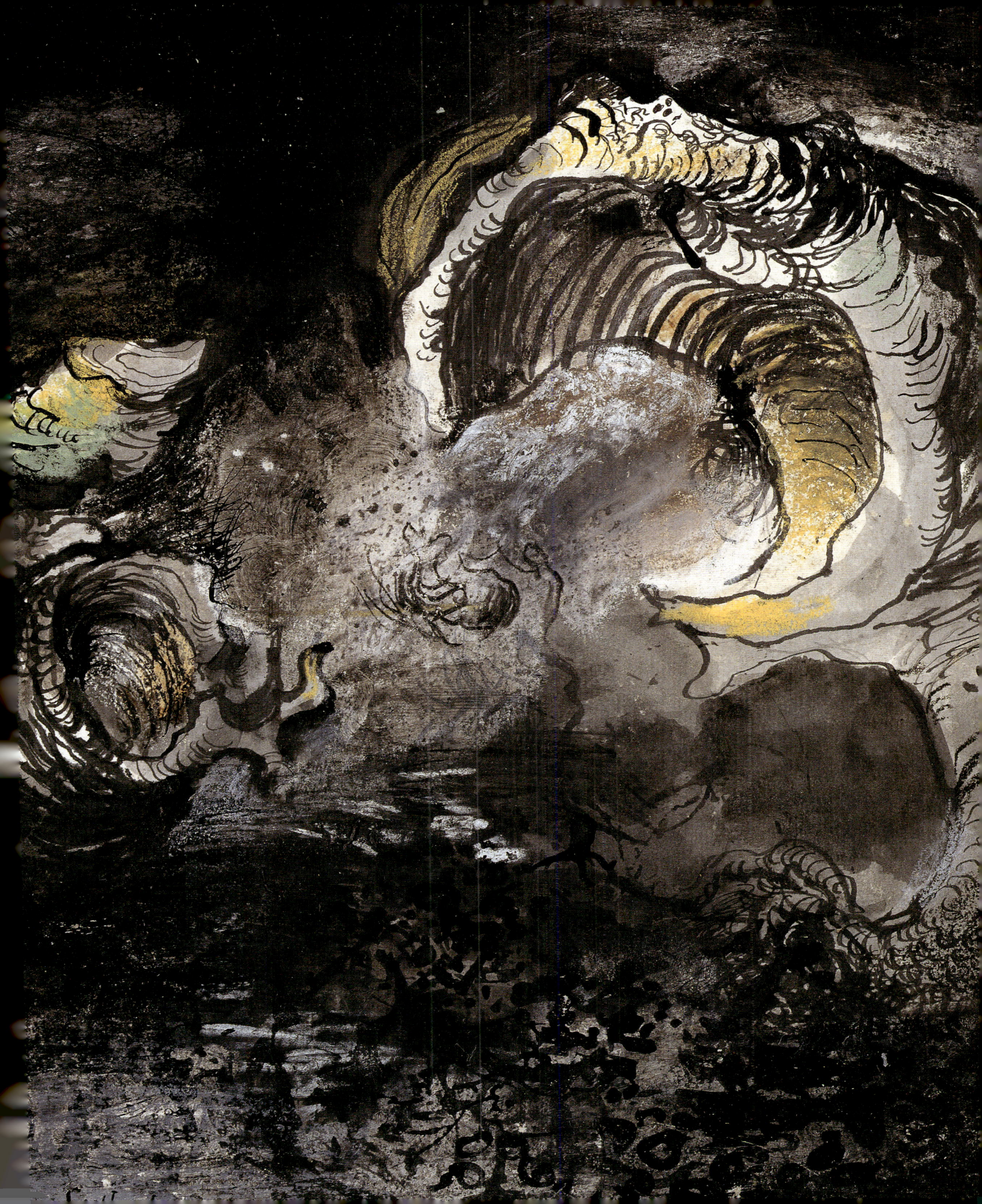

produced on war subjects, which had to go through censorship, as well as for reproduction rights, Sutherland received a decent salary, starting at the equivalent of £650 a year and rising later on to £750. By 1944 Sutherland had produced an extensive body of work variously depicting the devastation of bomb-damaged streets and buildings in south Wales and London; the process of manufacturing armaments associated with steel foundries in south Wales, Cornish tin mines and open-cast mining in Derbyshire; and finally the damage inflicted by the bombers of the Royal Air Force on German military sites in France. Aside from gaining Sutherland a steady income, working as a war artist prevented him, of course, from being called up for other forms of war service.

Through his friendship with Clark, it is likely that Sutherland was able to exert some influence over the themes recommended by the WAAC. He later acknowledged that he 'couldn't make much' of the kinds of subjects that he was initially asked to tackle: 'not only did I feel that I had to give value for money, but to contrive somehow to reflect in an immediate way the subjects set me. It was not until the advent of the air raids that I could see any way open to combine the aims of my work before the outbreak of war with the task then in front of me.'[44] Working with imagery of cataclysmic bomb damage enabled Sutherland to find a new channel for his existing artistic concerns, in much the same way that in London's Underground stations Moore found a poignant echo of the monumental reclining figures in his pre-war sculpture, or John Piper a new variation on the Romantic trope of the ruined decaying building in imagery of buildings shattered by German bombs. Sutherland remarked in February 1941: 'Nearly everyone says that the war has been a "good thing for me" as my war pictures are "so much more understandable" than my landscapes. It's hard to convince people that the degree of abstraction – if you can call it that – is identical!'[45] Certainly he adapted an established creative process, proceeding from notes and drawings on the spot, usually in pencil, through compositional studies made at a remove from the site, which in turn formed the basis for finished pictures. In the latter, we find strong continuities with Sutherland's mainstream production, including, for example, the theatrical lighting employed in much of his landscape and war work between 1940 and 1942. His tendency to focus in on specific elements, extracted from a wider spectacle, was elaborated in his images of lift and ventilator shafts, dangling, broken machinery, rolls of paper and pieces of foundry equipment (Cats 43–46). Equally, the writhing contortions of *Gorse on Sea Wall* and *Midsummer Landscape* recur in images of horribly twisted lift shafts and warped girders (Cats 47–48), evoking perhaps the skeletons of human or animal life forms that have been subject to destructive violence. Such forms read as surrogates for the human lives lost in German bombing raids, which it would have been both crass and demoralizing for Sutherland to show. The artist's fascination with narrow, enclosed spaces, with their connotations of fear and confinement, is carried over from the landscapes to the long dark tunnels of the Cornish tin mines (Cats 49–53).

In the war pictures, as in his landscapes, the artist believed that, by submitting the raw materials of observation to a process of stylistic intensification, it might be possible to arouse a deeper emotional and imaginative response in the viewer. In a 1941 radio discussion with Kenneth Clark and Henry Moore, Sutherland described his approach:

> It's the force of the emotion in the presence of such a subject that determines and moulds the pictorial form one chooses … the sordidness and the anguish implied by some of the scenes of devastation will cause one to invent forms which are the pictorial essence of sordidness and anguish – dirty-looking forms, tormented forms, forms which take

Fig. 7
William MacQuitty
(1905–2004)
c. 1944
Photograph from the set of *Out of Chaos*
MacQuitty International Photographic Collection.

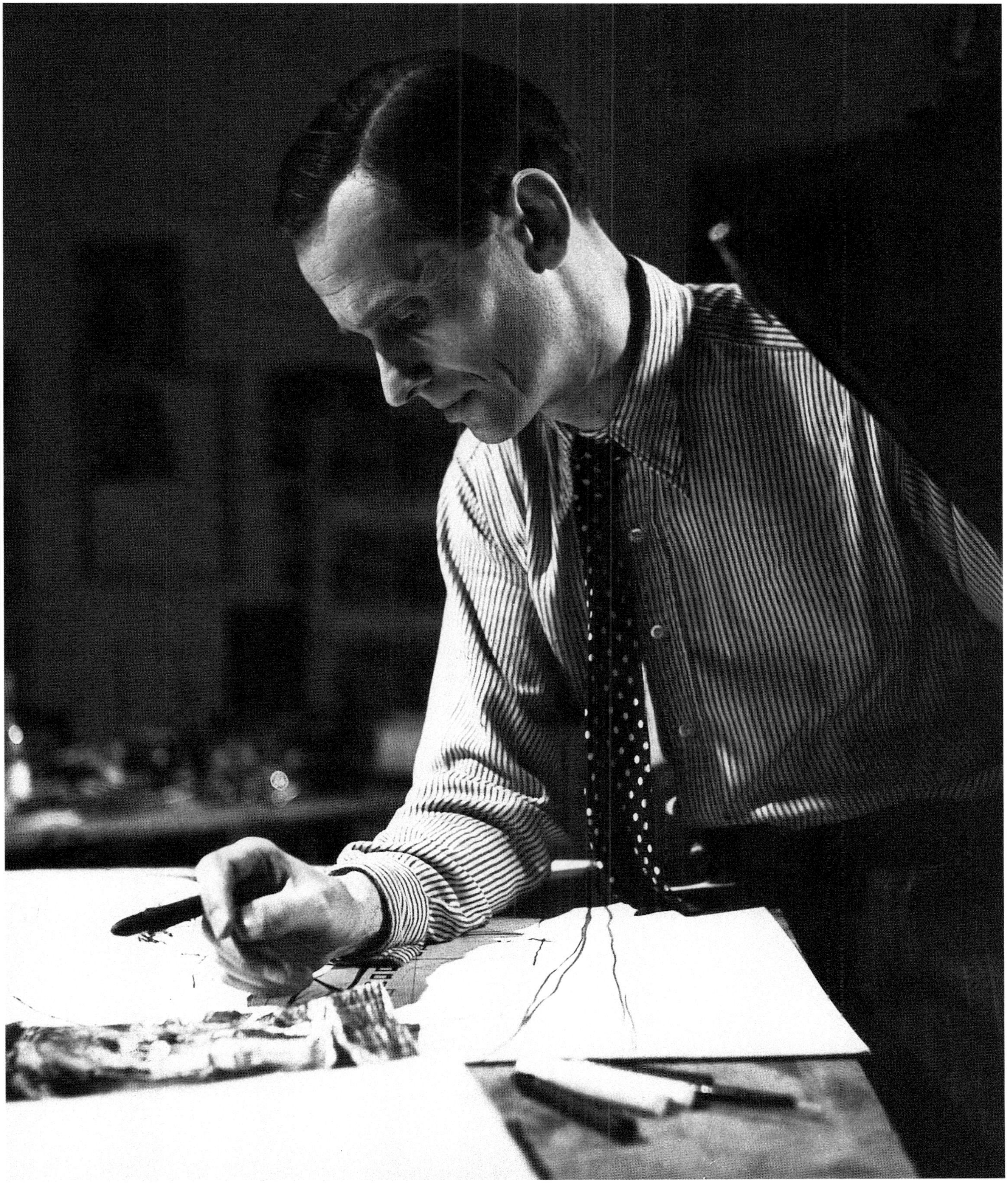

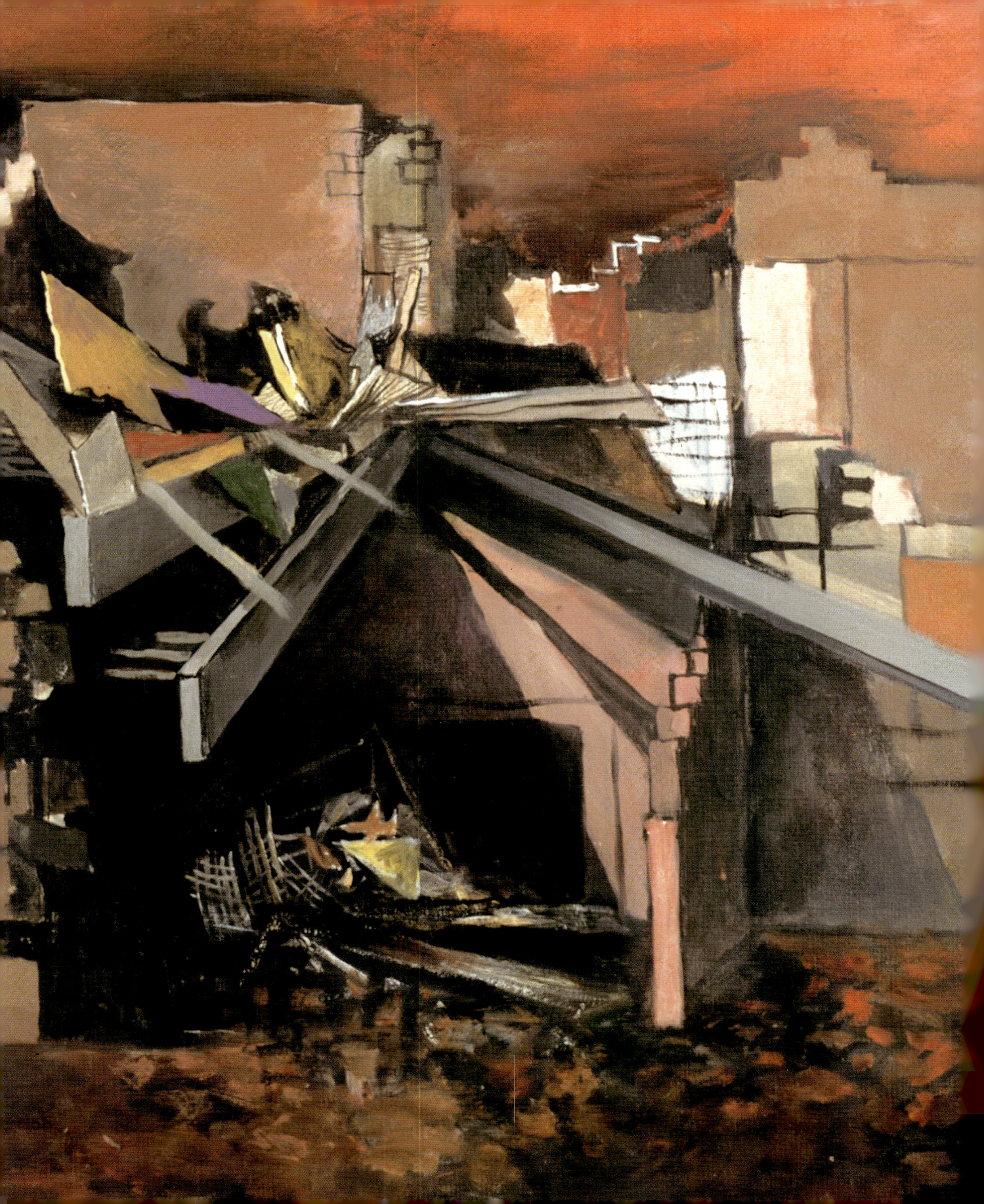

> on an almost human aspect – forms, in fact, which are symbols of reality, and tragic reality at that ... the point is, I think, that the forms which the artist creates, according to his inner capacity, will transcend natural appearances. To quote Maritain, such an art will recompose its peculiar world with that poetical reality, which resembles things in a far more profound and mysterious way than any direct evocation could possibly do.[46]

The continuing element of poetic generalization in Sutherland's war work was epitomized by his use of the title 'Devastation' for his bomb damage pictures, with its implications of a state of mind as well as a physical condition. Indeed, at the end of the conflict, Sutherland explained the more universal or mythic significance inherent in all the different kinds of war imagery that he had tackled:

> At the beginning of the war the forms of destruction moved me tremendously. After that I began to feel drawn towards basic industries such as furnaces, mines and latterly quarries. These things seemed to symbolise a kind of eternal war; a constant of conflict between the forces of man and nature, intensified greatly during a war between nations, and in which man can only just emerge on top. The turning of iron ore into steel seemed so much a primitive combat (still, in spite of modern machinery, an elemental and almost crude process, with the floor of the teeming pit like some tremendous field). So too with the mines, quarries – perpetual conflict with intractable material. The sensation of conflict, therefore, was what I had to unload in pictorial terms. In each set of pictures I have expressed something perhaps of the same vision. But you will notice that the atmosphere is very different.[47]

Devastation: House in Wales
1940
(Cat. 40, detail).

Work by Sutherland featured regularly in the exhibitions of official war art that became a regular feature in the vacated rooms of the National Gallery. Critical responses indicate that his approach fulfilled an expectation that artists should combine vivid description with projecting more metaphorical resonances. In the series of popular books 'War Pictures by British Artists', we find Stephen Spender celebrating Sutherland's ability to express the 'tragic and triumphant side of destruction' in the volume devoted to air raid imagery: 'There is an unearthly glory about Graham Sutherland's study of *Devastation in an East End Street*; and his pictures of twisted girders have something in them of twisted humanity.'[48] Introducing the images of 'those Vulcan forges of the armament workshops and aircraft production factories' in *Production*, Cecil Beaton indicated how artists had an advantage over photographers like himself:

> In this world of molten metals, of glowing furnaces, soot and firework sparks, that only the painter can interpret, Graham Sutherland has reverently seized his opportunity to capture this fleeting phenomenon of sequined brilliance, of mystery, of glowing magic ... Sutherland has also shown us the strange architecture that the necessity of war has built for us – an architecture that resembles something built in Babylon, or some other city of which no trace is now left.[49]

At times, Sutherland's work also converged with that of his fellow contributors to the scheme. For example, his initial emphasis on architectural subjects brings the art of John Piper to mind, while the emphatic linear perspective of *Devastation 1941: An East End Street* (1941; Cat. 42) finds an echo in certain Henry Moore drawings of people sheltering in the London Underground stations. Sutherland and Moore came closest in their studies of miners, though their interpretations of such imagery might also seem quintessentially those of a painter and a sculptor respectively (Cats 53–54). Moreover, Sutherland almost certainly took a hint from Moore in starting to apply water-based paints on top of drawing with a waxy crayon, resulting in suitably blotchy atmospheric effects. In 1941 Sutherland showed an extensive selection of the pictures he had made since 1936 at Temple Newsam in Leeds, alongside work by Moore and John Piper. The use of dramatic chiaroscuro and rough, mottled textures in the work of all three artists suggests something of a shared wartime style.[50]

Once an end to the war was finally in sight, Sutherland began to think about picking up where he had left off. His independent work needs to be considered both as a resumption of his existing concerns and in relation to the broader climate of post-war art. One is immediately aware of a greater toughness and boldness, initially apparent in wartime images of production themes and then in his independent landscapes. His use of colour during this period becomes more strident, and the application of paint more fluid and uninhibited: it is as though he was no longer using oil in the same way as water-based paints – as a means of filling in the shapes within linear contours – but was starting to exploit more fully its inherent surface and textural possibilities. Such a development can be observed in works like *Feeding a Steel Furnace* (1941–42; Cat. 59), *Folded Hills* (1943; Cat. 68) and the new versions of the *Entrance to a Lane* motif (1945–46; Cats 74–75). Sutherland was able to show such work in a host of group exhibitions, at home and abroad. The British Council showed his pictures in group shows touring around Europe and acquired an impressive selection of works. Sutherland also benefited from a brief infatuation with British art in the United States. The Buchholz Gallery in New York gave him a one-man show in spring 1946, and nine pictures were sold to private collectors and museums, including the Museum of Modern Art.

Sutherland's reputation as the leading progressive British painter, ranking alongside Moore in sculpture, was further apparent from his pervasive influence on younger artists. For critic Robert Melville, who produced a major monograph on Sutherland in 1950, the artist's 1938 one-man exhibition not only launched his career but also 'founded a new school of British painting almost overnight'.[51] It is certainly true that his work was the single key point of departure in the early to mid-1940s for the likes of Prunella Clough, Robert Colquhoun, John Craxton, John Minton and Keith Vaughan, figures who by the end of the war were being widely touted as the rising generation. Several were taken up by the wealthy collector Peter Watson, who had lived in Paris before the war and on his return to Britain provided generous support to struggling artists and writers. At Watson's flat they could look at two major Sutherlands, *Gorse on Sea Wall* and *Entrance to a Lane*, along with an unrivalled collection of avant-garde journals.

Watson's more public contribution was funding and helping to edit *Horizon*, which became the house journal of the British intelligentsia in the 1940s. Under the primary editorship of Cyril Connolly, *Horizon* sought during the war to keep the flame burning for internationalism and high cultural values, especially in literature. As part of the continuous coverage of the visual arts, Sutherland's essay 'Welsh Sketch Book' appeared in spring 1942, in the guise of an open letter to Colin Anderson, another early collector of his work, although the draft had actually been headed 'Dear Peter'.[52] In 1945 a special issue of *Horizon* was produced, in French translation, to be distributed in liberated France, with the aim of highlighting British cultural achievements during a period in which contacts had largely ground to a halt. The account of the visual arts took the form of a little known essay by Watson focusing on Sutherland and, more briefly, John Craxton. The essay indicates what

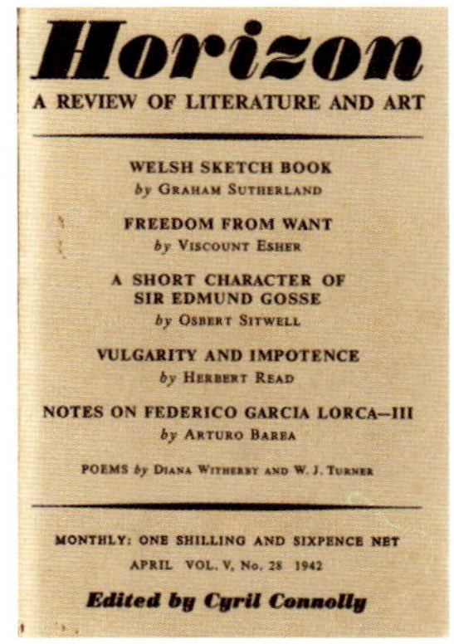
Horizon
A REVIEW OF LITERATURE AND ART
WELSH SKETCH BOOK
by GRAHAM SUTHERLAND
FREEDOM FROM WANT
by VISCOUNT ESHER
A SHORT CHARACTER OF SIR EDMUND GOSSE
by OSBERT SITWELL
VULGARITY AND IMPOTENCE
by HERBERT READ
NOTES ON FEDERICO GARCIA LORCA–III
by ARTURO BAREA
POEMS by DIANA WITHERBY AND W. J. TURNER
MONTHLY: ONE SHILLING AND SIXPENCE NET
APRIL VOL. V, No. 28 1942
Edited by Cyril Connolly

Fig. 8
Cover from *Horizon* Vol. V, No 28. April 1942.

Sutherland's art meant to its most enthusiastic and sophisticated audience. Watson emphasized the impact of the artist's visit to Pembrokeshire in 1936:

> It is in the observation of nature that Graham Sutherland has found his favourite subjects: rocky landscapes at sunset, large boulders covered in moss, the twisted forms of tree roots, the tendrils of plants – all of this stored up, ordered, abstracted from its context, and painstakingly transformed into luminous and mysterious entities. In these entities he has created a poetry of form of a powerful emotional intensity, where the emphasis is on the unity of the organic and the inorganic, and where the logic of associations only has secondary importance. He aspires to a synthesis where the usual appearance of things is boldly eliminated and where there only remains a complex of relationships. These relationships are less symbols than the fusion of an image with reality; and it is with these that he has created this very personal poetry of forms, without ever making the least concession to the decorative composition of a motif. It is clear that Sutherland works outside of all contemporary conventions, in a certain isolation; one cannot discern any distinct influence on him, and his uncompromising originality can only arouse profound admiration or violent antipathy. And yet, however paradoxical this may be, he has exercised on his contemporaries and on a whole generation of younger painters a greater influence than any other English painter of our time.[53]

The direction of influence is somewhat less clear in the case of Francis Bacon, who became a close friend of Sutherland's during the latter part of the war. Between 1944 and 1946 there seems to have been a good deal of give and take between the work of the two artists.[54] The interplay between ambiguous, metamorphic forms and flat orange backdrops, as well as a technical combination of oil and pastel on board, are among the striking common denominators between pictures the two men produced in 1944, including Bacon's *Three Studies for Figures at the Base of a Crucifixion* (Fig. 9) and Sutherlands such as *Twisted Tree Form* (Cat. 73) and *Horned Forms* (Cat. 72). There is also evidence to suggest that an awareness of Bacon's *Painting* (Fig. 10), completed by the summer of 1946,

Fig. 9
Francis Bacon (1909–1992)
Three Studies for Figures at the Base of a Crucifixion, 1944
Oil on board
Tate. Presented by Eric Hall 1953.
(N06171)

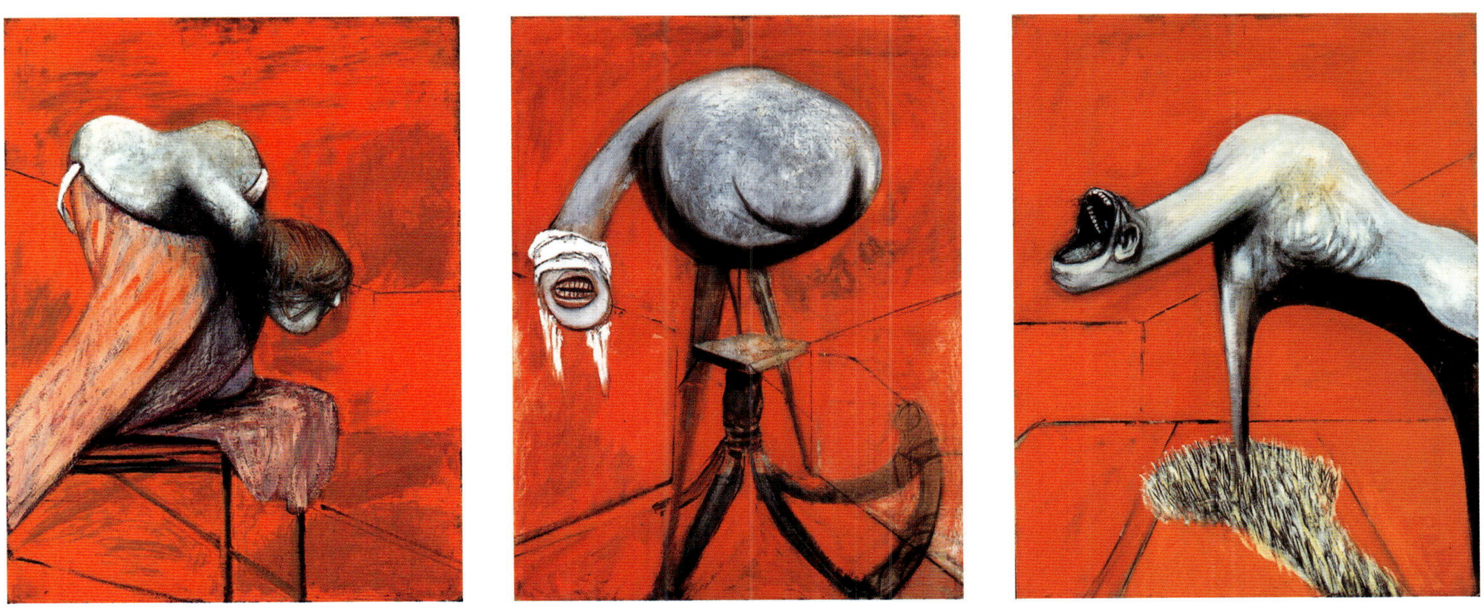

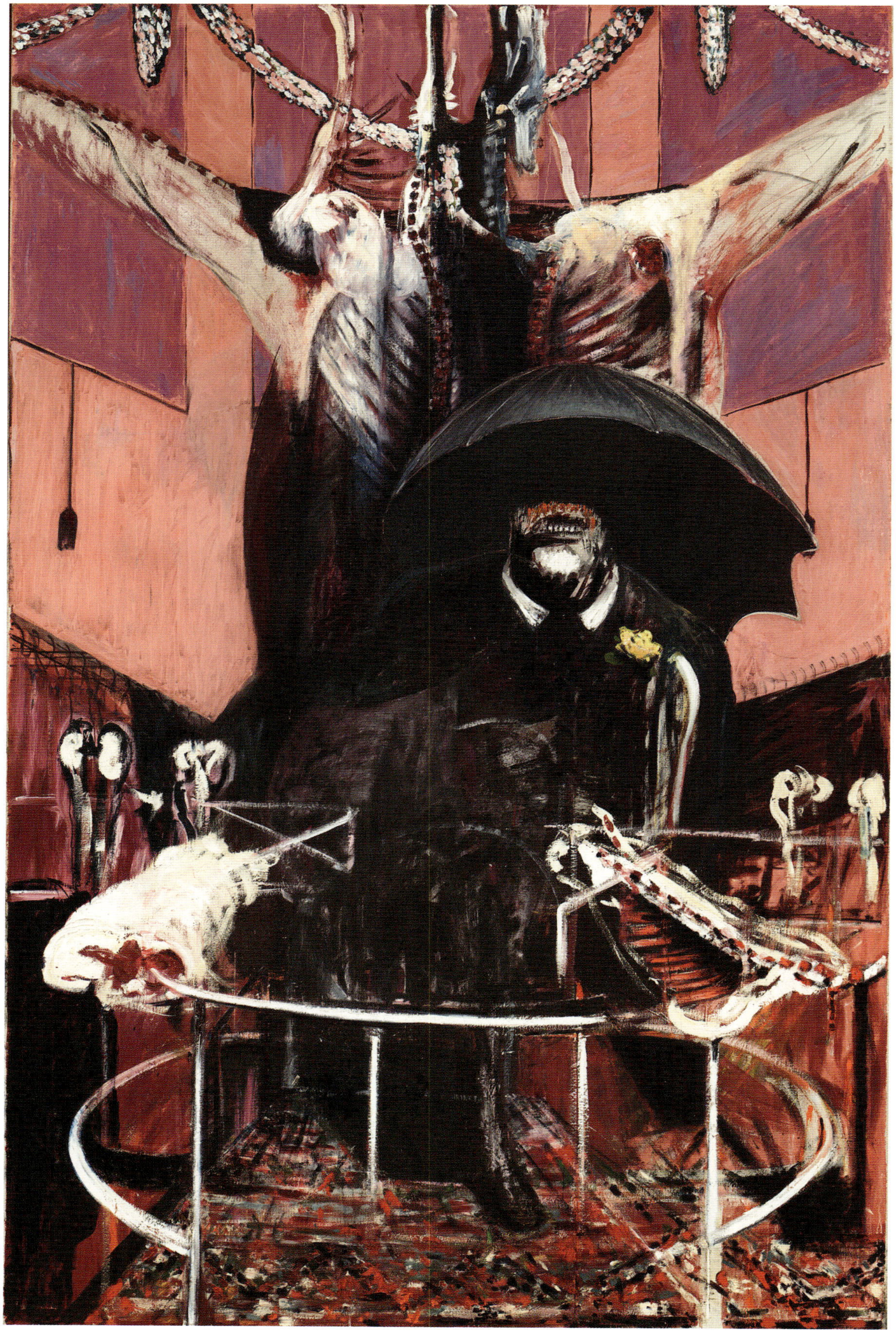

Fig. 10
Francis Bacon (1909–1992)
Painting
1946
Oil and pastel on linen
Museum of Modern Art,
New York.
(229.1948)

Fig. 11
Crucifixion
1946
Oil on hardboard
St Matthew's Church,
Northampton.

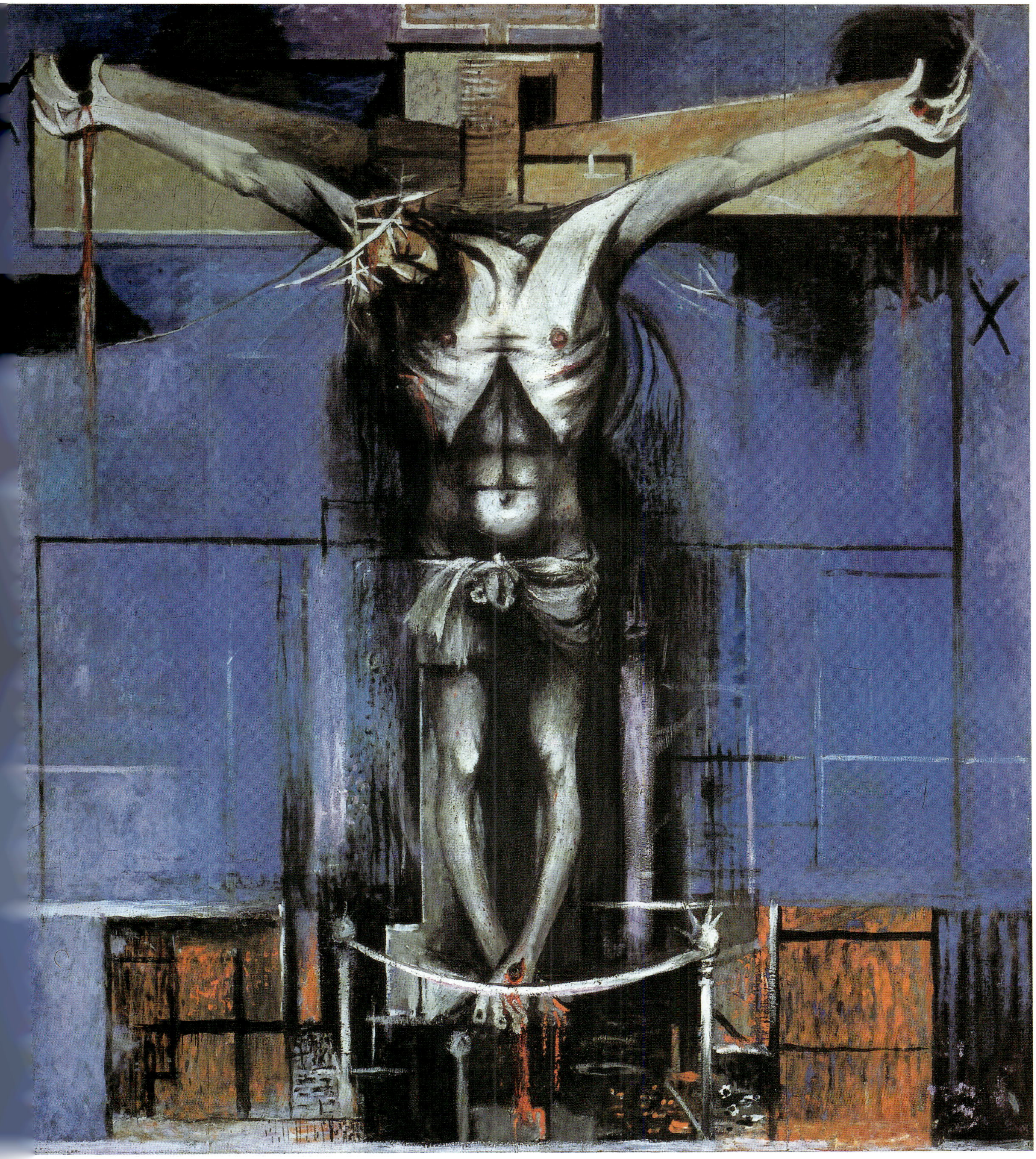

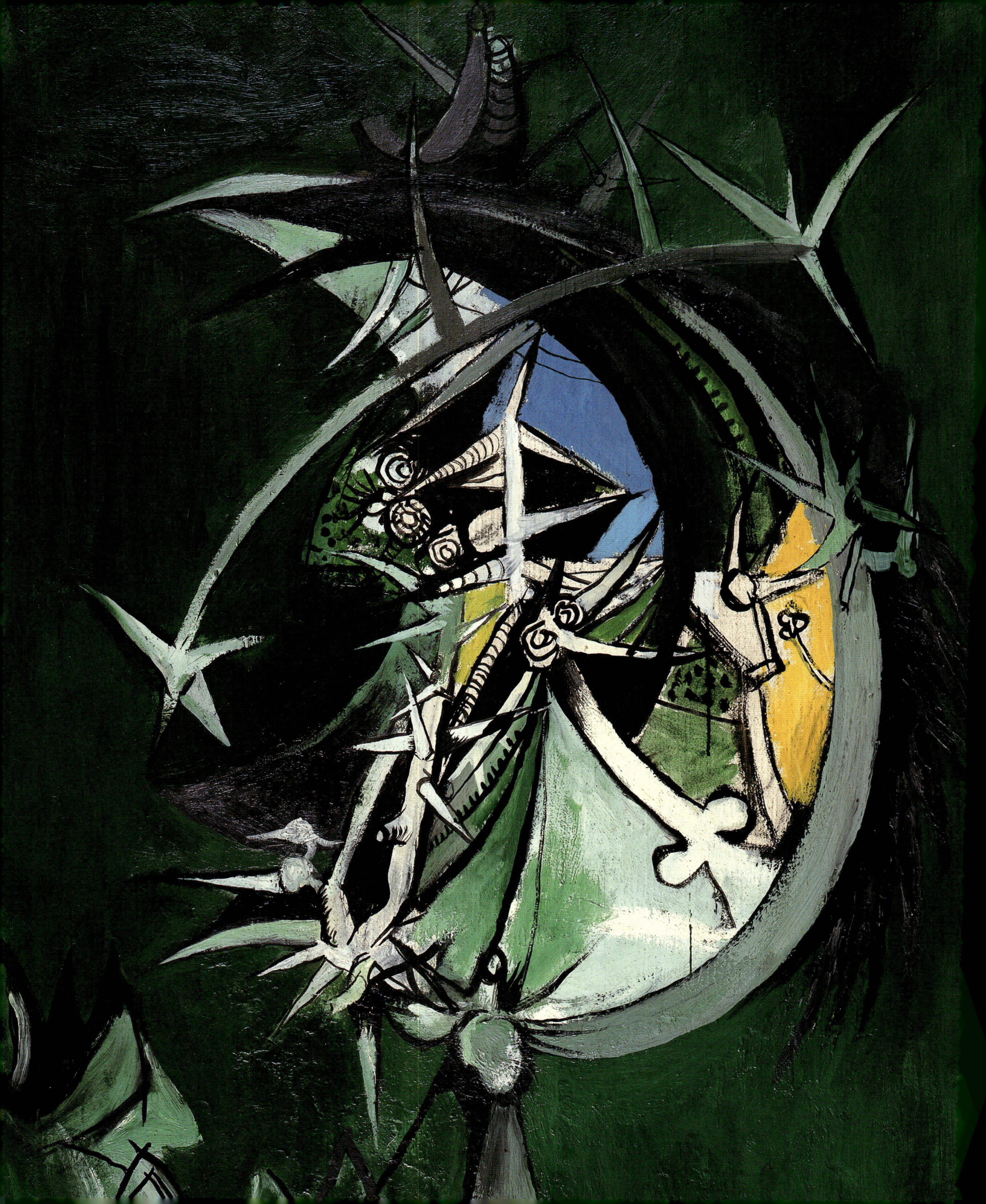

informed the big *Crucifixion* altarpiece that Sutherland produced during the second half of the year for St Matthew's Church, Northampton (Fig. 11).

The idea for the altarpiece originated in early 1944, when Sutherland attended the unveiling of Henry Moore's *Madonna and Child* sculpture in the transept. The Rev. Walter Hussey mooted the idea of a painted altarpiece to hang in the opposite transept, and suggested an Agony in the Garden. The Crucifixion, however, was Sutherland's own preferred theme, and it clearly held for him a powerful resonance of man's present inhumanity, as it did for many writers and artists of the period (including Bacon). Indeed, he may well have drawn some inspiration from David Gascoyne's 'Ecce Homo' in the collection *Poems 1937–1942*, which Sutherland had recently illustrated:

> Whose is this horrifying face,
> This putrid flesh, discoloured, flayed,
> Fed on by flies, scorched by the sun?
> Whose are these hollow red-filmed eyes
> And thorn-spiked head and spear-stuck side?
> Behold the Man: He is Man's Son.
>
> ... He is suspended on the cross-tree now
> And we are onlookers at the crime,
> Callous contemporaries of the slow
> Torture of God. Here is the hill
> Made ghastly by His scattered blood
>
> Whereon He hangs and suffers still:
> See, the centurions wear riding-boots,
> Black shirts and badges and peaked caps,
> Greet one another with raised-arm salutes...[55]

Although Sutherland vacillated for two years about how to respond to the challenge of a large figurative painting, intended for a public setting, his contemplation of the idea affected his independent landscape pictures, as he himself acknowledged in a published letter of 1946 (see p. 156). In the series of *Thorn Tree* and *Thorn Head* pictures (see Cats 76–78), on which Sutherland worked from the mid-1940s onwards, the forms of thorn bush and human head become inextricably fused, creating an inventive generalization of the image of the 'thorn-spiked head' which might also contain intimations of barbed wire or instruments of torture. When the thorn pictures were first exhibited, in early 1946, they seemed highly expressive of the current mood, and one critic was moved to quote Shelley:

> I do not know how far Graham Sutherland's thorns are deliberately symbolical.
> Oh, lift me as a wave, a leaf, a cloud!
> I fall upon the thorns of life! I bleed!
> Certainly these jagged forms are the flora appropriate to a crucified world in which atrocity has become endemic.[56]

Chimère I (Cat. 79) epitomizes Sutherland's growing confidence and ambition, and his desire at this stage to escape from the shackles of his own war work and the prevailing sense of traditionalism in English art. Compositionally, the work marks a further development of the organization of the *Thorn Tree* pictures, with their internal framing devices. Its starting point was an unimposing fallen tree trunk, with an eye-like knot, which Sutherland had come upon in Wales. He initially made some more literal, horizontal studies, but the eventual picture evokes a mysterious semi-human presence, perhaps some malevolent deity gazing imperiously in the direction of the viewer, although, judging from the title, it also alludes to the classical Chimera, a terrible monster with a dragon's tail, the body of a lion and a goat's head sprouting from its back, which was eventually fought and killed by the hero Bellerophon.[57] Whatever the picture's intended associations, Sutherland seems to have been willing here, more than in any other picture from the period, to dispense with reference to legible components of the visible world. One might again speculate

Thorn Head
1947
(Cat. 78, detail).

that his friendship with Bacon was a stimulus. The disquieting atmosphere of *Chimère I* is more than matched by Bacon's *Painting*, and the two pictures are almost exactly contemporary and identical in scale.

After 1947, the south of France replaced Pembrokeshire in Sutherland's affections. He was one of many who experienced a deep desire to escape the drabness and deprivation of life at home, after five and a half years of enforced isolation. A *Horizon* editorial lamented the signs that Britain had lost the economic war, despite military victory; London was 'now the largest, saddest and dirtiest of great cities'.[58] Doris Lessing recalled the antidote: 'there is no way now of telling how powerful a dream France was then ... it is hard to remember how people yearned for France, as for civilisation itself'.[59] Sutherland had visited Paris briefly in December 1944: 'It was the first time I'd been abroad in my life. Before the war I hadn't been able to afford it and before that I was living a really insular English life.'[60] In April 1946 he returned and visited some of the main galleries and collections devoted to modern art.[61] He first visited the south of France in April 1947, and thereafter made regular extended visits to the Côte d'Azur, leading eventually to the purchase of a house in Menton in 1955. He clearly took enormous pleasure in the climate and the landscape, not to mention meeting up with friends like Bacon in order to gamble at the Monte Carlo casino.

The south of France pictures created between 1947 and 1949 mark a reasonably coherent phase in Sutherland's evolution. His trips resulted in pictures of such unfamiliar imagery as vine pergolas, palm palisades, banana leaves and insects (Cats 80–81). These were the themes that dominated Sutherland's one-man show in 1948, which served to launch the Hanover Gallery in London. Founded by Erica Brausen, the gallery became for a number of years the most significant shop window for progressive British artists. Brausen's choice of Sutherland for her first exhibition was clearly a shrewd move, reflecting the consensus that he was the 'most important painter working in England today'. Aside from their novel subject matter, Sutherland's works from this time display a more linear definition of form, and a flatter application of bright colour. Understandably, reviewers tended to comment on the inspiration that he had absorbed from artists whom he had encountered in the Midi, notably Matisse and Picasso. Sutherland himself recalled that he felt a renewed affinity with Van Gogh, who had of course worked in the area.[62] Yet the extent to which Sutherland had changed direction can be exaggerated. In the south of France he encountered very different kinds of light and vegetation, but also an environment as 'primitive' and unspoilt as Pembrokeshire, though one might not think this now. He later remarked that by 1944 he was already painting pictures that were 'very bright and light in colour': 'When I did start working in France, in 1947, I must confess that I did wonder how I had come to anticipate, by this lightening of key, the clarity of the steady southern light'.[63] The palm pictures extended the heightened palette, spiky contours and anthropomorphic treatment of natural forms that had characterized the thorn paintings of 1945–46. Raymond Mortimer, a long time admirer, noted that the affinity extended to the gloom-laden emotional register of Sutherland's recent work:

> Into the Mediterranean basin ... into this gravely harmonious landscape, Mr Sutherland seems to have brought an obsessive, though unconscious, sense of tragedy ... A world lacerated by wars, pustulent with concentration camps, is hardly calculated to produce idyllic painting ... Mr Sutherland, moreover, is a fervent Catholic and almost all the Catholic art of our time is tragic; the writings of Mauriac, Graham Greene ... Their sense of what man might be fills them with disgust for what he is.

> Mr Sutherland's earlier works seem infused with an almost pantheistic love of nature. He painted Welsh mountains as if they were animate beings with which he identified himself. But now more usually he seems to find in nature symbols of human suffering and cruelty. The Southern vegetation hardens into instruments of torture. The palm – traditional emblem of the martyr's victory – is degraded into a weapon for his executioner.[64]

A comparably bleak reading was offered by Geoffrey Grigson in his *Horizon* essay 'Authentic and False in the New "Romanticism"', though the author's attitude to the value of Sutherland's work was very different.[65] For Grigson, a tradition of life-enhancing art had passed from nineteenth-century predecessors such as Blake and Palmer to contemporaries such as Moore. Sutherland's pictures were 'sharply impressive in their sharp clattering of colour and darkness', but from nature the artist could only extract images of death, just as in his war pictures 'devastation and destruction ... are accurately and powerfully horrible; are hell, which is his province ... In St Matthew's Church at Northampton, Henry Moore's affirmative tenderness of the Madonna and Child faces the twists and cruelty of Sutherland's little-headed, crucified Christ who suggests no resurrection.'[66] In the painter's art, 'life sinks without tension into the black death of a denatured rock and a sapless claw'.[67] In sum, the art of Sutherland represented surrender rather than resistance to the spirit of the age: 'if this is an evil time and a time of the prevalent wish for death, that is no great reason for surrendering to a deathly admiration for its expression either in language or in paint'.[68] Such responses to Sutherland epitomize the wider climate of the late 1940s, in reaction not just to the experience of the war but also to post-war revelations of the Holocaust and the terrors associated with the Cold War. Cyril Connolly drew the curtain down on *Horizon* magazine with the lament: 'it is closing time in the Gardens of the West and from now on an artist will be judged only by the resonance of his solitude or the quality of his despair'.[69] Appropriately enough, the same issue featured the first major published essay, by Robert Melville, on the art of Francis Bacon.[70]

Whilst commentators could readily assimilate his art to the prevailing atmosphere, Sutherland found himself dissatisfied with what he saw as the overly descriptive and decorative aspects of his recent work, a reservation with which one can perhaps sympathize. In a letter from the south of France, he articulated his frustration:

> It has been very lovely down here ... In spite of this, I do not seem to have produced much work, although I have been working regularly every day. To start with I think I have been experiencing a wave of really horrifying disgust and dissatisfaction with nearly all my work, and I'm afraid with some of recent date: it all seems too easy and superficial. Perhaps it is good that I should feel like this for such a thing usually precedes a period of getting closer to what I think I can and should do and therefore, also, a consistent seam of work. I can only hope so. Several ideas are simmering in the back of my mind: but they are not clear enough yet & I must solve this figure question ...
>
> ... I'm afraid I'm now convinced that English painting ... is entirely off the rails ... I think Lucian F. miles ahead of the rest although he's horribly restricted in ideas. Francis B. has done two remarkable canvases – depressing & attenuated, – but his painting I think real & containing the germ of recovery & the possibility of a post-Picasso development – at all events, to me, he makes nearly all the others look whimsy or folksy or schematic or just simply dead ...[71]

The letter gives a fascinating insight into Sutherland's

outlook towards the end of the period under consideration. His subsequent work appears, for example, to stem from this impulse to 'solve the figure question', which presumably involved inserting into his work more direct references to human imagery. At any rate, the letter comes just a few months before his first experiment with portraiture.[72] Thanks to a mutual friendship with Kenneth Clark, Sutherland and Somerset Maugham met socially in spring 1947, when the Sutherlands were staying near Maugham's villa on the French Riviera. There is some uncertainty about whether the idea of a portrait came from the artist or the sitter, and when precisely it was broached. The picture was executed, on the basis of numerous drawings from the life, during the spring of 1949 (Cat. 84). Sutherland clearly struggled somewhat with the relationship between the figure and the format of the canvas, which is slightly awkward and top-heavy here but is handled more effectively in subsequent portraits such as that of Edward Sackville-West (Cat. 85). Both portraits reveal a concern to convey the distinctive physical and psychological aura of their sitters. It is often said that Sutherland characterized, or even caricatured, Maugham as aloof and sardonic, a human equivalent to the gnarled and prickly forms that had littered his Provençal landscapes. Yet the sitter does not come across so very differently in portraits by photographers such as Yousuf Karsh (Fig. 12), and one wonders, therefore, how far Maugham's own projection and performance of self was a determining factor. What is clear is that the sharply focused realism of *Somerset Maugham* strikes an incongruous note in the context of Sutherland's work to date. In considering why he embarked upon this new direction, one might also wish to take account of the artist's informed awareness of the contemporary art scene. In Britain, the obvious precedent for a close-up, psychologically penetrating portraiture, highly descriptive in approach, was provided by the recent work of Lucian Freud, an artist Sutherland knew well and admired. Such imagery was also a significant strand in Alberto Giacometti's post-war figurative work, as in the painted and drawn images of his brother Diego. Given Sutherland's support, as a trustee, for the Tate Gallery's acquisition of several Giacomettis in 1949, as well as the known interest in this artist on the part of figures in his milieu such as Francis Bacon and Peter Watson, one might speculate that he was also encouraged by the example of Giacometti to experiment with portraiture.[73]

Sutherland presumably embarked upon his vertical *Standing Form* series in order to strengthen the figurative resonance of his work, as well as to rediscover a vein of drama and mystery that had been lacking, he felt, in his recent production. *Standing Form against a Hedge* (1950; Cat. 83), which comes near the start of this new strand of imagery, can also be seen as the culmination of a direction in Sutherland's work since the mid-1930s, when he had become obsessed by the possibility of extracting strange, hidden motifs from the countryside, as a vehicle for projecting disquieting, metamorphic imagery in the resulting pictures. Here, the principal form seems to evoke, at one and the same time, the banded, swelling trunk of a palm tree, a characteristic feature of the Midi; the abdomen of a cicada, as portrayed in his work a couple of years previously; a piece of fruit, perhaps a fig that has been sliced open; some obscure mechanical or metallic contraption; stone garden statuary; a kind of primitive fetish or totem, set on a mount; and a simplified rendition of the human figure itself. The nocturnal illumination confers a sinister atmosphere on the picture. On another level, it seems to register Sutherland's awareness of the muted, monochromatic use of colour and smeary application of paint in Francis Bacon's latest work, as presented in an acclaimed one-man show at the Hanover Gallery in late 1949. Indeed, as the *Standing Forms* evolved in the new decade, it became increasingly obvious that Sutherland was in thrall to the younger artist's work, to the detriment, one might argue, of his own art. In the 1950s, the example of Bacon seems to have prompted Sutherland to work on an expansive scale, and to indulge in

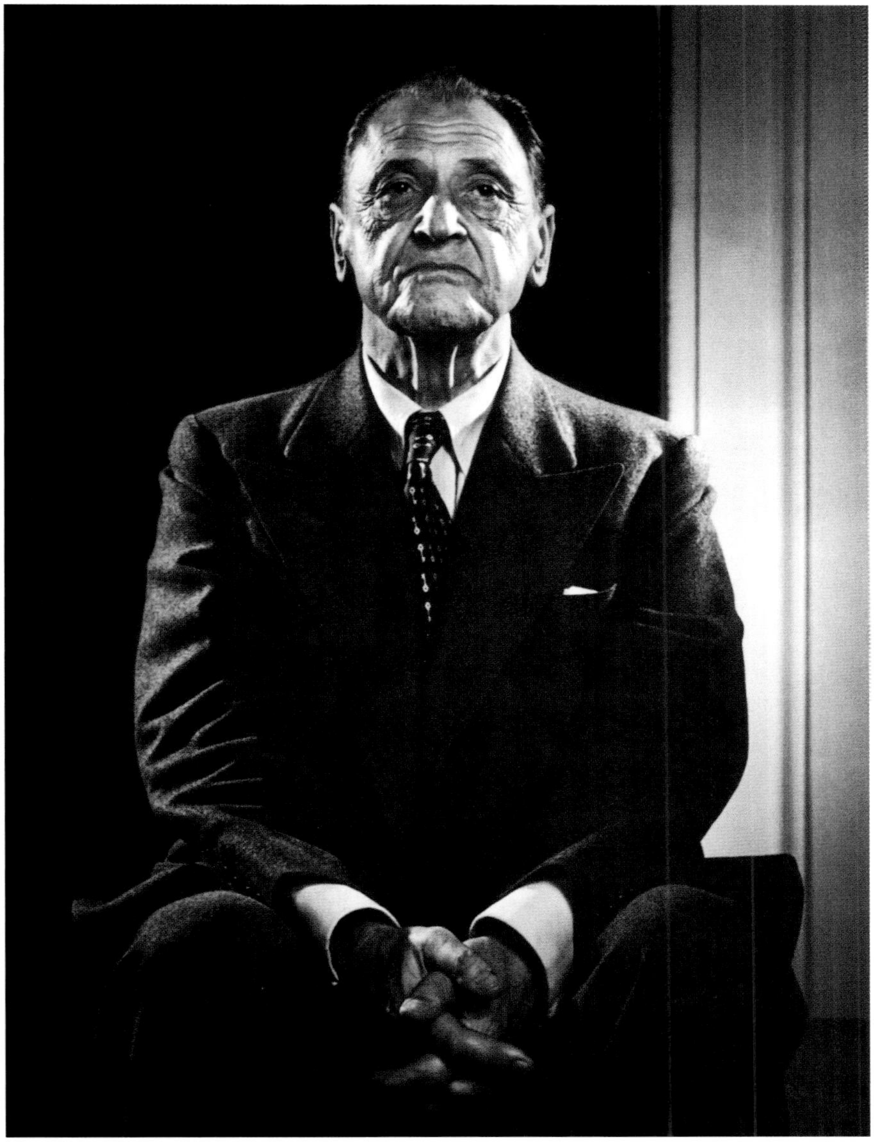

Fig. 12
Yousuf Karsh (1909–2002)
c. 1950
William Somerset Maugham
Camera Press Ltd.

a painterly rhetoric that ran contrary perhaps to his real instincts and inclinations as an artist. The relative absence of tension in the later work prompts consideration of how such a quality manifests itself in his earlier, more fully convincing pictures.

In 'Thoughts on Painting', a radio broadcast printed in 1951 in *The Listener* magazine, Sutherland talked about recent developments in his work, including the emergence of portraiture and the *Standing Form* pictures (see pp. 142–45). One passage in particular highlights a distinctive pattern of thinking. At the height of Cold War tensions, and with the Second World War and the Nazi death camps still a very recent memory, Sutherland talked about the notion that his work encapsulated the tragic tenor of the times. Up to a point, he was willing to concede this: '... the painter is a kind of blotting paper; he soaks up impressions ... and is very much part of the world. He cannot therefore avoid soaking up the implications of the outer chaos of twentieth century civilisation. By that token tragic pictures will be painted – subconsciously perhaps, and without necessarily having a tragic subject.' Nevertheless, Sutherland was at pains to resist too simplistic and one-dimensional a reading of his work, which identified art with projecting unequivocal messages, and the viewer's experience of pictures with a process of passive consumption. This was typical. In 1948 Raymond Mortimer had felt obliged to qualify his apocalyptic interpretation by noting that the bright colours of Sutherland's pictures allowed for a contrary, more optimistic reading – the artist 'goes so far as to consider them replete with gaiety'.[74] When the Catholic reading was recapitulated by Robert Melville, Sutherland refused to be drawn one way or the other (see pp. 170–72). Likewise, in 'Thoughts on Painting', he held out for ambiguity and equivocation: 'People have said that my most typical images express a dark and pessimistic outlook. That is outside my feeling. ... the precarious tension of opposites – happiness and unhappiness, beauty and ugliness, so near the point of balance – are capable of being interpreted according to the predilections and needs of the beholder – with enthusiasm and delight, or abhorrence, as with the taste of bitter-sweet fruit.'

It transpires that a tendency to savour the 'precarious tension of opposites ... near the point of balance' pervades Sutherland's outlook and art, underpinning the more conspicuous visual and thematic continuities that have already been noted. On a formal level, we frequently encounter dramatic oppositions of acidic green or pink against more neutral expanses of yellow ochre or black. Strident colour and vigorous brushwork coexist in many pictures with careful linear draughtsmanship and the visible evidence of a meticulous squaring-up process by means of which images were carried over from preparatory studies to finished paintings. In looking at Sutherland's pictures we may well, as noted, sense allusions both to English Romanticism, notably Blake and Palmer, and to the idioms of international contemporary art. Equally, the imagery of his paintings frequently relies upon a 'condensation of contrasts'.[75] Configurations might simultaneously evoke landscape imagery and bodily forms, whether human or animal. The image of the sunset, which haunts so many pictures, suggests the conjunction of day and night, and the mysterious transition between the two. In the *Entrance to a Lane* pictures, tree-lined paths become, in Sutherland's hands, dark prison-like enclosures, relieved by luminous pockets of space that intimate the possibility of imaginative escape or transcendence. Darkness and light, then, perhaps take on metaphorical connotations of suffering and redemption, death and life. For Sutherland and his audience, who had felt the full weight of the appearance of Sigmund Freud's psychoanalytical writings in English translation, such contrasts might have intimated the precarious equilibrium between conflicting instinctive forces, as described by Freud. Indeed it was possible to read the dire and unfolding crisis of the late 1930s in the light of the psychoanalyst's wide-ranging later writings, such as *Civilization and its Discontents*. These involved an explicit projection onto the social fabric at large of ideas initially developed in the context of investigations of the individual psyche. Freud came to believe that the interplay between two basic instincts, Eros (love) and the destructive, or death, instinct, was fundamental to human society. Civilization comprised:

> A process in the service of Eros, whose purpose is to combine single human individuals, and after that families, then races, peoples and nations, into one great unity, the unity of mankind. But man's natural aggressive instinct, the hostility of each against all and all against each, oppose this programme of civilization. This aggressive instinct is the derivative ... of the death instinct which we have found alongside of Eros and which shared world-dominion with it. And now, I think, the meaning of the evolution of civilization is no longer obscure to us. It must present the struggle between Eros and Death, between the instinct of life and the instinct of destruction as it works itself out in the human species.[76]

Such thinking provides a context for reading Sutherland's *Red Tree* (1936; Cats 17–18), with its suggestion of vital forces seeming to gush forth from within a dead tree root. The picture might equally be seen as a pictorial equivalent to the meditation on the inextricability of creative and destructive energies in a celebrated Dylan Thomas poem, first published in 1933 and itself informed by Freudian attitudes, which Sutherland would almost certainly have known:

> The force that through the green fuse drives
>   the flower
> Drives my green age; that blasts the roots of
>   trees
> Is my destroyer. And I am dumb to tell the
>   crooked rose
> My youth is bent by the same wintry fever.[77]

Sutherland's own writings further indicate the value he placed on polarities of sensation, held in taut balance. In September 1938, the moment of the Munich crisis when war against Germany seemed imminent, he communicated characteristically mixed feelings in a postcard to Nash: 'We are in Pembrokeshire,

Chimère I
1946
(Cat. 79, detail).

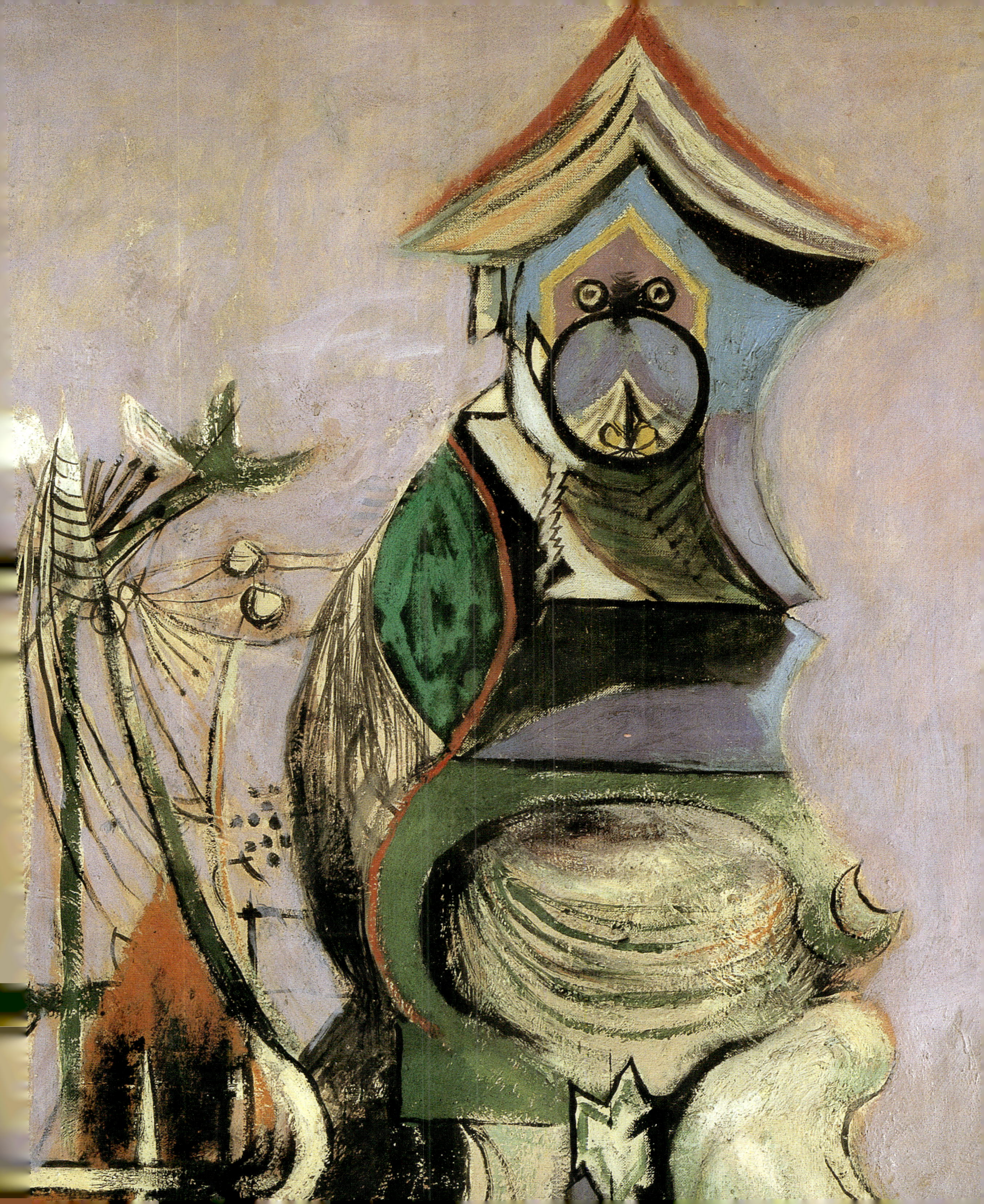

alternating between enjoyment of this superb countryside and desolation as we scan the European horizon.'[78] 'Welsh Sketch Book' indicates that the particular places to which Sutherland was drawn embraced, in a remarkably small compass, such contrary qualities as 'exultant strangeness', darkness and light, decay and life. At Brimham Rocks, he had noticed how the colours of the sunset, normally viewed as tranquil and benign, 'assume tones as of blood'.[79] From Robert Melville's illuminating account of a conversation in Sutherland's studio (see pp. 170–72), we learn of the artist's fascination with W. B. Stanford's study of Aeschylus's use of language in his classical tragedies, and in particular with the line 'The reek of blood smiles out at me', as extreme an example as one could wish for of the expressive charge of dissonant associations.[80]

In Sutherland's war work, an emphasis on oppositions is conveyed most schematically in his design for a poster for the WAAC scheme (Cat. 39), where a bombed building in nocturnal lighting is juxtaposed with a sun-drenched English landscape. Elsewhere, the forms of bombed buildings often take on bodily connotations, as noted, and 'one gets a feeling that the destruction is not final but that the organic principle of life remains; that the principles of growth and decay are almost inseparably inter-mixed'.[81] Towards the end of the conflict, Sutherland was drawn to the image of the Crucifixion because if its 'duality': 'It is the most tragic of all themes yet inherent in it is the promise of salvation. It is the symbol of the precarious balanced moment, the hair's breadth between black and white.' This emotional ambiguity was originally to have been reinforced by the use of a 'blue sky' for the Crucifixion background, though the colour he finally chose, 'a bluish royal purple, traditionally a death colour', was 'partly dictated by certain factors already in the church' (Fig. 11).[82]

A comparable approach informed the thorn pictures (Cats 76–78). For Sutherland, these were, in essence, 'about cruelty': 'The thorns sprang from the idea of potential cruelty – to me they *were* the cruelty; and I attempted to give the idea a double twist, as it were, by setting them in benign circumstances: blue skies, green grass, Crucifixions under warmth – and blue skies are, in a sense, more powerfully horrifying.'[83] One might speculate that this vein of imagery distilled Sutherland's imaginative and emotional response to the particular circumstances of spring 1945, when the idea for the pictures first crystallized in studies made in Pembrokeshire. That April, Allied forces were advancing towards the heart of the crumbling Nazi empire. Russian troops finally entered Berlin, Hitler committed suicide on the 30th, and formal celebrations of victory were held in Britain on 8 May, VE Day. Yet the news of military success was tempered by the discovery of the concentration camps. British tanks first entered Belsen, for example, on 15 April, and by the end of the month photographs, films and verbal accounts of the horrors encountered there were widely circulated. This was, indeed, a 'double twist', and Sutherland's images register the presence of unimaginable cruelty and suffering in what might otherwise have seemed benign circumstances.

Looking back at these wartime pictures sixty years later, we may well find that they evoke, vividly and often movingly, what it felt like to be living through such horrendous times and attempting to come to terms with such extreme sensations and emotions. Sutherland's art demonstrates, too, how a bleak wartime mentality took hold before the actual outbreak of hostilities, and lasted well beyond the military conflict. As we have seen, it opens up a perspective on the wider artistic and literary sensibilities of the period, as filtered through one particular body of work. Finally, from the evidence of his most inventive and fully realized pictures, one may gain some sense at least as to why Graham Sutherland was so extravagantly admired – why for some 15 years he was regarded by artists and other observers as the most remarkable British painter of his time.

Notes

1 Fuller (1988). The negative impression made by the Tate retrospective comes across in, for example, R. Shone, 'Sutherland at the Tate Gallery', *Burlington Magazine*, July 1982, pp. 461–62.

2 G. Sutherland, 'The Visionaries' [1973], reprinted in Andrews (1982), p. 26.

3 'Landscape and Figures: Graham Sutherland, O.M., discusses his art with Andrew Forge', *The Listener*, 26 July 1962, p. 132.

4 Sutherland, 'The Visionaries'.

5 For a general account of the period, see C. Harrison, *English Art and Modernism*, New Haven and London, 1994.

6 Alley (1982) gives a good representation of the design work.

7 G. Grigson, *Samuel Palmer: The Visionary Years*, London, 1947, pp. 171–72 (No. 67). Clark is given as the previous owner, and it seems likely that he would have given the drawing to Sutherland. The work was subsequently donated by Kathleen Sutherland to the British Museum, along with two late Palmer prints that Sutherland owned (Cats 3–4).

8 G. Sutherland, letter to Kenneth Clark, 27 December [1939?], Tate Gallery Archive (hereafter Tate).

9 E. and P. Lewis, *The Land of Wales*, London, 1937, p. 3.

10 *Ibid.*, p. 34.

11 G. Sutherland, cited in Barber (1964), p. 44.

12 D. H. Lawrence, *Selected Essays*, Harmondsworth, 1950, p. 62.

13 See J. Montagu (ed.), *Paul Nash: Modern Artist, Ancient Landscape*, London, 1982.

14 In this context, one might recall the general argument concerning continuities between Romanticism and Modernism in Rosenblum (1975). Sutherland is one of many artists discussed by Rosenblum within this framework.

15 'Graham Sutherland Explains his Art', *Illustrated London News*, CCXVIII, 19 February 1966, p. 30.

16 'Landscape and Figures', p. 132.

17 'Exhibition of Works by André Masson', exh.cat., Wildenstein Gallery, London, 12 February to 6 March 1936.

18 See W. Rubin and C. Lanchner, *André Masson*, exh. cat., New York: The Museum of Modern Art, 1976, p. 215.

19 'Landscape and Figures', p. 132.

20 *Ibid.*, p. 133.

21 H. Read, 'Picasso's *Guernica*', *London Bulletin*, No. 6, October 1938, p. 6.

22 G. Sutherland, cited in Berthoud (1982), p. 92.

23 Sackville-West (1944), p. 9. The example cited was *Landscape with Sullen Sky*, then in Clark's collection, now in the Harris Museum and Art Gallery, Preston.

24 G. Sutherland, 'Images Wrought from Destruction' (see pp. 102–05).

25 A. C. Sewter, 'Round the Art Exhibitions', *The Listener*, 16 May 1940, p. 980.

26 H. Read, 'Introduction', *The International Surrealist Exhibition*, exh. cat., London: New Burlington Galleries, 11 June – 4 July 1936, p. 13.

27 For a wide-ranging discussion of this phenomenon in British culture, see S. Smiles, 'Equivalents for the Megaliths', in Corbett, Holt and Russell (2002), pp. 199–224.

28 Newton (1950), p. 85.

29 R. Mortimer, 'Painting and Humanism', *New Statesman and Nation*, 28 March 1942, p. 208.

30 J. Piper, *British Romantic Artists*, London, 1942, p. 48.

31 Sackville-West (1944), pp. 9 and 10.

32 See A. Powers, 'The Reluctant Romantics: *Axis* Magazine 1935–37', in Corbett, Holt and Russell (2002), pp. 264–65.

33 G. Sutherland, letter to Sackville-West, 20 April 1942, Tate.

34 *The Tate Gallery's Wartime Acquisitions*, exh. cat., London: National Gallery, April–May 1942, Nos. 135 (Sutherland) and 8, 10 and 11 (Blake).

35 G. Sutherland, letter to Keith Vaughan, 7 February 1943, cited in Berthoud (1982), p. 108.

36 Sackville-West (1944), p. 9.

37 'Landscape and Figures', p. 132.

38 J.-P. Sartre, *The Diary of Antoine Roquentin*, London, 1949, translated by Lloyd Alexander (thereafter *Nausea*), p. 182. First published in France in 1938.

39 *Ibid.*, p. 185.

40 *Ibid.*, pp. 185–86.

41 K. Raine, 'The Poet of our Time', in R. March and Tambimuttu (eds), *T. S. Eliot*, London, 1948, p. 78.

42 *The Complete Poems and Plays of T. S. Eliot*, London, 1969, p. 24.

43 *Ibid.*, p. 61.

44 Sutherland, 'Images Wrought from Destruction'.

45 G. Sutherland, letter to Edward Sackville-West, 8 February 1941, Tate.

46 'Art and Life. Part of a discussion between V. S. Pritchett, Graham Sutherland, Sir Kenneth Clark, and Henry Moore', *The Listener*, 13 November 1941, p. 657.

47 G. Sutherland, draft letter to Eric Newton at the time of the making of 'Out of Chaos', Sutherland Archive, National Museum and Gallery of Wales, Cardiff (hereafter Cardiff).

48 S. Spender, 'Introduction', *Air Raids*, 'War Pictures by British Artists' (Second Series, No. 4), London, 1943, p. 7.

49 C. Beaton, 'Introduction', *Production*, 'War Pictures by British Artists' (Second Series, No. 2), London, 1943, p. 6.

50 For recent accounts of their war work, see J. Andrews, *London's War: The Shelter Drawings of Henry Moore*, London, 2002; D. Fraser Jenkins, *John Piper: The Forties*, London, 2000.

51 R. Melville, 'A Panorama of Modern Art', *World Review*, March 1949, p. 44.

52 G. Sutherland, draft manuscript, Cardiff.

53 P. Watson, 'Note sur deux peintres anglais', *La Littérature anglaise depuis la guerre*, London, 1945, pp. 24–27 (author's translation).

54 Discussed in greater depth in Hammer (2005).

55 Gascoyne (1943), p. 5.

56 R. Marvell, 'New Pictures', *The New Statesman and Nation*, 16 February 1946, p. 119. The quotation is from Shelley's 'Ode to the West Wind'.

57 Sutherland's title presumably signals a further reference to the sonnet sequence *Les Chimères* by Gérard de Nerval, the French Romantic poet who was much admired in wartime literary circles in London

58 C. Connolly, 'The Coming of the Crisis – I', reprinted in his *Ideas and Places*, London, 1953, p. 142.

59 Cited in P. Conradi, *Iris Murdoch: A Life*, New York and London, 2001, p. 214.

60 Sutherland, 'Images Wrought from Destruction'.

61 Berthoud (1982), pp. 125–26.

62 Barber (1964), p. 49.

63 G. Sutherland, 'Thoughts on Painting' (see pp. 142–45).

64 R. Mortimer, 'Graham Sutherland's New Paintings', *Harper's Bazaar*, July 1948, p. 71.

65 G. Grigson, 'Authentic and False in the New "Romanticism"', *Horizon*, No. 99, March 1948, pp. 203–13.

66 *Ibid.*, pp. 205 and 206–07.

67 *Ibid.*, p. 209.

68 *Ibid.*, p. 208.

69 [Cyril Connolly], 'Comment', *Horizon*, Nos 120–21, December 1949 – January 1950, p. 362.

70 R. Melville, 'Francis Bacon', *Ibid.*, pp. 419–23.

71 G. Sutherland, letter to the Melvilles, 20 November 1948, Robert Melville Papers, Tate.

72 For a detailed account of the project see Berthoud (1982), pp. 133–43.

73 This argument is elaborated and illustrated in Hammer (2005).

74 Mortimer, 'Graham Sutherland's New Paintings', p. 71.

75 Soby (1948), p. 136.

76 Cited in A. Storr, *Freud*, Oxford, 1989, p. 53.

77 D. Jones (ed.), *Dylan Thomas. The Poems*, London and Melbourne, 1974, p. 77.

78 G. Sutherland, postcard to Paul Nash, 16 September 1938, Paul Nash Papers, Tate.

79 G. Sutherland, 'An English Stone Landmark' (see pp. 64–65).

80 This was an inspiration that Sutherland shared with Francis Bacon, whose interest in Stanford's book has often been discussed.

81 Art Critic [Keith Vaughan], 'War Artists and the War', *The Penguin New Writing*, No. 16, March 1943, pp. 115–16.

82 Sutherland, 'Thoughts on Painting'.

83 *Ibid.*

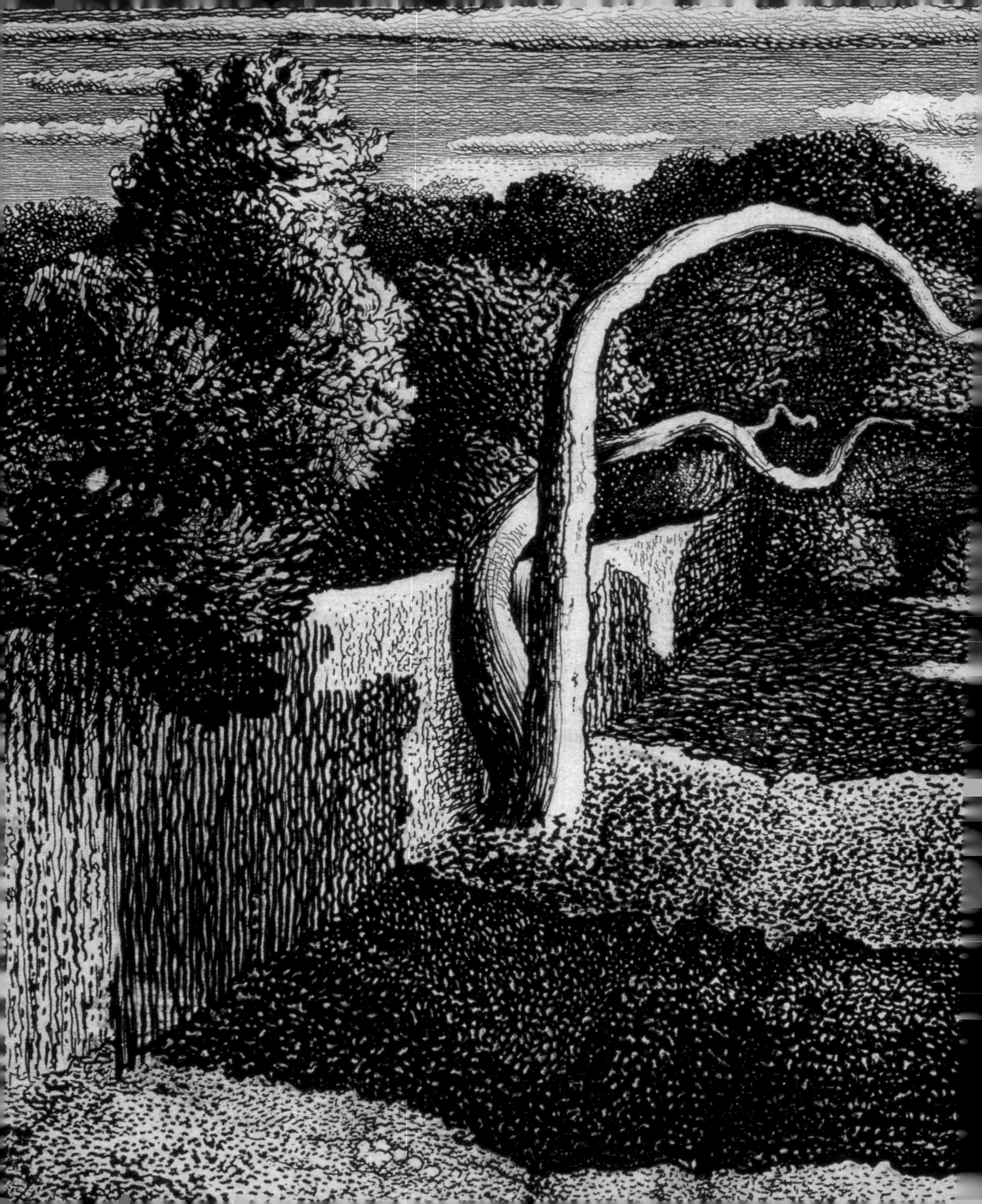

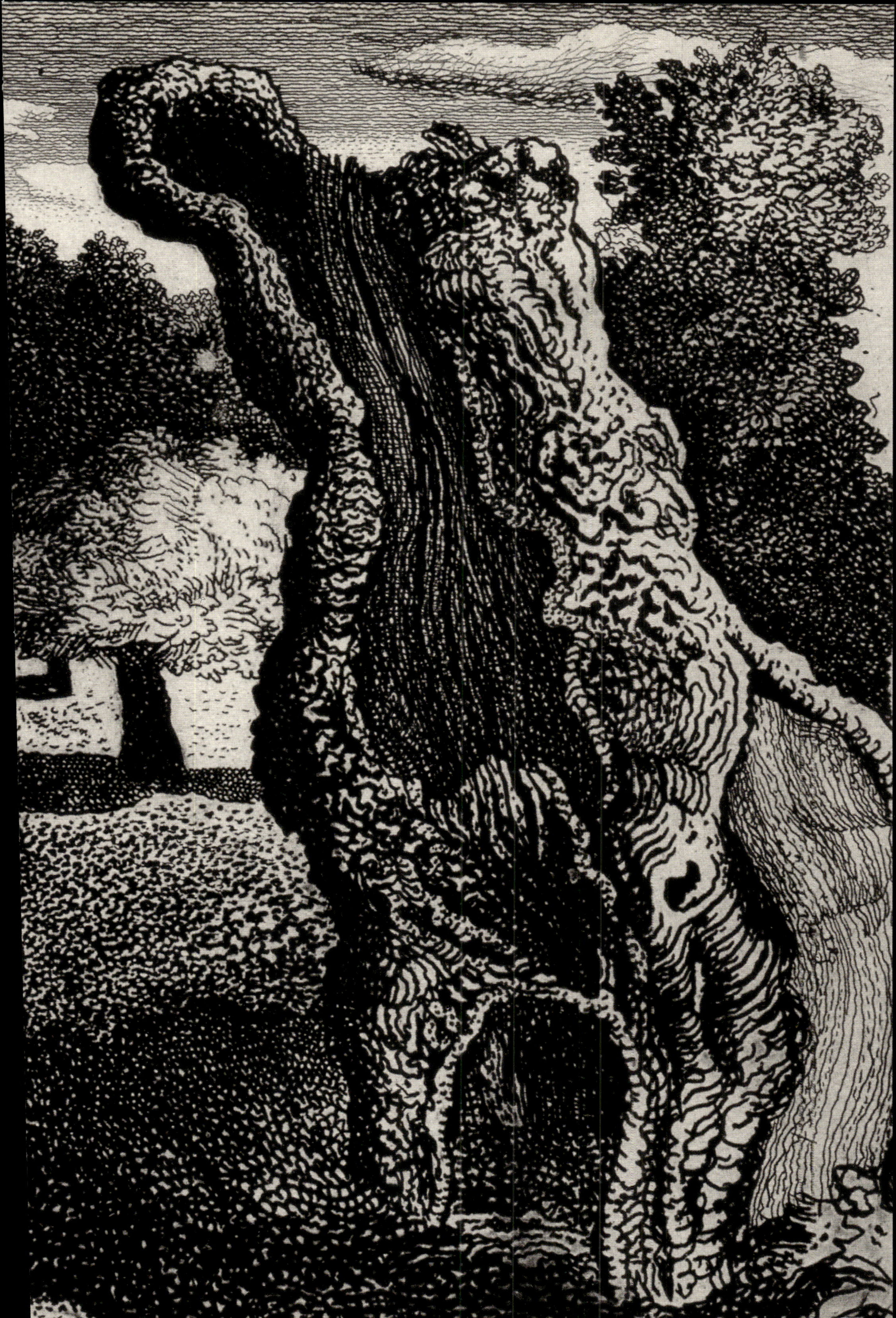

1

Early Prints
1924–1932

Pastoral
1930
(Cat. 10, detail).

A Trend in English Draughtsmanship

Graham Sutherland

> Then I asked: 'Does a firm persuasion that a thing is so, make it so?'
> He replied: 'All poets believe that it does, and in the ages of imagination this firm belief moved mountains; but many are not capable of a firm belief in anything.'
>
> William Blake, *Marriage of Heaven and Hell.*

It is our wont, nowadays, in attempting to discuss the nature of things, to make categories. This, however, is often an imperfect method of identification, and particularly so when we attempt to discuss the nature of art; for the very qualities which we regard as being especially characteristic of a particular type of art are, in fact, elusive, and may be found to be a constituent of another type of art. Yet if we wish to communicate our enthusiasms, we must adopt some means of distinguishing them.

Mr Herbert Read has already given us an exhaustive and masterly analysis of the whole field of art in its various divisions and subdivisions.[1] My intention in this essay is to simplify the issue by limiting the conception of draughtsmanship to two heads only. The one head is objective, extrinsic, and, broadly speaking, may be said to depend on direct visual experience; the other is subjective, and depends on the disposition of the artist to design from his inner consciousness.

It is my intention in this article to discuss the second head only, but in order to do this it will first be necessary for me to describe the divergencies between the two heads.

I have said that the objective outlook depends on the experience of the eye. Such experience may lead an artist of this type to make a representation of what he sees, or it may induce him to make a painted pattern derived from the forms before his eyes. In either case his inspiration is limited objectively, and his enjoyment is bound up with his choice and apprehension of the rhythms which he abstracts from the visual field.

In theory it is easy to distinguish our second type of draughtsman, but in practice this is difficult. We may assert that an artist working objectively depends on the experience of his eye, but so, to a certain degree, does an artist who works from within. The real difference, however, between the objective and the subjective artist lies in the fact that the function of the latter is akin to that of the poet, since he is essentially creative. But since he cannot create *ex nihilo*, he is objective in the sense that he is continually gathering material from his experience of physical things.

This extrinsic material may comprise the component parts of the scene before him, or he may find it in isolated forms. But the parts of the scene, as they reach his mind, lose their normal contiguity, the isolated forms their identity, and all become absorbed in the reservoir of the subconscious mind out of which emerge the reconstructed and re-created images.

Thus an artist of this type must be possessed of a lively visual curiosity. We shall not find him searching for ideas. We shall find him in a receptive mood, awaiting the ideas which well up from his subconscious mind. He is on a voyage, out of touch with the land, and sails in uncharted seas. His ship carries him where it will; his discoveries sometimes frighten him, but are always exciting. Sometimes that which he sees may be, like a mirage, non-existent. 'I do not seek,' said Picasso, 'I find.' In short, the production of work of this kind is less an active than a passive and involuntary process. That is not, however, to say that the brain does not take a hand. It assesses the value of and selects from the images as they rise, rejects any which are paltry, and contrives the selected ones in terms of the material employed.

In a short essay of this sort it is only possible to select a few individuals as types partially or wholly representative of the subjective trend. If we look in this country among artists of the past for an example of this tendency, the most obvious is William Blake. As he is, perhaps, the first and most characteristic example of the type, it would, perhaps, be fitting to give a short analysis of his development.

His mind was directed early into the habit of religious mysticism. Poet and painter as he was, much of his earlier pictorial work has a literary association which his students, no doubt, believe they have discovered. That this theological ideography at times adulterated the inherent spiritual quality of the designs themselves, there can be no doubt; and in this sense the literary significance intended can hold little interest for us.

In addition to this disadvantage Blake had other difficulties to meet. During the earlier part of his life we find inconsistencies of style which mar the unity of his designs. More often than not his work was filled with incongruous elements; he was unable to relate the human figure to the landscape, and this itself was confused in expression.

It must be assumed that these vagaries of style were due, not so much to his inability to draw out of his mind a unity of those forms which inhabited it, as to the fact that these forms themselves derived little nourishment from the natural world; while others inspired by various and incongruous sources, were insufficiently assimilated. Frequently their origin is to be found in the pictorial style of other artists, a legitimate, useful and necessary source of inspiration, provided the style is understood. But Blake more often than not received material of this kind direct and failed to adapt it to his needs and temperament. Further, he rarely refreshed his imagination by making studies from natural phenomena. He is reputed to have said that 'Nature put him out'. It is not difficult to understand what he meant by this: the two activities – drawing from nature and from a conceived mental image – are not reconcilable. Blake may have tried at one time to combine both these practices. Had he nourished his conceptual ideas by familiarizing himself with the ways of nature, his art might have reached the perfection of its maturity at an earlier period. But be this as it may, it is almost solely in the Dante drawings and the wood-engravings executed for Ambrose Philips' imitation of Virgil's 1st Eclogue – works executed towards the end of his life – that we see Blake at the height of his powers, and achieving complete unity of expression. In these works, too, the pictorial life is so little adulterated with literary associations that nothing matters except the self-contained vitality which they manifest. Here there is no trace of the earlier inconsistencies.

In them we see a mysterious grandeur and a flaring ecstasy. What strange and exciting vistas they open up for us! This tree, so like yet so unlike the trees of our visual knowledge, so universal yet so intimate, obeys no laws except those of its creator. These stark forms clothed in rich lambent colours, blithe or grave, are strangely familiar yet disturbingly unprecedented. What power they have to move us!

Blake's direct influence appears to have been confined to a small group of disciples of whom the most distinguished was Samuel Palmer. Palmer's significance as a type is based on a small collection of drawings made during the space of five years. I mention these drawings because they are comparatively little known; moreover, their character is such as amply to fulfil our attempted definitions. A few may be seen either in the Tate Gallery or the Victoria and Albert Museum, but most of them are in private collections.

No estimate of this type of work would be complete, I feel, without mentioning the later work of Turner. I say later work, because while it is there that his genius shows its greatest purity, it is there, too, that we can trace the evidence of his subjective mind.

We shall find, perhaps, better examples of this among his paintings than among his drawings (if in an article on draughtsmanship we may allude to paintings). In his Petworth Interior in the National Gallery, and his 'Sunrise and the Sea Monster' in the Tate Gallery, we recognize the quality of that excitement which their remote and intangible ecstasies arouse in our minds.

Both Blake and Turner were born out of due time, but to-day we have reached a stage at which we can appreciate their genius and, at least, their influence has made it possible for us to understand work of contemporary artists whose method of approach is comparable with theirs.

In our time and in this country this approach has derived an immense stimulus from abroad, but the best English work, whilst retaining its essential universality, shows definite native characteristics. 'The more a poet sings in his genealogical tree,' said Jean Cocteau, 'the more his singing is in tune.' As far back as 1917 Paul Nash was painting with individual taste and sensibility – and later with far more than this; we find him producing work of a strangely moving kind, and asserting in unmistakable terms his imaginative personality. Not only do we see this in a series of paintings of extraordinary significance and power, but we find in his drawings for books – such drawings as 'Mansions of the Dead' and 'Summer', from Sir Thomas Browne's *Urne Buriall and the Garden of Cyrus* – a poetic and imaginative achievement without equal to-day in this country.

It would be difficult to find clearer evidence of the subjective tendency than that shown in the work of the sculptor Henry Moore. His drawings are of two kinds, and both are intimately connected with his sculpture.

On the one hand he makes drawings from nature; on the other he produces drawings of a kind which may be said to be a prelude to his sculpture, and in these we are astonished at the fertility of the invention displayed. There the forms certainly derive their shape from the exigency of representing the sculptor's ideas in terms appropriate to the material in which he will be working, for, like all good artists, Moore never does violence to his material. For this reason the drawings, as such, possess a self-contained vitality of their own. They are not merely studies for proposed sculpture, but have the qualities, textures and colour proper to a drawing. If we examine the drawings, of which the accompanying reproduction is one, we see Moore's art, to quote Maritain, 'recomposing its peculiar world with that poetic reality which resembles things in a far more profound and mysterious way than any direct evocation could possibly do'. We find Moore discovering one thing with the help of another, and by their resemblance making the unknown known.

It will have been apparent that the purpose of this article is not to index a list of artists, but to describe and distinguish a type of art. It is not claimed that all pictorial art is entirely objective or subjective in approach. Frequently an artist whose approach may be said to depend on direct visual knowledge will experience an imaginative excitement governing the manipulation of his medium. Other instances could be given of an overlapping of the two types of activity; in many cases the line of demarcation is difficult to analyse. But that there is work conforming more closely to the one type of approach than the other there can be no doubt; and not only must the artist have as clear as possible an idea of the character of his aims, but those who possess themselves of his drawings should have an equally clear idea of those aims. Those who are in sympathy with the characteristics of the approach more particularly discussed above will doubtless meet with work possessing attributes conforming to this type. If when they meet it they can recognize it for what it is, this article will not have been written in vain.

1 *Art Now*, by Herbert Read. Faber & Faber, 12s. 6d.

(*Signature*, July 1936, pp. 7–13)

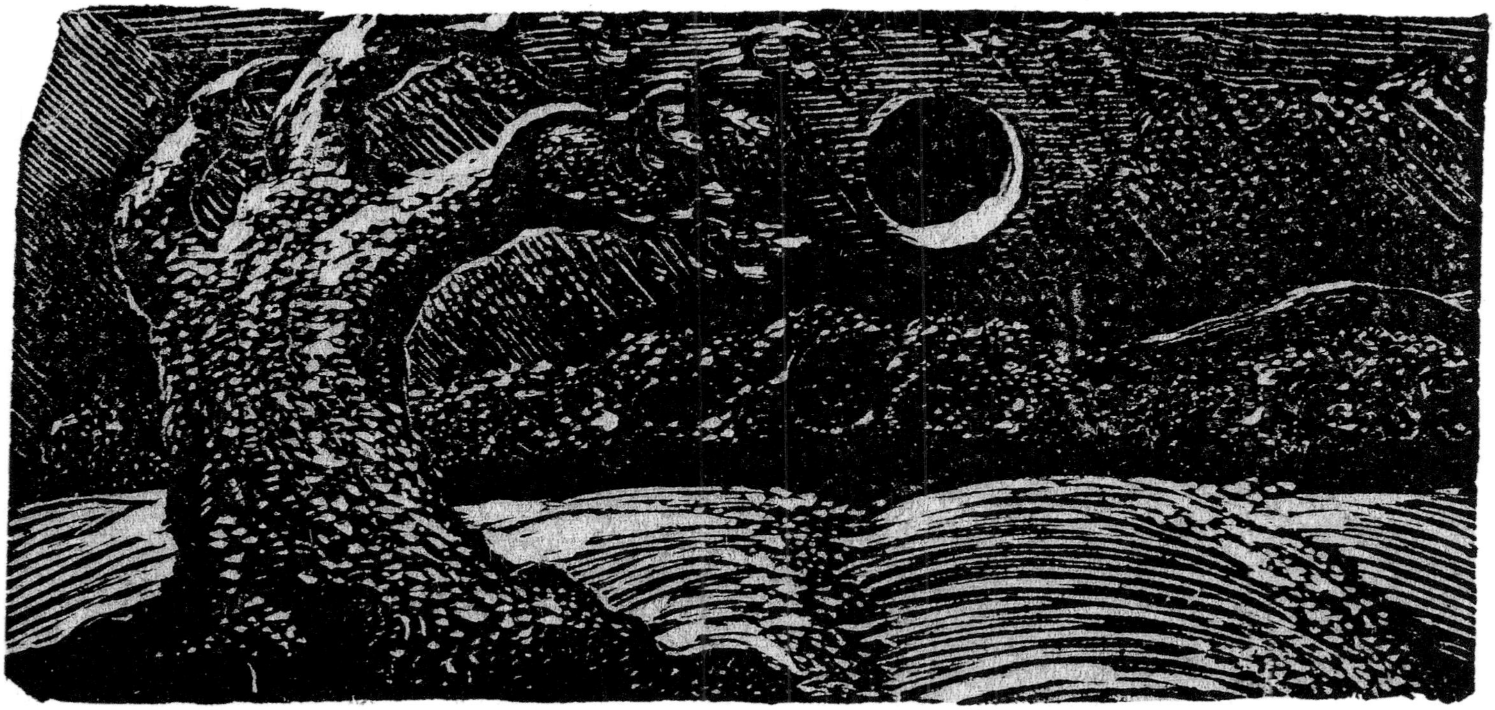

1.
WILLIAM BLAKE
(1757–1827)
The Blighted Corn from Thornton's *Pastorals of Virgil*
1821/c. 1830
Wood engraving
34 x 73 mm
Tate. Presented by Herbert Linnell 1924
A0116.

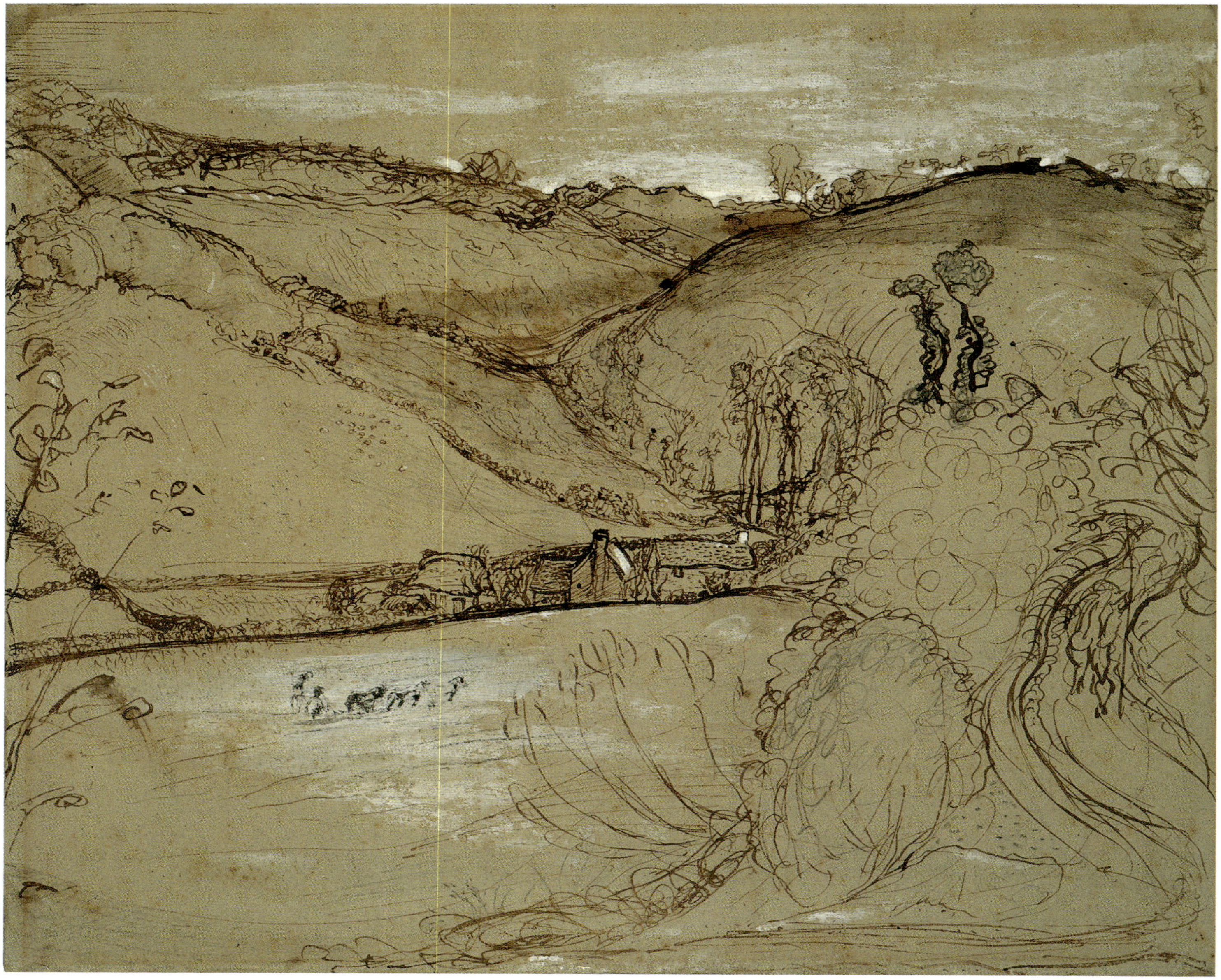

2.
SAMUEL PALMER
(1805–1881)
The Valley Farm
c. 1828
Pen and brown ink, with graphite, heightened with Chinese white; on brown-grey paper
220 x 275 mm
British Museum
1980-10-11-224
Formerly Graham Sutherland collection.

This drawing was acquired by Kenneth Clark, who at some point gave it to Sutherland.

3.
SAMUEL PALMER
(1805–1881)
The Herdsman's Cottage,
or **Sunset**
1850
Etching
98 x 78 mm (image size)
British Museum
1980-10-11-226.
Formerly Graham Sutherland collection.

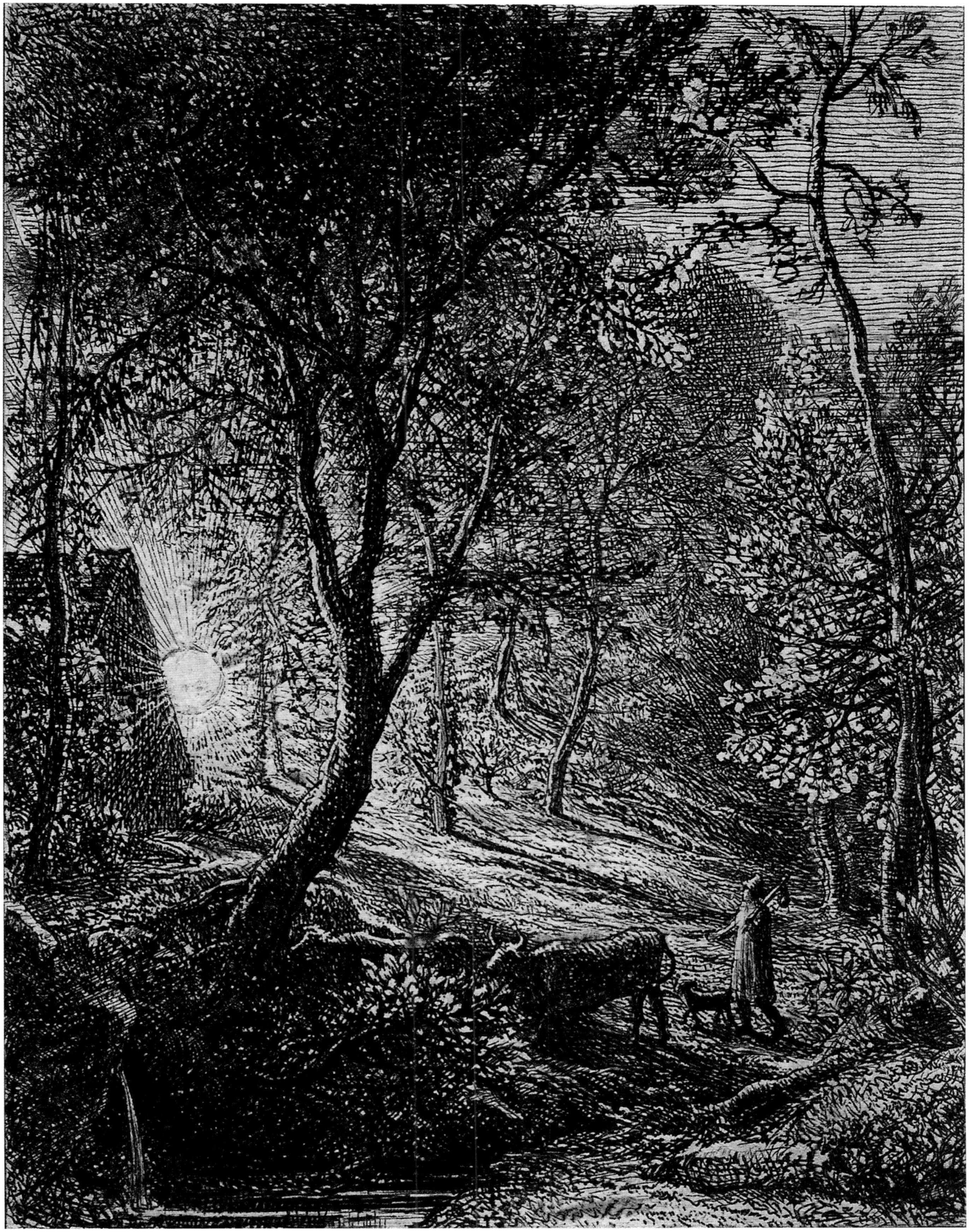

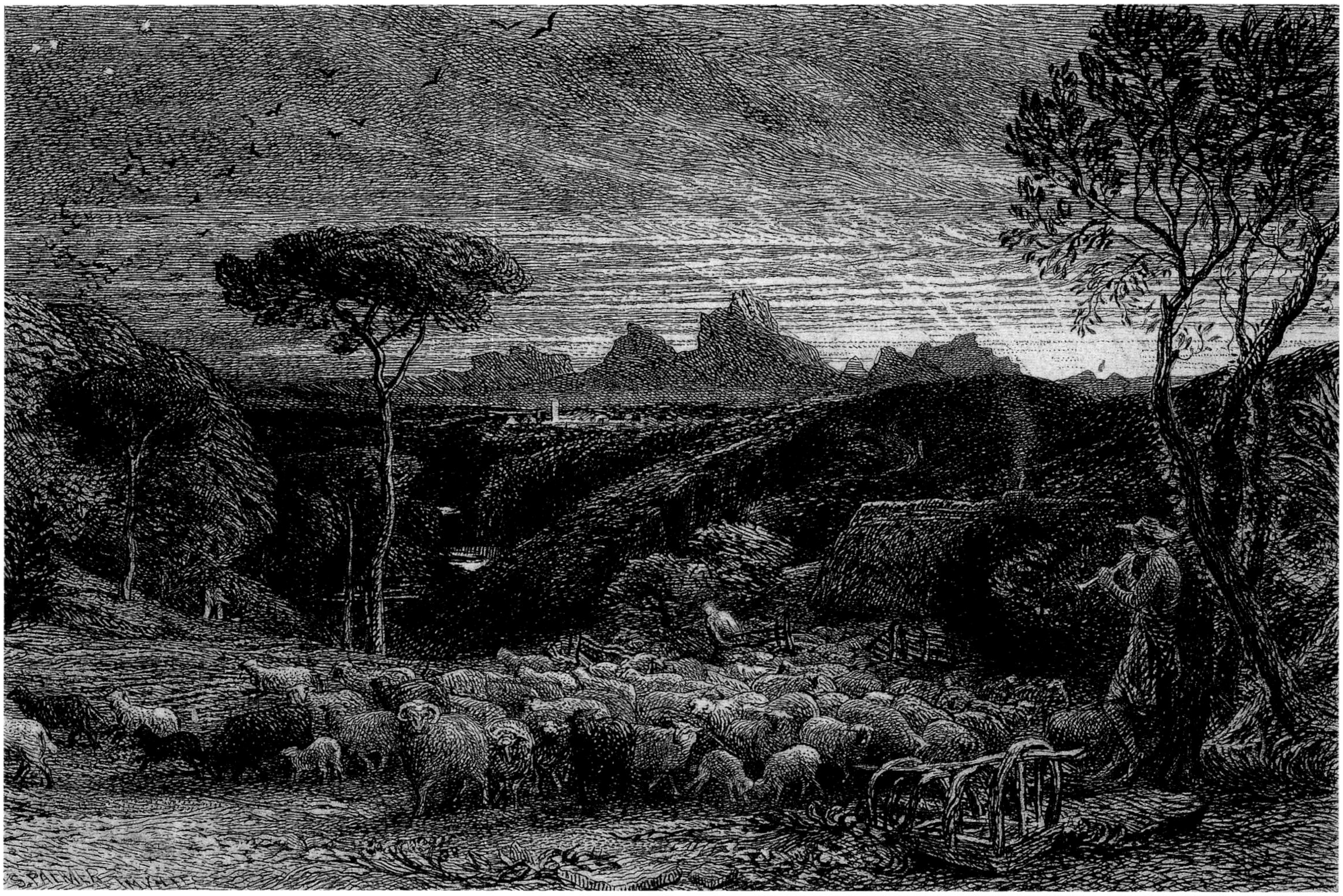

4.
SAMUEL PALMER
(1805–1881)
Opening the Fold, or **Early Morning**
1880
Etching
118 x 176 mm (image size)
British Museum
1980-10-11-227
Formerly Graham Sutherland collection.

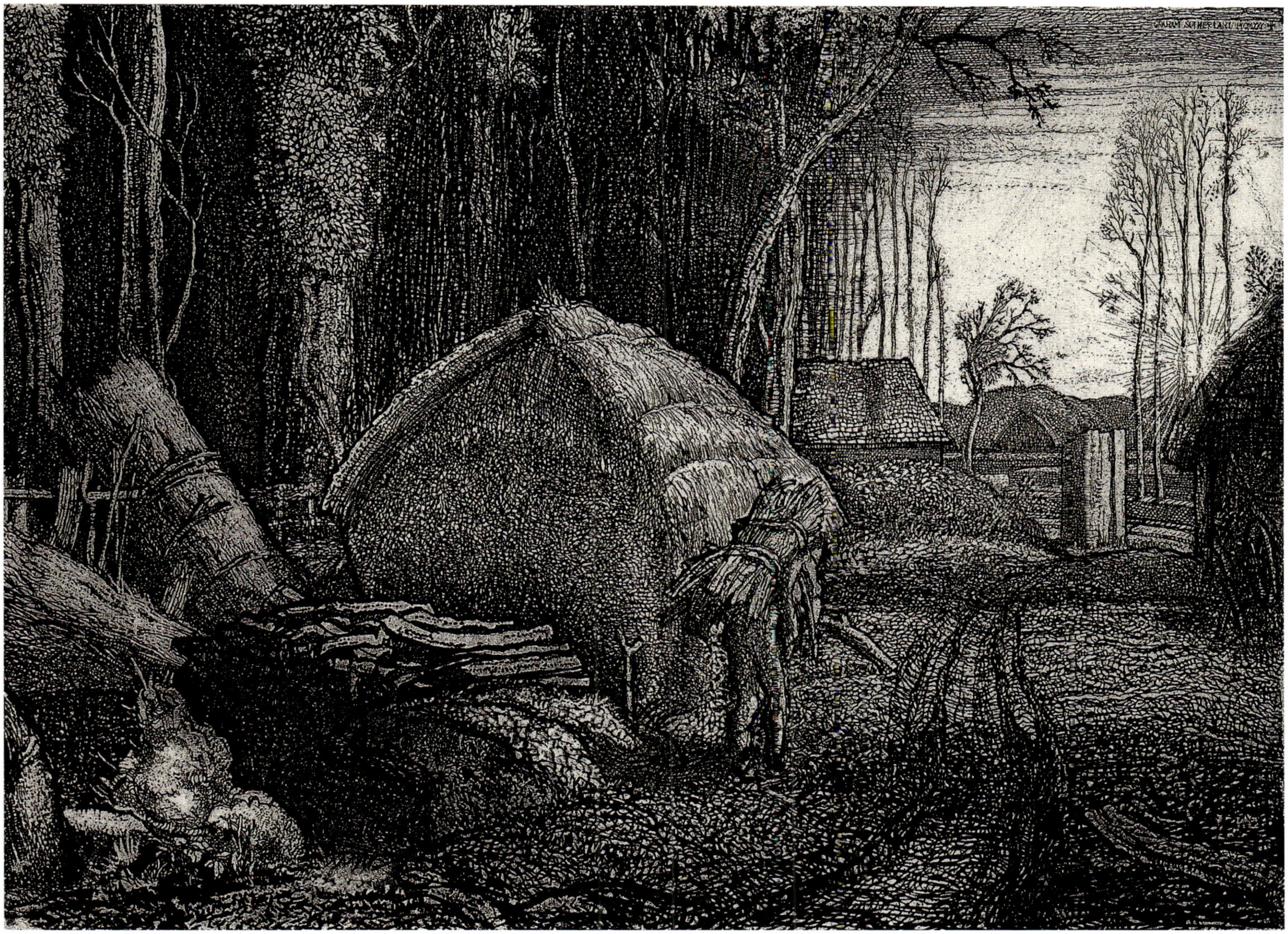

5.
Pecken Wood
1925
Etching
136 x 188 mm (image size)
The Scottish National Gallery
of Modern Art, Edinburgh
GMA 765.

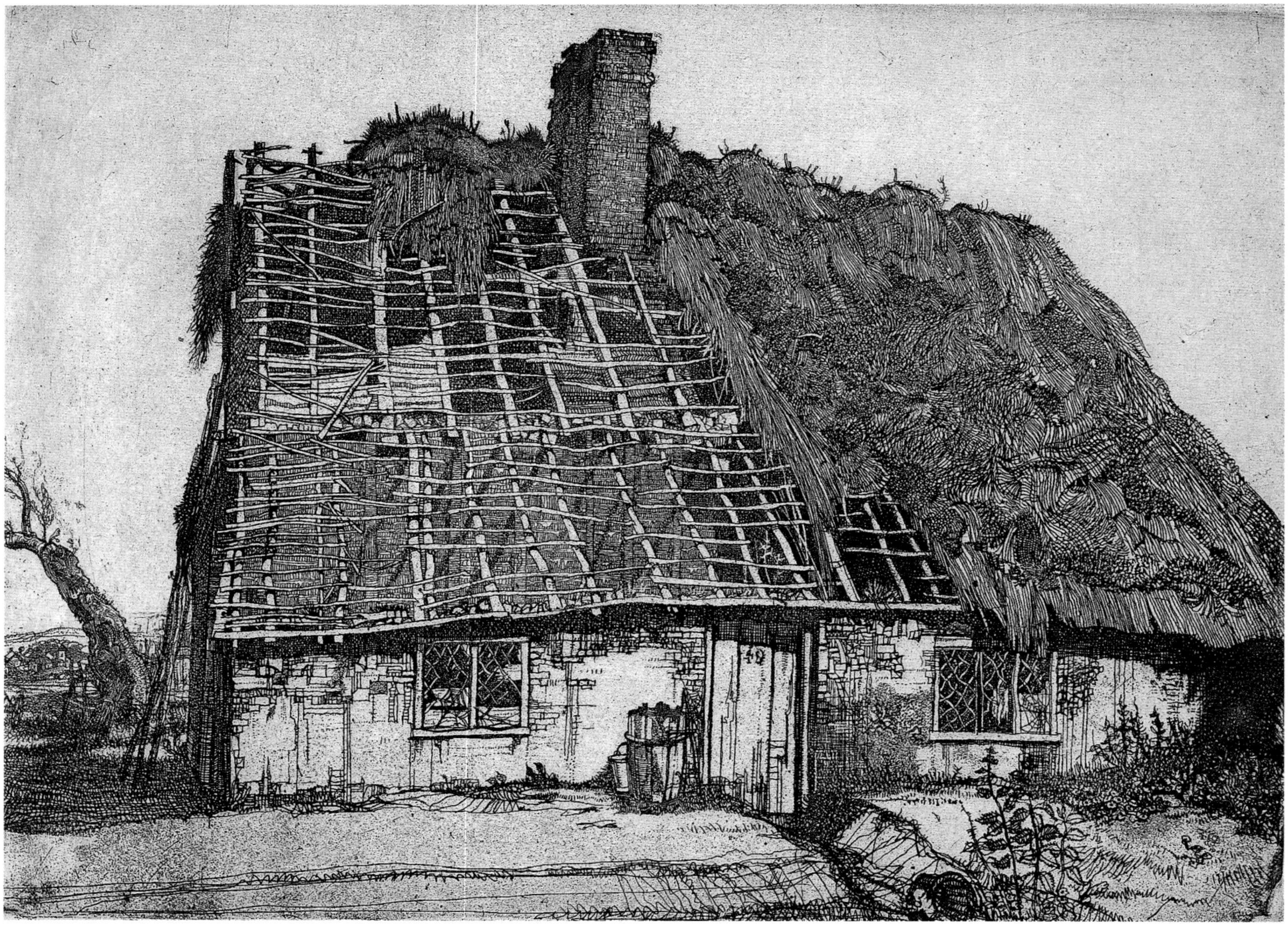

6.
Number Forty-nine
1924
Etching
178 x 250 mm (image size)
The Scottish National Gallery
of Modern Art, Edinburgh
GMA 764.

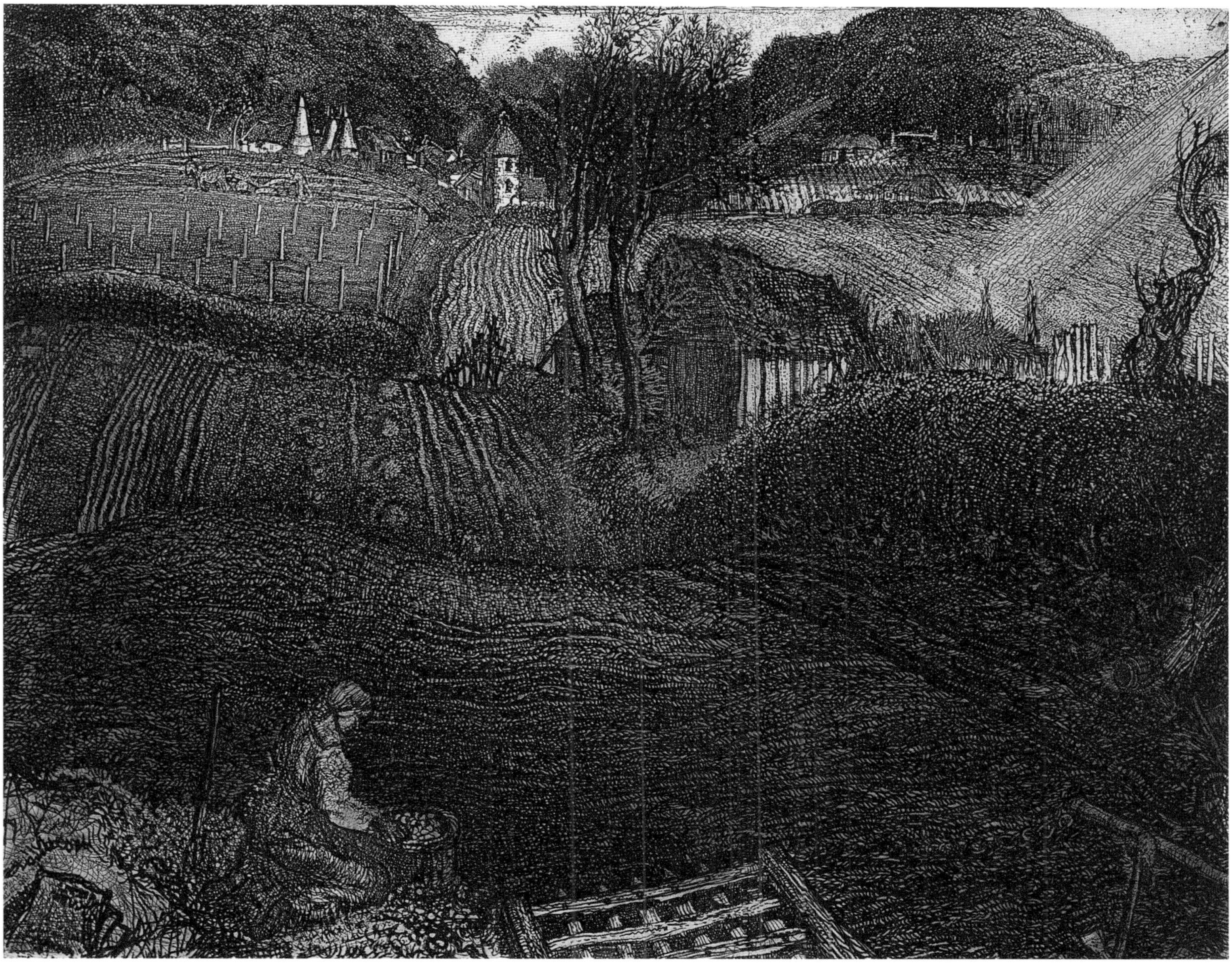

7.
The Village
1925
Etching
176 x 225 mm (image size)
The Scottish National Gallery
of Modern Art, Edinburgh
GMA 766.

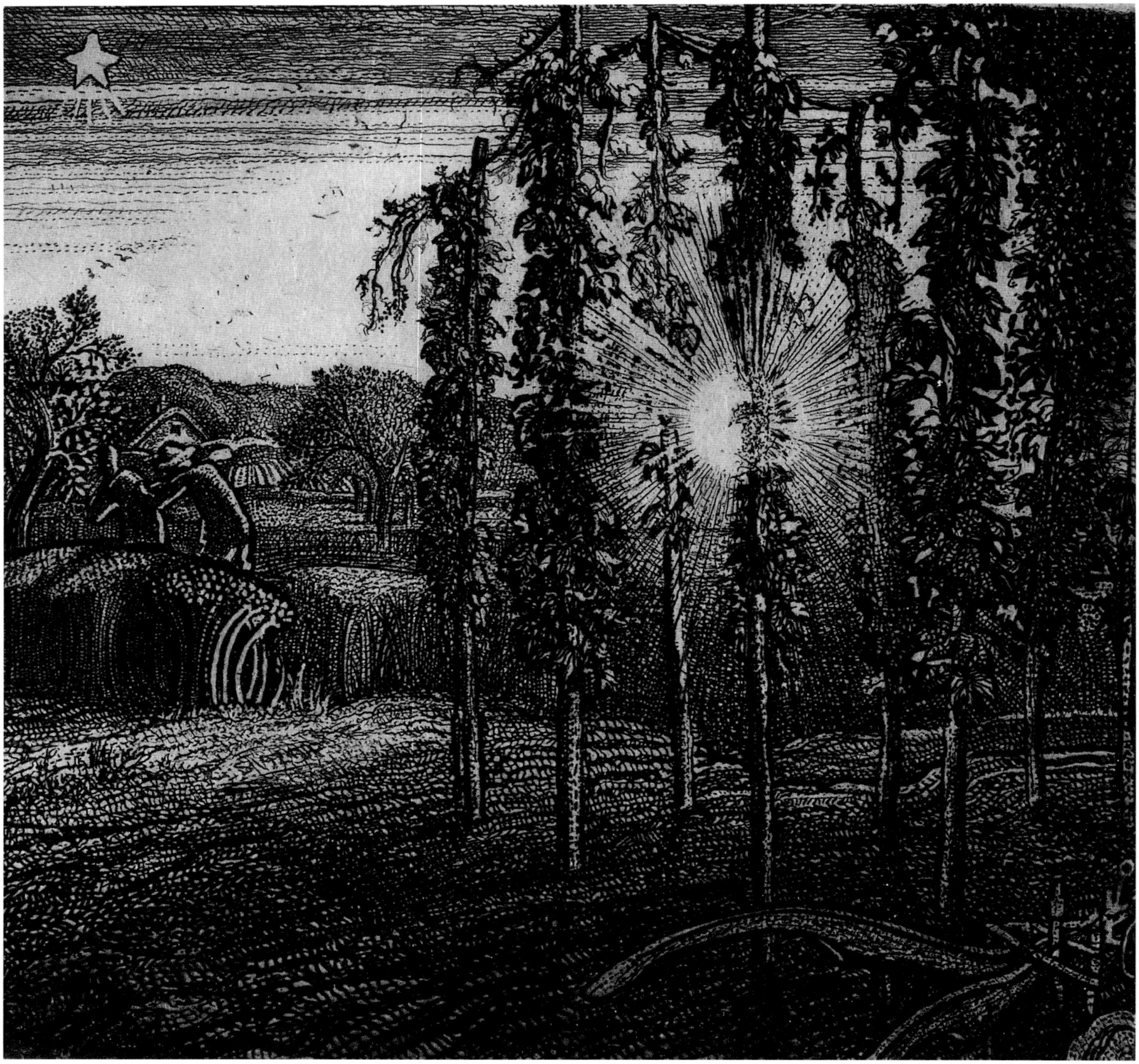

8.
Cray Fields
1925
Etching
117 x 124 mm
Tate. Presented by the artist
1970
P02067.

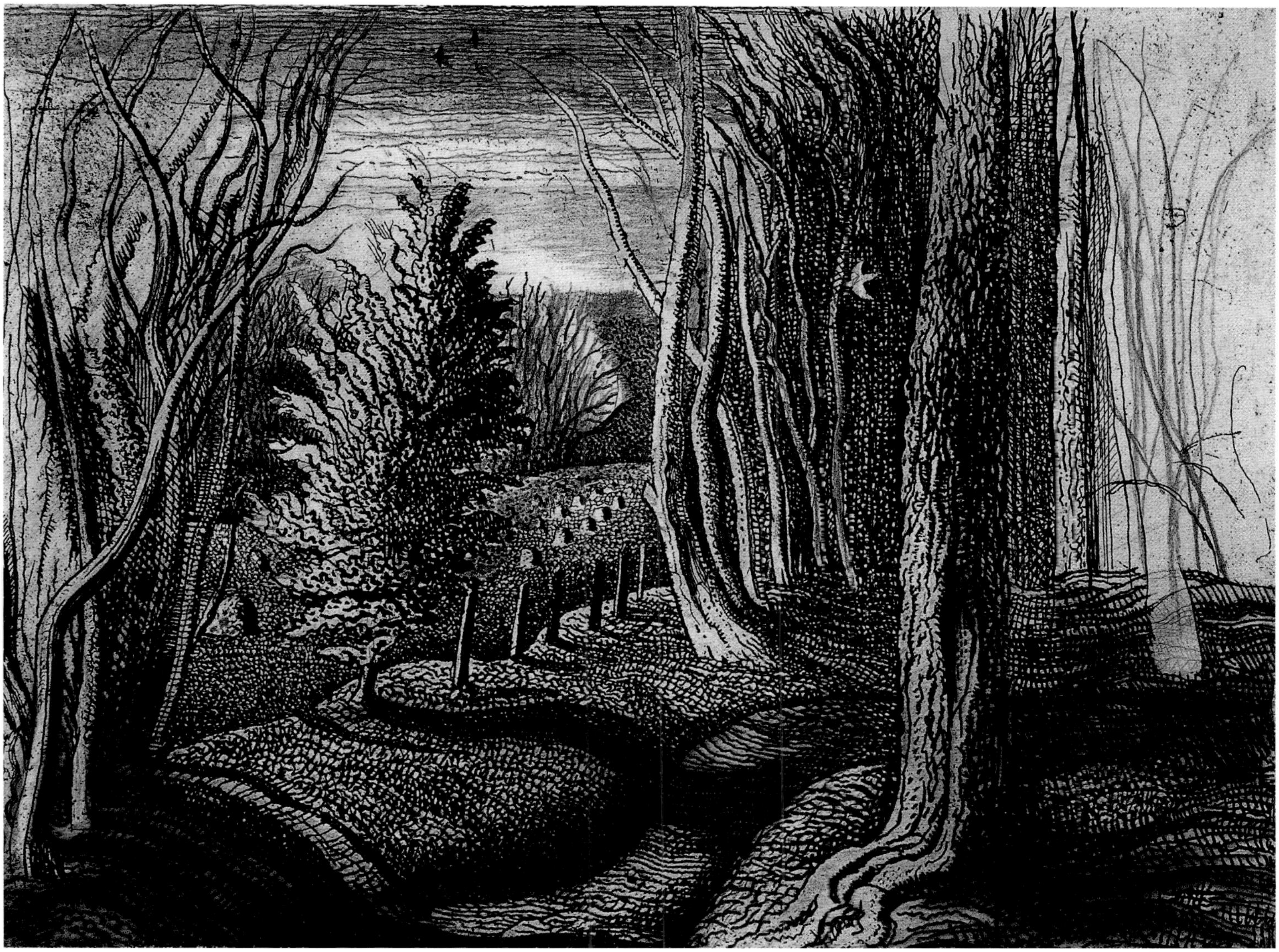

9.
Wood Interior
(also known as **The Forest**)
1929–30
Etching
118 x 163 mm
British Museum
1930-8-19-1.

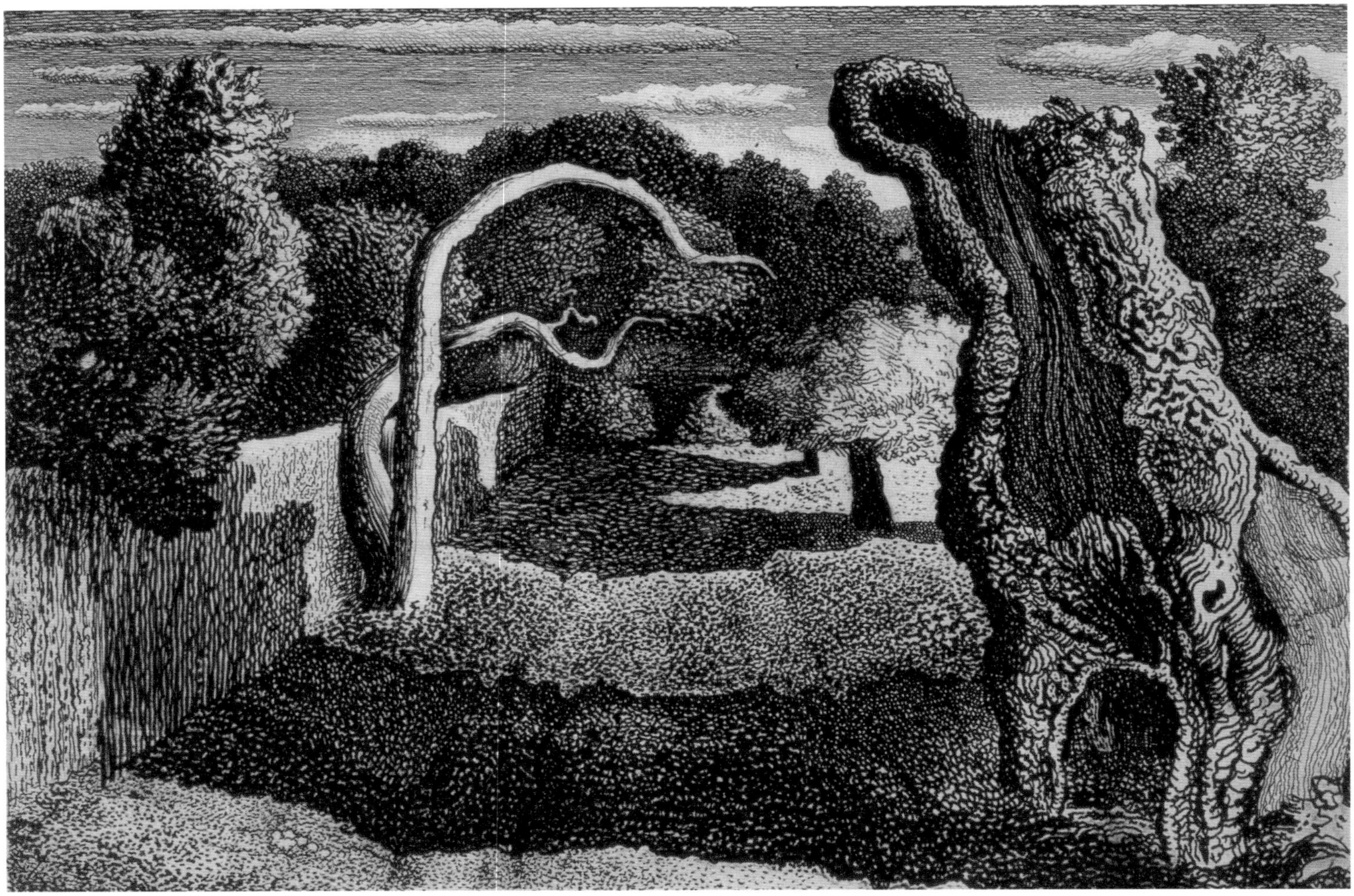

10.
Pastoral
1930
Intaglio print
130 x 190 mm
Tate. Purchased 1970
P07117.

11.
The Garden
1931
Etching
261 x 196 mm
The Ashmolean Museum, Oxford. Purchased with the assistance of Prof. Francis Comstock, 1970
WA 1970.38.

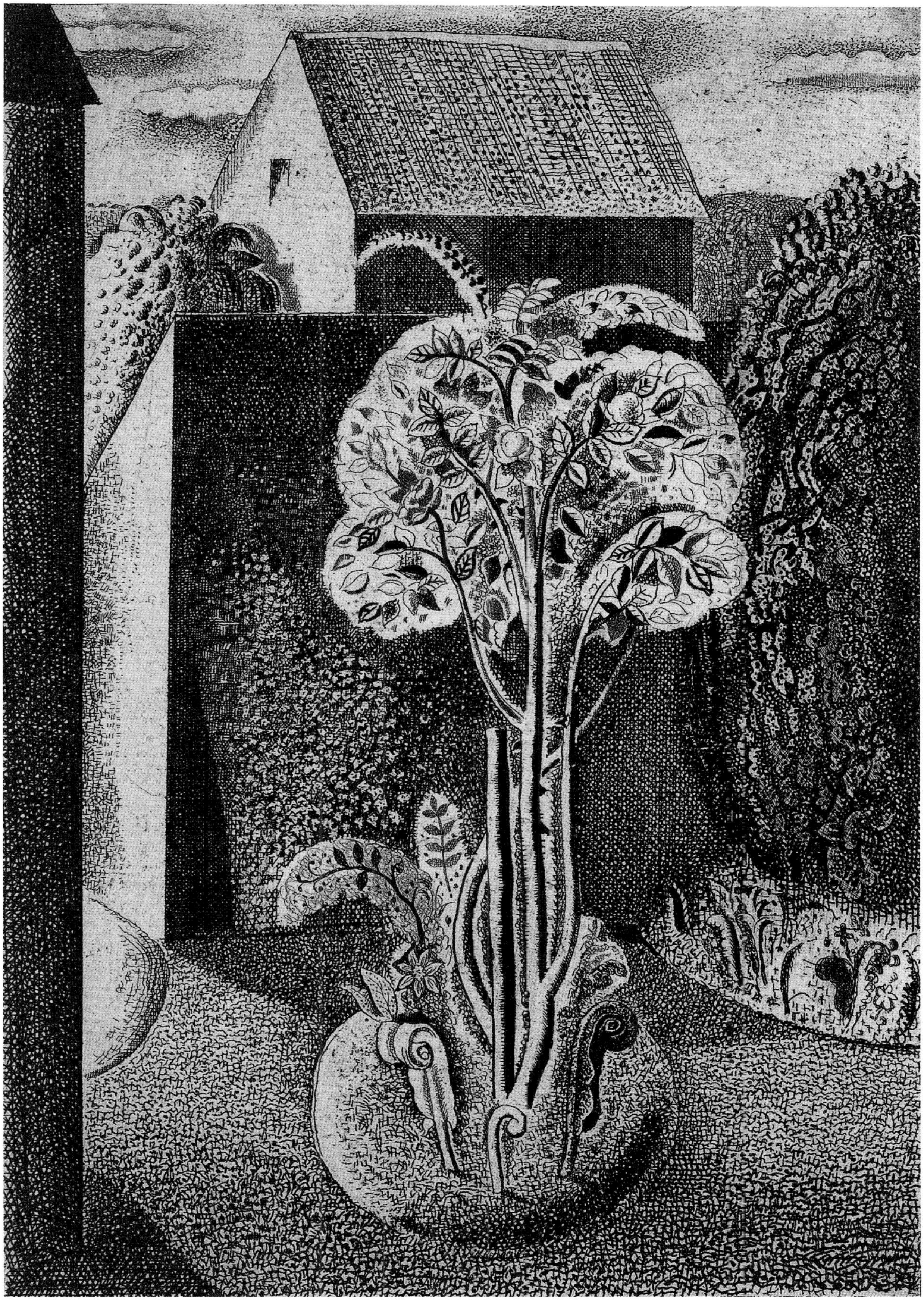

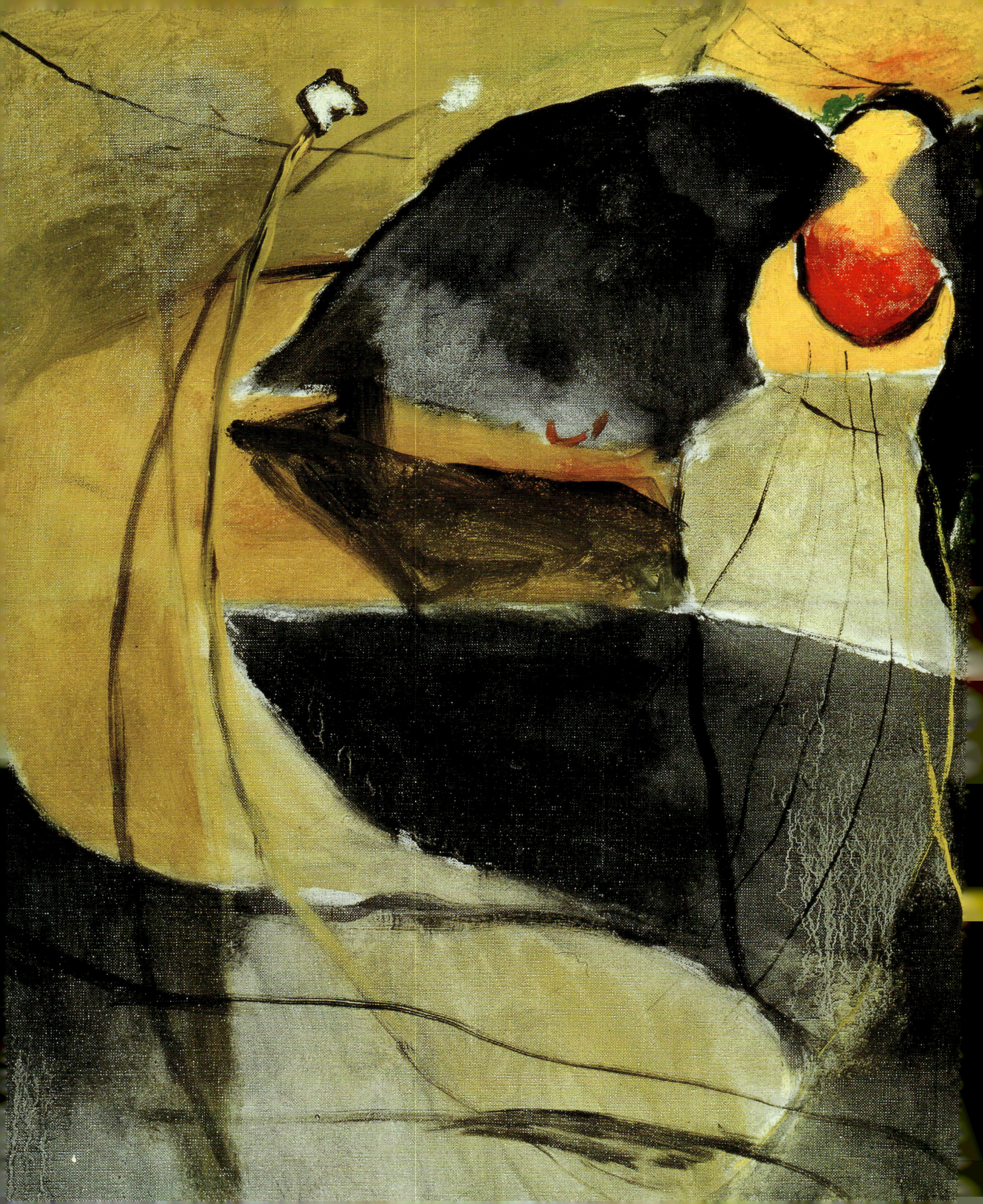

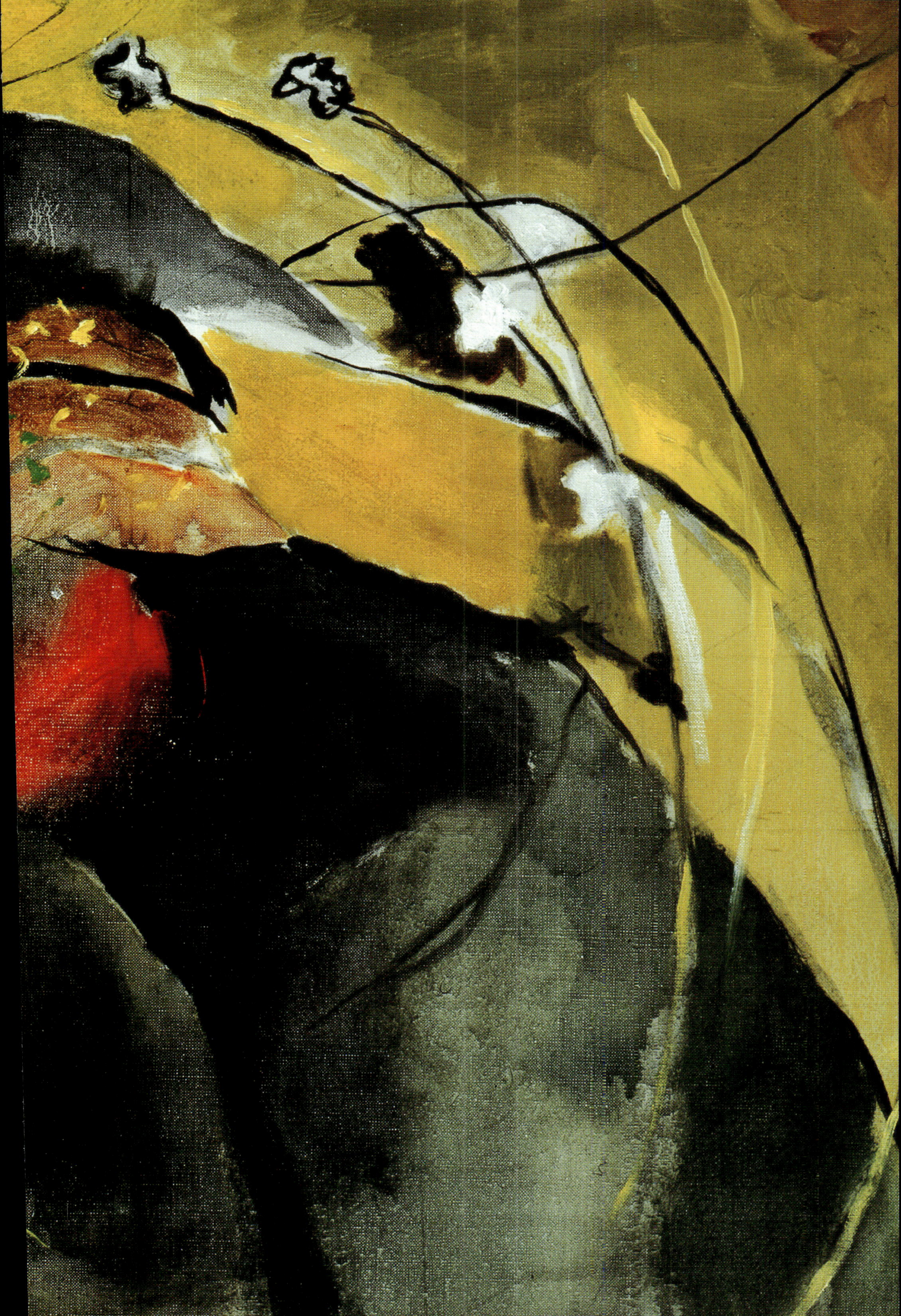

2

Landscapes
1936–1942

Sunrise between Hedges
1939
(Cat. 25, detail).

An English Stone Landmark

Graham Sutherland

It is a primitive environment. A wide plain surrounds us. It is redeemed from emptiness by the road which curves across it. The attention becomes drawn to an irregularity of contour on the horizon. Lit by the effulgent figure of the sun which hangs low behind, innumerable sharp forms cut brightly into the sky. Their outlines, devoid of order or rhythm, confuse the eye as the crazy cacophony of village church bells confuses the ear.

This confusion clarifies; we are approaching a vast congregation of rock forms. Passing through the outer stones the road is soon joined by another, which, running straight like an arrow, leads us to the centre of the area. Standing here on the higher ground there by degrees becomes apparent the real vastness of the assemblage which a cursory view from the outside was apt to obscure.

The rocks lie in every direction. They obscure the earth and the sky with their forms which cross and re-cross in innumerable combinations. Yet now the whole effect seems to form a single entity. Each intricate grouping unfolds the limit of another. Every space establishes that interval which gives to each form its significance.

The dismal privacy which these forms impose is at the highest point offset by the intrusion of a house. This single evidence of the presence of man not only gives scale, but quickens by its implications and associations our apprehension of the strangeness of the scene. Built of stone, it casts its square shadow across the walled paddock adjoining, in which, restless, as if disturbed by the foreboding atmosphere of the place, cattle graze. Nearer and still more incongruous, a patch of corn stands partially out. Were it not for the familiarity of these things appearing among those so strange and unreal, the eye might tire or, at least, fail to grasp the character of the experience for want of some known object with which to compare it.

The largest stones lie near the house; many of them rise, like unmentionable bathers, from pools of water. Supporting on their backs small rocks like little slothful heads, they bend forward casting their huge shadows into the depths which half obscure their bulk.

Here, too, are monoliths. The corrosion of their surfaces has produced perpendicular fissures, which gives them the appearance of bound bundles of wood; of bamboo in fact, for their sides are undulant and scooped in a way which we associate with this wood.

Most singular of all is the huge conglomerate mass of stone to the right. Shaped like a growth which one sometimes sees attached to the nose of a peasant, it is divested, owing to the fact that it exists in stone, of the horror that such an affliction inspires. It is round in plan and divided into three distinct sections. The lowest and largest section is shaped like a flattened sphere, rather broader than it is long, and the middle section is attended by much corrugation and eruption, which, extended to the section above, almost attains to an efflorescent character. The whole mass is poised, like an acrobat's ball on his stick, on a small inverted cone of stone.

The setting sun, as it were precipitating new colours, turns the stone, rising from its undulating bed of bright green moss and blackened heather, yellow, pink and vermilion. The coloured patches which streak the surfaces give emphasis to the form and variety to the eye. These patches are warm, even in a cold light. But now they assume tones as of blood. In addition the surfaces are speckled with lichens. Some are yellow red and sparkle unnaturally from the cool tones of the shadows, while others shading from white at their centres to blackish green evoke the texture and form that we associate with the uncontrolled blots on French marbled papers. Indeed, the pleasure derived from such textures is comparable with that produced by all decoration added to and not contained in a material. Here it is as if, by a kind of prodigality of nature, the natural processes must add to the patterns inherent in matter.

A path leads us to the edge of the area and now we see that there is a limit to the plain. For here the ground itself is rock which precipitates itself to the fields, three hundred feet below.

* * *

This, then, is the outline attempted; but what of the significance of the scene? 'Is it the natural beauty of proportion ... contrasted with the more studied or ecstatic proportion of mental or spiritual consciousness we are accustomed to?'[1]

Melancholy, impressive and integral such as this, is the basis of sculpture.

1 D. H. Lawrence.

(Myfanwy Evans, ed., *The Painter's Object*, London: Gerald Howe, 1937, pp. 89–93)

Fig. 13
Graham Sutherland
Brimham Rock (published poster), 1937
Shell Advertising Art Collection.

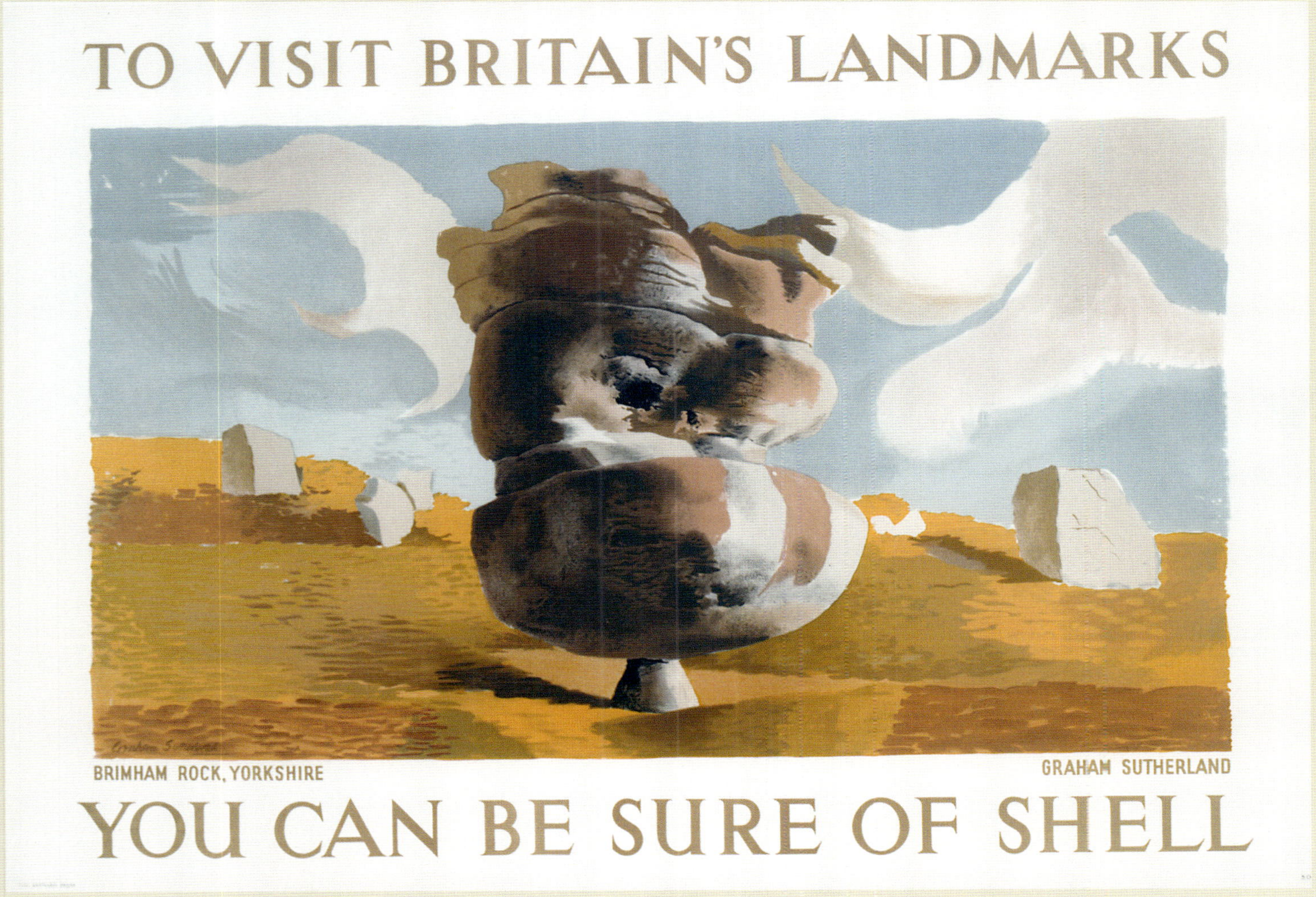

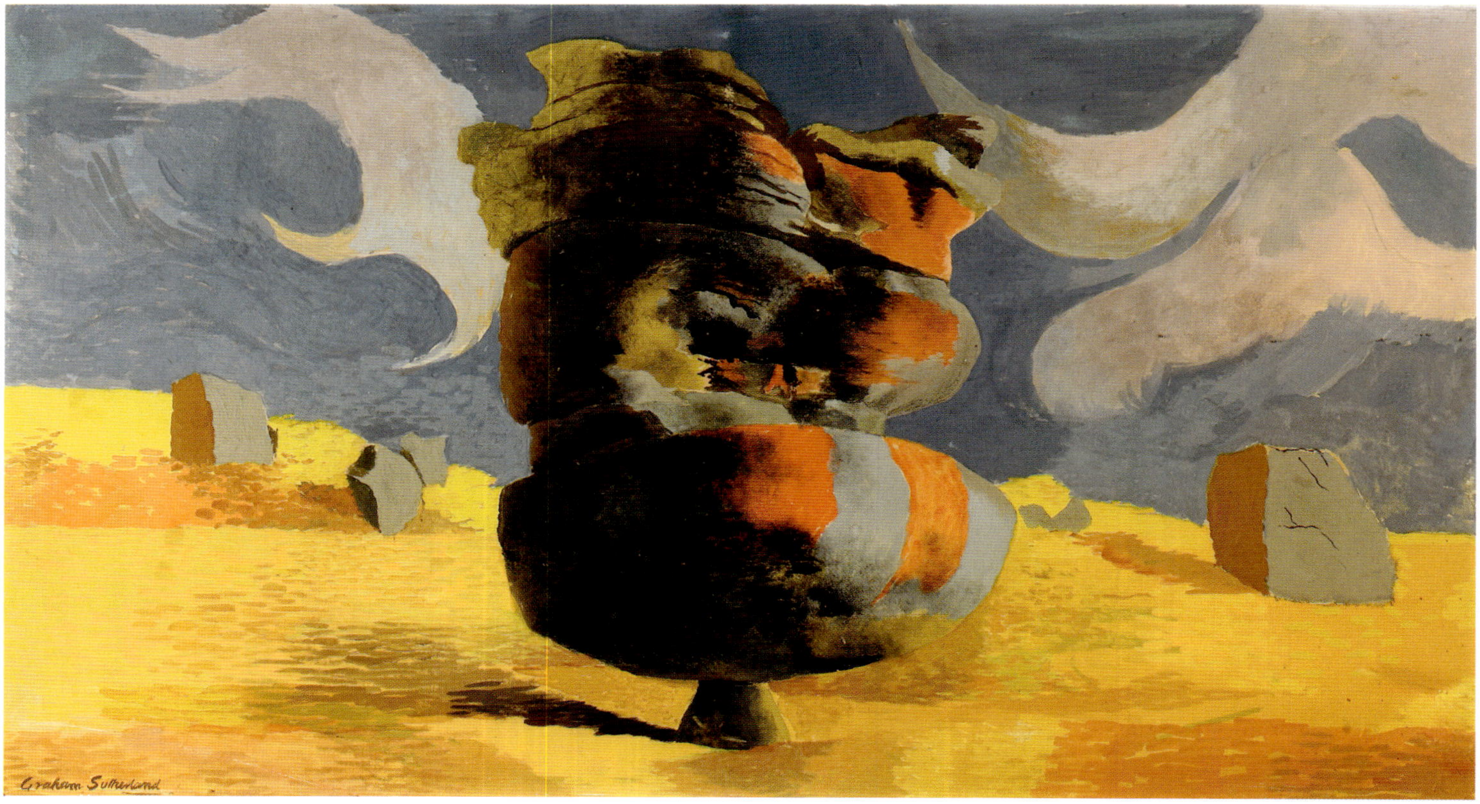

12.
Brimham Rock – study for poster
1937
Gouache on paper
533 x 975 mm
Courtesy of the Shell Art Collection.

The basis for a poster that Shell produced in 1937 (reproduced on p. 65).

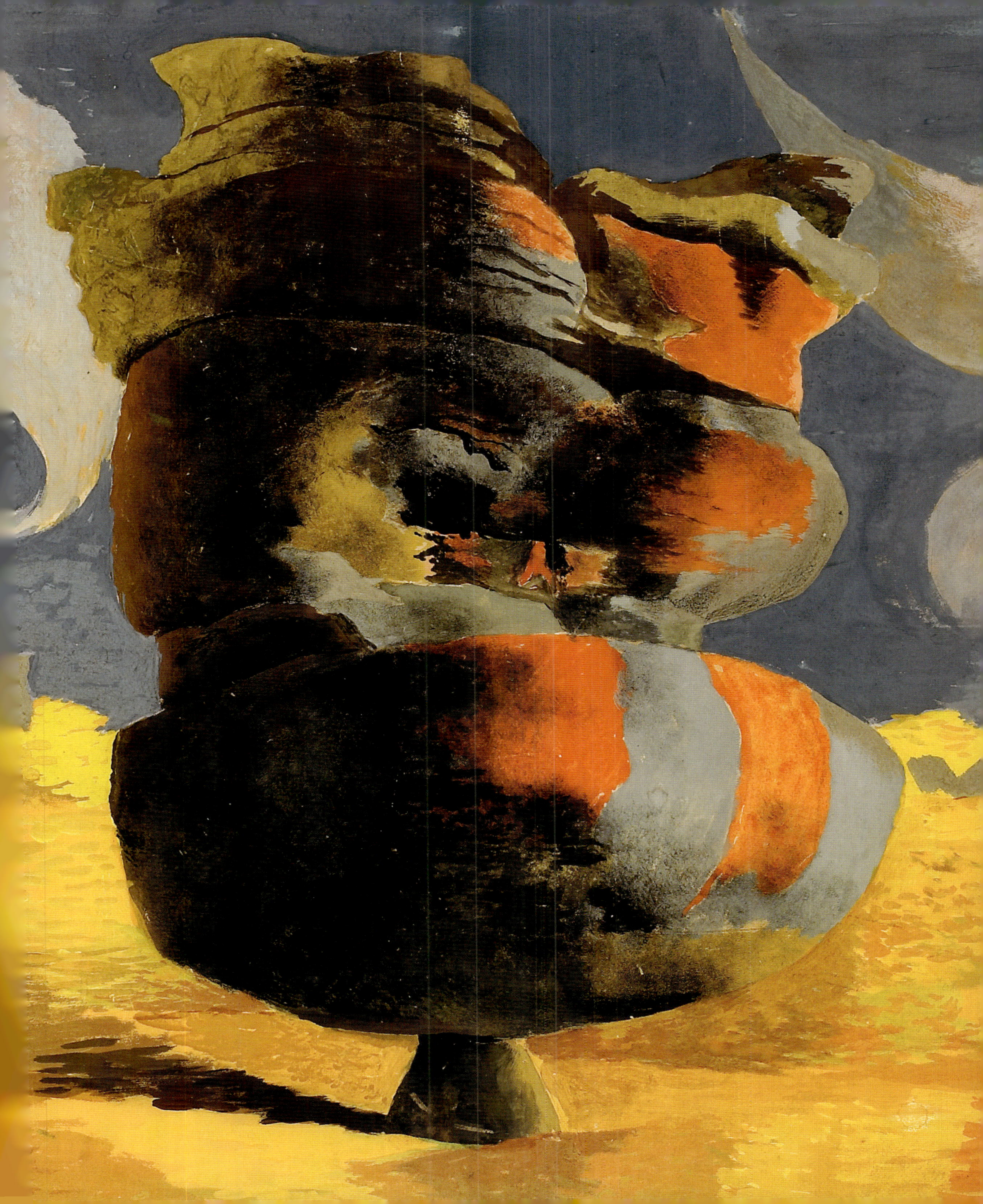

Welsh Sketch Book

Graham Sutherland

Dear Colin,

You ask about the places which have started me off – which have started ideas for my paintings. Certainly I would rather write to you about such places than about the paintings themselves; for how can a painter explain his paintings? The onlooker may come to like them through familiarity, or he may hate them. It is quite impossible to follow with any exactitude the path taken by the brain in the fixing of images seen by the eye, stored in the mind, and drawn out of the subconscious. But in describing the sort of things that start one off – the country that one likes, perhaps, and its peculiarities, it may be possible to give some kind of hint as to the genesis of the paintings.

The mind of a painter, of course, is a reservoir for *all* kinds of emotions and impressions. He who is over-discriminating becomes narrow in achievement. Yet a singleness of purpose over certain periods of time is necessary. A painter will have certain preoccupations with regard to his subject, and a passion for it.

I expect that you may have noticed that for the last few years I have been preoccupied with a particular aspect of landscape – and not only that, but, for the most part, with a particular area of country.

It was in 1934 that I first visited Pembrokeshire. I was visiting a country, a part of which, at least, spoke a foreign tongue, and it certainly seemed very foreign to me, though sufficiently accessible for me to feel that I could claim it as my own.

After a good deal of wandering about, I came upon two very remarkable passages of country situated in the arms of land which embrace the great area of St Bride's Bay. The arm towards the north is like an isosceles triangle on its side, the narrowest angle forming St David's Head to the west. One approaches across a wide plain from the north, its emptiness relieved by the interlocking of tightly-packed strips of field and their bounding walls of turf-covered rocks. One soon notices an irregularity of contour on the horizon which resolves itself into what appears to be two mountains. As one approaches still closer one sees that these masses of rock scarcely attain a height of more than seven hundred feet. But so classically perfect is their form, and so majestic is their command of the smoothly-rising ground below, that the mind comfortably corrects the measurement of the eye, and holds their essential mountainous significance. A rocky path leads round the slopes of the nearer mountain, where, to the west, the escarpment precipitates itself to a rock-strewn strip of marsh, marked out with the crazy calligraphy of the foundations of primitive hut dwellings; from here the ground rises to a vast congregation of rocks, fallen cromlechs, and goats' caves, which continue their undulating and bewildering disorder, until they plunge, in the terraces of St David's Head, into the table of the sea. The southern slopes yield to the plain again; but here the land, gradually sloping to the sea, is studded with rocky cairns of every size. Between these are fields, each with a spear of rock at its centre. It is as if the solid rock foundation of the earth had thrown up these spears to transfix and hold the scanty earth of the fields upon it. Farms and cottages – glistening white, pink, and blue-grey – give scale and quicken by their implications our apprehension of the scene.

In this direction, nearer the sea, the earth is comparatively flat, but this flatness is deceiving and makes the discovery of little steep valleys more surprising. These valleys possess a bud-like intricacy of form and contain streams, often of indescribable beauty, which run to the sea. The astonishing fertility of these valleys and the complexity of the roads running through them is a delight to the eye. The roads form strong and mysterious arabesques as they rise in terraces, in sight, hidden, turning and splitting as they finally disappear into the sky. To see a solitary human figure descending such a road at the solemn moment of sunset is to realize the enveloping quality of the earth, which can create, as it does here, a mysterious space limit – a womb-like enclosure – which gives the human form an extraordinary focus and significance.

At the risk of talking like a guide-book, I must tell you of the area to the south. I shall never forget my first visit. We approached by a flat winding road and had slipped into one of the little valleys such as I have attempted to describe. To the left this opened out to reveal what appeared to be a watery inlet narrowing to its upper end. As the road progressed we caught further glimpses of this and curiosity was roused. We had intended making for a village called Dale, marked on the map as lying to the north side of the mouth of Milford Haven. Fortunately, we missed the road and found ourselves descending a green lane buried in trees, which, quite unexpectedly, led to a little cove and beach by the banks of a narrow estuary.

Here is a hamlet – three cottages and an inn crouch under the low cliffs. A man is burning brushwood cut from a tree, bleached and washed by the sea. The flame looks incandescent in the evening light. The tide in the estuary (or pill, as such inlets are called here) is out, and we walk across the sandy bed of the opening and look down its winding length to the place where it narrows to the upper end.

I wish I could give you some idea of the exultant strangeness of this place – for strange it certainly is, many people whom I know hate it, and I cannot but admit that it possesses an element of disquiet. The left bank as we see it is all dark – an impenetrable damp green gloom of woods which run down to the edge of low blackish moss-covered cliffs – it is all dark, save where the mossy lanes (two each side) which dive down to the opening, admit the sun, hinged, as it were, to the top of the trees, from where its rays, precipitating new colours, turn the red cliffs of the right-hand bank to tones of fire. Do you remember the rocks in Blake's 'Newton' drawing? The form and scale of the rocks here, and the minutiae on them, is very similar.

The whole setting is one of exuberance – of darkness and light – of decay and life. Rarely have I been so conscious of the contrasting of these elements in so small a compass.

The right bank has fields above the cliff, some covered with ripe corn, others with rough gorse-clad pasture. The life-giving sound of the mechanical reaper is heard. Cattle crouch among the dark gorse. The mind wanders from contemplation of the living cattle to their ghosts. It is no uncommon sight to see a horse's skull or horns of cattle lying bleached on the sand. Neither do we feel that the black-green ribs of half-buried wrecks and the phantom tree roots, bleached and washed by the waves, exist but to emphasize the extraordinary completeness of the scene. Complete, too, is the life of the few inhabitants – almost biblical in its sober dignity. The people in this part appear quite incurious of the activities of a foreigner. The immense soft-voiced innkeeper and his wife, small as he is big, sit, when they are not working, bolt upright, on a hard bench in the cool gloom of the parlour which forms the only 'bar' of the inn, or they sit – for he is ferry-man and fisherman, as well as innkeeper – gazing across the ferry.

The quality of light here is magical and transforming – as indeed it is in all this country. Watching from the gloom as the sun's rays strike the further bank, one has the sensation of the after tranquillity of an *explosion* of light; or as if one had looked into the sun and had turned suddenly away.

Herons gather. They fly majestically towards the sea. Most moving is the sound of snipe which flicker in their lightning dash down the inlet, to and from the sea.

These and other things have delighted me. The twisted gorse on the cliff edge, such as suggested the picture 'Gorse on Sea Wall' – twigs, like snakes, lying on the path, the bare rock, worn, and showing through the path, heath fires, gorse burnt and blackened after fire, a tin school in an exuberant landscape, the high overhanging hedges by the steep roads which pinch the setting sun, mantling clouds against a black sky and the thunder, the flowers and damp hollows, the farmer galloping on his horse down the estuary, the deep green valleys and the rounded hills and the whole structure, simple and complex.

It was in this country that I began to learn painting. It seemed impossible here for me to sit down and make finished paintings 'from nature'. Indeed, there were no 'ready made' subjects to paint. The spaces and concentrations of this clearly constructed land were stuff for storing in the mind. Their essence was intellectual and emotional, if I may say so. I found that I could express what I felt only by paraphrasing what I saw. Moreover, such country did not seem to make man appear little as does some country of the grander sort. I felt just as much part of the earth as my features were part of me. I did not feel that my imagination was in conflict with the real, but that reality was a dispersed and disintegrated form of imagination.

At first I attempted to make pictures on the spot. But soon I gave this up. It became my habit to walk through, and soak myself in the country. At times I would make small sketches of ideas on the backs of envelopes and in a small sketch book, or I would make drawings from nature of forms which interested me and which I might otherwise forget. The latter practice helped to nourish my ideas and to keep me on good terms with nature. Sometimes, through sheer laziness, I would lie on the warm shore until my eye, becoming riveted to some sea-eroded rocks, would notice that they were precisely reproducing, in miniature, the forms of the inland hills. At all events, I never forced myself here, or consciously looked for subjects. I found it better to visit this country because I liked it – and ideas seemed to come gradually and naturally.

I have confined myself to writing about a particular area and I do this because it was in this area that I learned that landscape was not necessarily scenic, but that its parts have an individual figurative detachment. I found that this was equally true of other places which I visited later; but the clear, yet intricate construction of the landscape of the earlier experience, coupled with an emotional feeling of being on the brink of some drama, taught me a lesson and had an unmistakable message that has influenced me profoundly. Well, I think there is not much else – it is only a rough outline, but it may go some way towards answering your request.

(*Horizon*, April 1942, pp. 225–35)

13.
Pembrokeshire Landscape – Valley above Porthclais
1935
Black ink, chalk, crayon and watercolour on buff paper
280 x 230 mm
Peter Nahum at the Leicester Galleries.

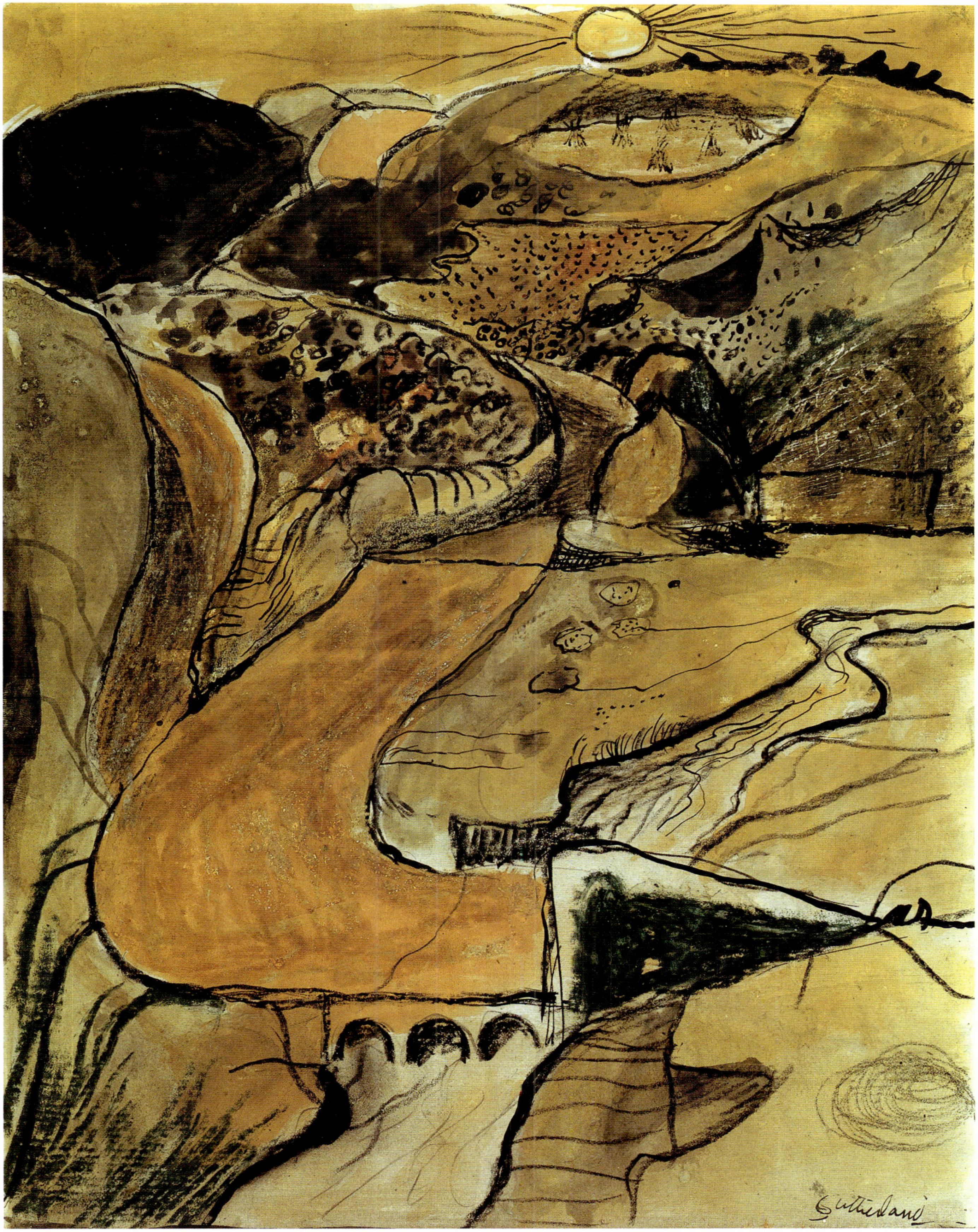

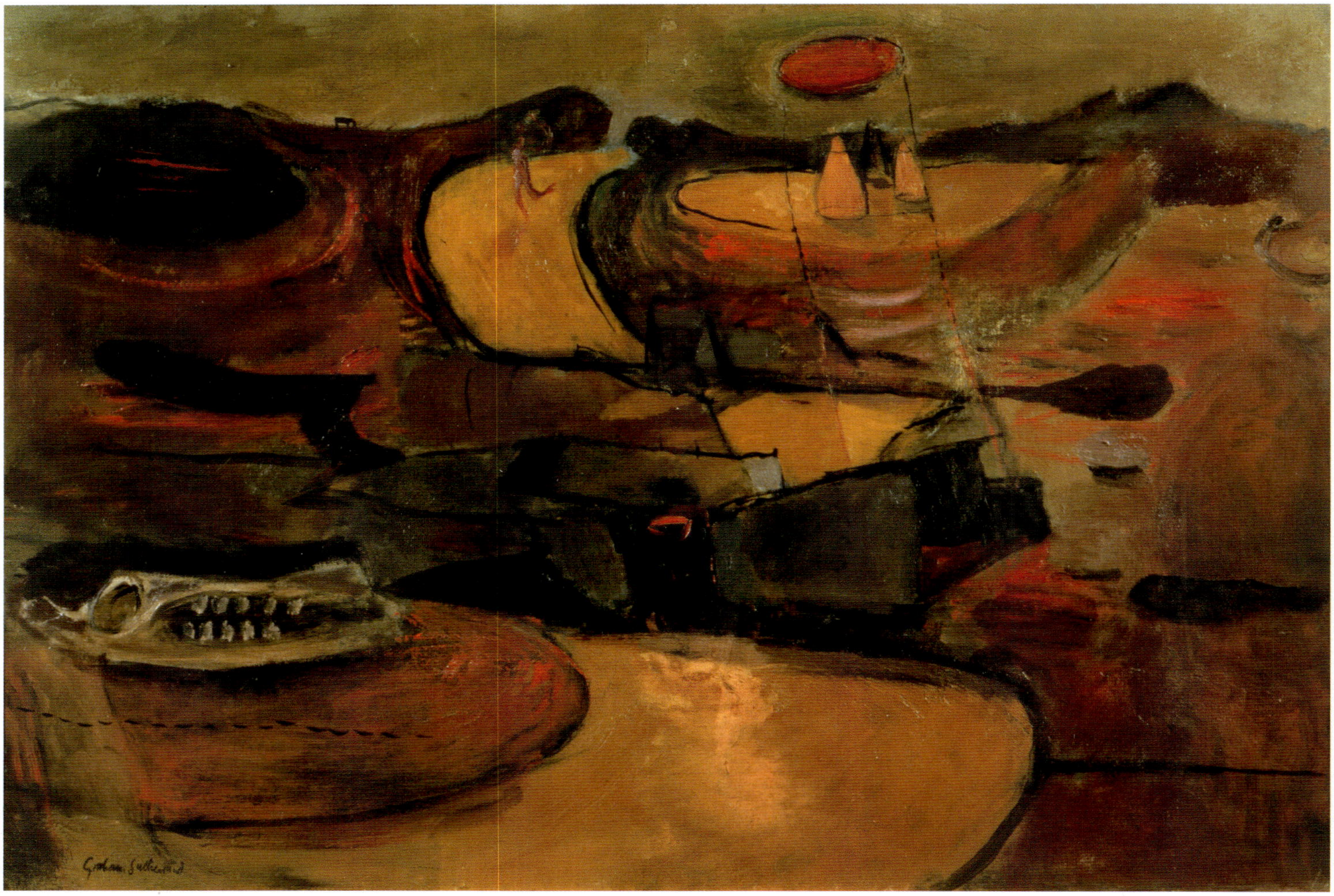

14.
Welsh Landscape with Roads
1936
Oil on canvas
610 x 914 mm
Tate. Presented by the
Contemporary Art Society
1946
N05666.

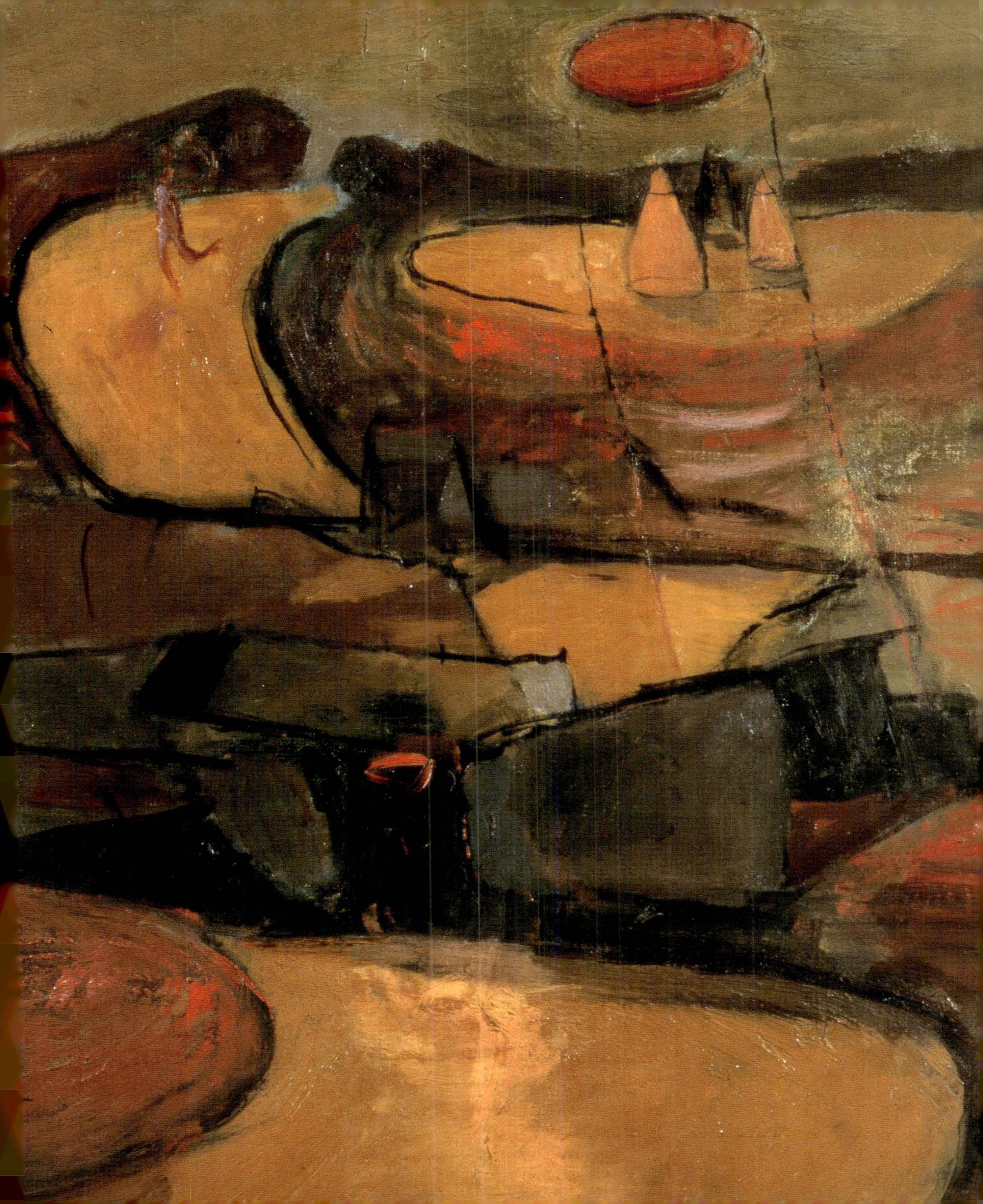

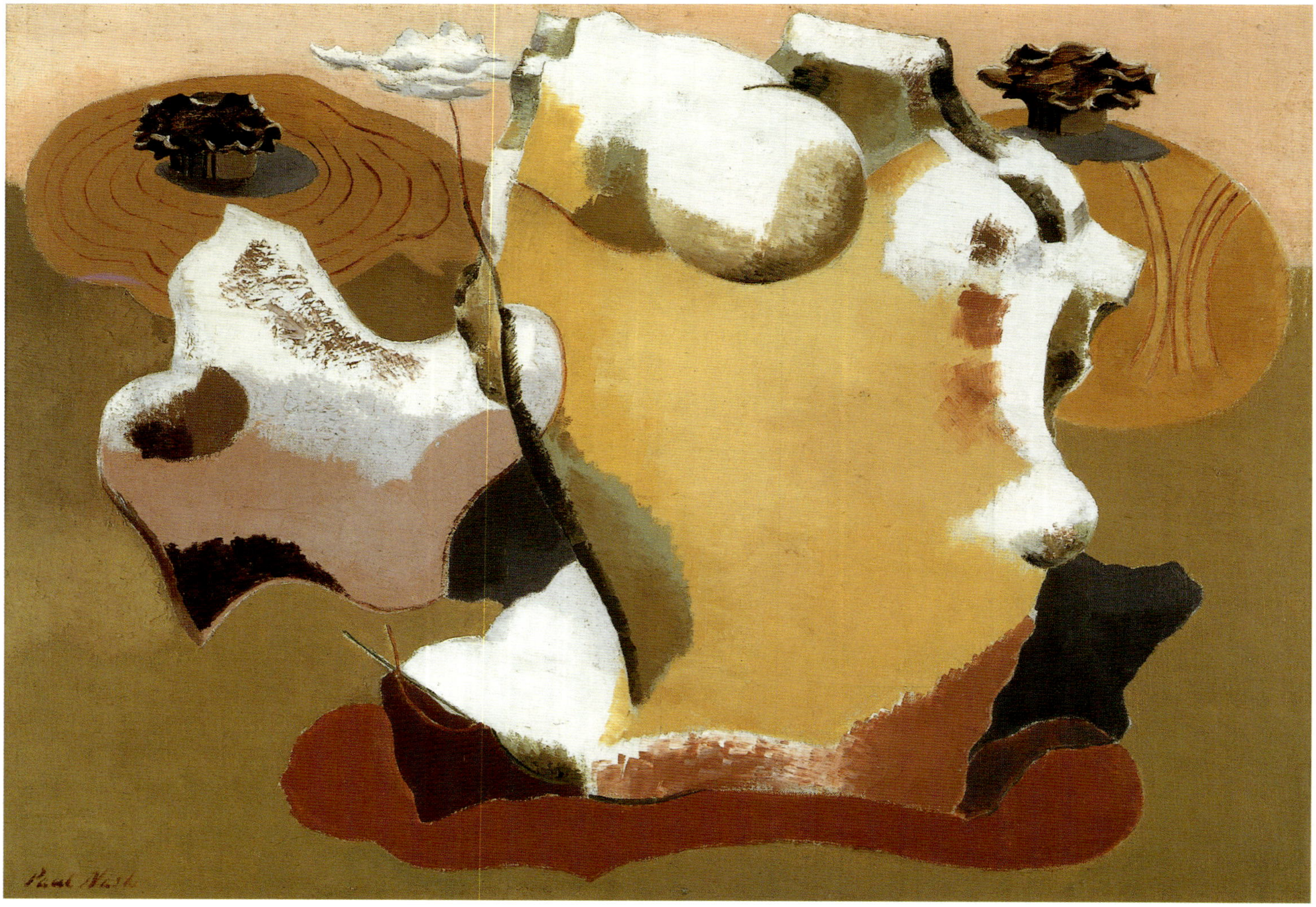

15.
PAUL NASH (1889–1946)
Landscape of the Megaliths
1934
Oil on canvas
445 x 732 mm
British Council.

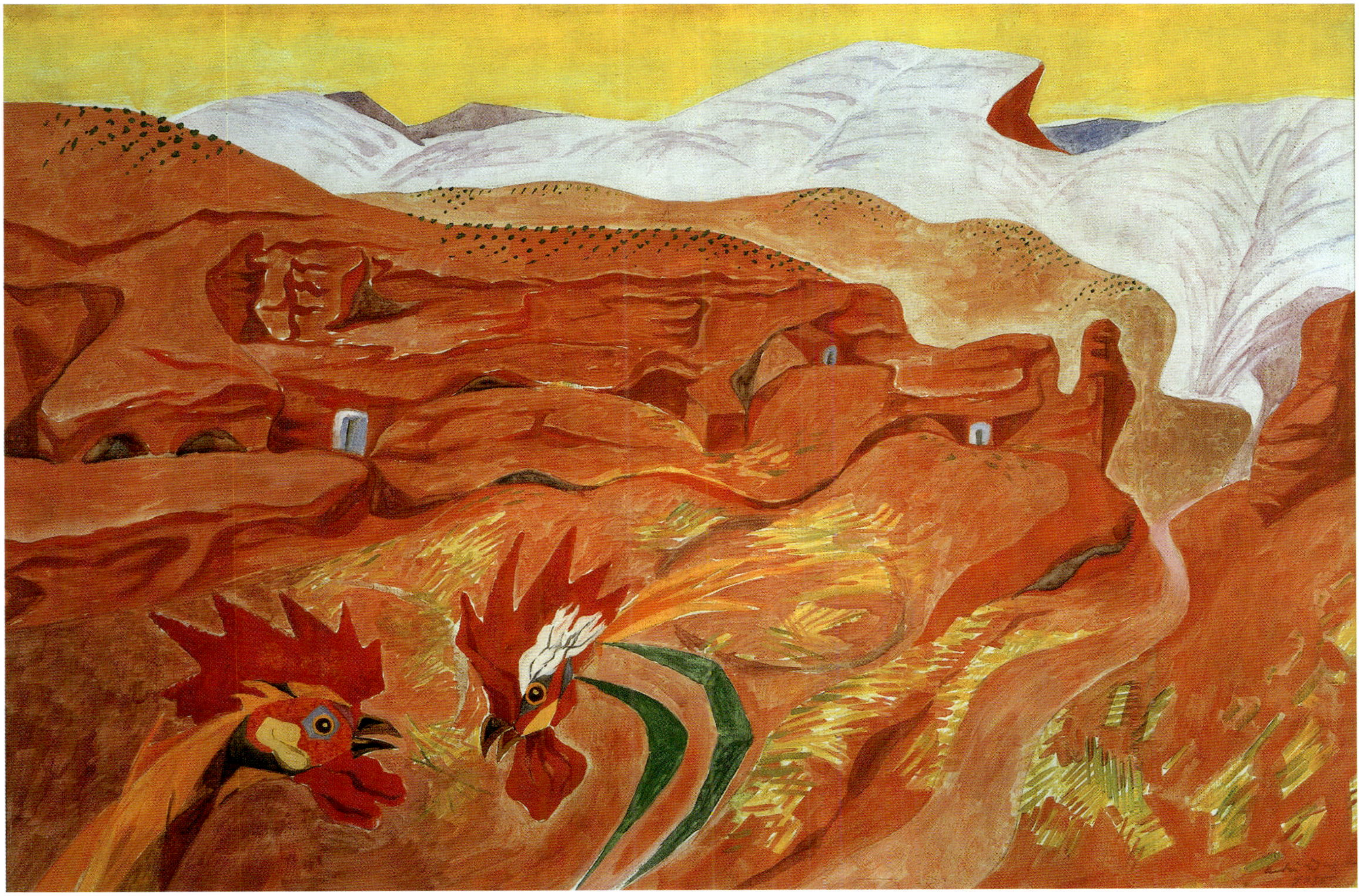

16.
ANDRE MASSON
(1896–1987)
Ibdes in Aragon
1935
Oil on canvas
600 x 924 mm
Tate. Presented by the Contemporary Art Society 1946
No5646.

Acquired by Kenneth Clark in 1937.

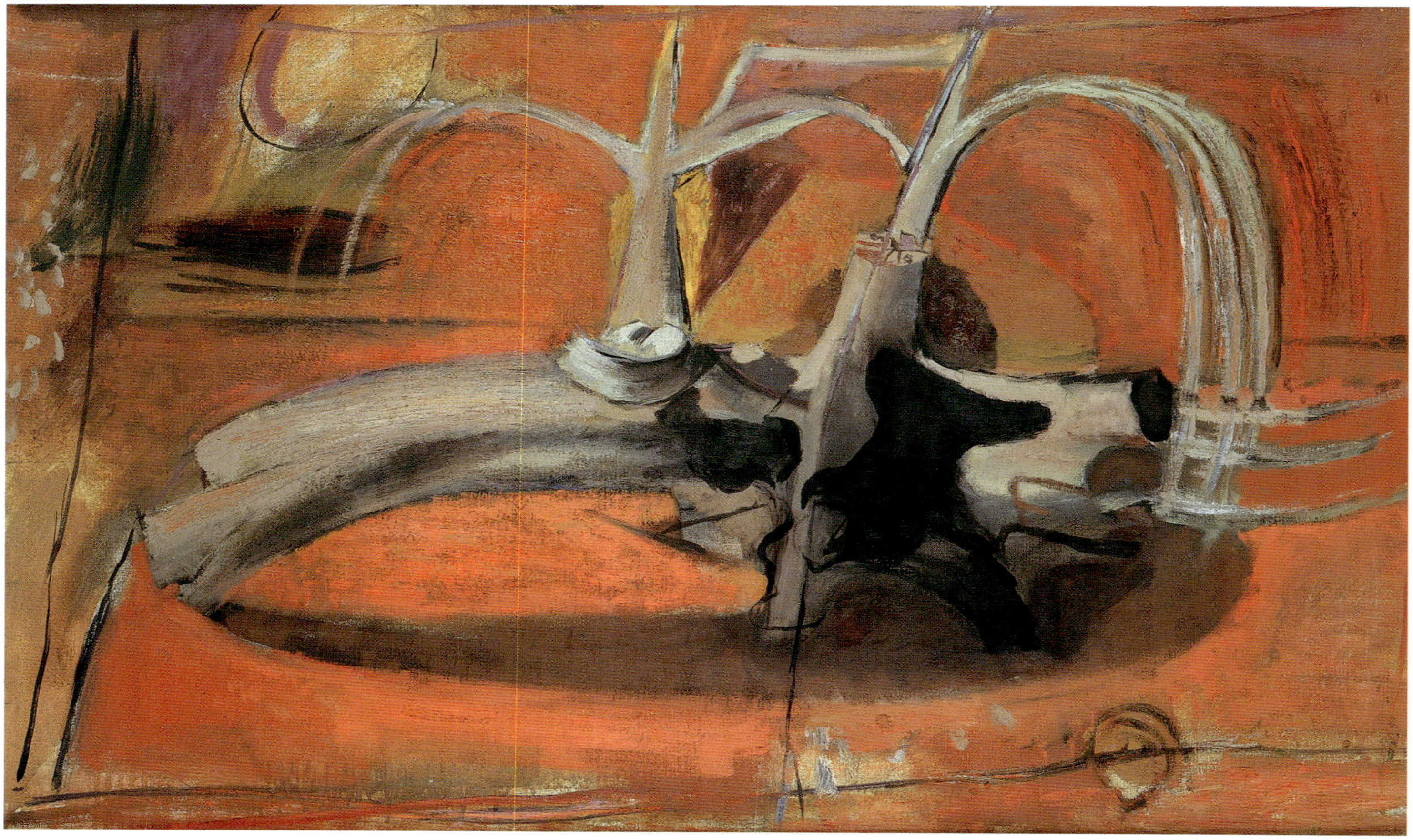

17.
Red Tree
1936
Oil on canvas
560 x 920 mm
Private Collection.

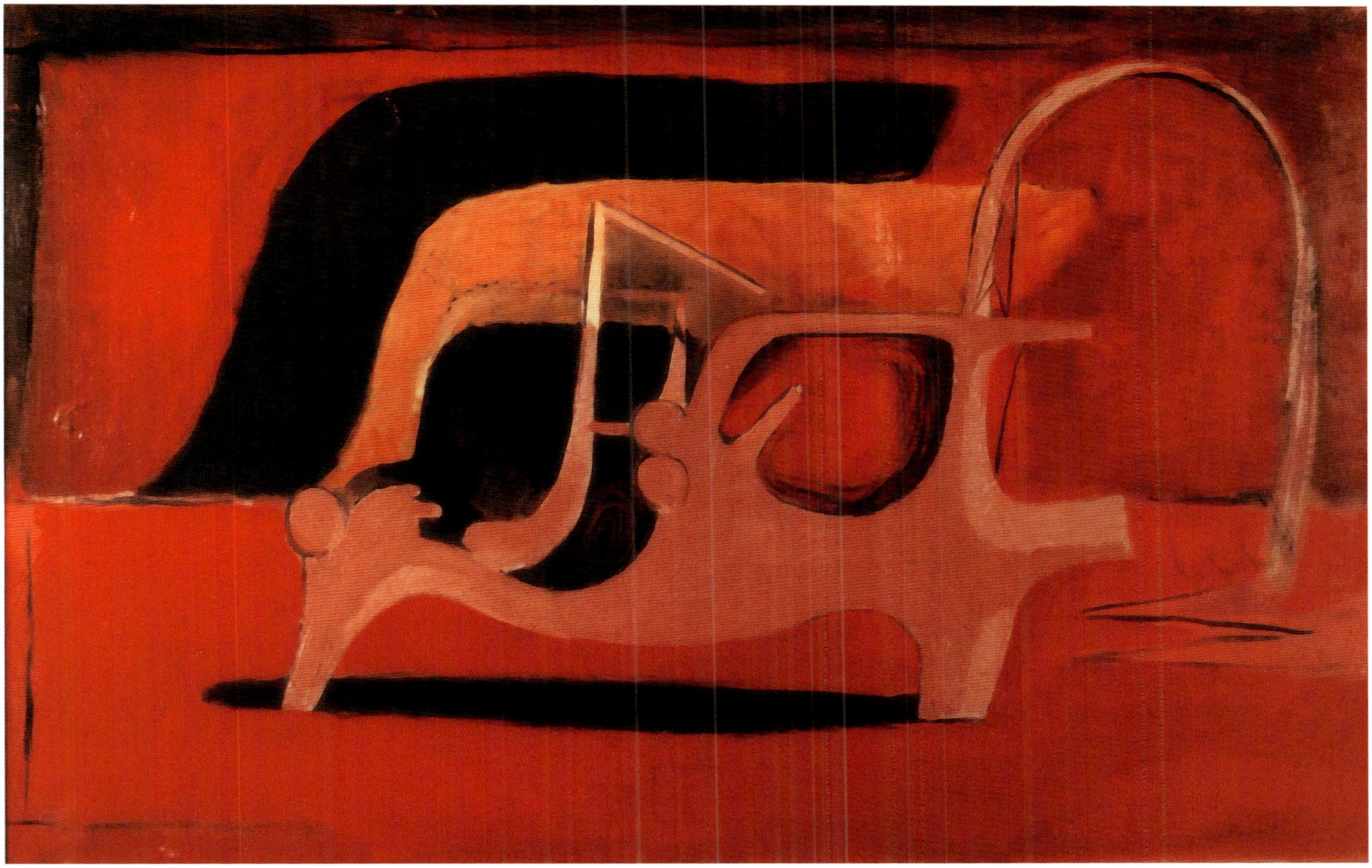

18.
Red Tree
1936
Oil on canvas
550 × 910 mm
BP International Art Collection.

Graham Sutherland

Kenneth Clark

Poetical painting should come naturally to the English; actually it is rare. Many English painters have attempted poetical subjects, few have painted poetically. Turner did so in some of his later works, Blake did so in his illustrations to Dante, Palmer in his paintings of Shoreham. Graham Sutherland does so. His colour and design are a joy to the eye, but they exist and acquire their force through his magical vision of nature. The strangeness of this vision – and it must seem strange to those who experience it for the first time – is completely unforced, and gradually convinces the spectator, who ends by discovering Graham Sutherland in nature. Nearly all the pictures in this exhibition have been painted from small, careful drawings done on the spot, squared for enlargement and followed most accurately. As a result Sutherland's work is the reverse of abstract. Nor is it Sur-realist, for he never consciously introduces images on account of their psychological associations. Indeed those who like to arrange pictures into categories and influences will find his work hard to place. But those who are prepared to trust their eyes will recognise one of those rare and precious talents which can furnish the mind with memorable images.

(Anonymous essay [by Kenneth Clark] from *Recent Works of Graham Sutherland*, exhibition catalogue, Rosenberg & Helft Gallery, London, 20 September to 8 October 1938)

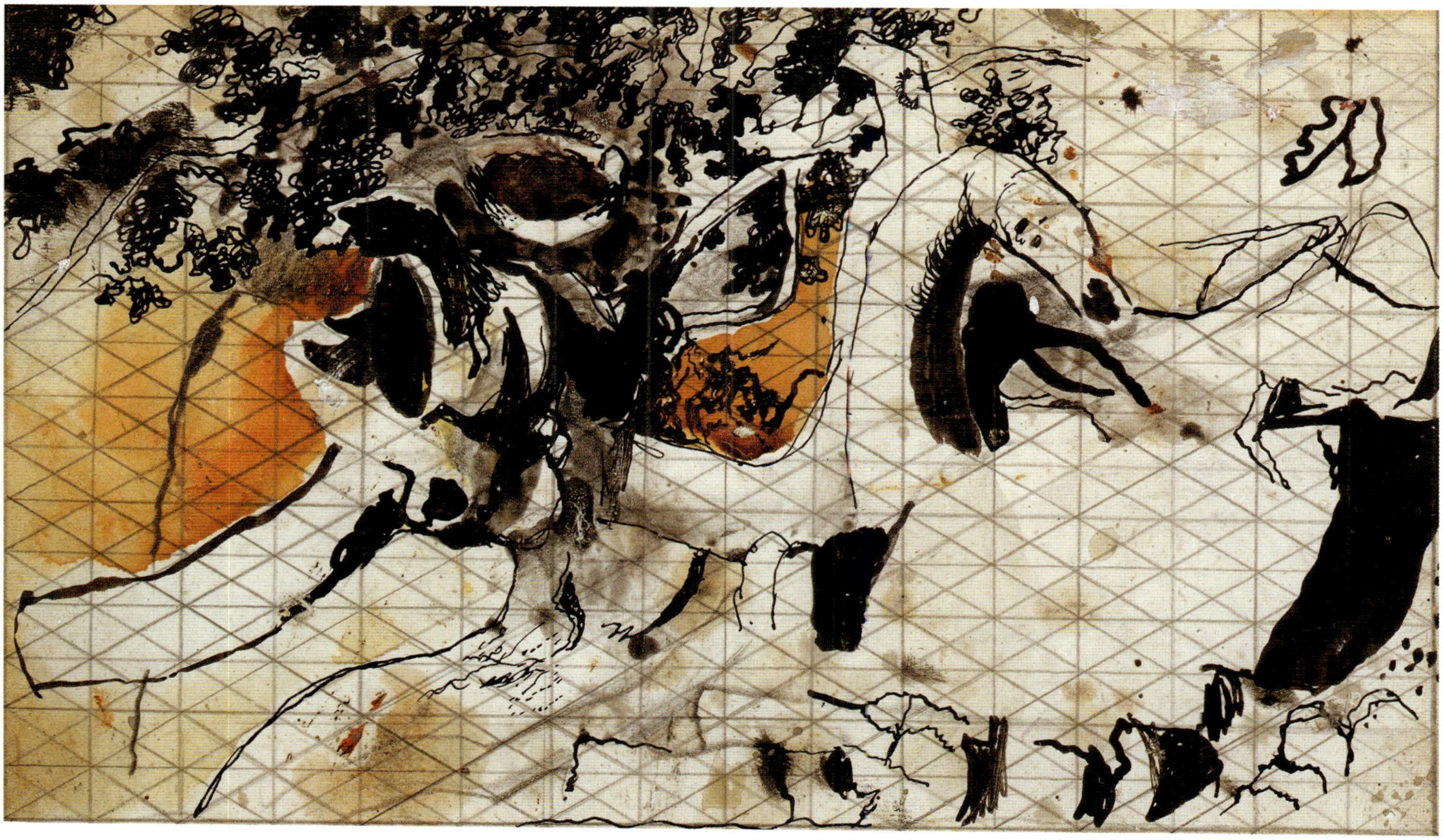

19.
Drawing of Tree Roots (with squaring)
c 1938
Pencil, ink and watercolour on paper
105 x 186 mm
Private Collection.

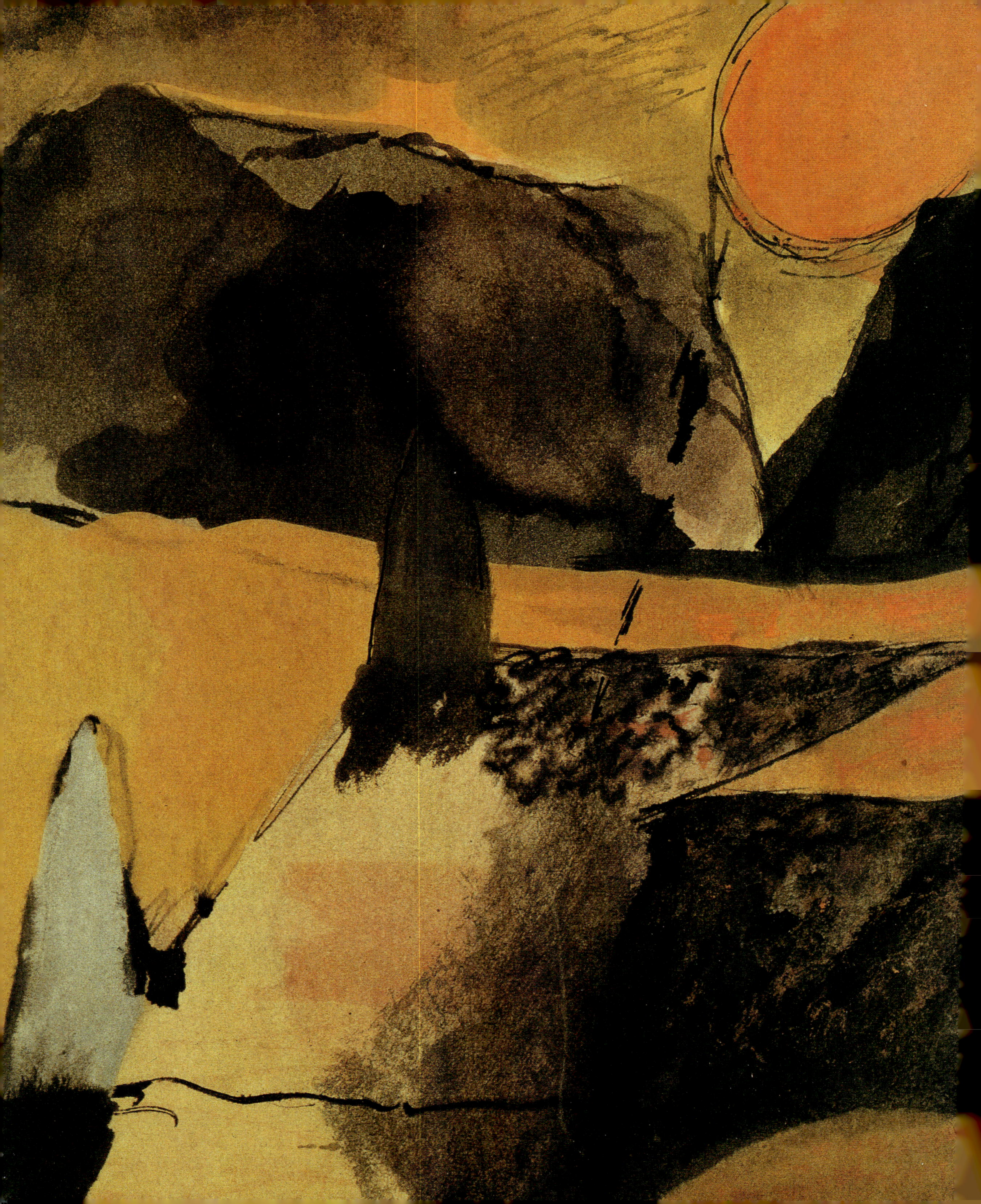

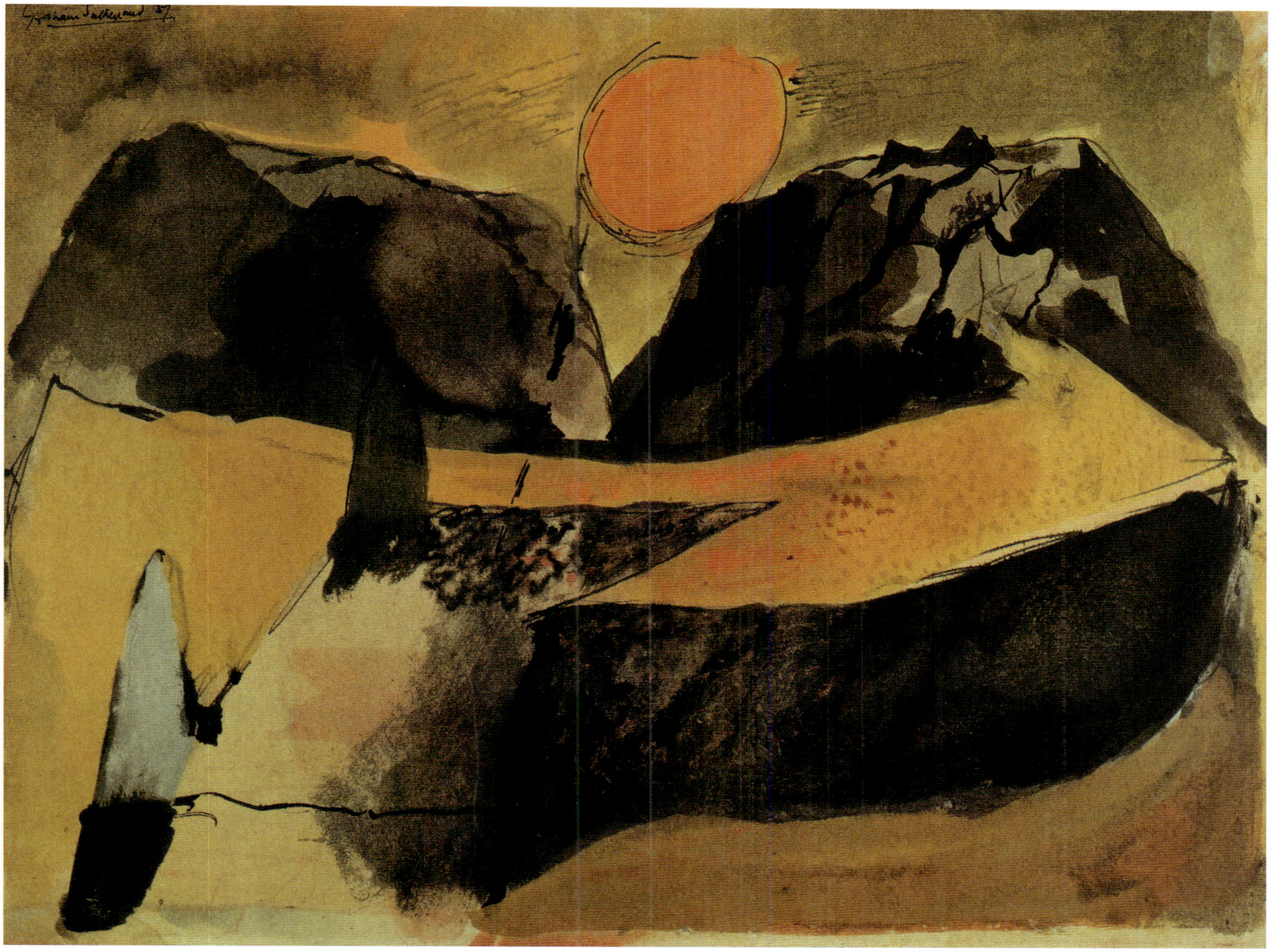

20.
Sunset in-between Hills
1938
Watercolour on paper
265 x 360 mm
Private Collection.

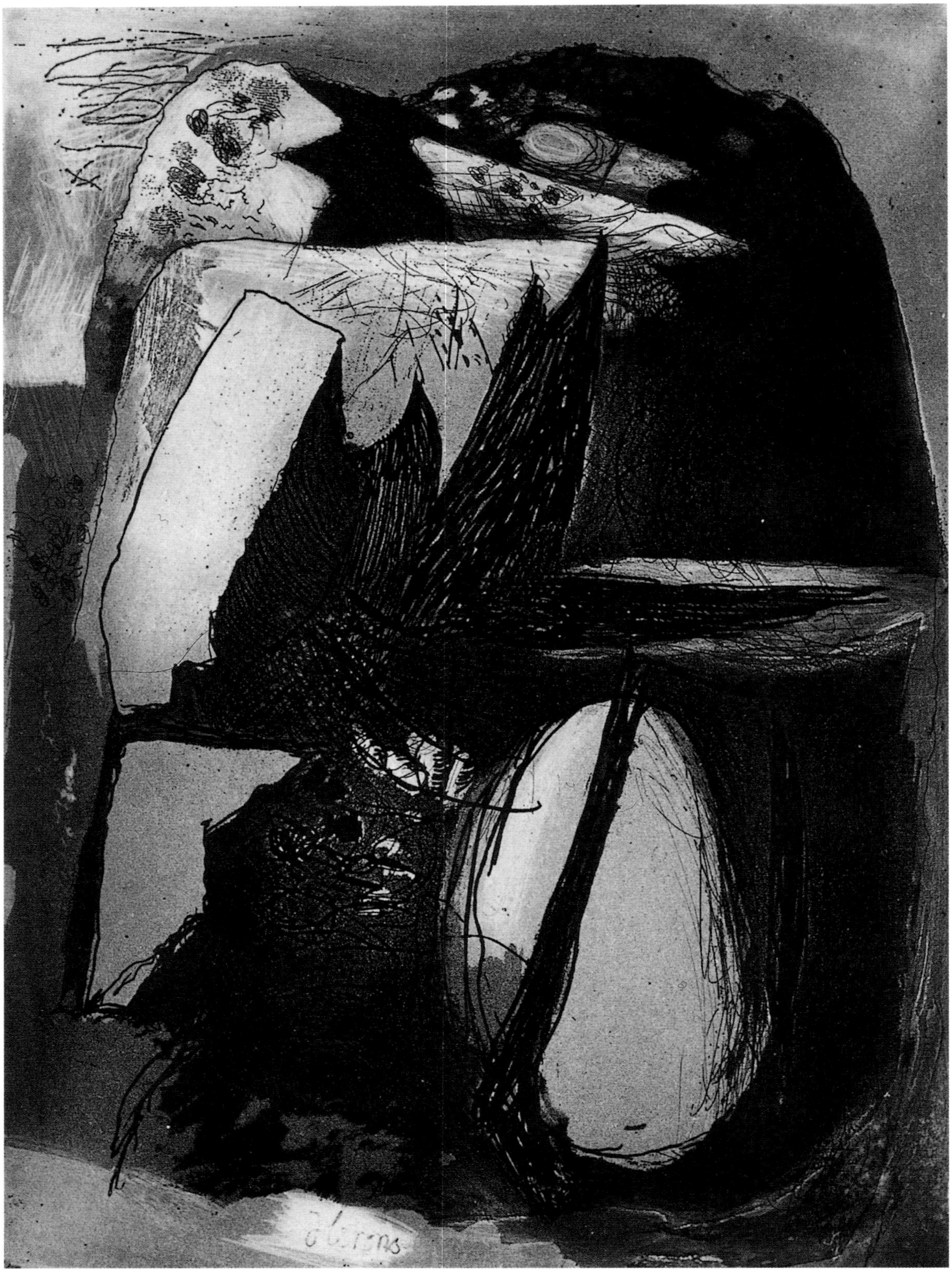

21.
Clegyr-Boia
1938
Intaglio print
197 x 146 mm
Tate. Presented by the artist
1970.
P02068.

22.
Tree Forms in Estuary
1939
Watercolour on paper
290 x 225 mm
Doncaster Museum Service,
Doncaster M.B.C.

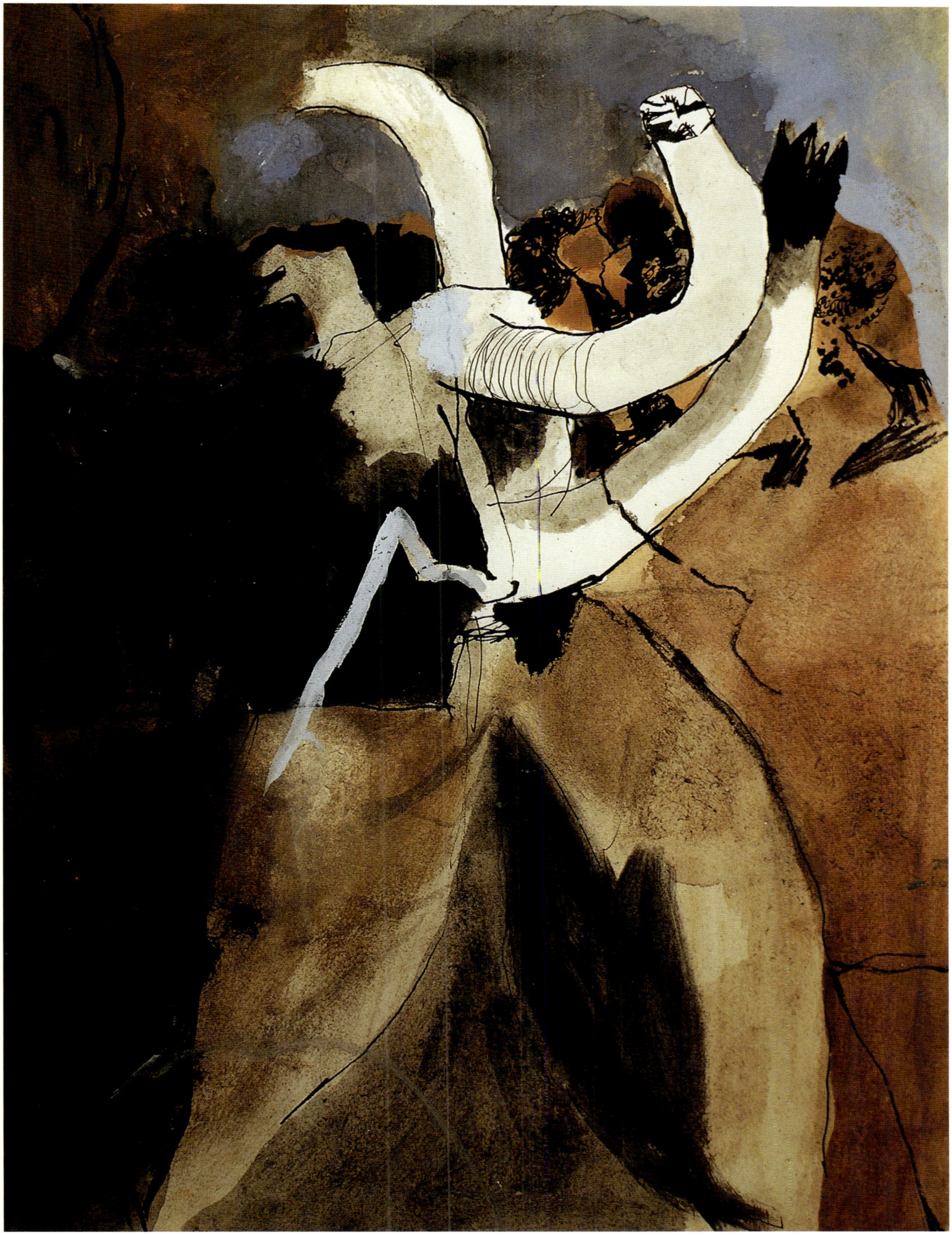

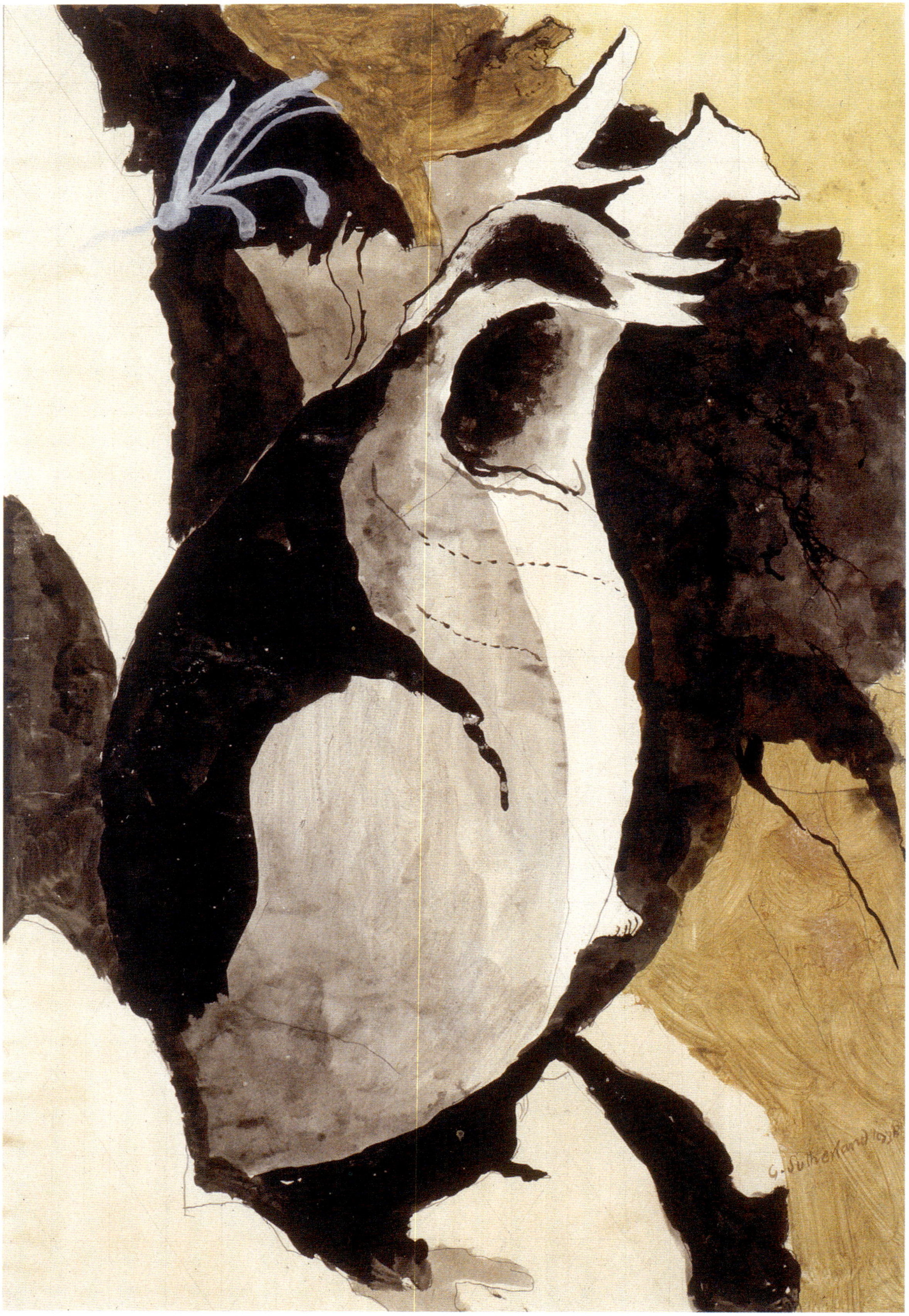

23.
Hollow Tree Trunk
1938
Pencil, watercolour and bodycolour on paper
624 x 456 mm
Laing Art Gallery, Newcastle upon Tyne (Tyne and Wear Museums)
E5274.

24.
Gorse on Sea Wall
1939
Oil on canvas
622 x 483 mm
Collection Ulster Museum, Belfast.

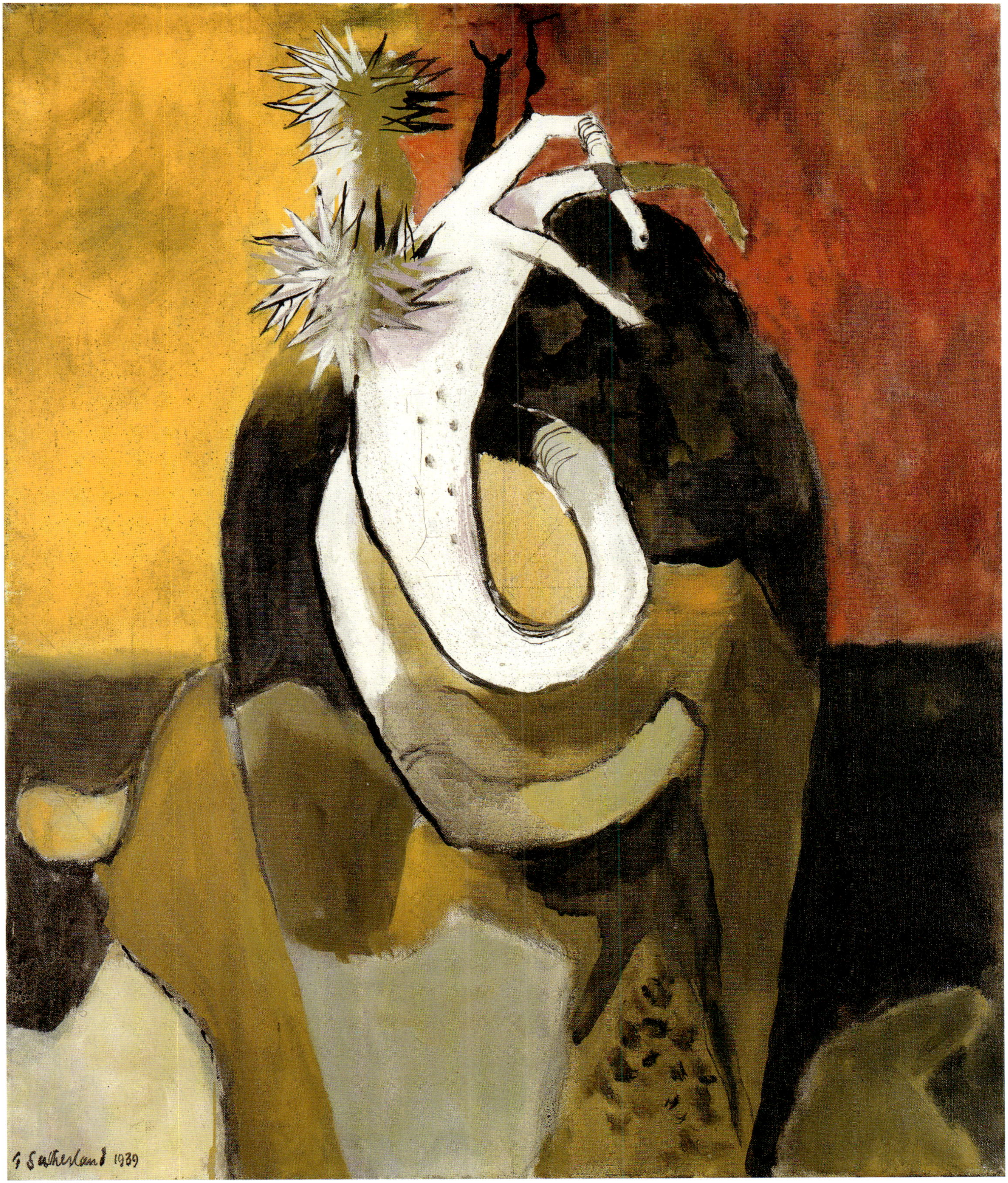
G Sutherland 1939

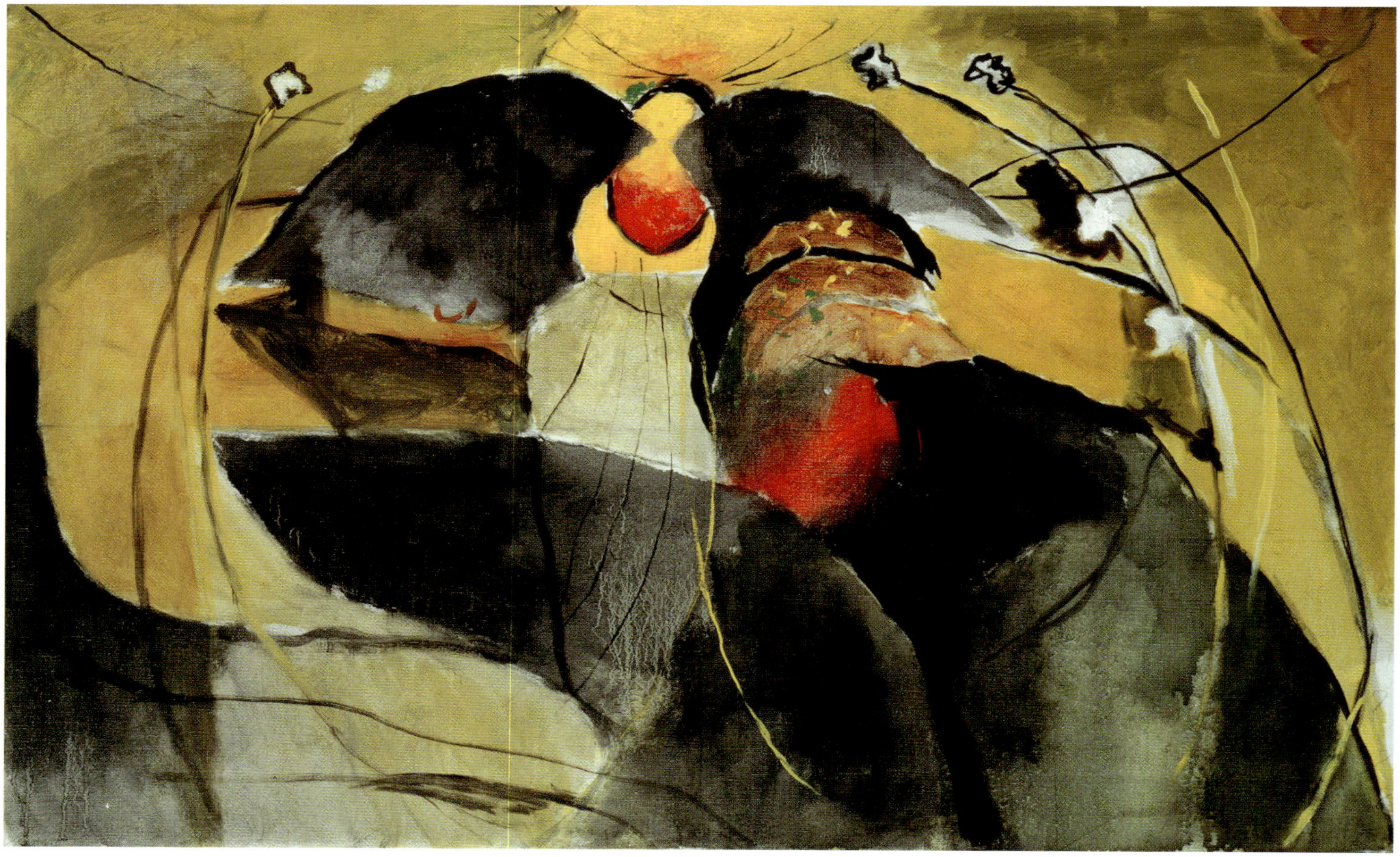

25.
Sunrise between Hedges
1939
Oil on canvas
546 x 902 mm
Leeds Museums and Galleries
(City Art Gallery)
2/41.

26.
Study of Road Rising between Hedges
1940
Gouache, pen and wash on paper
110 x 87 mm
Private Collection.

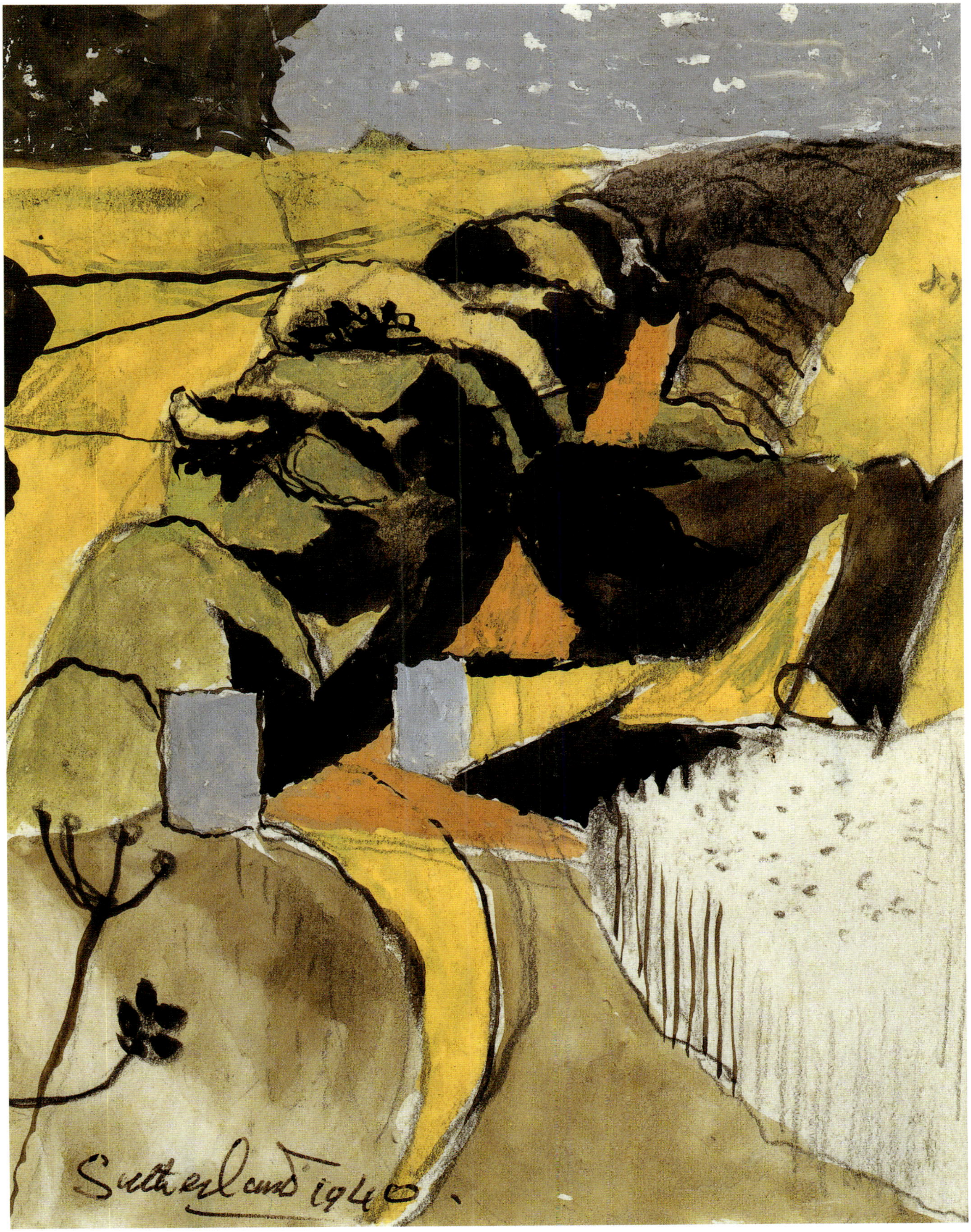
Sutherland 1940.

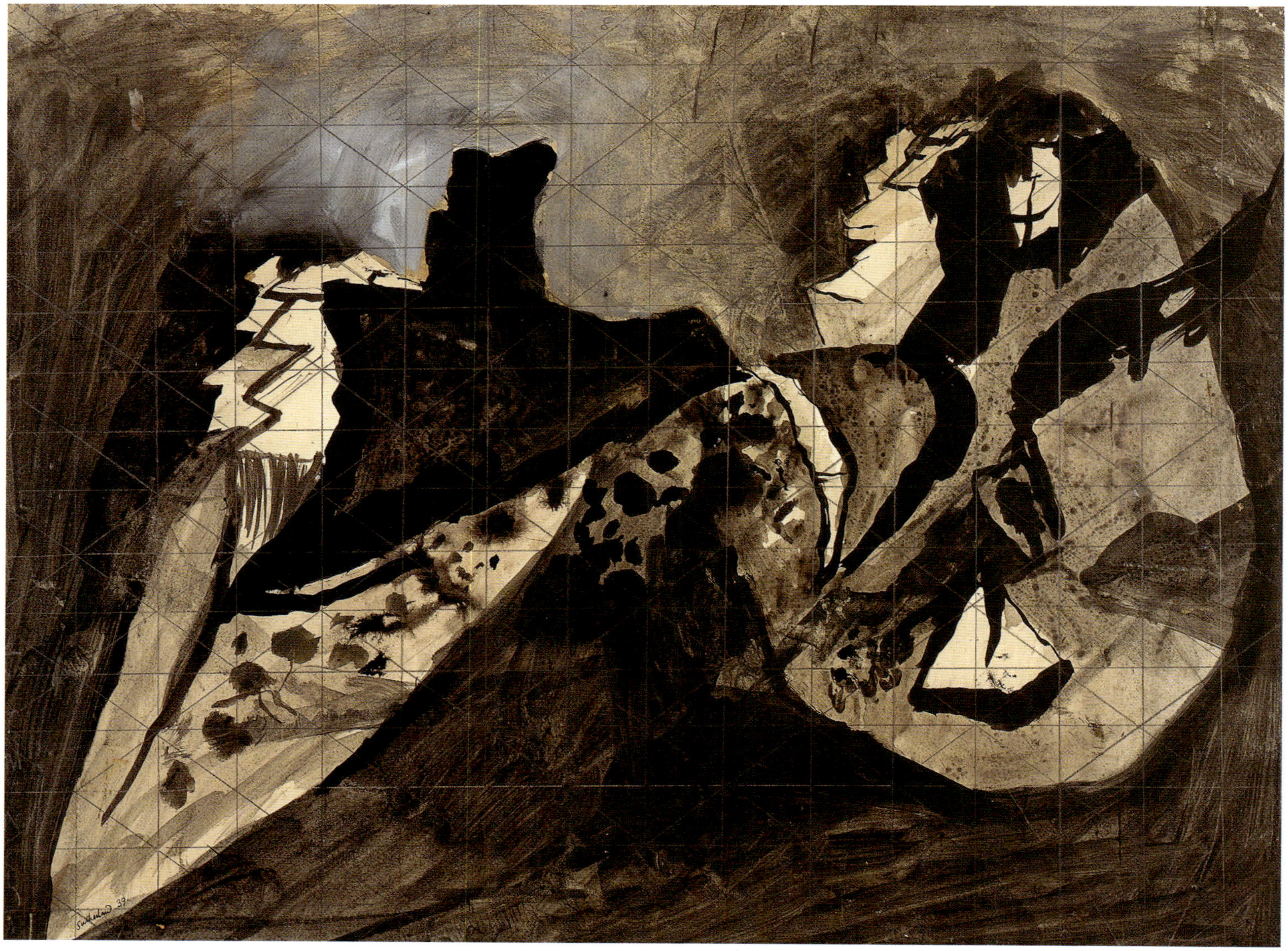

27.
Landscape with Rocks
(Wolf's Castle)
1939
Gouache, ink and pencil on
paper
500 x 683 mm
The Scottish National Gallery
of Modern Art, Edinburgh
GMA 894.

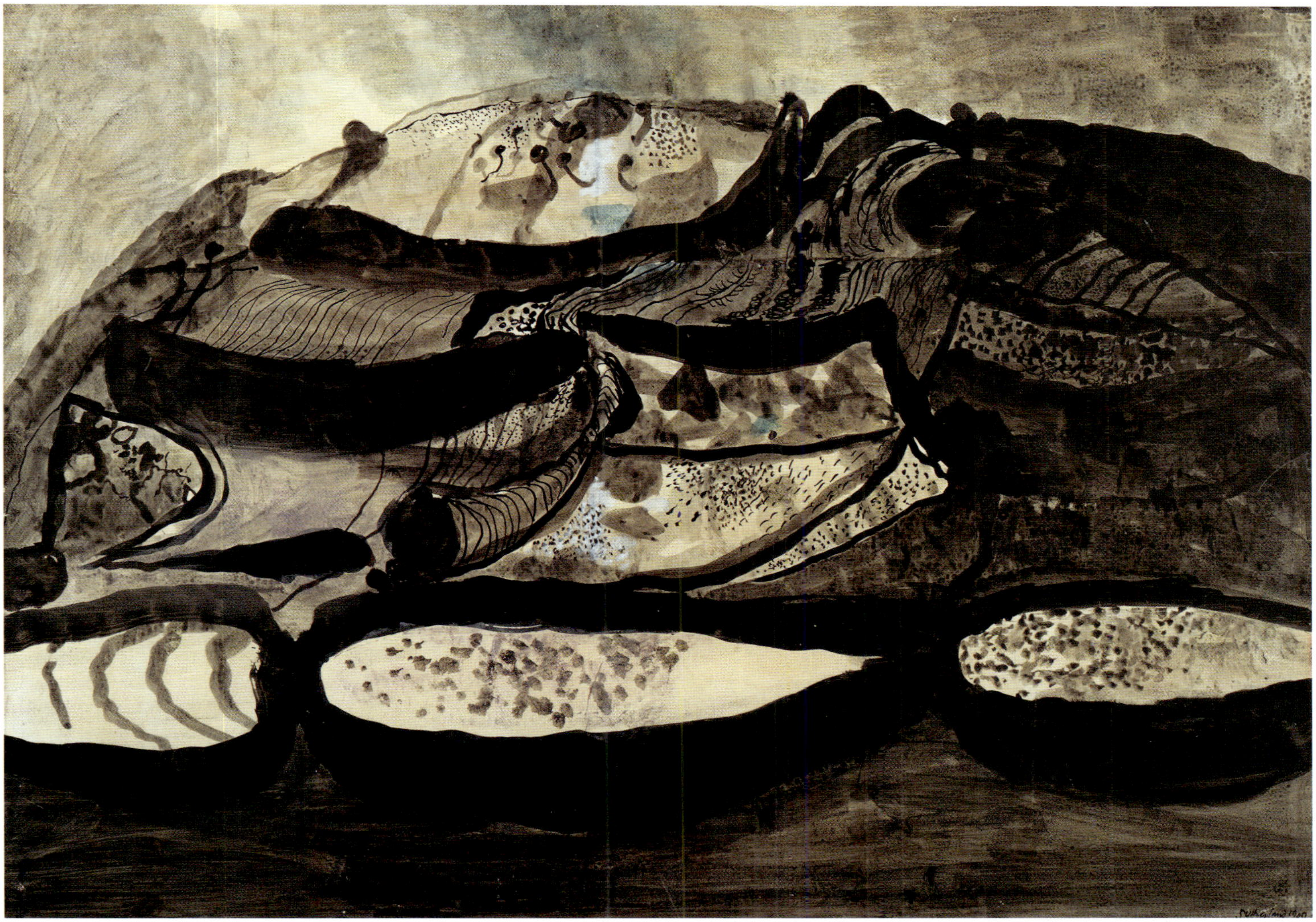

28.
Dark Hill
1940
Watercolour, gouache on paper
439 x 698 mm
Swindon Museum and Art Gallery
AG 1978/25.

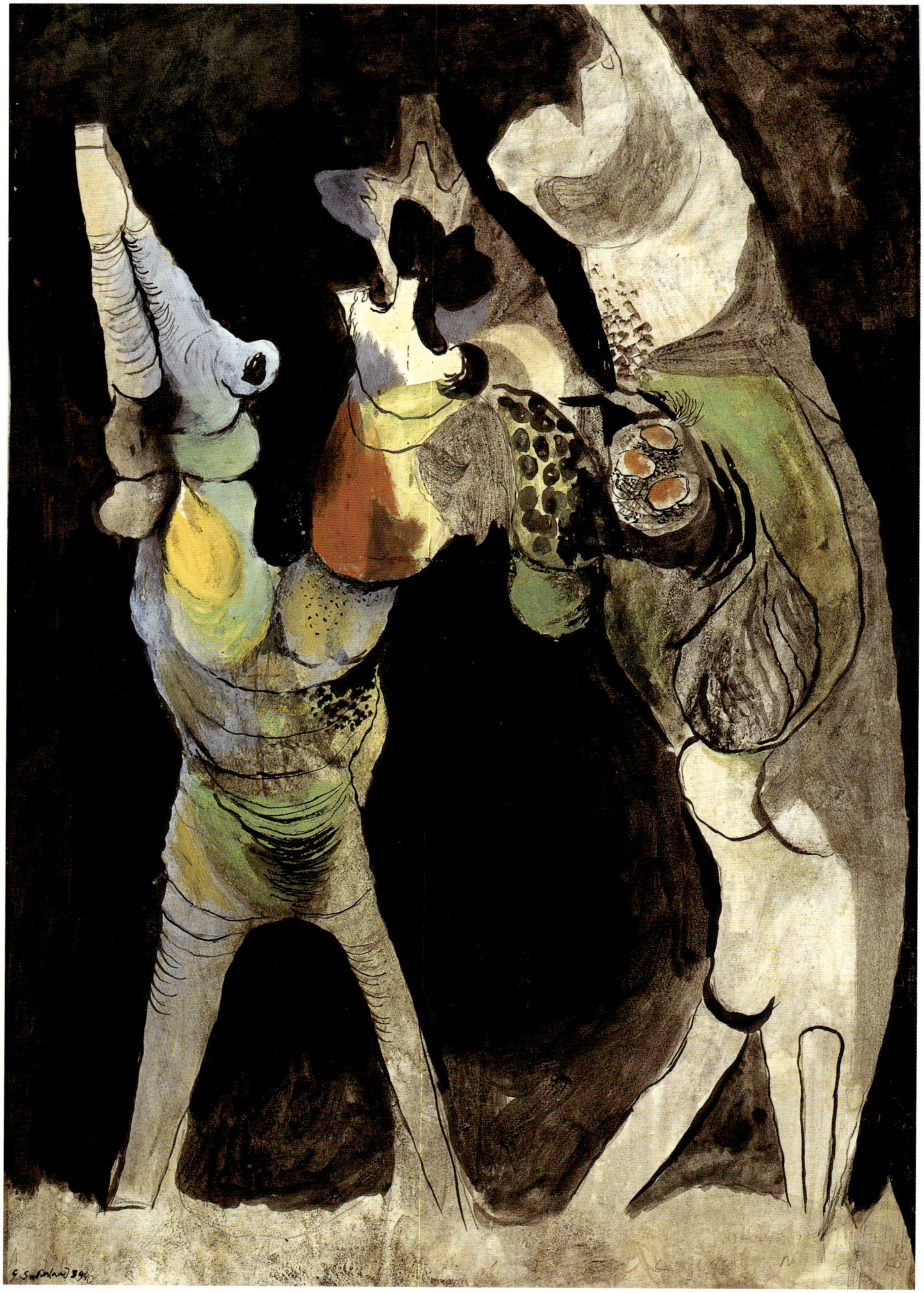

29.
Association of Oaks
1940
Gouache, watercolour and pencil on paper
686 x 486 mm
The Scottish National Gallery of Modern Art, Edinburgh
GMA 2219.

30.
Fallen Tree against Sunset
1940
Oil on canvas
673 x 508 mm
Darlington Arts Centre.

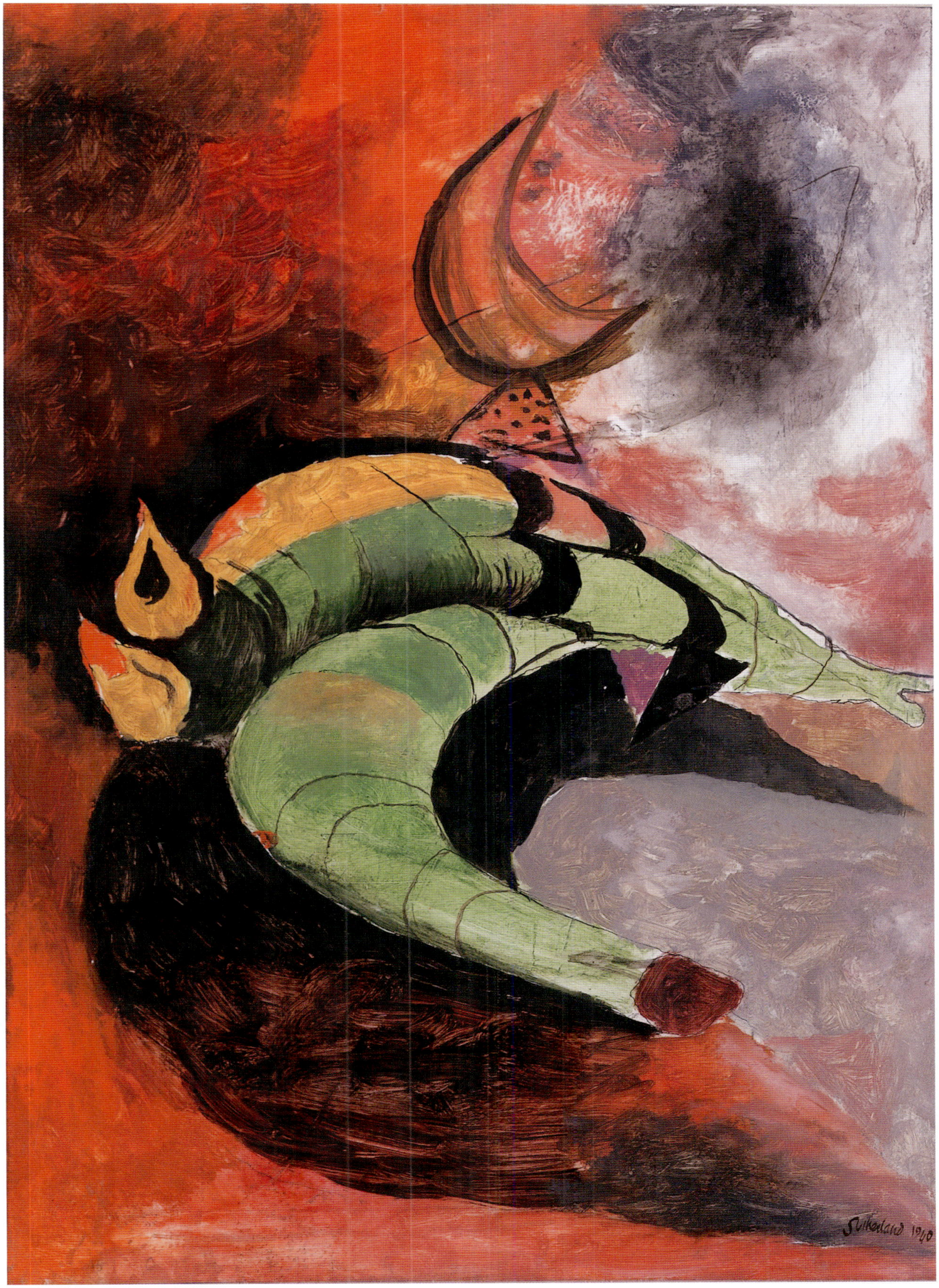

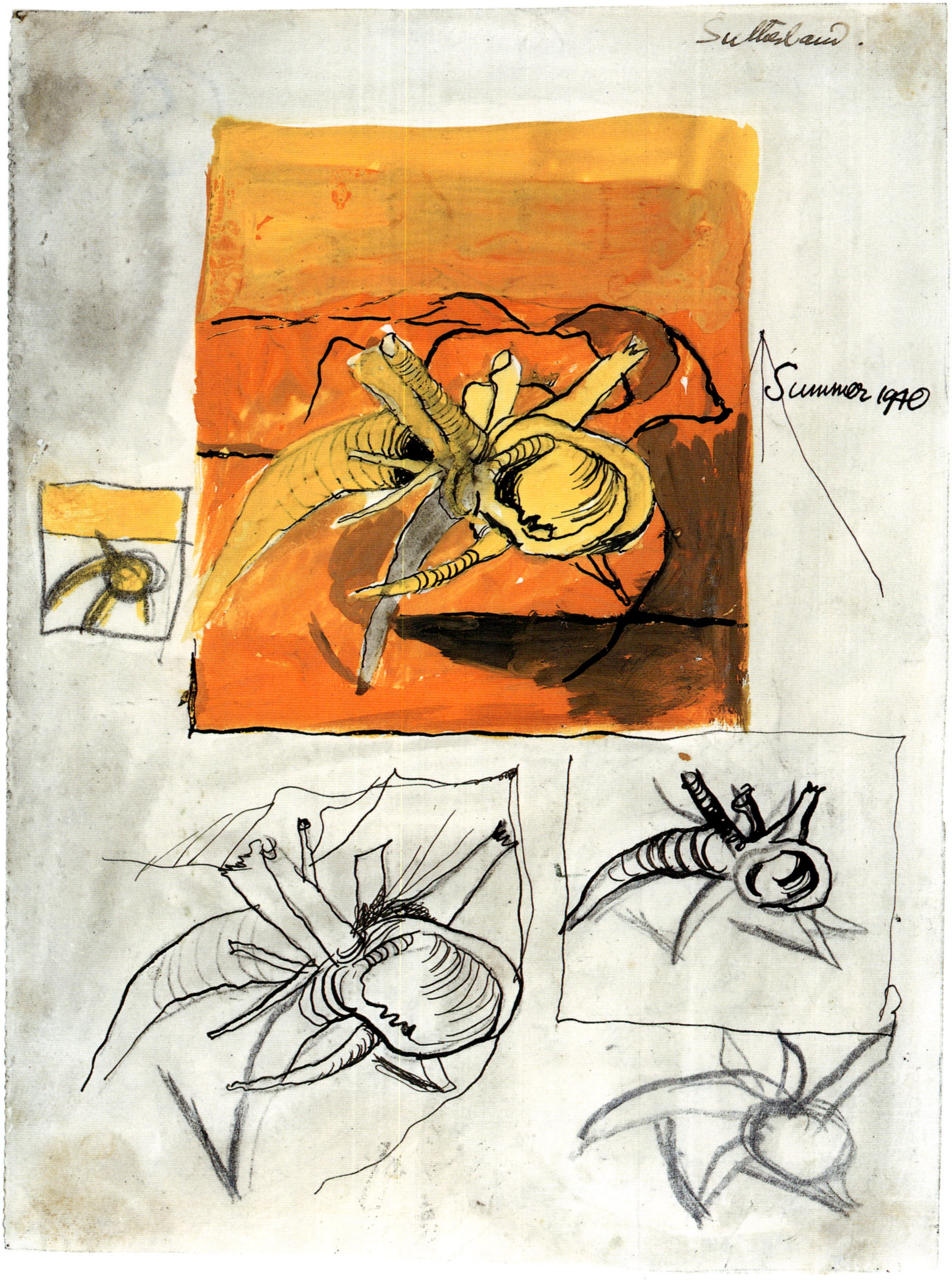
Sutherland.
Summer 1940

31.
Studies for Midsummer Landscape
1940
Pen and gouache on paper torn from notebook, perforations down left hand edge
200 x 155 mm
Birmingham Museums and Art Gallery
1962P36.

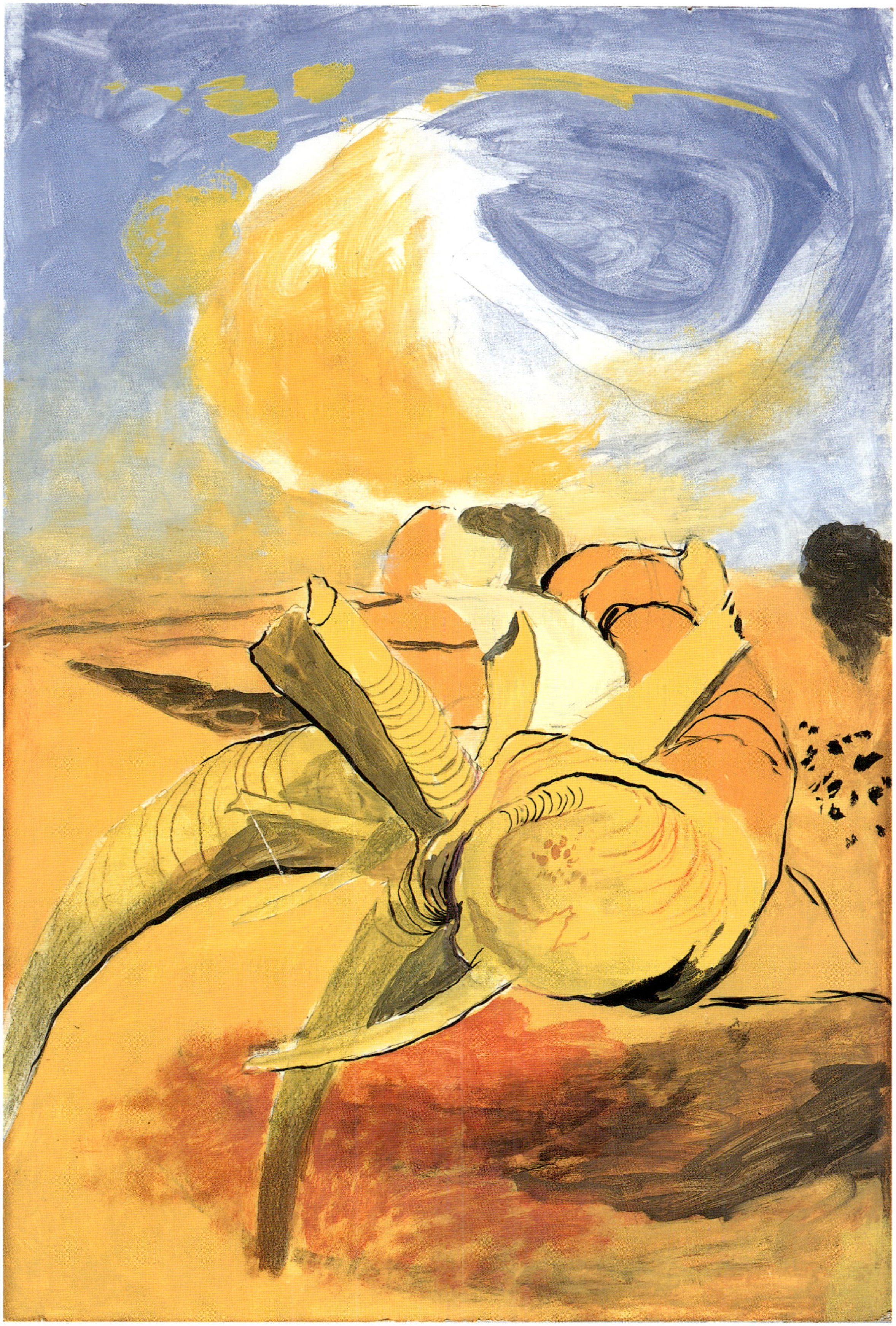

32.
Midsummer Landscape
1940
Pencil, ink and gouache
686 x 483 mm
Birmingham Museums and Art Gallery
1946P37.

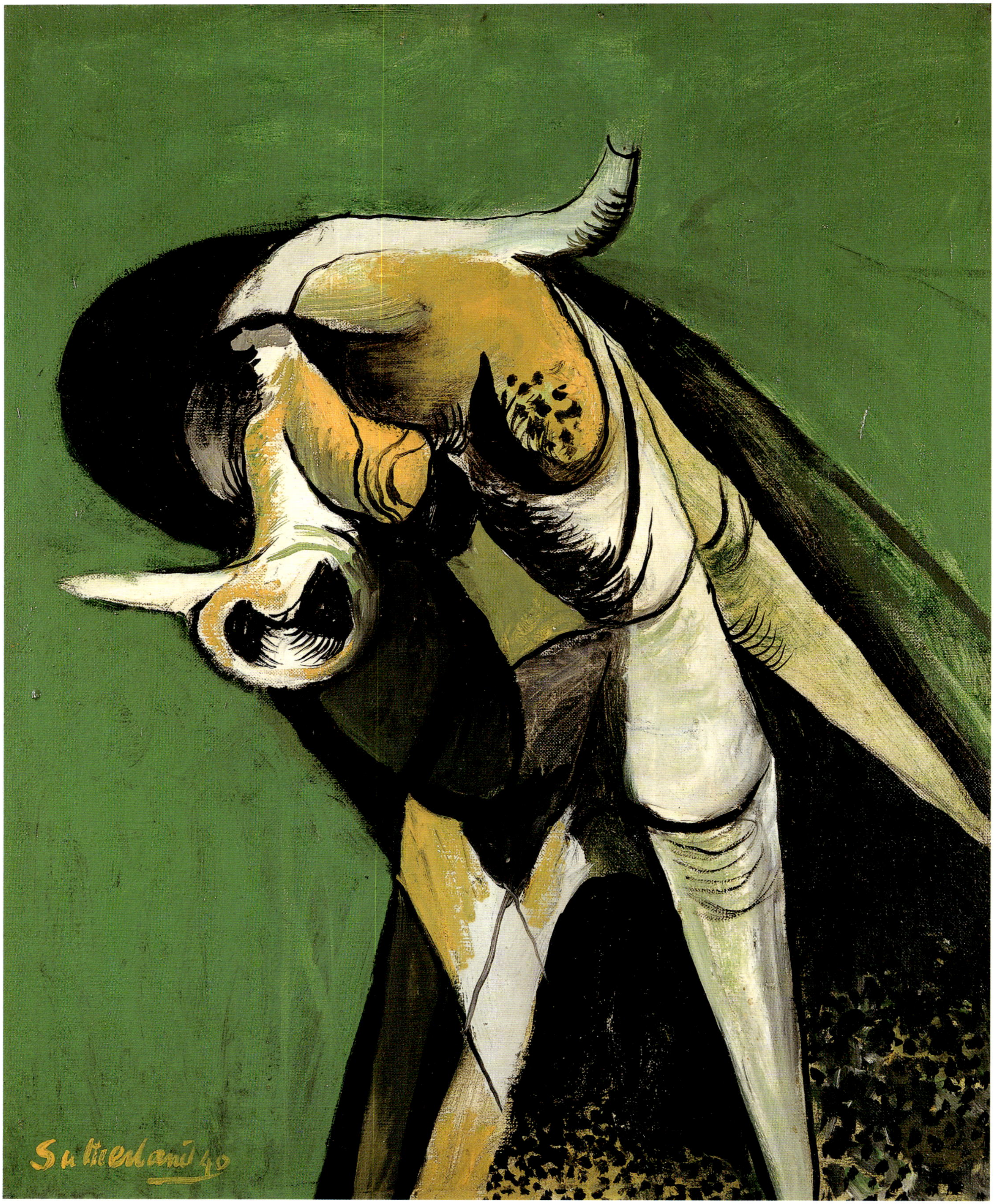
Sutherland 40

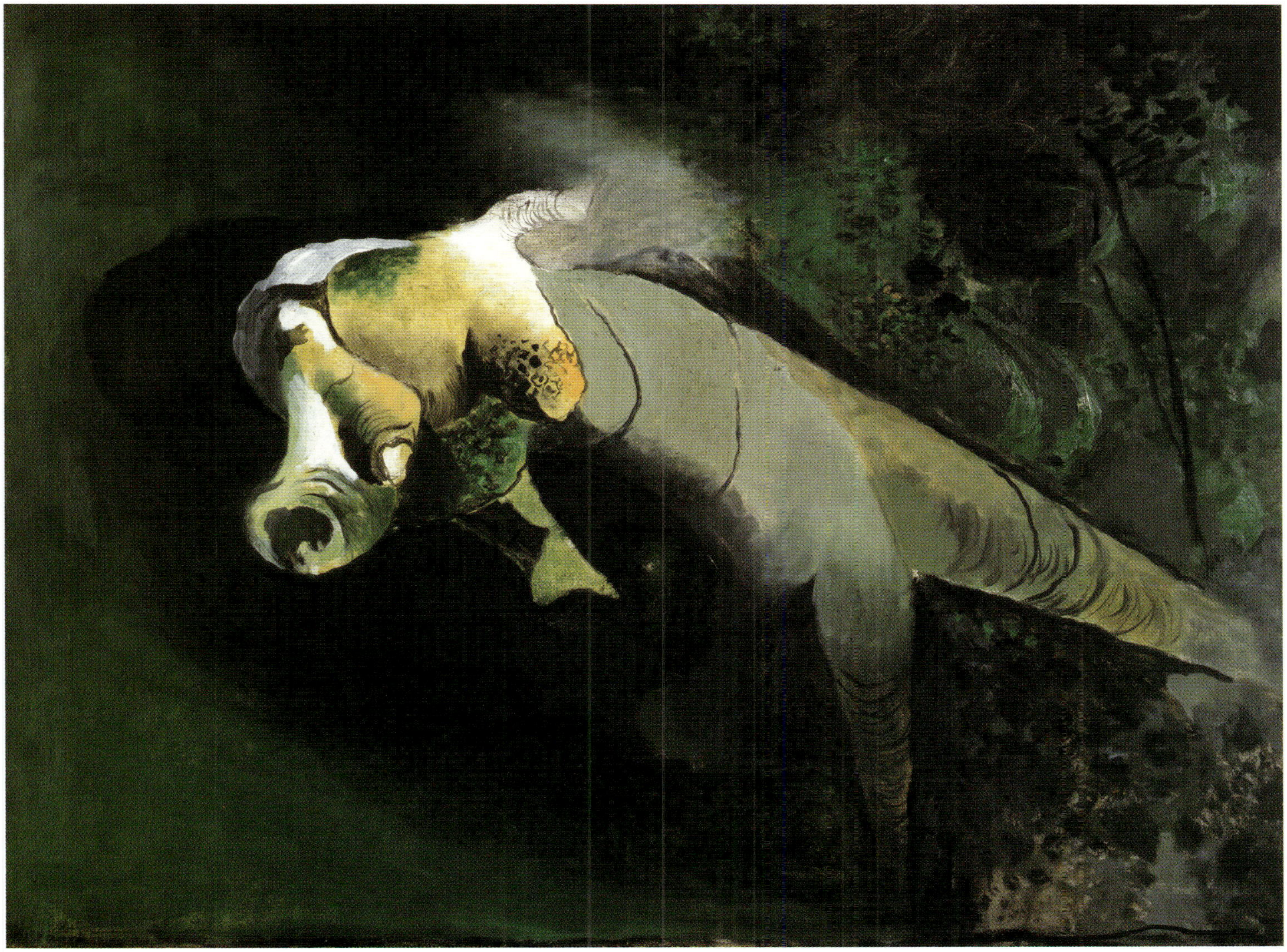

33.
Green Tree Form
1940
Oil on canvas
605 x 545 mm
British Council
P177.

34.
Green Tree Form: Interior of Woods
1940
Oil on canvas
787 x 1079 mm
Tate. Purchased 1940
N05139.

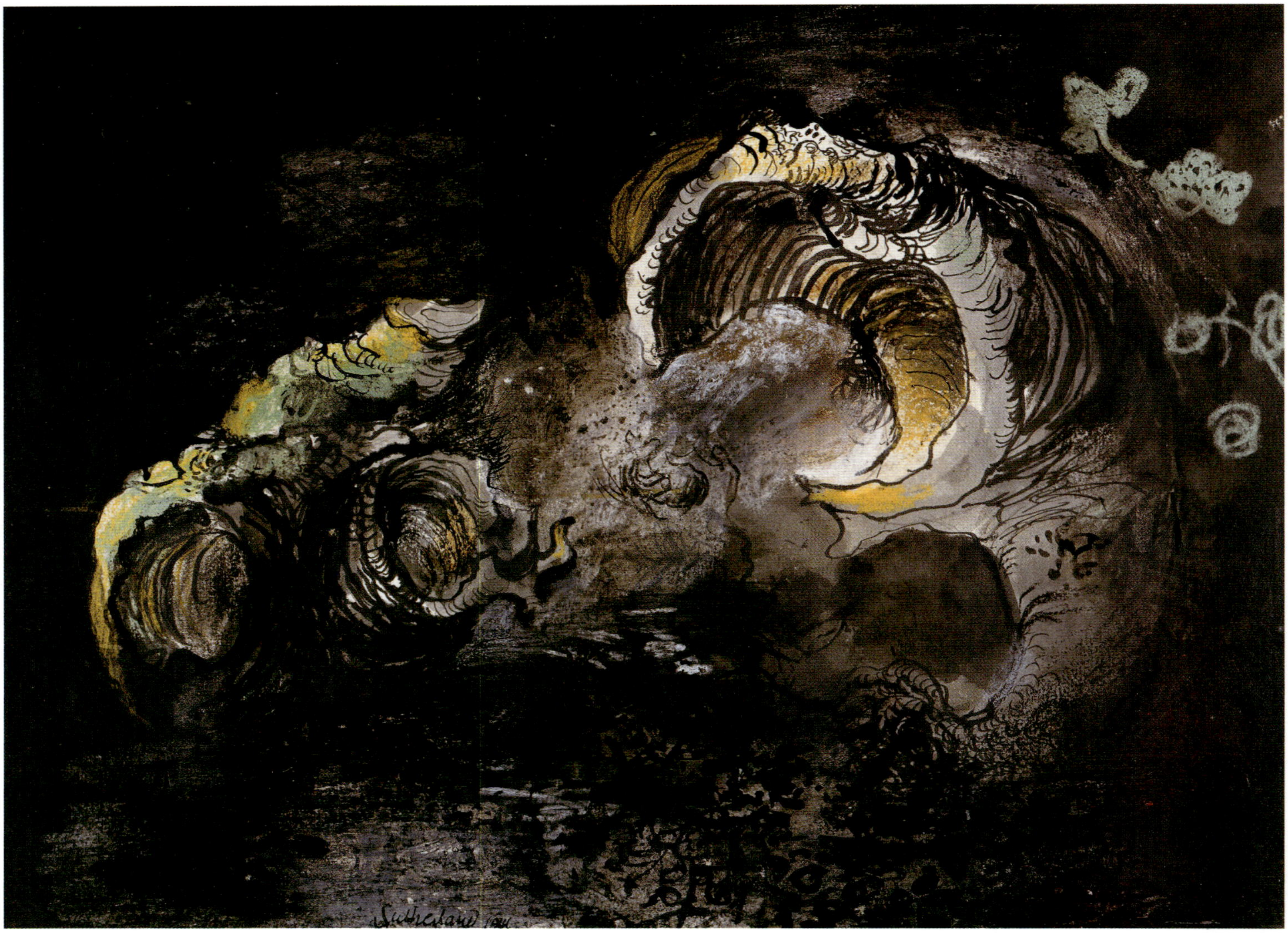

35.
Dwarf Oaks
1941
Coloured chalk, Indian ink
and gouache on paper
260 x 355 mm
Private Collection.

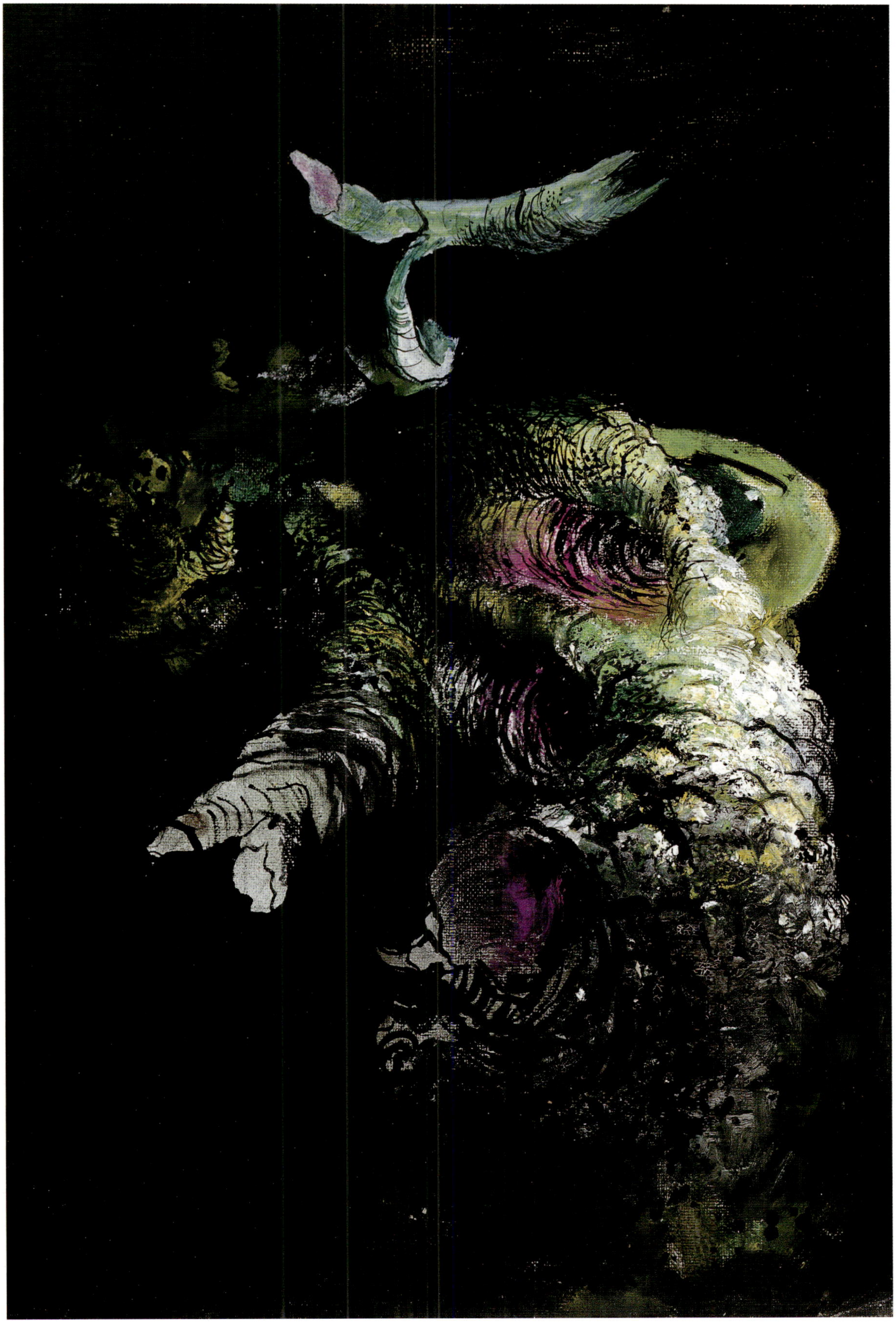

36.
Tree Form
1941
Canvas on board
393 x 305 mm
Leeds Museums and Galleries
(City Art Gallery)
15/41.

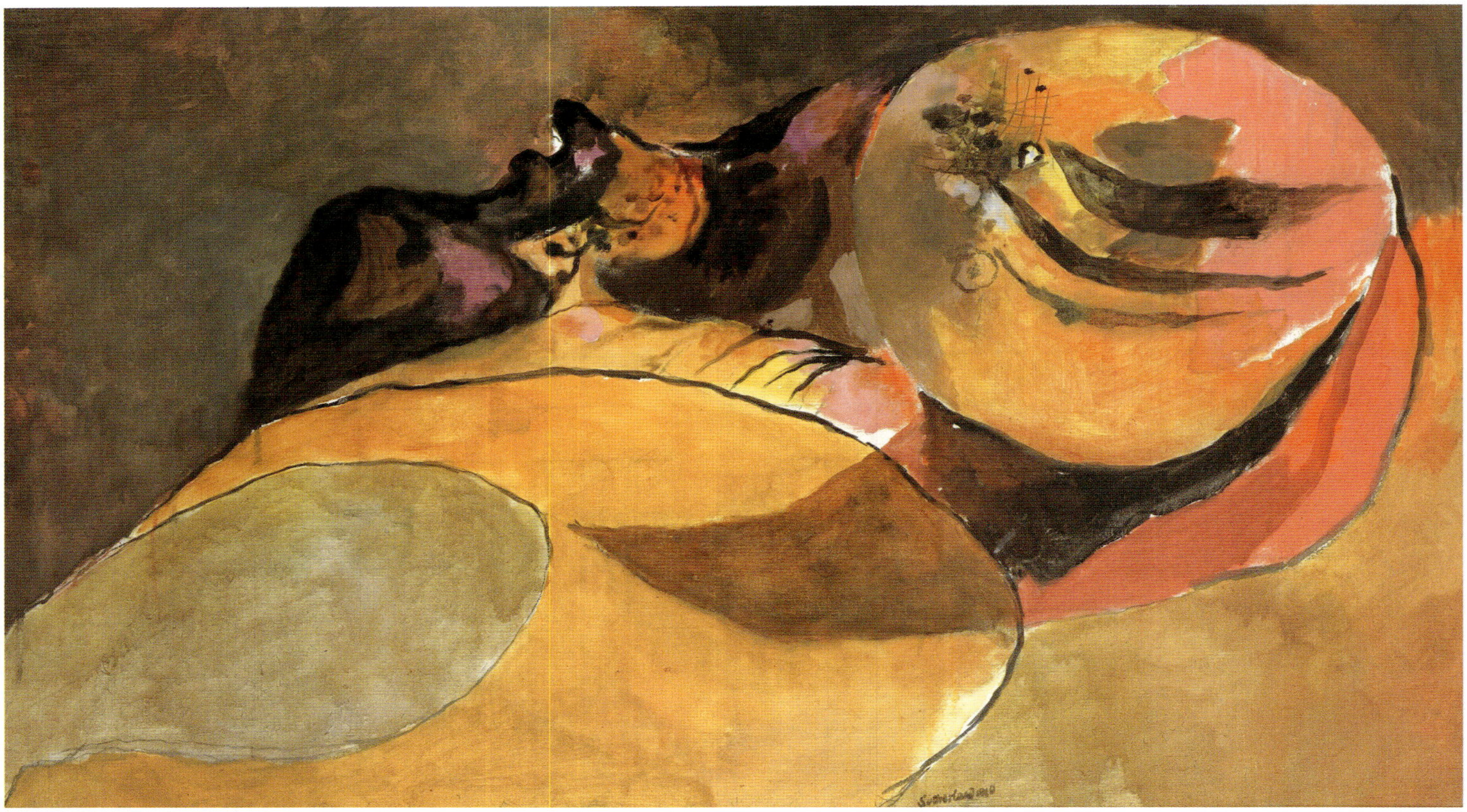

37.
Mountain Road with Boulder
1940
Oil on canvas
622 x 1117 mm
Private Collection.

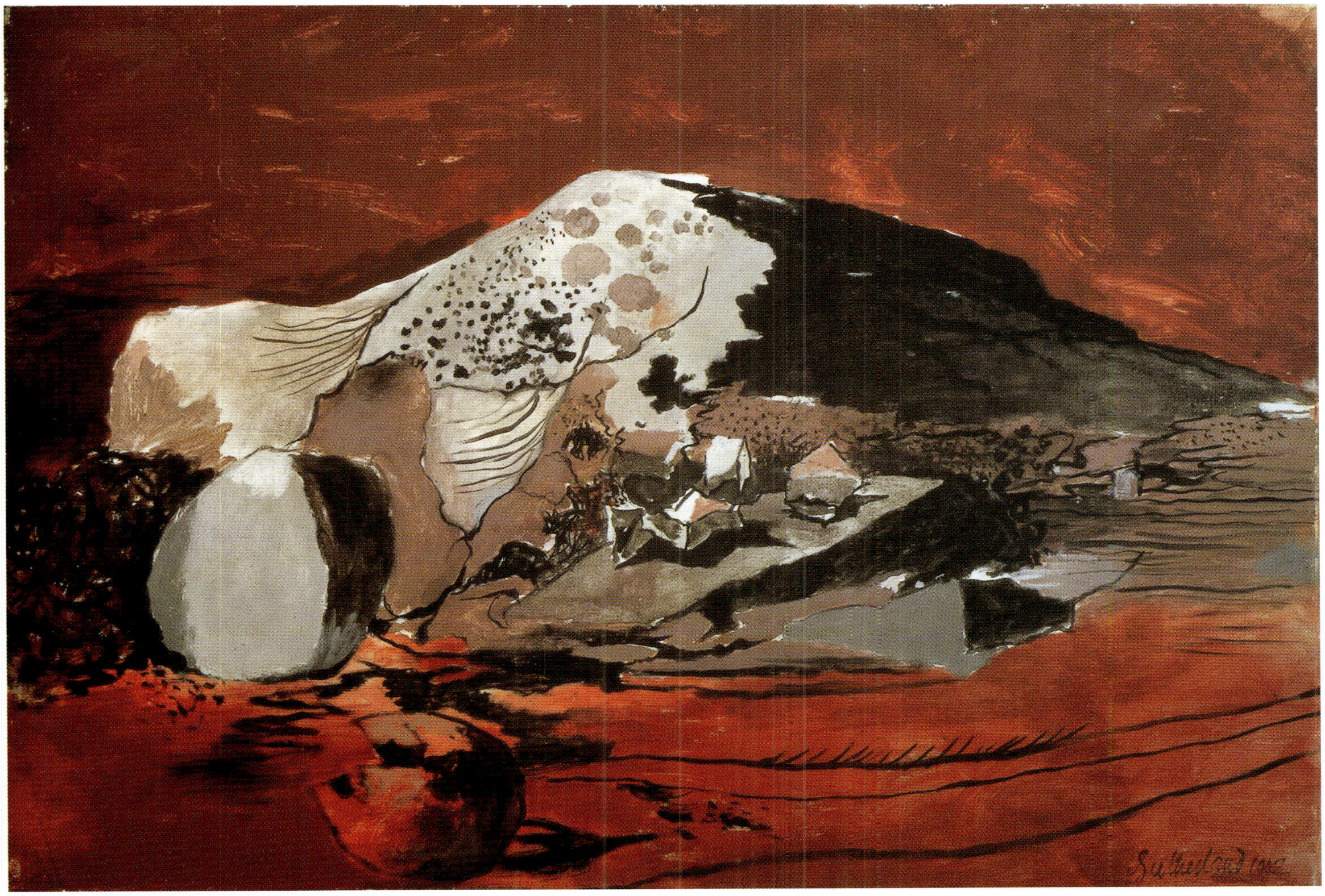

38.
Red Landscape
1942
Oil on canvas
680 x 998 mm
Southampton City Art Gallery
1369.

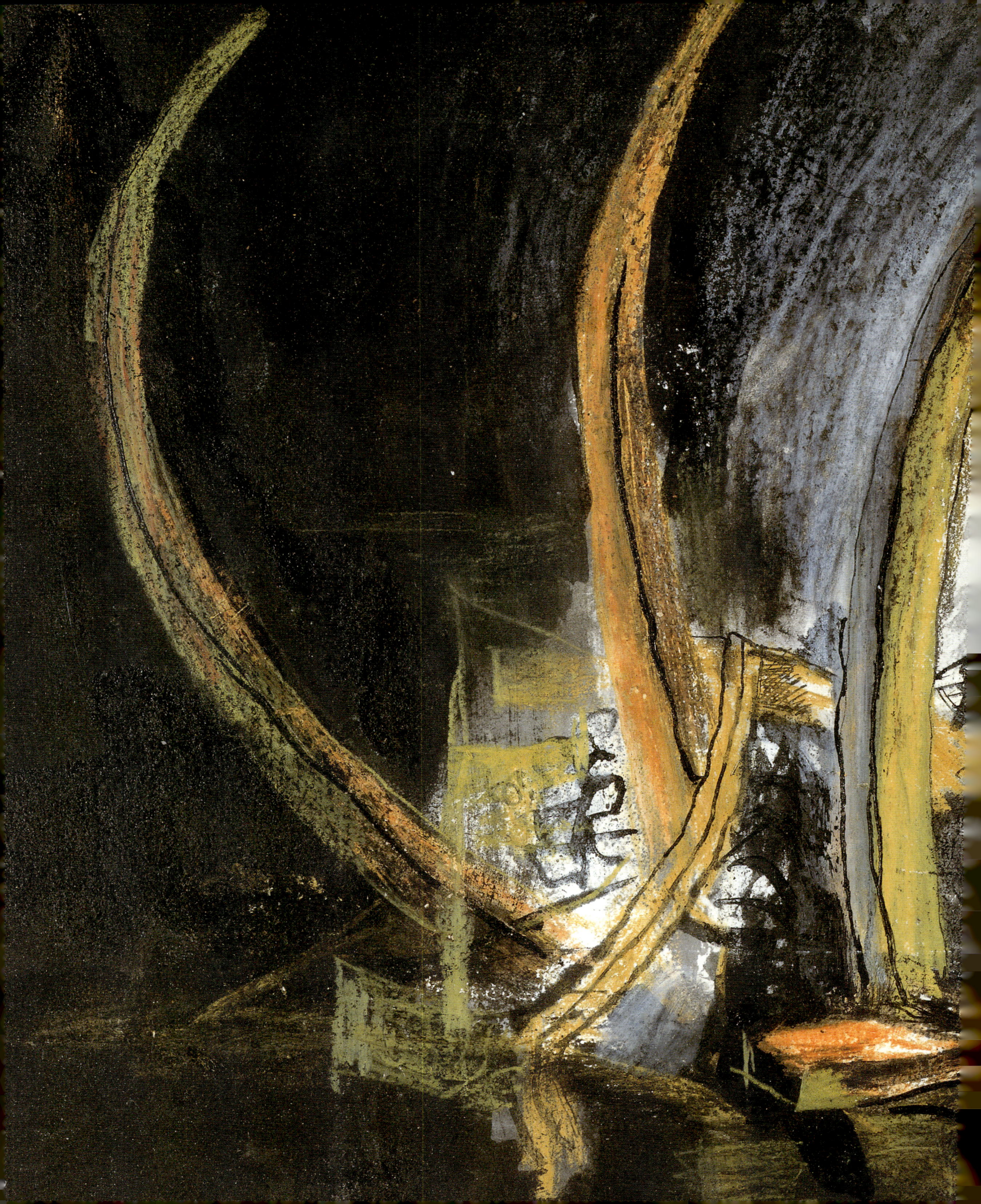

3

War Artist
1940–1944

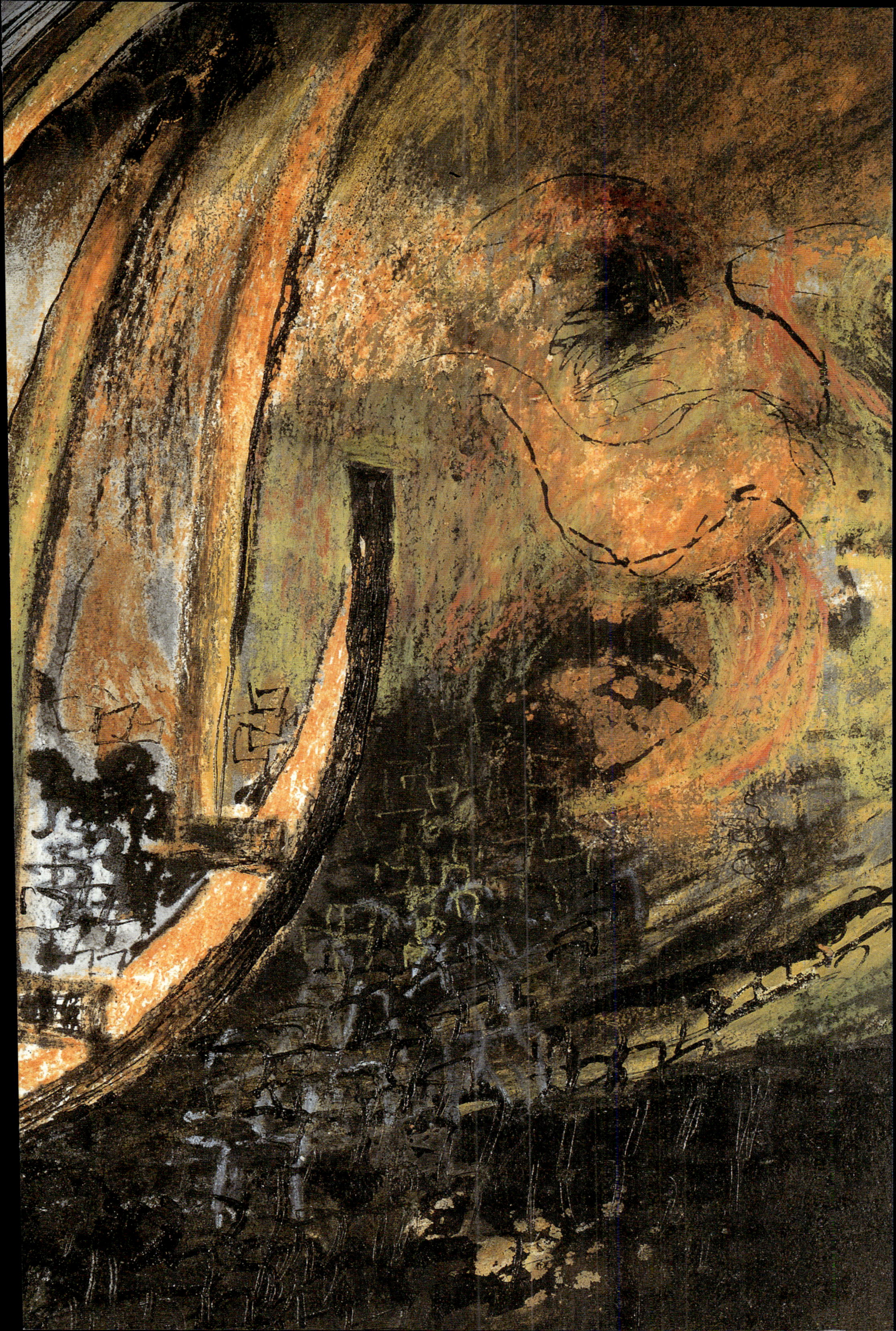

Devastation in the City: Twisted Girders Against a Background of Fire
1941
(Cat. 47, detail).

Images Wrought From Destruction

Graham Sutherland

Dear Edwin,

You ask me questions about my war paintings and I will try to answer.

During the bombardment of London, on a typical day, I would arrive there from Kent where we had resumed living, with very spare paraphernalia – a sketch book, black and two or three coloured chalks, a pencil – and with an apparently watertight pass which would take me anywhere within the forbidden areas. It wasn't watertight at all, I was arrested several times, especially in the East End.

And once there I would look around. I will never forget those extraordinary first encounters: the silence, the absolute dead silence, except every now and again a thin tinkle of falling glass – a noise which reminded me of some of the music of Debussy.

The first place I went to was the big area just north of St Paul's – I suppose about five acres – which had been almost completely flattened; here and there within this flattened field remains were left. Sometimes fires were still burning. Everywhere there was a terrible stench – perhaps of burnt dirt; and always the silence. There was nobody about; just a few police. Very occasionally there would be the crash of a building collapsing of its own volition.

I would start to make perfunctory drawings here and there; gradually it was borne on me amid all this destruction how singularly one shape would impinge on another. A lift-shaft, for instance, the only thing left from what had obviously been a very tall building: in the way it had fallen it was like a wounded animal. It wasn't that these forms *looked* like animals, but their movements were animal movements. One shaft in particular, with a very strong lateral fall, suggested a wounded tiger in a painting by Delacroix.

At the beginning I was a bit shy as to where I went. Later I grew bolder and went inside some of the ruins. I remember a factory for making women's coats. All the floors had gone but the staircase remained, as very often happened. And there were machines, their entrails hanging through the floors, but looking extraordinarily beautiful at the same time. And always there was the terrible smell of sour burning.

The City was more exciting than anywhere else mainly because the buildings were bigger, and the variety of ways in which they fell more interesting. But very soon the raids began in the East End – in the dock areas – and immediately the atmosphere became much more tragic. In the City one didn't think of the destruction of life. All the destroyed buildings were office buildings and people weren't in them at night. But in the East End one did think of the hurt to people and there was every evidence of it.

I don't really know what I expected, but even a mattress that had been blown out of a house into the middle of the street looked more like a body than a mattress. From butchers' shops which had been hit the meat spewed on the road and I remember feeling quite sick when seeing this for the first time because I thought that here was a body that hadn't been picked up.

I became tremendously interested in parts of the East End where the shells of long terraces of houses remained; they were great – surprisingly wide – perspectives of destruction seeming to recede into infinity and the windowless blocks were like sightless eyes.

On the few occasions when I stayed the night in London I was concerned with the City. I took a room at a railway hotel and I made my way from there to St Paul's (which was to be my centre when I needed it) on foot. If there was a raid I took to my heels: not belonging here I was not familiar with the shelters. Once, I went on the roof of St Paul's. The gathering place of authorities and others – architects and businessmen, who had volunteered to be there to put out incendiaries – was the gallery round the base of the dome. This passage between walls was probably the strongest place in the cathedral. All, when not on duty, slept or lolled on deck chairs and I remember thinking that it was like being on an ocean liner.

It had all begun with Kenneth Clark, Director of the National Gallery, conceiving the idea of reviving a war artists' body in much the same way as had existed during the First World War.

For the first year of the war the Clarks had asked Katherine and me to go and stay with them in a house they had taken in Gloucestershire. They thought, with the most sensitive consideration, and rightly, that I should be at this time in great financial difficulty. My teaching work had been completely cut off at the outset and all commissioned work for which I was engaged had been cancelled straight away.

At first it was difficult to decide what function I might undertake as a war artist and I couldn't properly call myself one for some time. My first job was to make drawings of camouflaged aeroplanes. I couldn't make much of them, I am afraid.

After that (and still the bombardment from the air had not as yet started) I was sent to a gun testing site near Melton Mowbray, and again I tried to find my way towards making something of the subject – this time guns, gun barrels and breech blocks. But I did nothing with any kind of heightened feeling. The people on the range were all helpful and the commandant played Bach to me in the local church in the evenings.

Suddenly, at nearby Leicester, there was a big raid and there was a round of diving under tables. Almost simultaneously, as I remembered it, there were raids on factories at Cardiff and Swansea. At this point I was made a salaried war artist.

Katherine and I could never bear to be separated: neither could I contemplate leaving her alone, even in Kent. We stayed in a small village just outside Swansea because the damage was both there and around the nearby aerodrome. In the bedroom over the shop in which we lived the bed backed on to a window and I remember that each night I covered this with my drawing board against the possibility of flying glass.

Swansea was the first sight I had of the possibilities of destruction as a subject. The architecture was florid and Victorian. At first I made as complete a record as I could of what I saw. I hadn't yet begun to feel any sense of what these remains really *looked* like. Later, as I have said, some were to become like great animals who had been hurt. After making my studies I would go to a farmhouse we knew to work them out. Finally, I delivered six or seven: a large painting and some gouaches.

After Swansea the bombardment of London started. Before then we had decided we should go back from Gloucestershire to our house in Kent. I used to go up daily from there, or occasionally stay overnight at one of the railway hotels in the City as I have already related.

During these terrible months I found I didn't inquire as to the future at all.

The daily atmosphere now and before this was to us particularly disturbing. Kenneth Clark, who was then in the Ministry of Information, knew just how serious the situation was becoming. Through him we had an idea of the true gravity of the situation and we knew how near to capitulation we were. The blackness of the atmosphere of war was like the prospect of death, and more and more funereal. We lived from day to day.

At the same time I was never completely desperate. I was never in the state where I thought our whole world would come to an end. Somehow or other, I felt, I would be able to return to my normal work.

My feeling at the beginning of the war from the point of view of my work was one of being thrown down in a totally unfamiliar field. There was I who, up to then, had been concerned with the more hidden aspects of nature. I had been attempting to paraphrase what I saw and to make paintings which were parallel to rather than a copy of nature. But now, suddenly, I was a paid official – a sort of reporter – and naturally not only did I feel that I had to give value for money, but to contrive somehow to reflect in an immediate way the subjects set me. It was not until the advent of the air raids that I could see any way open to combine the aims of my work before the outbreak of war with the task then in front of me. It was difficult too to see how anything I could do as a war artist could help the course of the war and – of course – it didn't. One cannot escape the fact that some of us were protected. Now as the raids subsided, how was I to continue?

Kenneth Clark had a lot of suggestions. One was – mines. All the tin mines were being opened in Cornwall – there was a great scarcity of tin which had been, in peacetime, obtained from overseas. Now it had to be found within the British Isles. To make drawings of the mines had only the vaguest relation to the war but I was certainly presented with a new world – and a world of such beauty and such mystery that I shall never forget it. There was none of the urgency of the war in this – unless you can call mining a perpetual war.

I was put through some hair-raising tests – to establish my nerve. One goes down the pit, normally, in a lift to the bottom. I was afraid that I would experience terrible claustrophobia (when I was an engineer, I was once trapped in a locomotive boiler for hours, so I hate enclosed places). The man who first took me round said, "Look now, we'll go down on the bucket, not in the lift – put your feet either side of the bucket and we'll hold on to the rope." We went down 1,300 feet like a bullet and I didn't like it at all. I disliked even more the fact that the last floor of all, the 14th, was not served by a lift. One had to go through a trap-door in the floor and down a ladder. The 'Captain' said, "You go first because I have to close the trap door." I thought to myself as my legs began to tremble "Pitch dark and underneath 100ft of ladder, I know I'm going to faint." What he didn't tell me was that there were stages every so often and I couldn't possibly have fallen the whole way.

Once down and walking through the various tunnels – some a mile along – the problem was to avoid getting lost. I would mark up my way in chalk on the walls. Later I found the geography of the place easier. Far from the main shaft the sense of remoteness was tangible and the distances seemed endless. Faintly, far away, was the sound of work on other levels.

Underground I did a number of portraits. This was mainly to distract the attention of the miners from what I was really drawing. I did not lack customers and the poses struck were splendidly incongruous in the environment. The heads I did were small and naturalistic, as suited their purpose; but the deeper significance of these men only gradually became clear to me. It was as if they were a kind of different species – ennobled underground, and with an added stature which above ground they lacked, and my feeling was that in spite of the hardness of the work in this nether world, this place held for them – subconsciously perhaps – an element of daily enthralment.

The search for the diagonally descending vein of metal took the miners through a hole in the floor of the level tunnels via a high and narrow passage, shored with struts, terminating through a similar hole in the roof of the tunnel on the level below. This passage revealed precipitous perspectives of extraordinary and mysterious beauty in which the men, brilliantly lit, would be seen from above. On a lower level tunnel, from an opening in the roof, would emerge a crouching figure; often too one would come across a miner sitting in a niche in a wall – like a statue, immobile. The distant sound of a miner or trucks approaching would herald itself long before arrival. One would flatten oneself against the wall when trucks passed. In places the tunnels would converge in a central junction where all was light and where there were many figures and trucks. All was humid: the walls dripped water and the only light normally was from the acetylene lamps fixed to each man's helmet. Even today the smell of acetylene transports me immediately to the mine.

This went on until the late summer of 1942 and in the autumn I went to Cardiff to work in the steelworks. The conception of the idea of stress, both physical and mental, and how forms can be modified by emotion had been, even before the war, much in my mind. It was crystallised and strengthened by my understanding of Picasso's studies for *Guernica*. Faces become distorted by tears and mouths open in fear. Even a hand supporting a head creates distortion, as does the placing of food in the mouth.

I had seen aspects of this idea in certain kinds of destruction. So did I too in the steelworks. As the hand feeds the mouth so did the long scoops which plunged into the furnace openings feed them, and the metal containers pouring molten iron into ladles had great encrusted mouths.

When the flying bombs started I was sent to France. This was in late November, 1944. It was the first time I'd been abroad in my life. Before the war I hadn't been able to afford it and before that I was living a really insular English life. When we were children it was thought by my family too much of an upheaval to travel abroad. I suppose my natural inclination is to resist a thing until eventually I taste it: when I do, I like it the better perhaps.

In France, my brief really was to draw both the devastation of marshalling yards and to find out what the flying bomb sites looked like. They hadn't even been photographed then. In fact, the RAF had finished bombing them only a few weeks before. The advancing troops had liberated Paris, which was my base, only recently.

Inside the hills the French had made caves – in which had been grown Champignons de Paris. The Germans had used these caves and fortified them to store their flying bombs. This was the place the RAF was intent on bombing; it did so very successfully. The caves were so high that the bombs made holes in the top of the hills. It was fascinating to look up inside the caves and see blue sky.

I've never seen such a panoramic piece of devastation in my life – for miles the bridges and remnants of houses on either side of the river were like black spokes. A lot of Germans had been killed inside the caves and there was a terrible sweet smell of death in them.

That was really the end of my work as a war artist. The visit to this place and to the marshalling yards at Trappes virtually marked the end.

Looking back on it, undoubtedly the war had an important effect on my consciousness. I never saw the concentration camps; I should in some ways have liked to have seen them. I remember receiving a black-covered American Central Office of Information book dealing with the camps. It was a kind of funeral book. In it were the most terrible photographs of Belsen, Auschwitz and Buchenwald. These photographs were to have a great effect on me; I saw them just before I received a commission to paint a Crucifixion – in them many of the tortured bodies looked like figures deposed from crosses. The whole idea of the depiction of Christ crucified became much more real to me after having seen this book and it seemed to be possible to do this subject again. In any case the continuing beastliness and cruelty of mankind, amounting at times to madness, seems eternal and classic.

But you will ask me at this point what might have been my attitude if I had been assigned a military or naval theatre. No one, let alone myself, can say what reaction I might have had or what I might have made of battle and all that it connotes.

I feel sure that my thinking would not have been aroused by fighting on a grand scale entailing all the speed and mechanisation of modern warfare; though no doubt individual battles, street and house fighting, might well have been another matter.

When, today, one sees in magazines the very remarkable photojournalism concerning sudden uprisings, revolutions, riots and the rest, one is struck by mysterious timeless qualities of drama which grip the imagination. A brawl in a café – starting with one glass thrown and igniting and electrifying in the space of seconds the whole company and quietening gradually, as does a thunderstorm – can give an unreasonable excitement.

But if the trappings in battle pictures, the uniforms, types of guns and the rest are unsympathetic to me, this may well be because the effect of seeing bad descriptive work is stronger than one thinks; great battle pieces have been done which utilise the same material (though in its time, of course, it was variously armour or bows and arrows etc.) but this material was always *recreated* and *represented*.

And while it is true that at the root of my work is memory, plus the sudden unaccountable emotion which modifies and transforms facts, none the less these facts – these objective vocabularies – are invariably for me the necessary starting point. And in the particular context of modern warfare it is more than likely that I would have found these facts difficult or impossible to gather.

Yours sincerely,
Graham Sutherland

(*The Sunday Telegraph Magazine*, 10 September 1971, pp. 27–28; the addressee was art critic Edwin Mullins, who reported that their extensive recorded conversations led to a typescript, which Sutherland finally chose to reshape into a letter format)

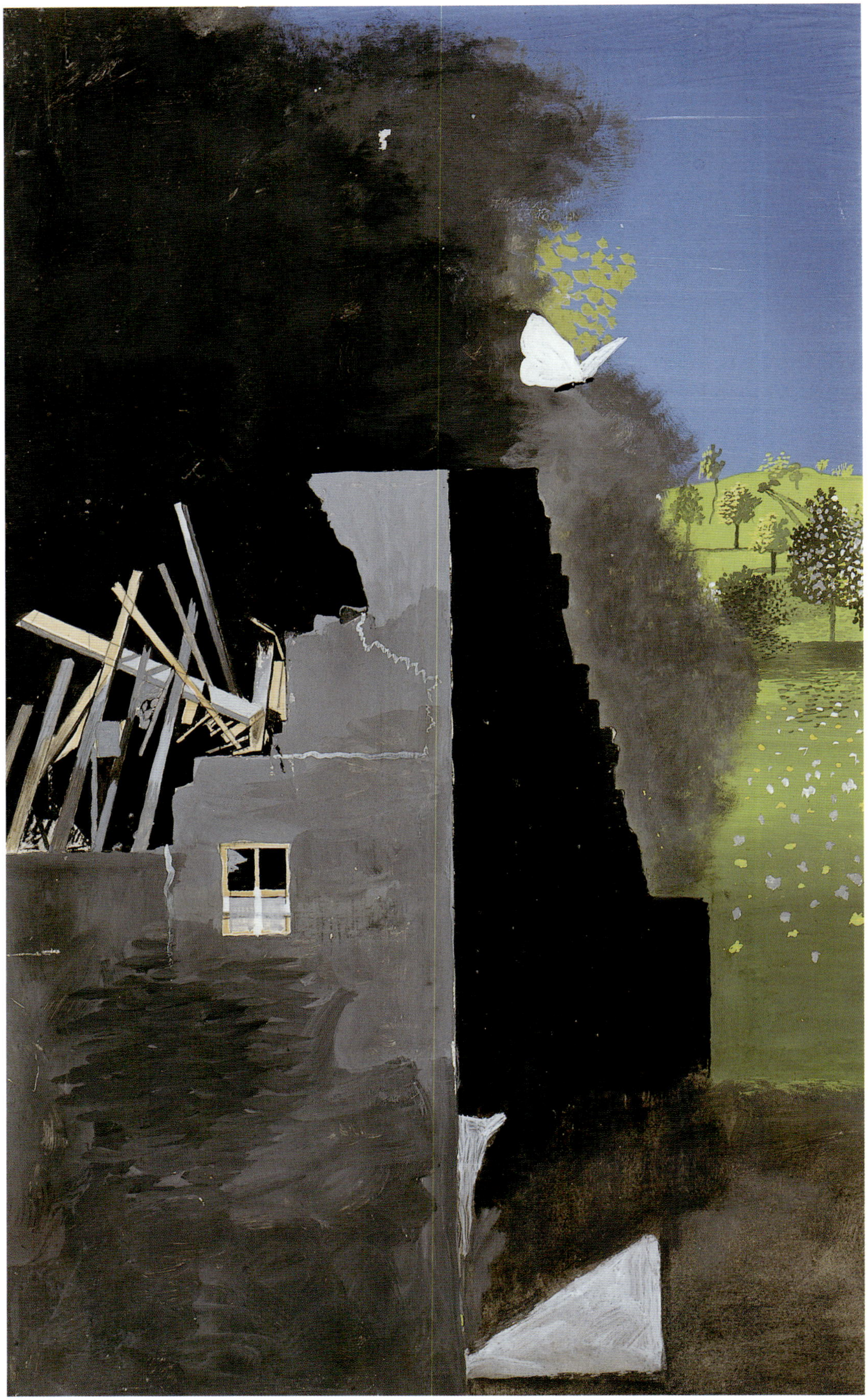

39.
Design for poster
c. 1940
Gouache on paper
360 x 265 mm
Private Collection.

According to a letter from Sutherland to Kenneth Clark, attached to the back of the picture, this was intended as a design for a poster, accompanied by the caption "can spring be far away[?]". The idea was presumably conceived in relation to a wartime propaganda project. There is no evidence that a poster was produced from the design.

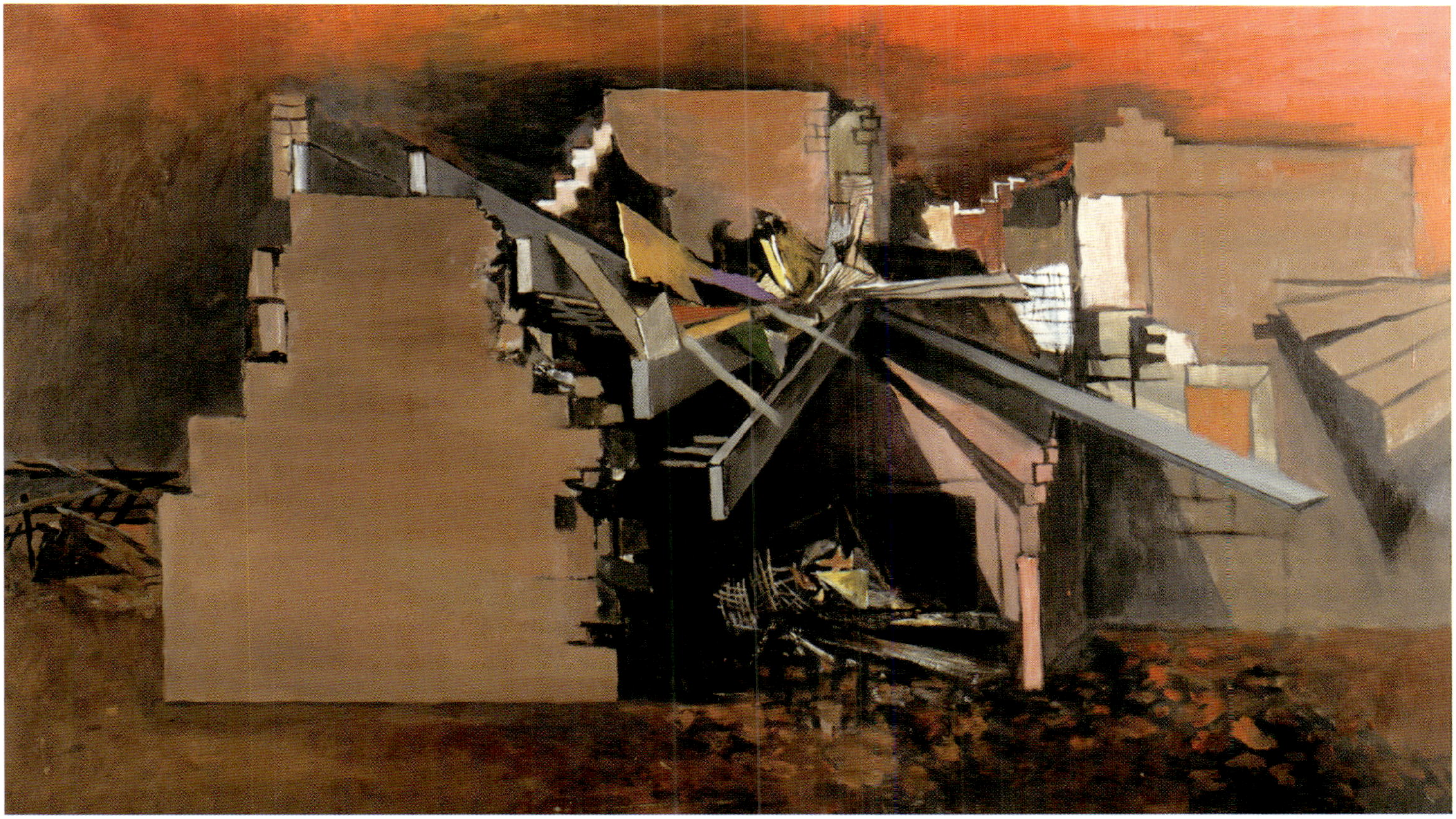

40.
Devastation: House in Wales
1940
Oil on canvas
625 x 1134 mm
Collection of Cheltenham Art Gallery and Museum
1947.141.

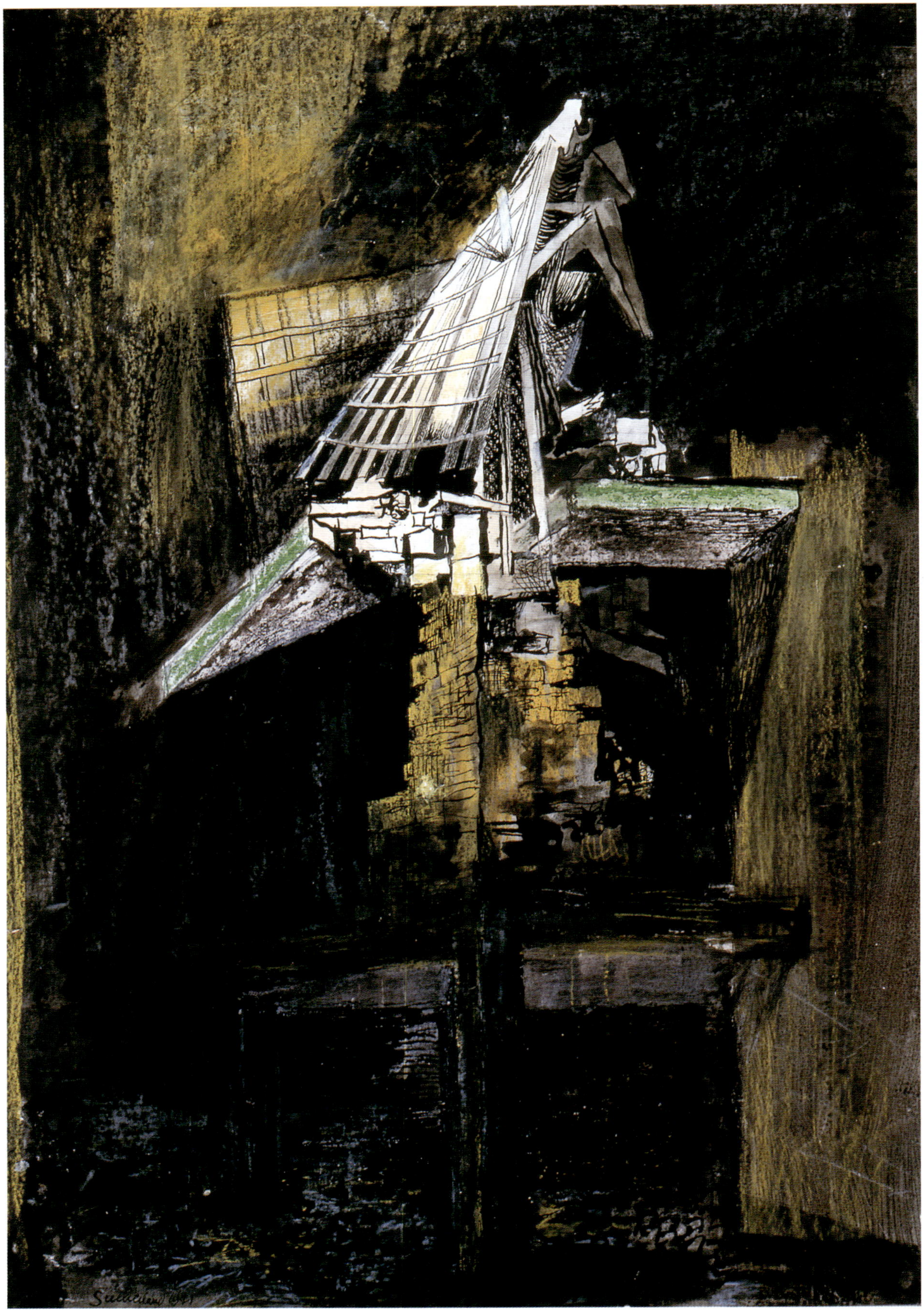

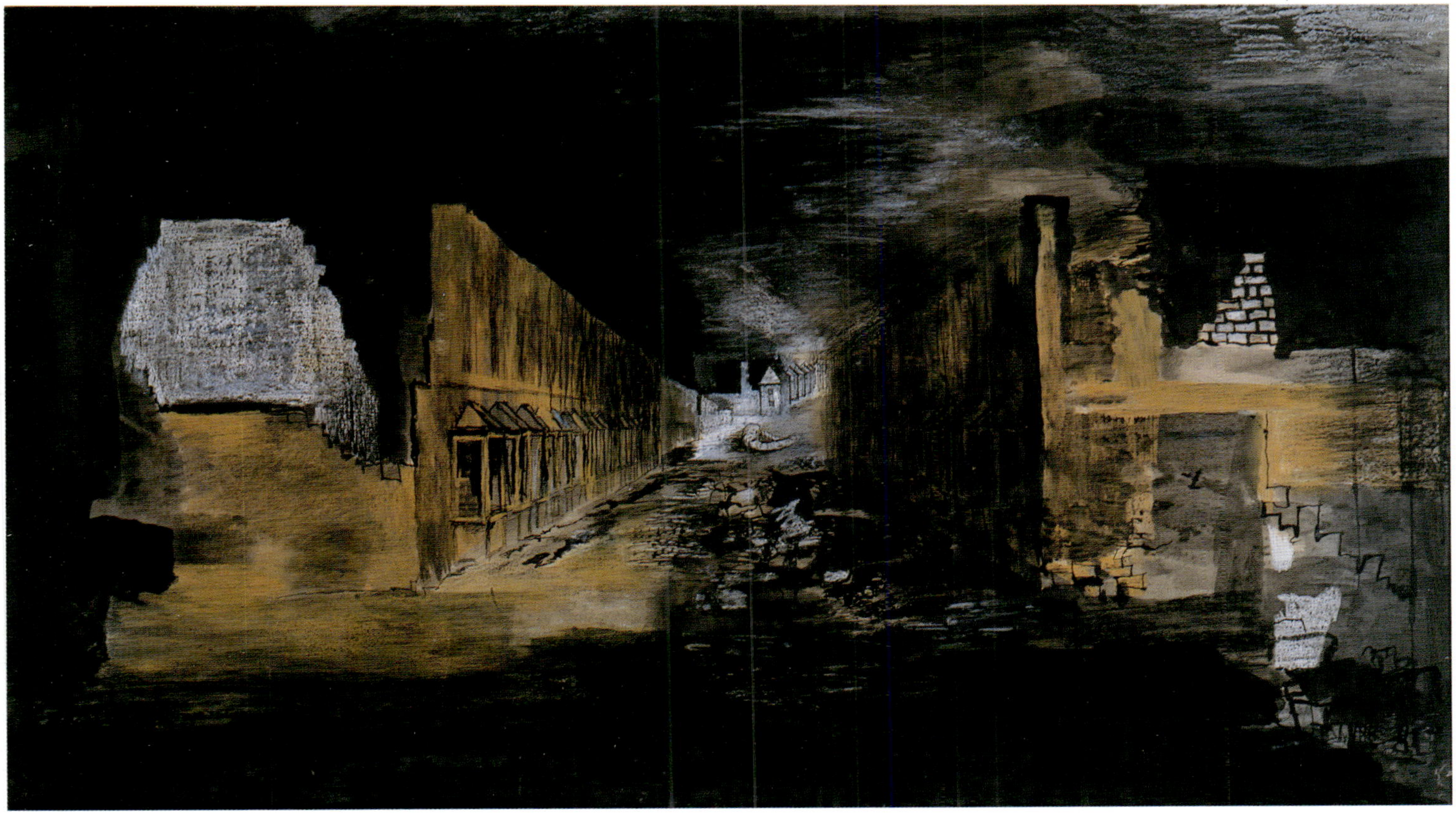

41.
Devastation 1941: East End, Wrecked Public House
1941
Crayon, pen and ink, pastel and gouache on paper
673 x 476 mm
Tate. Presented by the War Artists Advisory Committee 1946
NO5735.

42.
Devastation 1941: An East End Street
1941
Crayon, gouache, pen and ink, pencil and watercolour
648 x 1137 mm
Tate. Presented by the War Artists Advisory Committee 1946
NO5736.

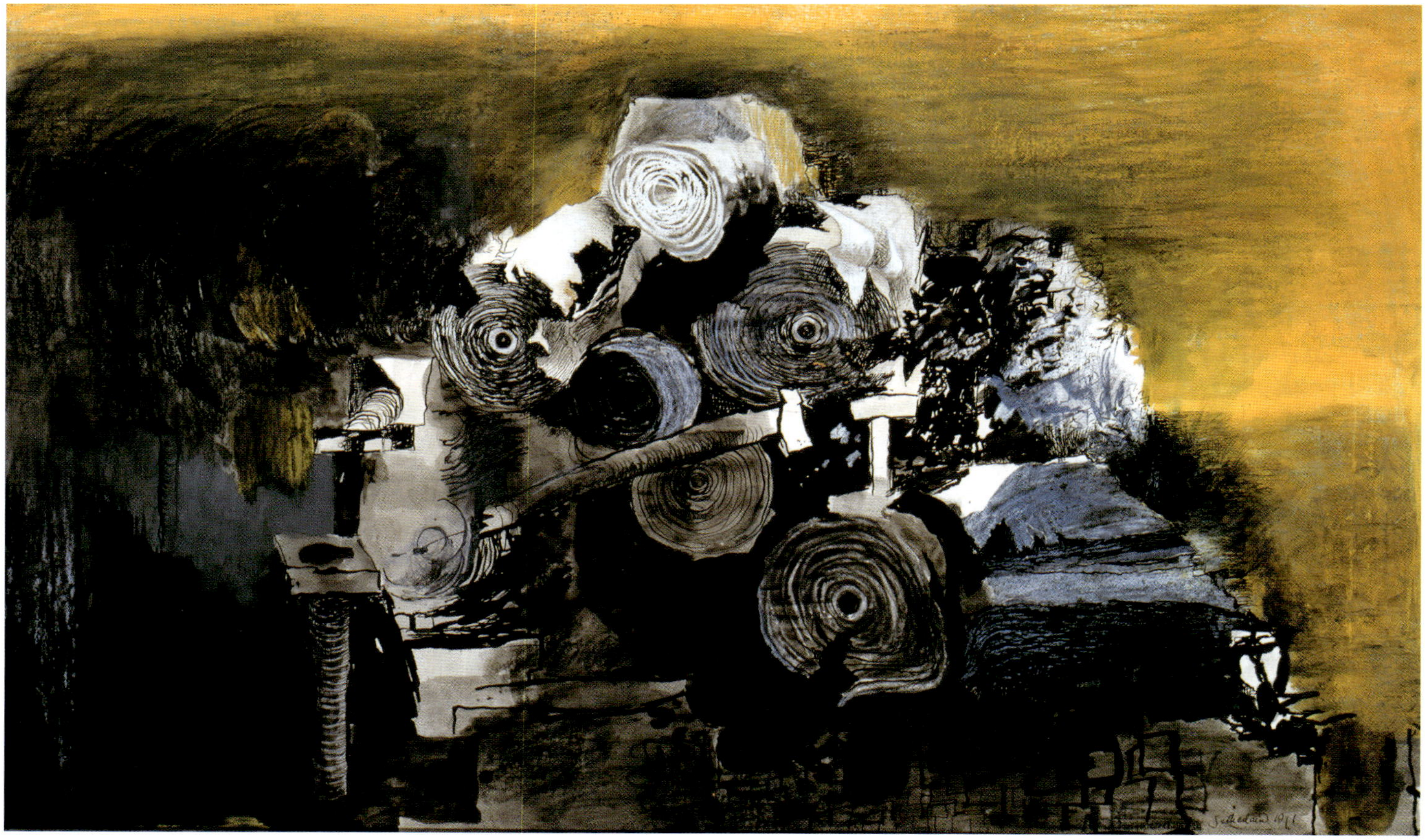

43.
Devastation 1941: East End, Burnt Paper Warehouse
1941
Gouache, pastel, pencil, pen and ink on paper mounted on card
673 x 1137 mm
Tate. Presented by the War Artists Advisory Committee 1946
N05737.

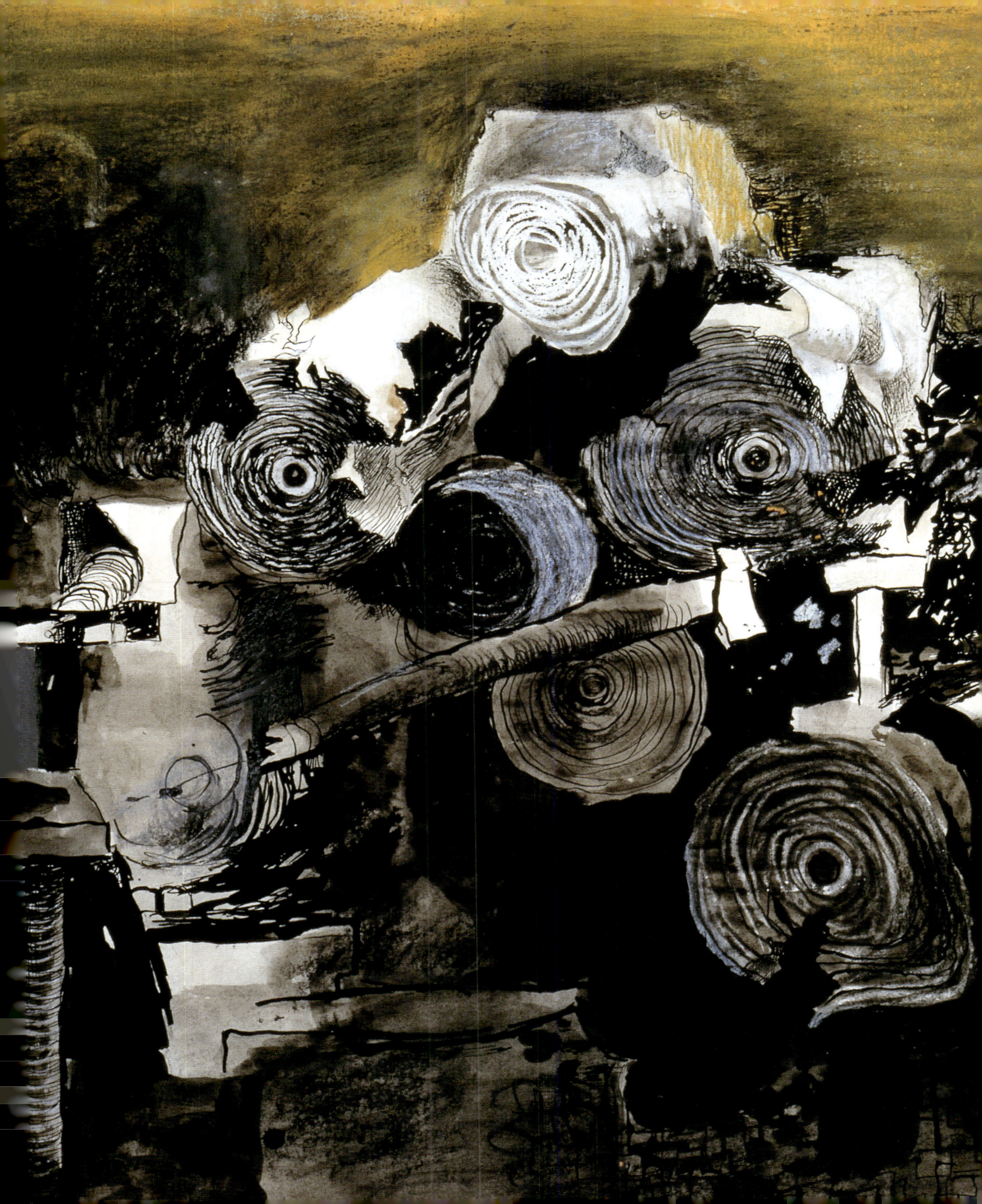

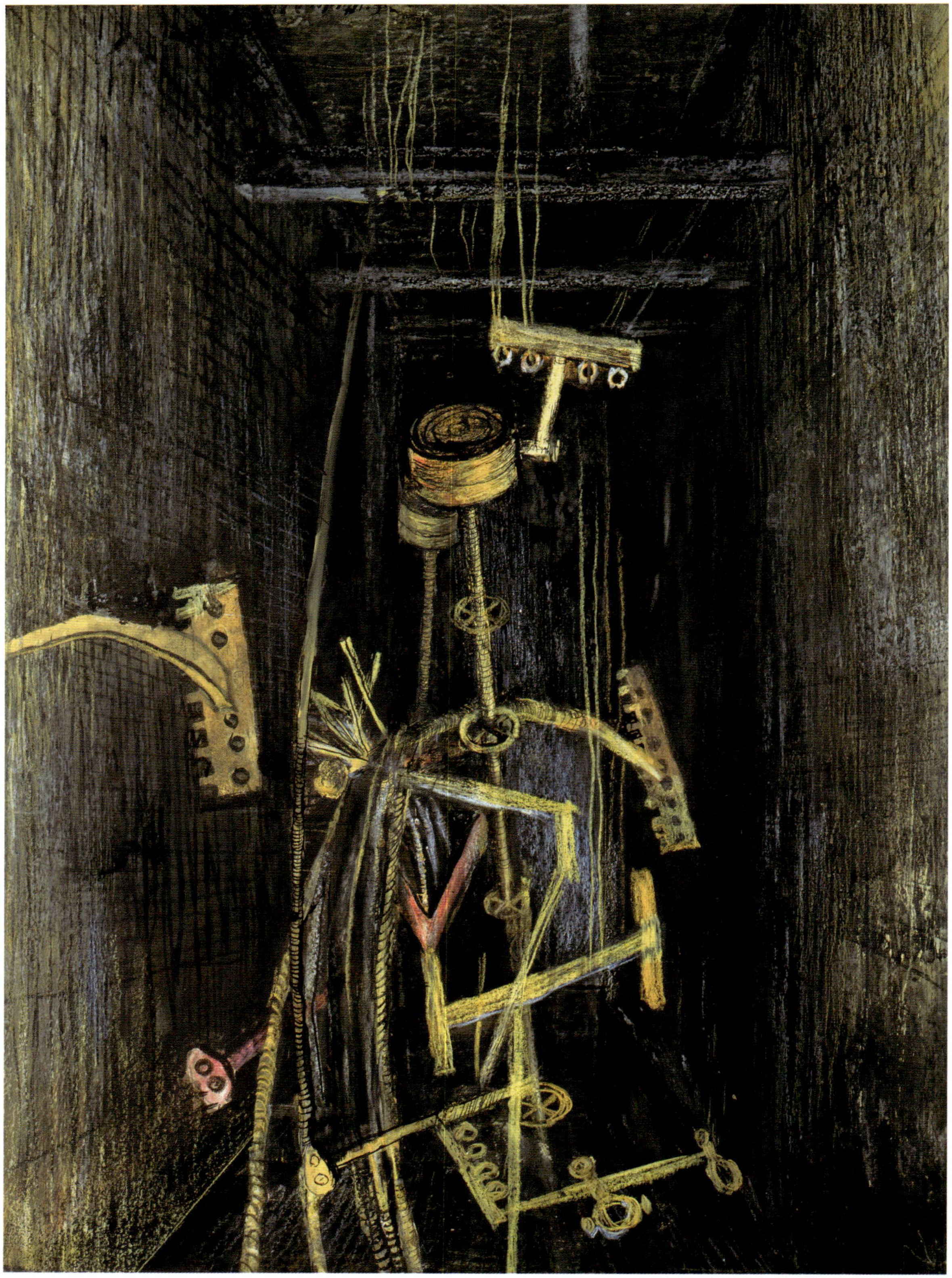

44.
Devastation: City, Ruined Machinery
1941
Pastel and ink on paper
720 x 540 mm
Collection of Cheltenham Art Gallery and Museum
1947.140.

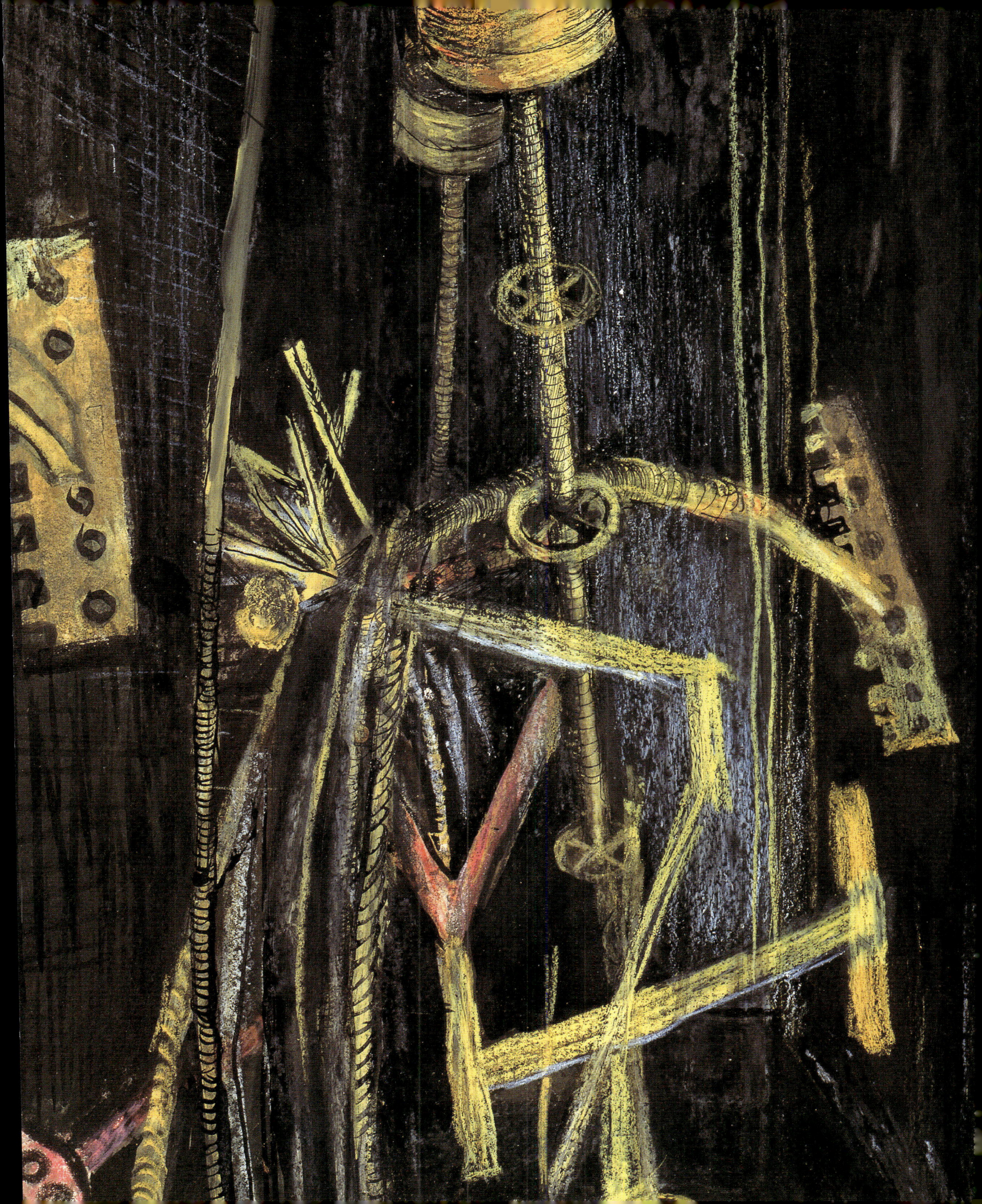

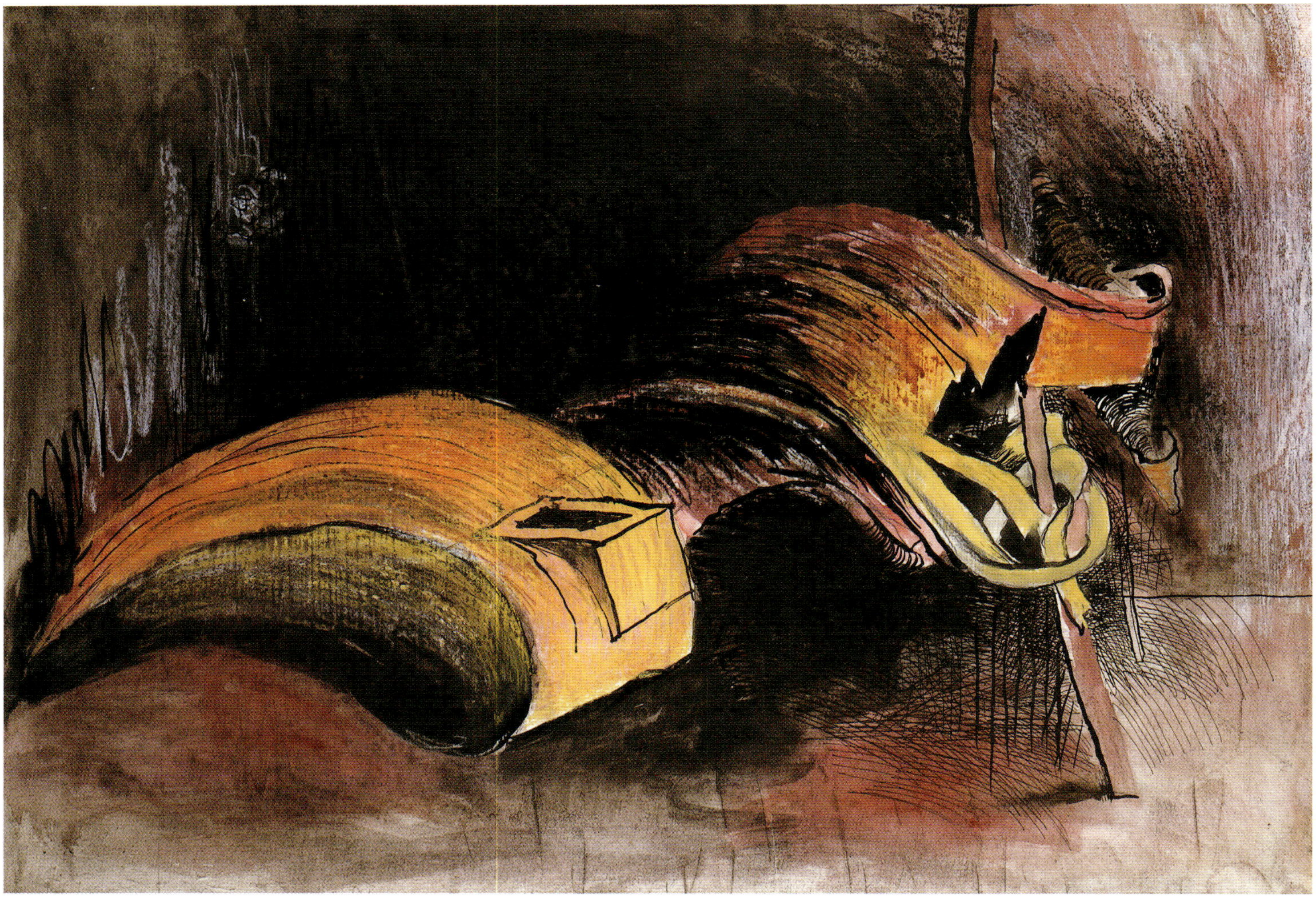

45.
Devastation: East End Factory Ventilation Shaft
1941
Crayon, charcoal, watercolour, pen and ink on paper
660 x 460 mm
Bolton Museums, Art Gallery and Aquarium
BOLMG 1987.1.

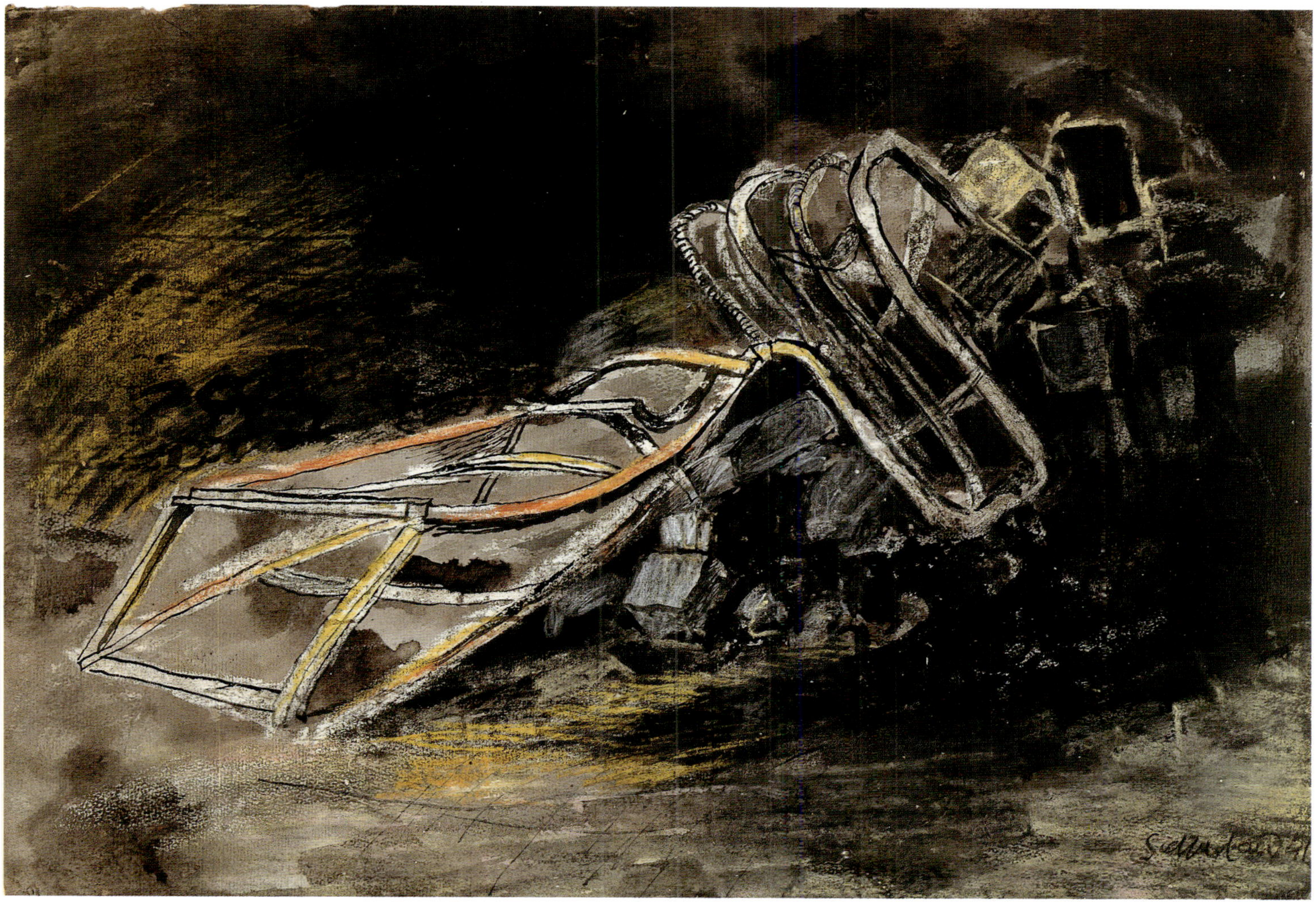

46.
Devastation, City 1941: Fallen Lift Shaft
1941
Pen and ink, watercolour and chalk (coloured) on paper
319 x 457 mm
The Whitworth Art Gallery, The University of Manchester
D.1947.28.

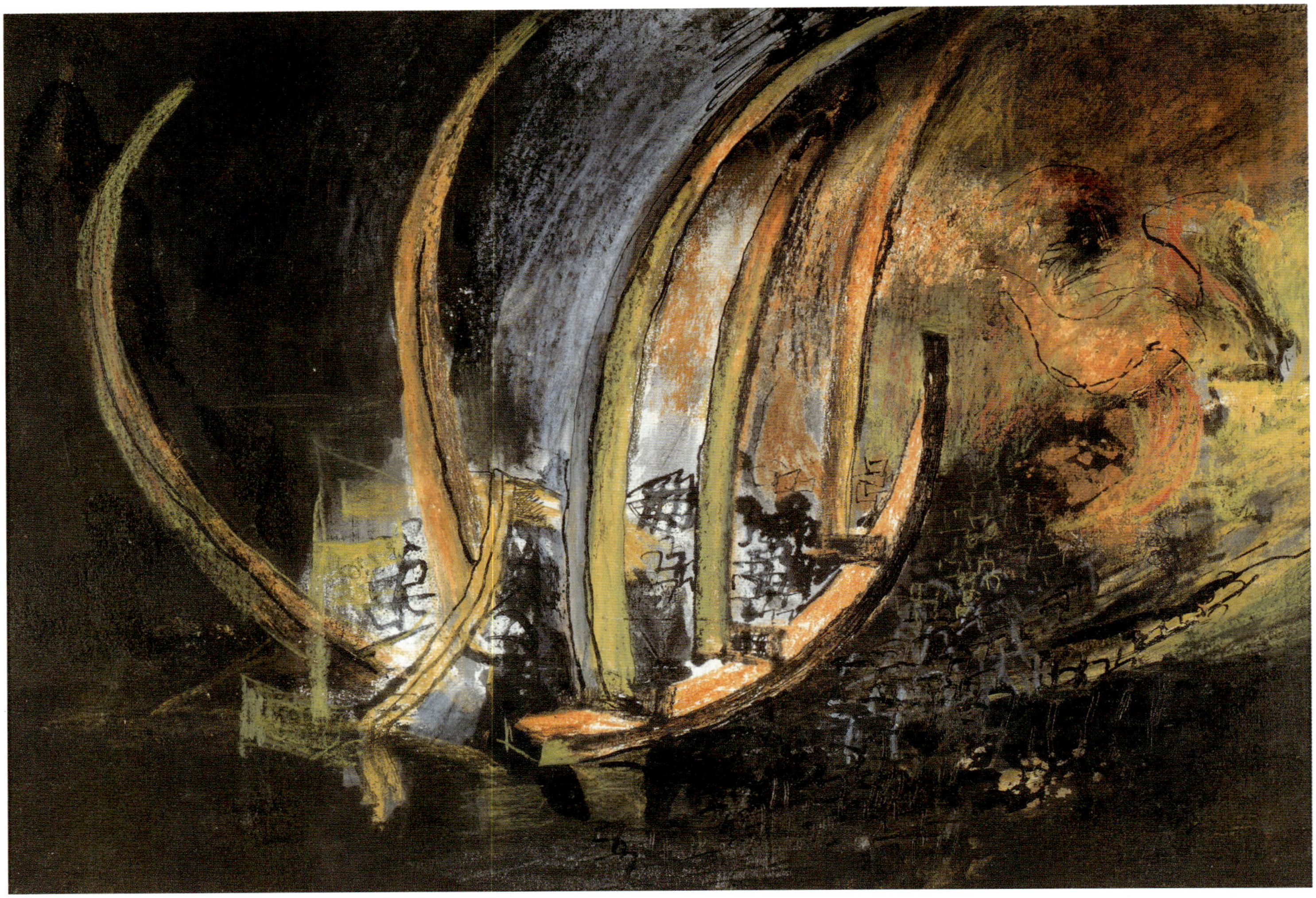

47.
Devastation in the City: Twisted Girders Against a Background of Fire
1941
Gouache on paper
368 x 457 mm
The Trustees of the Imperial War Museum
IWM ART LD 1379

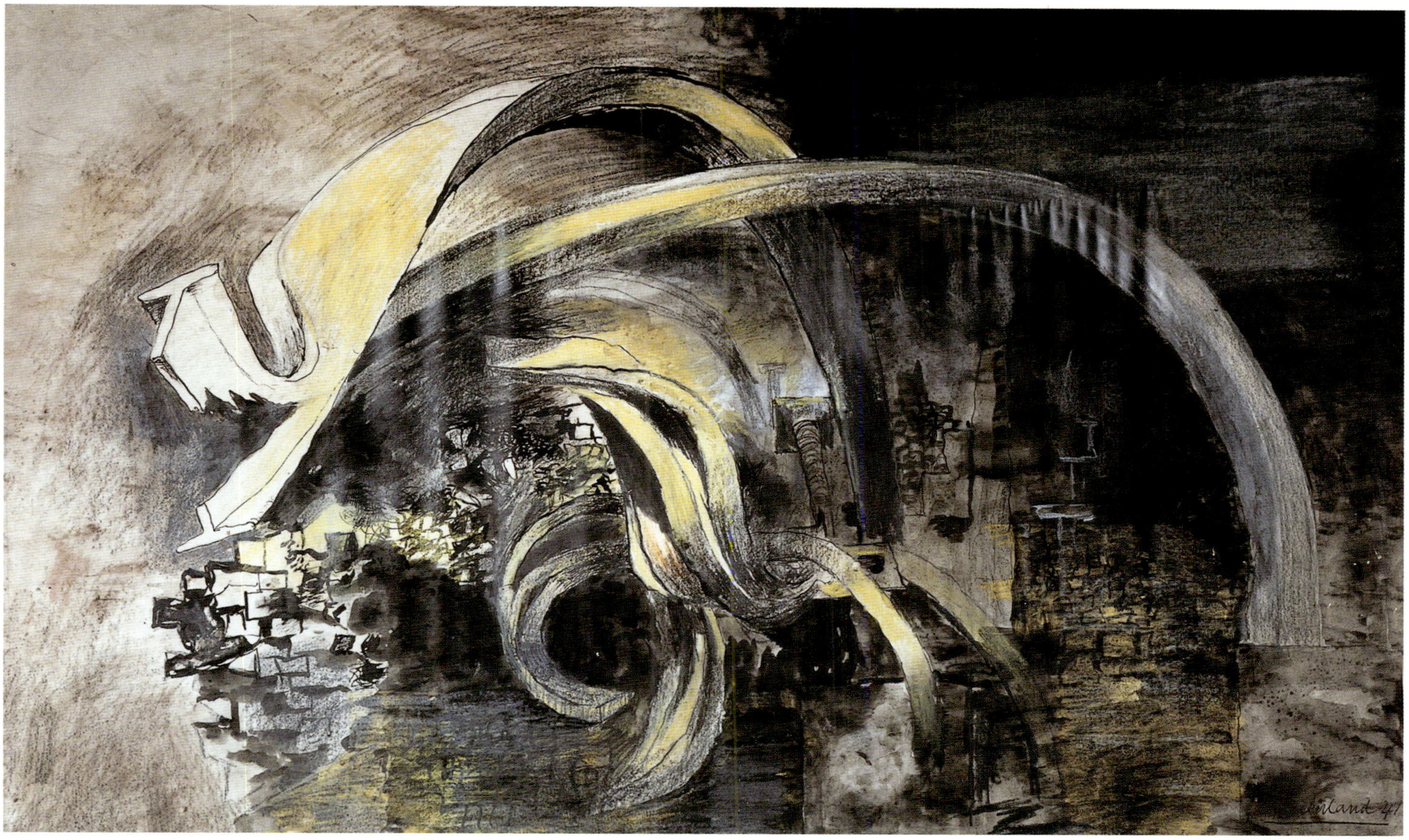

48.
Devastation 1941: City, Twisted Girders
1941
Gouache, charcoal and ink on paper
554 x 1123 mm
Ferens Art Gallery, Hull Museums and Art Gallery Service
W192

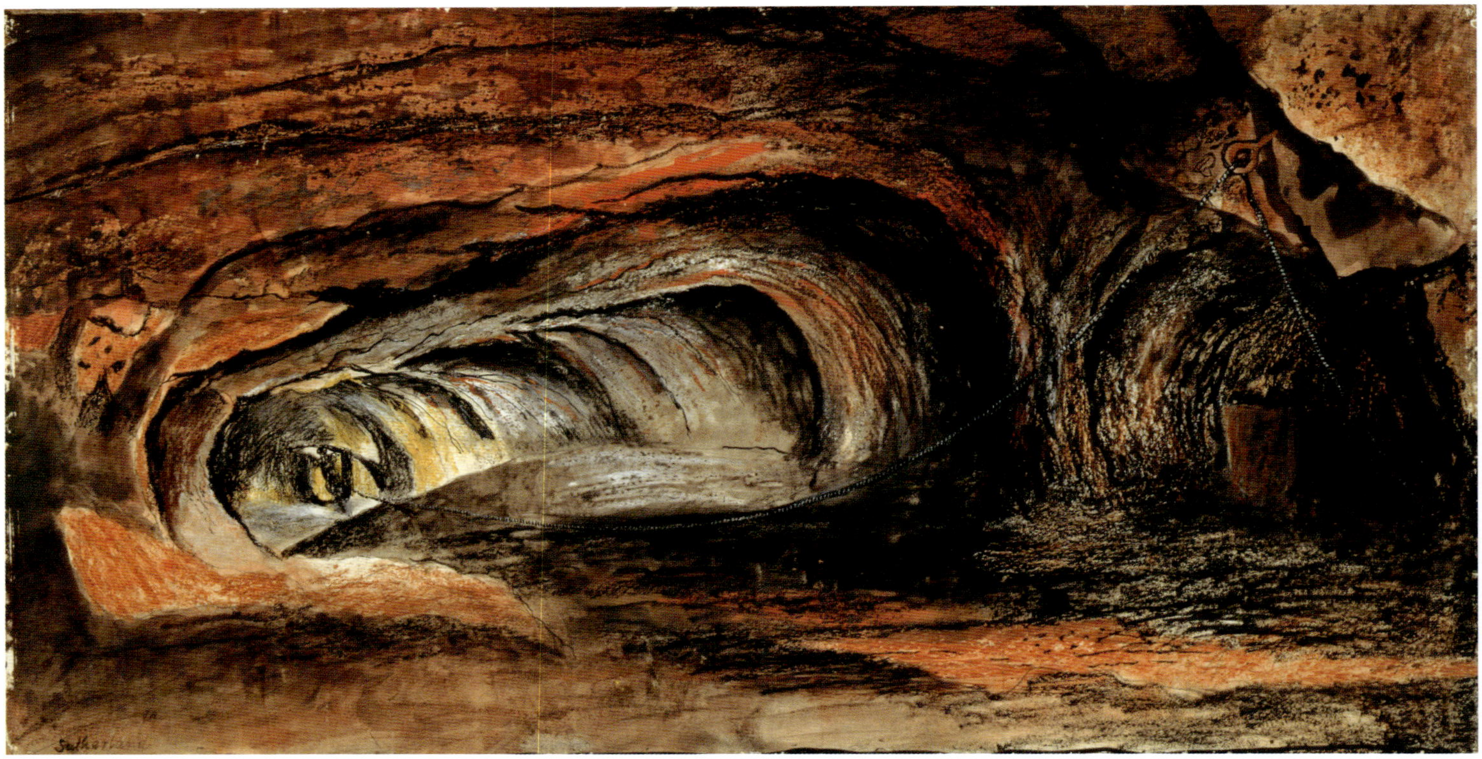

49.
Tin Mine – A Declivity
1942
Ink, gouache, chalk and
watercolour on paper
mounted on board
476 x 946 mm
Leeds Museums and Galleries
(City Art Gallery)
20.40/47.

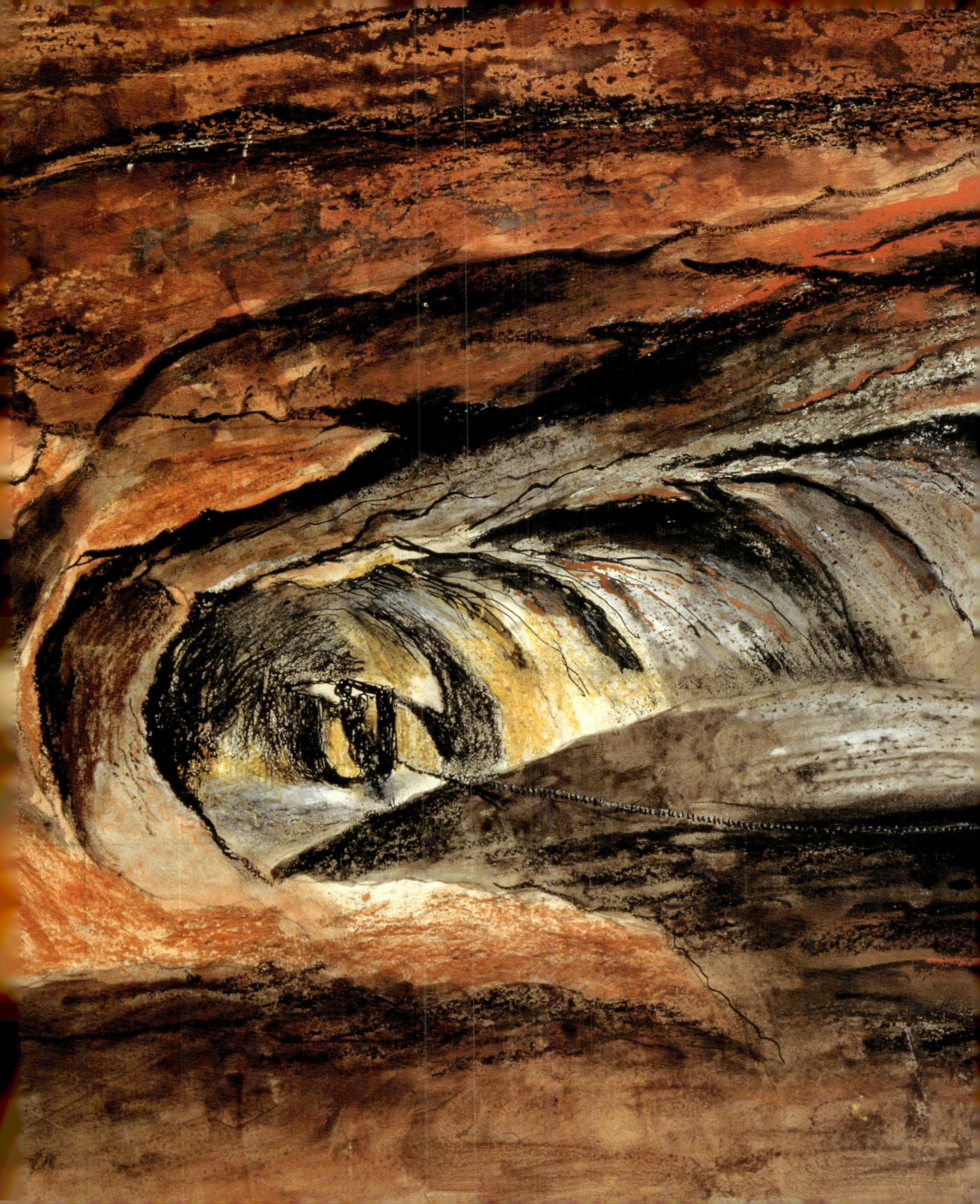

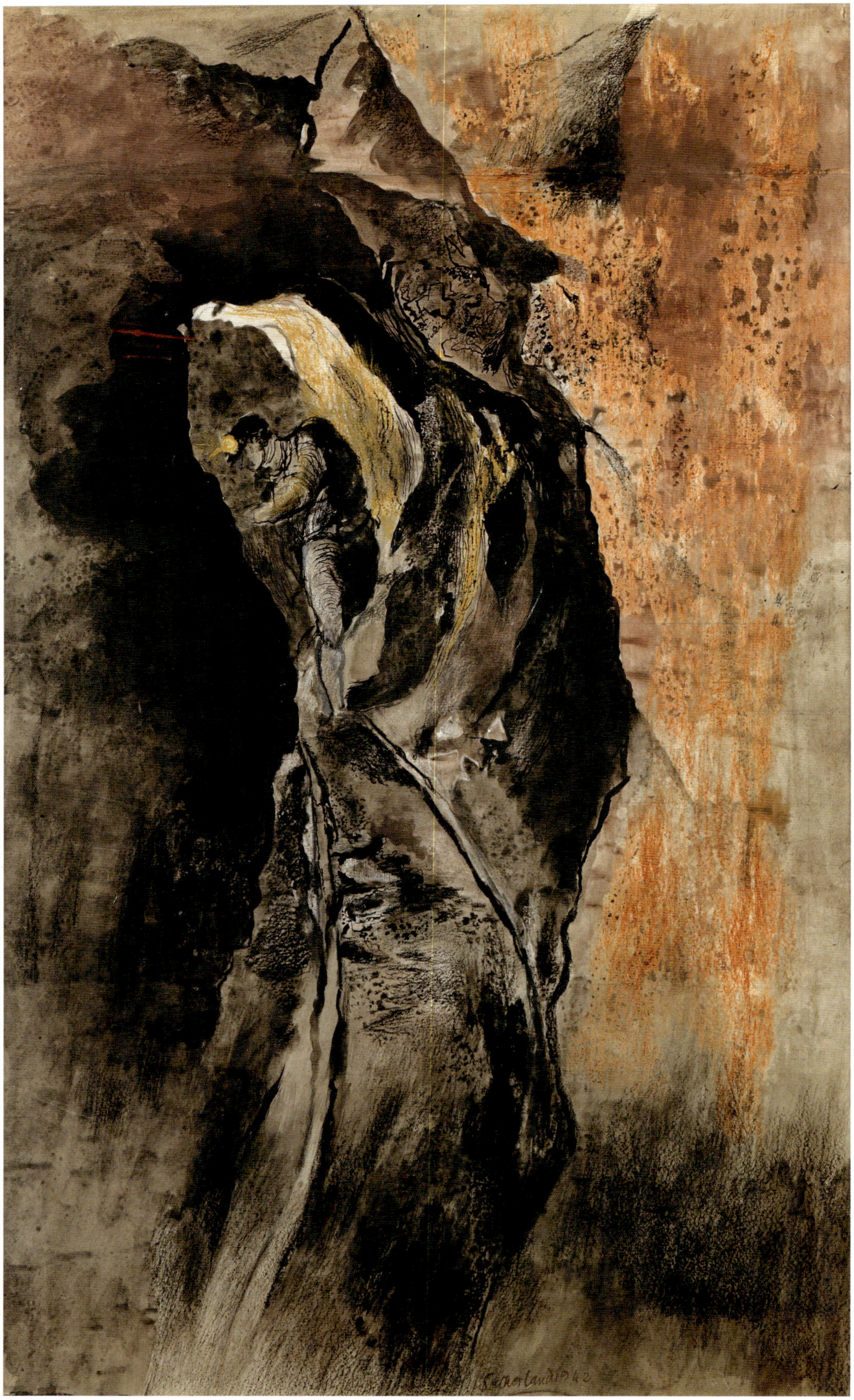

50.
Tin Mine – Miner Approaching
1942
Gouache, chalk and wax crayon on paper mounted on hardboard
1175 x 745 mm
British Council
P163.

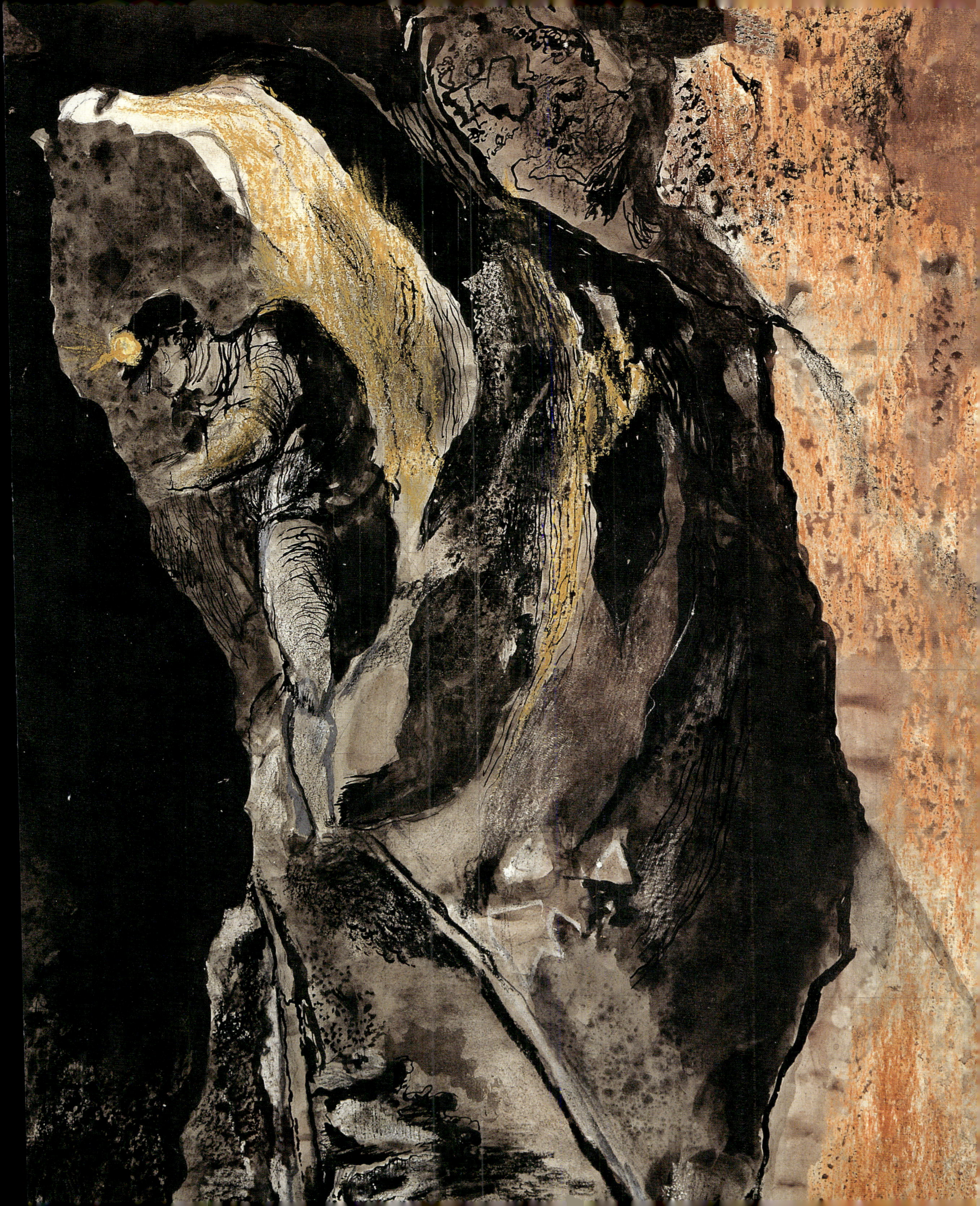

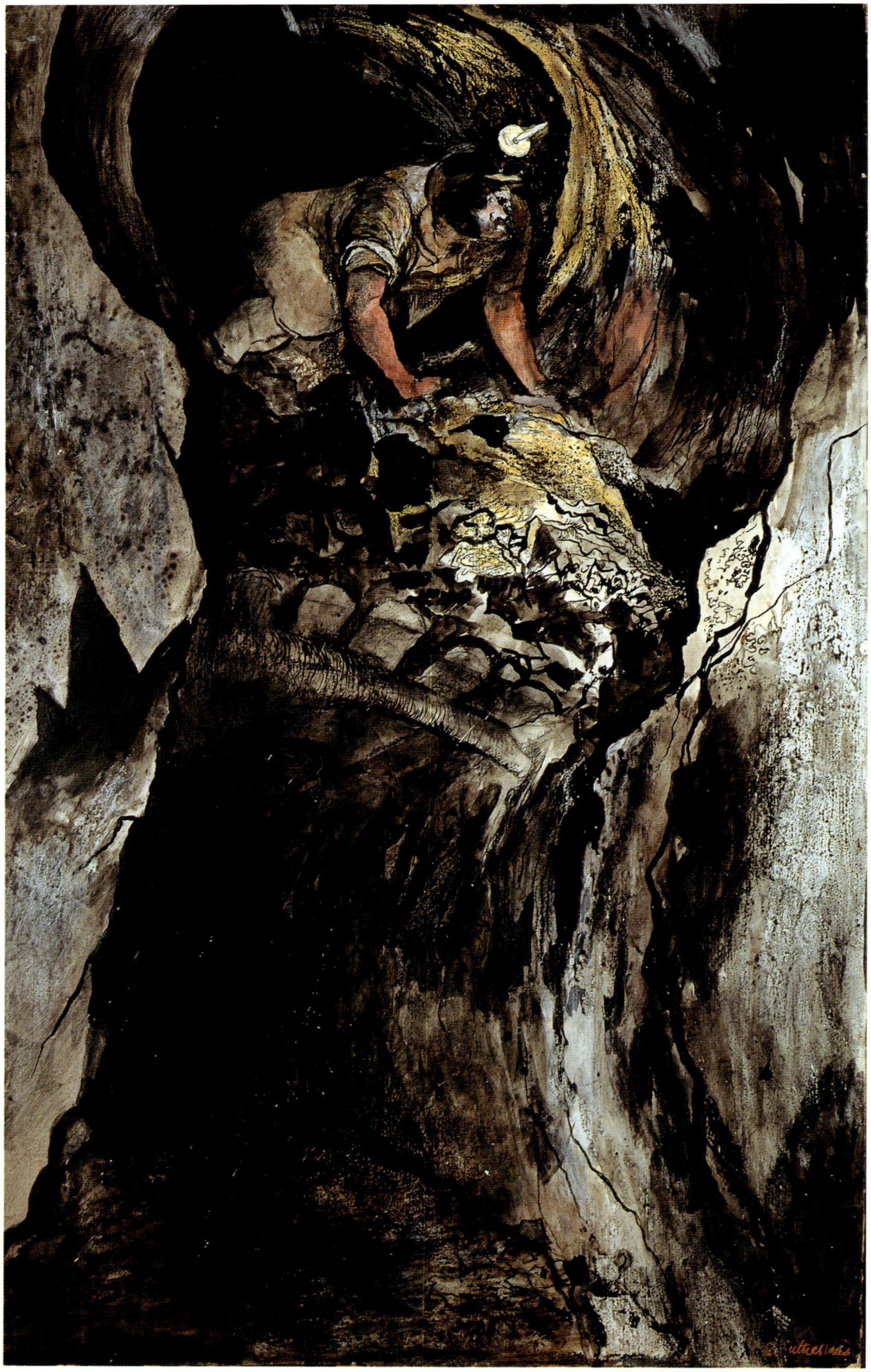

51.
Tin Mine: Emerging Miner
1942–43
Gouache on paper on board
1168 x 730 mm
Leeds Museums and Galleries
(City Art Gallery)
28.11/47.

52.
Two Miners Drilling
1942–43
Bodycolour, crayon and
watercolour on board
560 x 512 mm
Laing Art Gallery, Newcastle
upon Tyne (Tyne and Wear
Museums)
F3423.

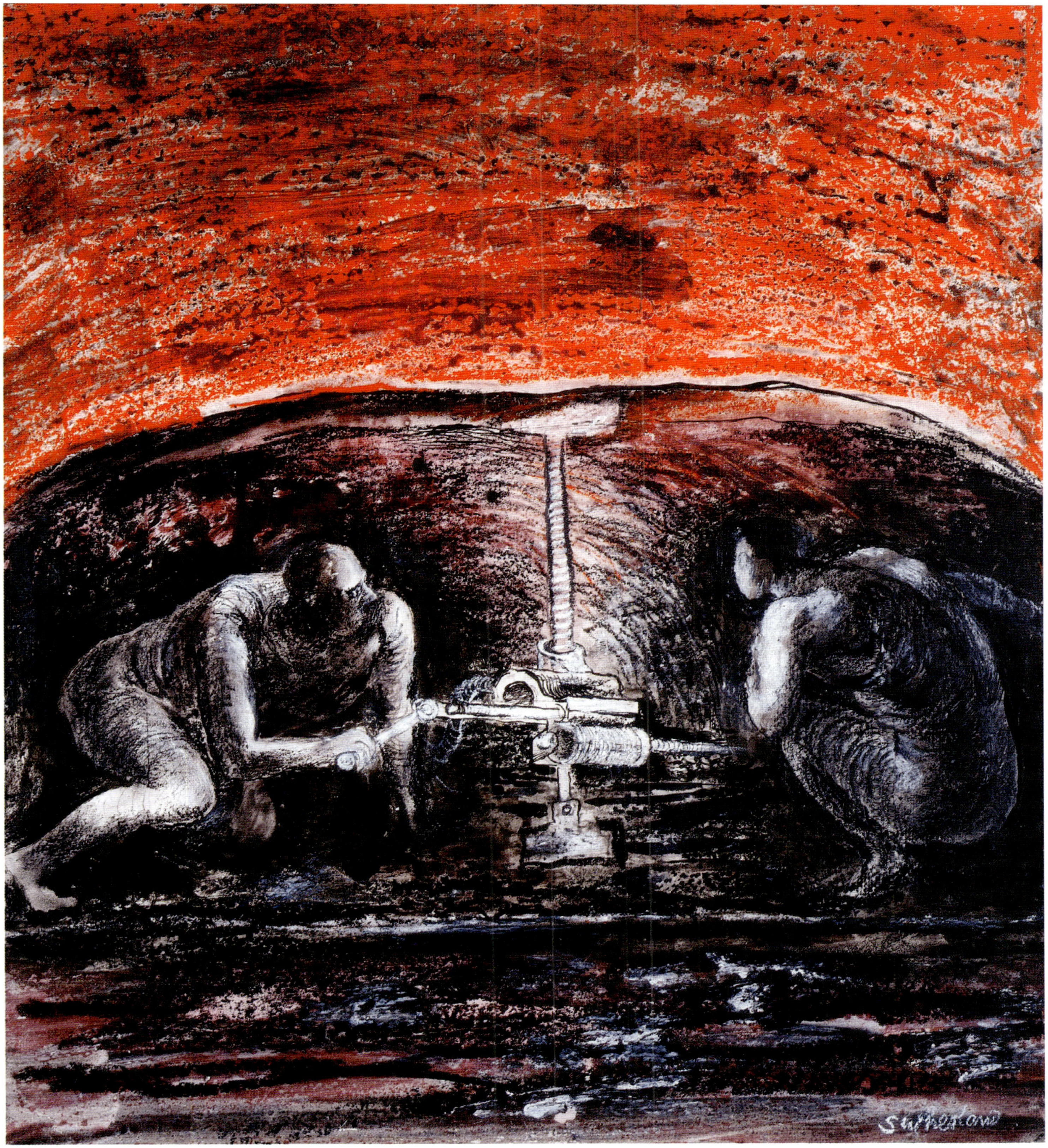
Sutherland

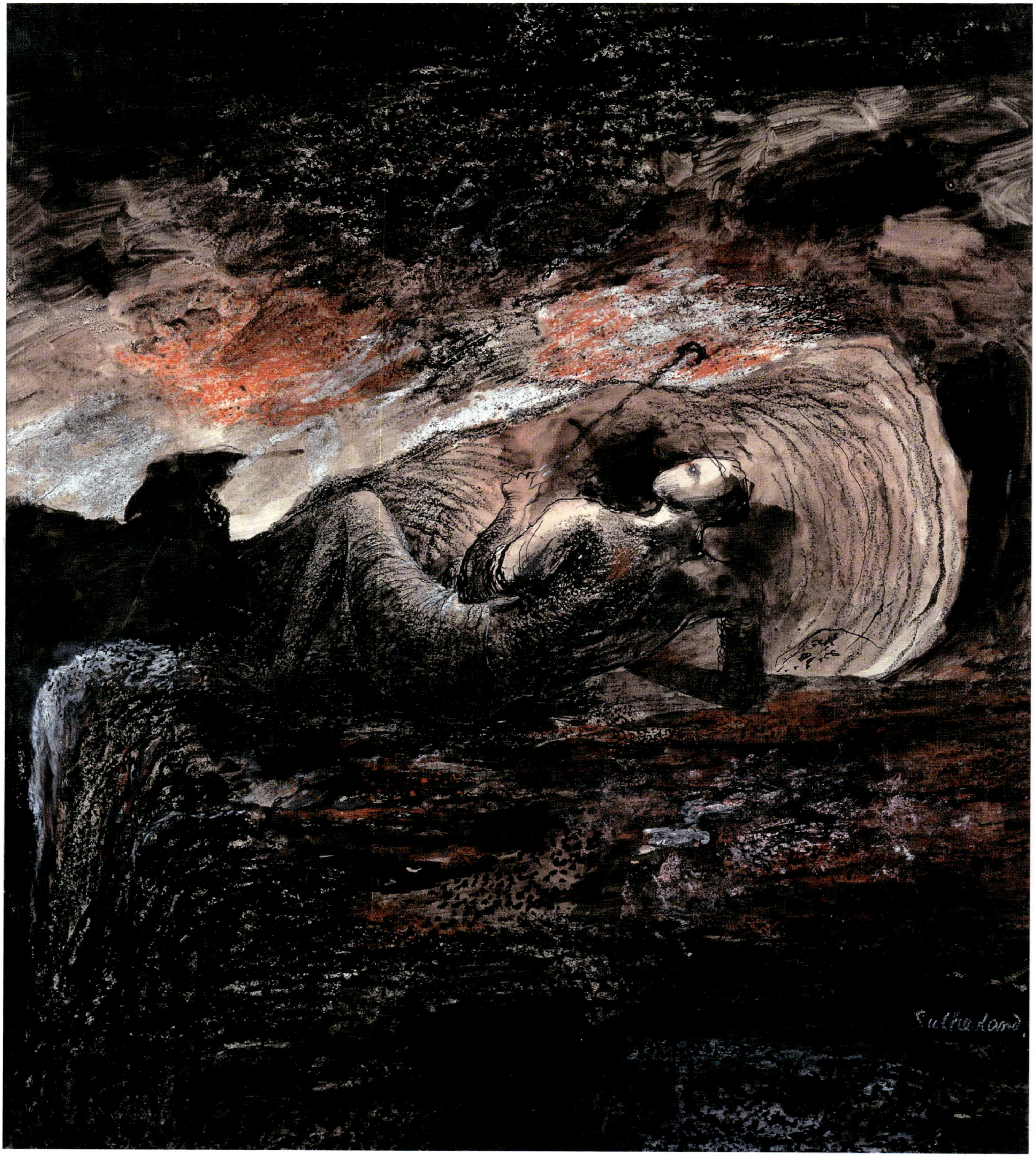
Sutherland.

53.
Miner Probing a Drill Hole
1942
Gouache, wax crayon, Indian ink on paper mounted on hardboard
559 x 508 mm
Tate. Presented by the War Artists Advisory Committee 1946
N05741.

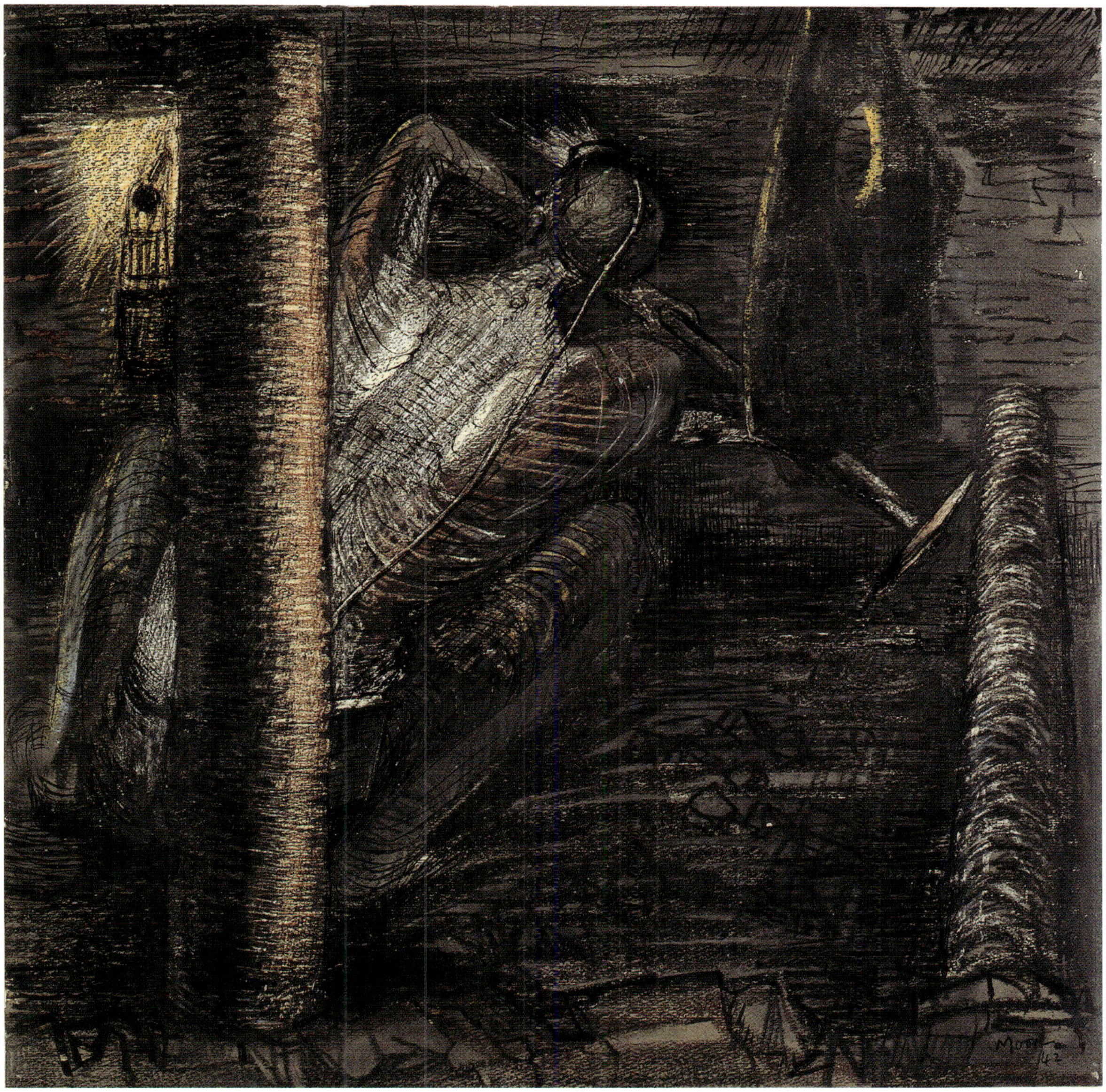

54.
HENRY MOORE (1898–1986)
A Miner at Work
1942
Ink, chalk and gouache on paper
495 x 495 mm
The Trustees of the Imperial War Museum
IWM ART LD 5947.

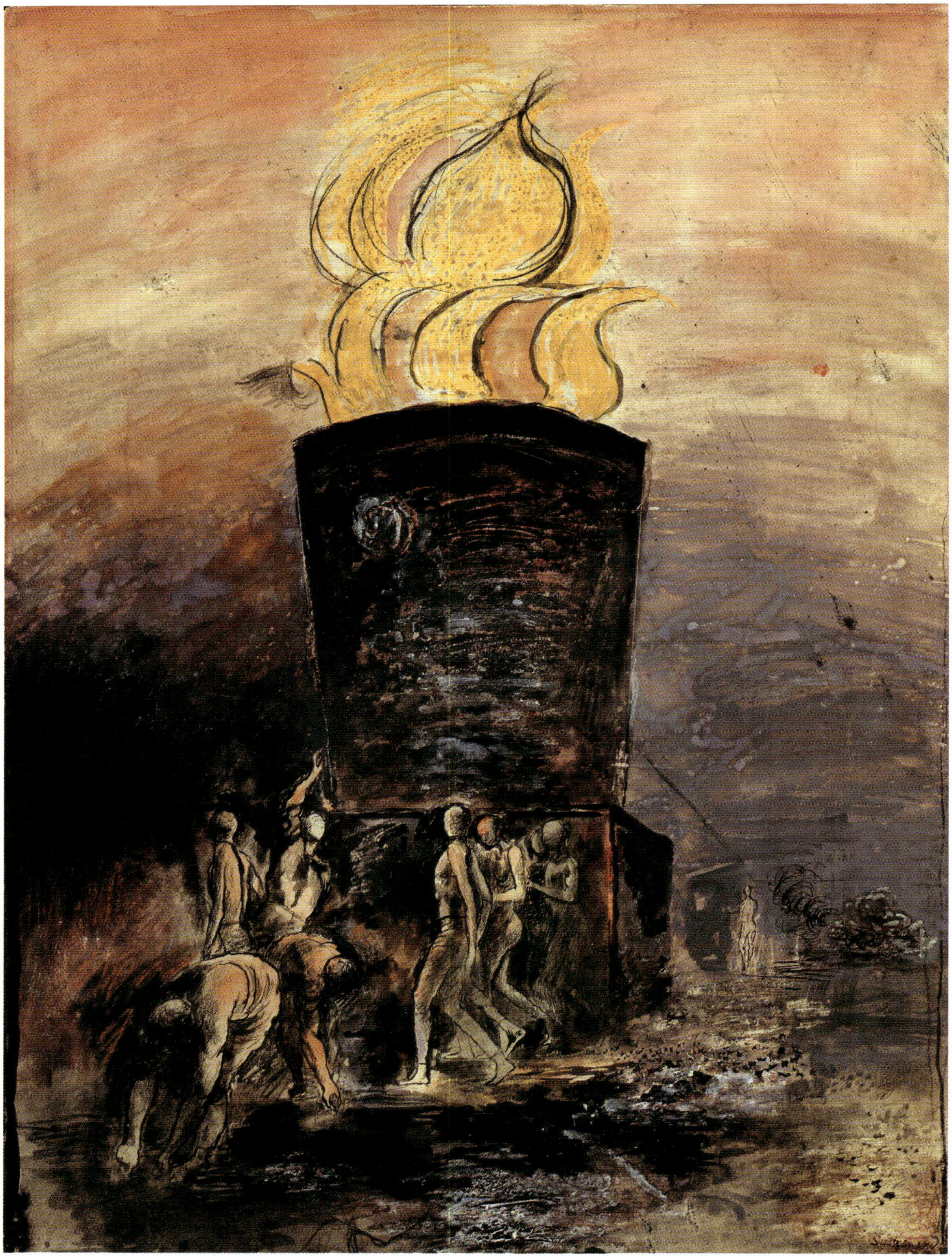

55.
Tapping a Steel Furnace
1943
Gouache, pen and ink on paper
550 x 380 mm
Private Collection.

56.
Slag Ladles
1942
Gouache on paper
514 x 377 mm
The Trustees of the Imperial War Museum
IWM ART LD 1773.

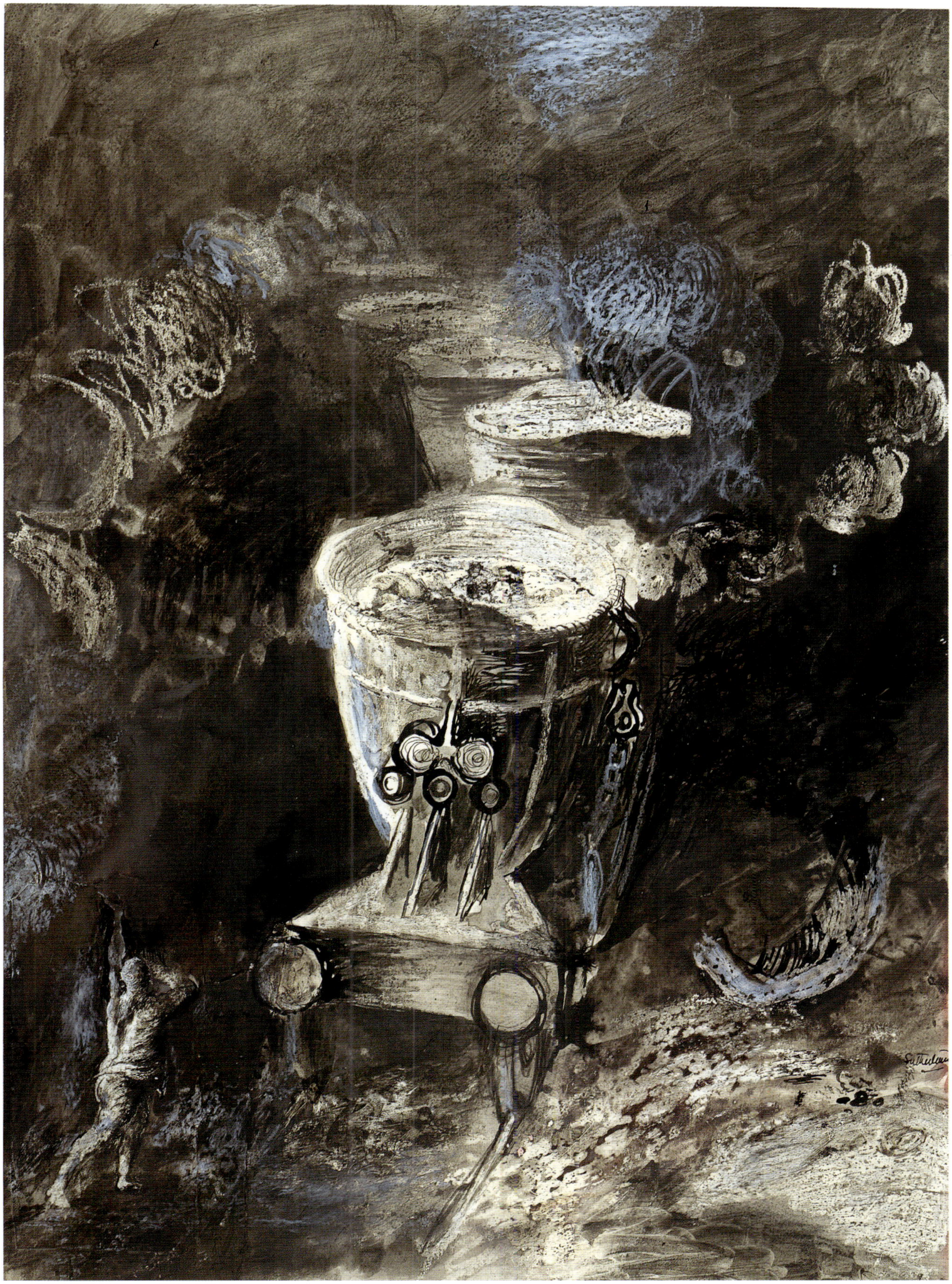

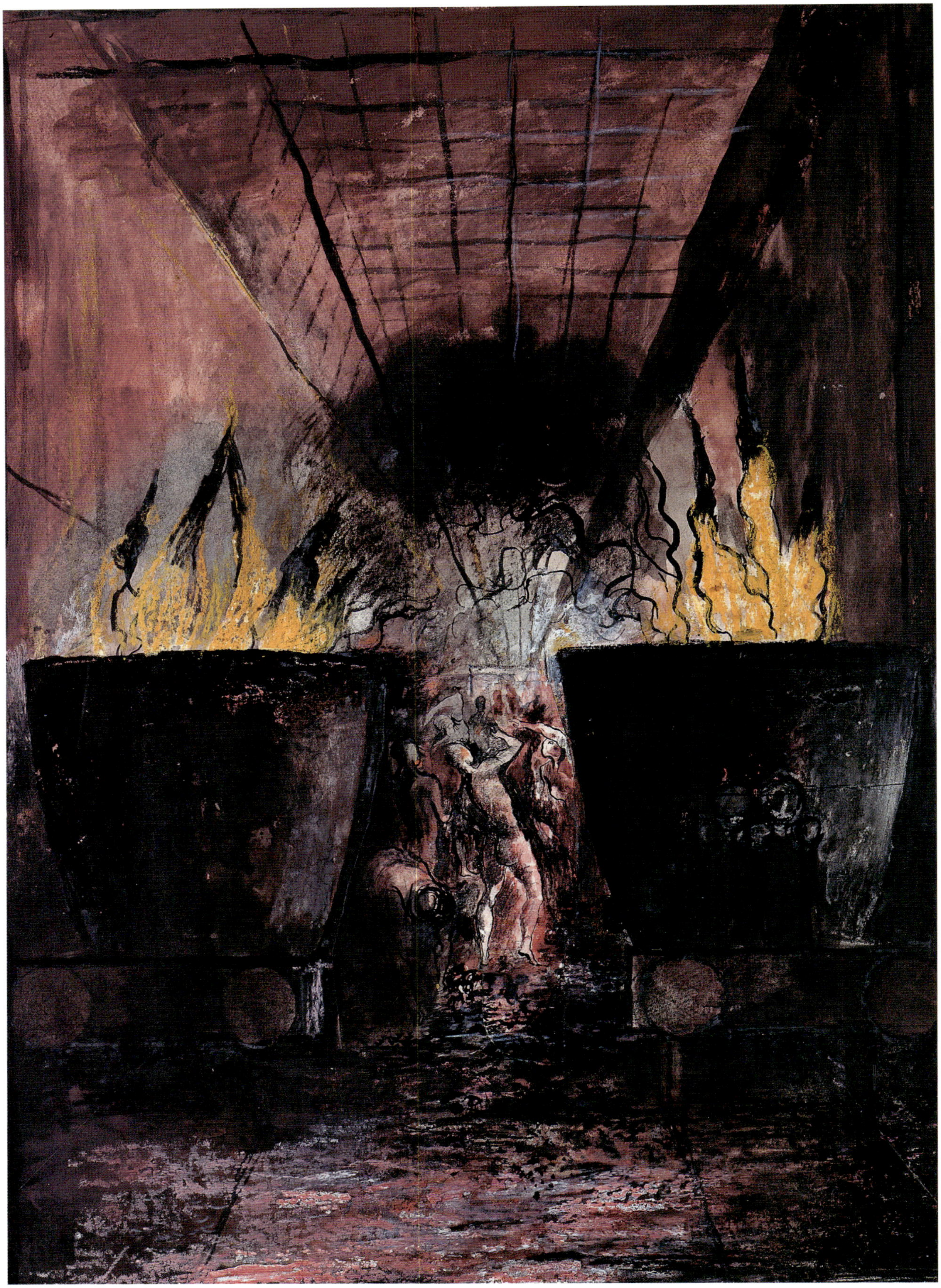

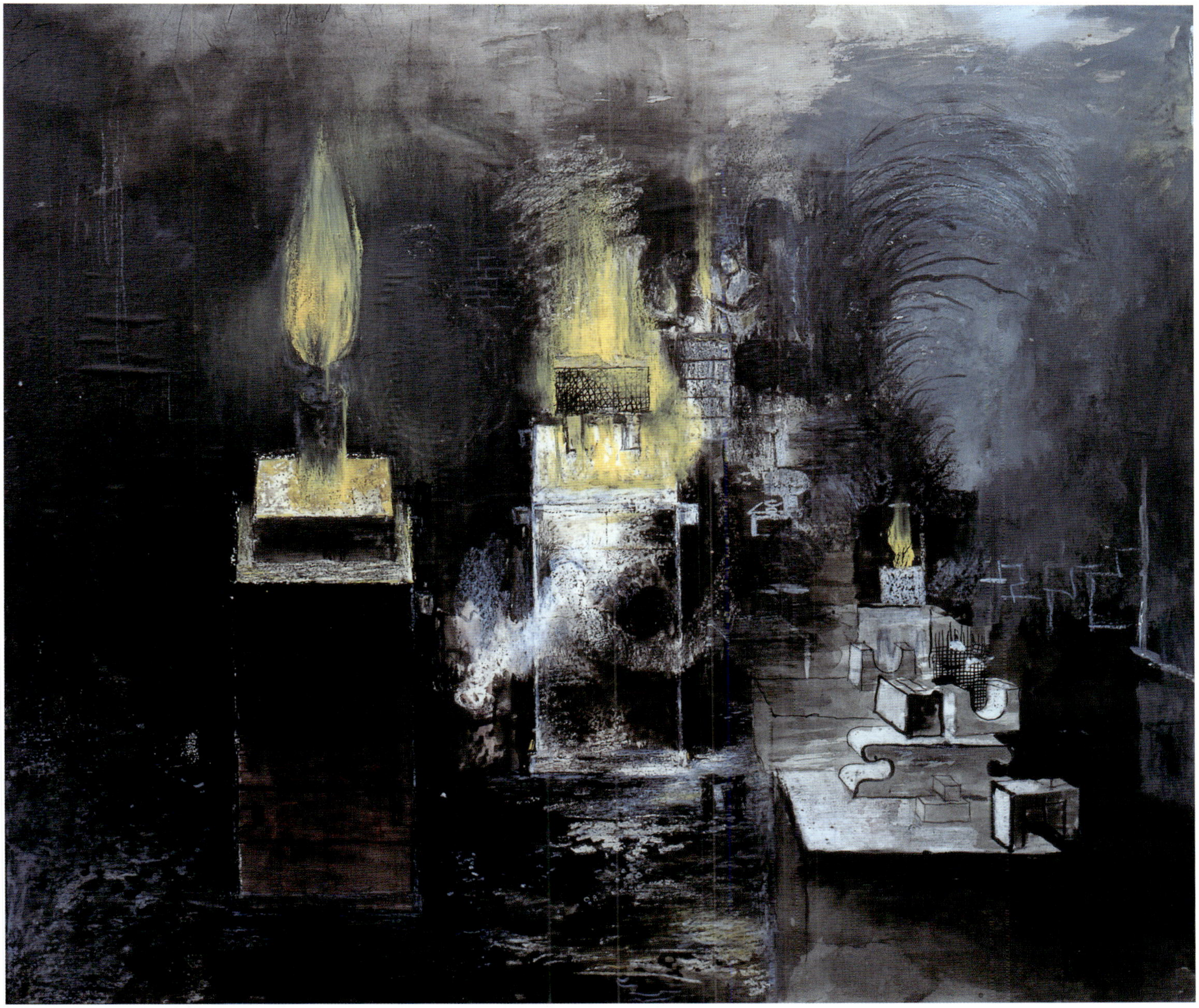

57.
Twin Ladles
1941
Watercolour and wax crayon with varnish and some pen and black ink on paper
505 x 366 mm
The Ashmolean Museum, Oxford. Presented by HM Government (War Artists' Advisory Committee) 1947
WA 1947.416.

58.
A Foundry: Hot Metal has been Poured into a Mould and Inflammable Gas is Rising
1941–42
Crayon and gouache on paper
518 x 1092 mm
Tate. Presented by the War Artists Advisory Committee 1946
N05739.

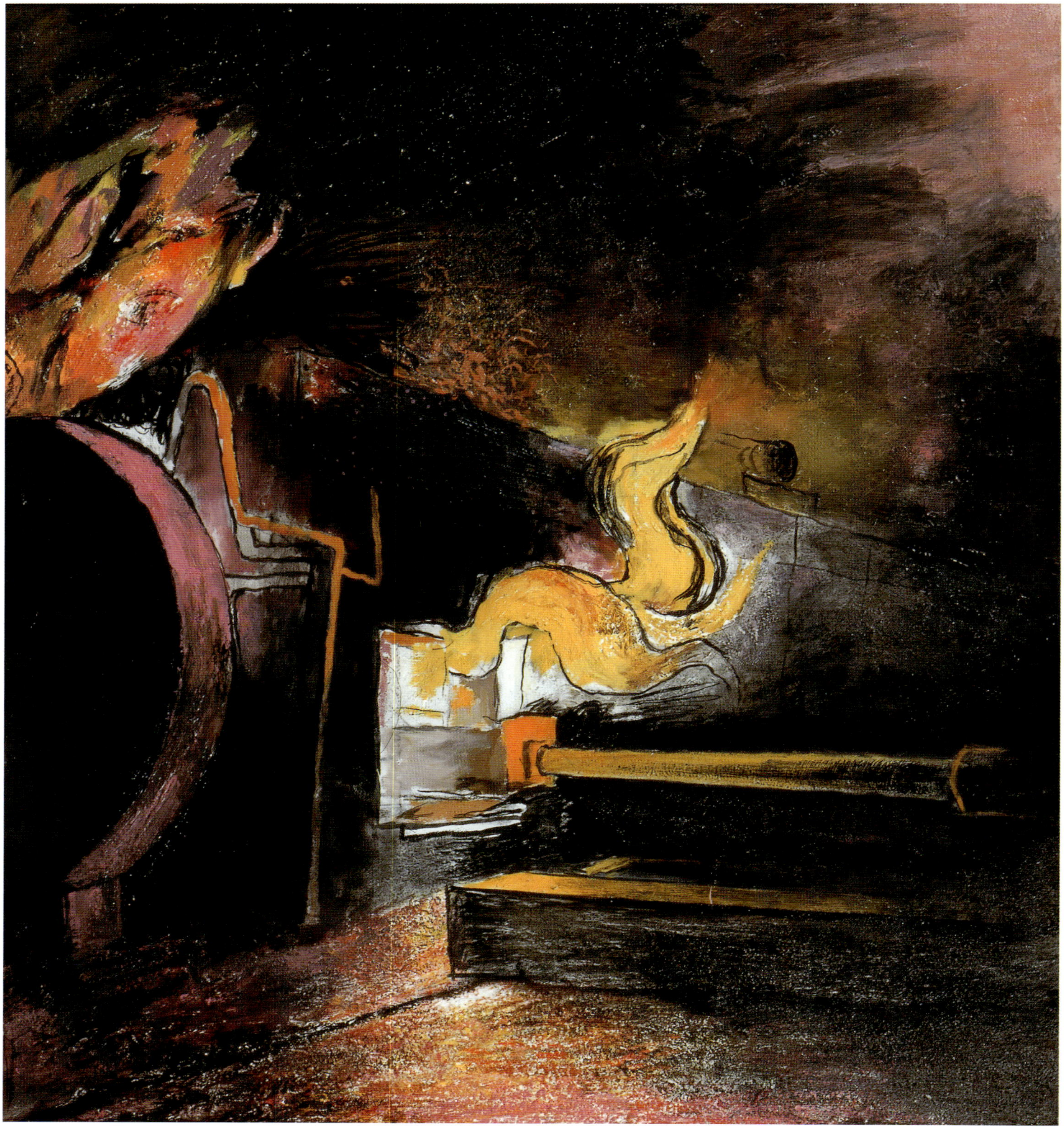

59.
Feeding a Steel Furnace
1941–42
Oil on canvas
902 x 864 mm
Tate. Presented by the War Artists Advisory Committee 1946
N05738.

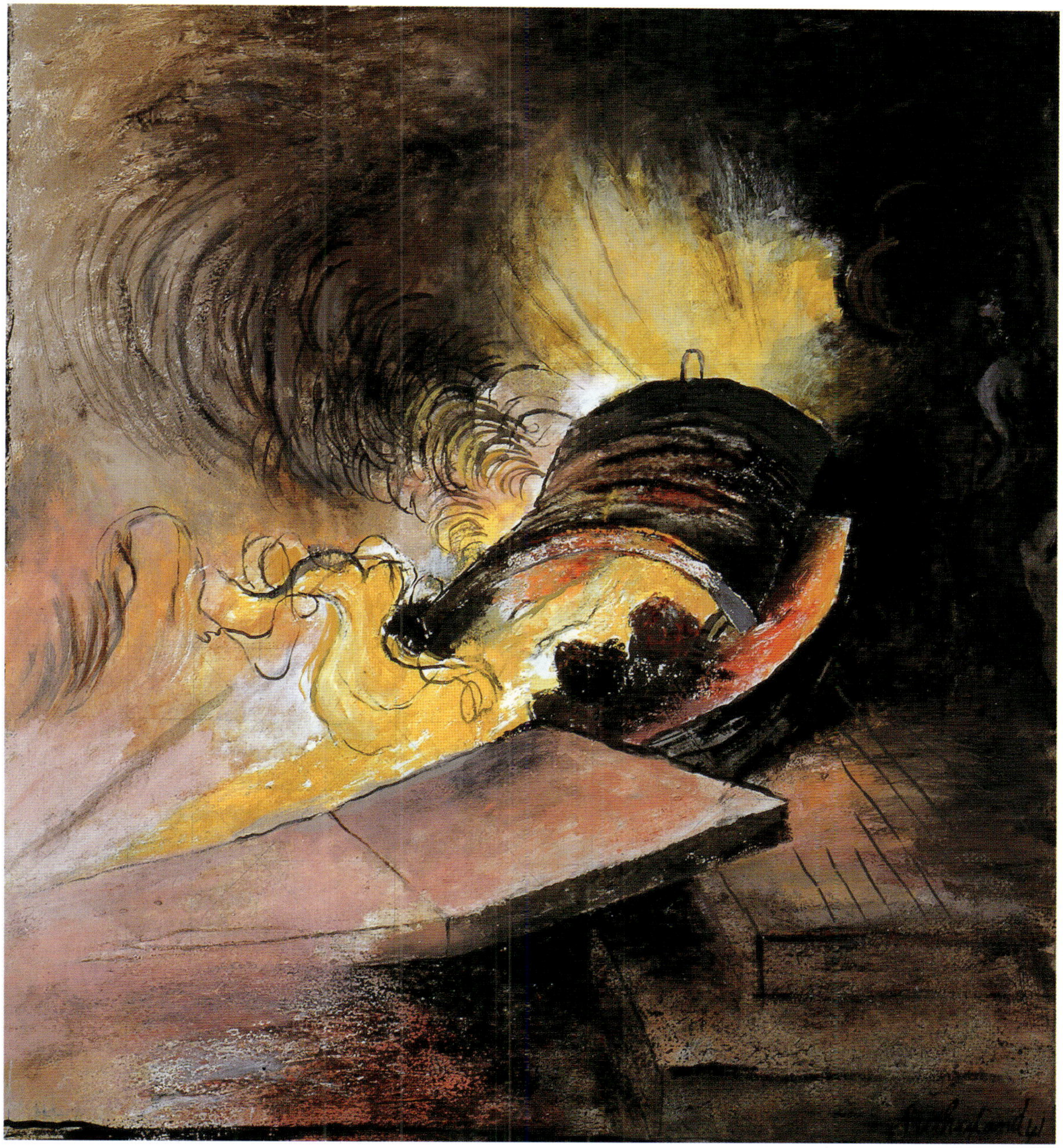

60.
Tapping a Blast Furnace
1941–42
Oil on canvas
921 x 860 mm
Tate. Presented by the War Artists Advisory Committee 1946
N05740.

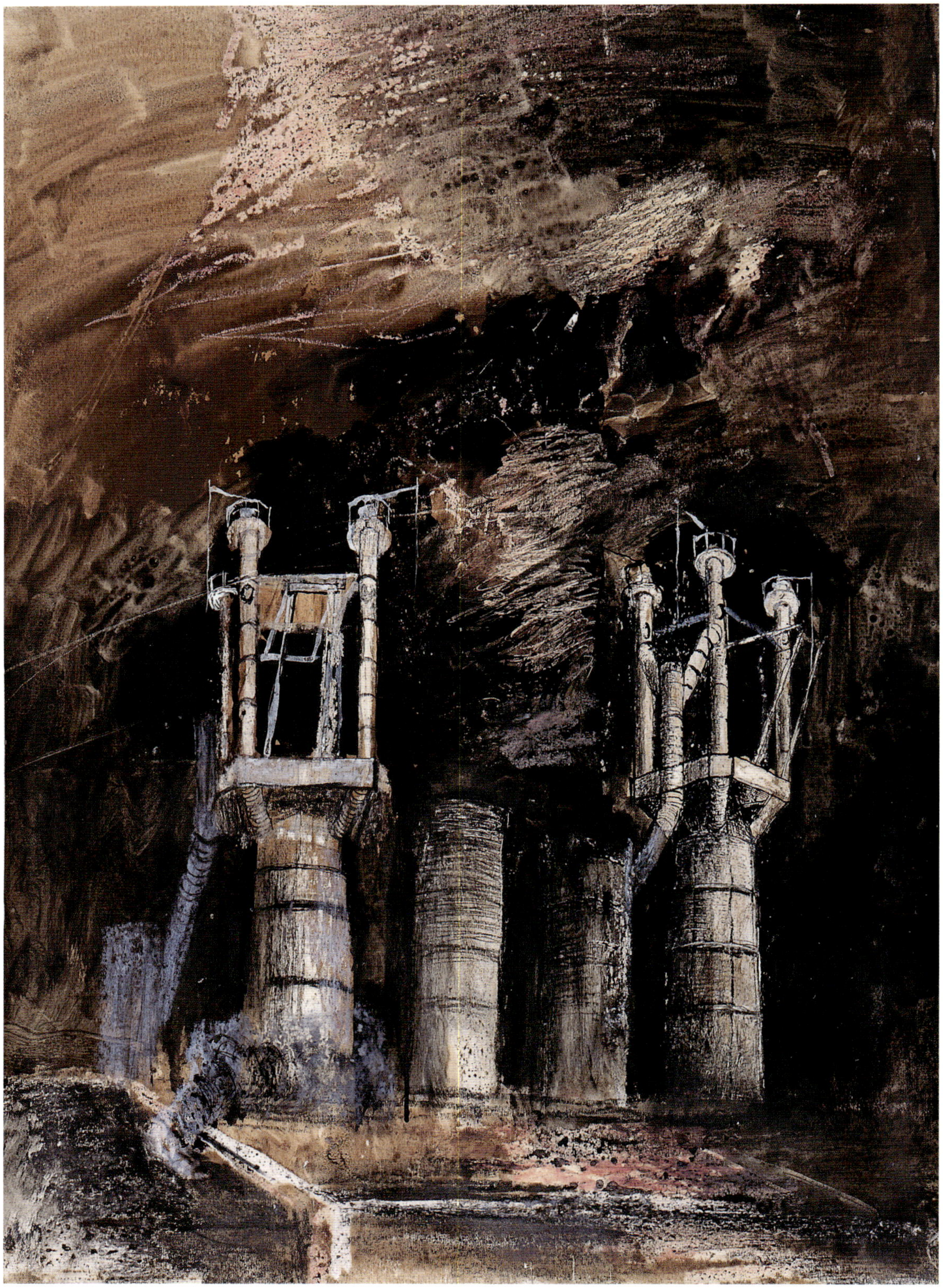

61.
Blast Furnaces
1942
Watercolour, gouache, pencil, wax crayon and Indian ink on paper
497 x 370 mm
Birmingham Museums and Art Gallery
1947P39.

62.
Limestone Quarry: Loosening Stone
1942
Gouache, wax crayon and pencil on cardboard
660 x 587 mm
British Council
P165.

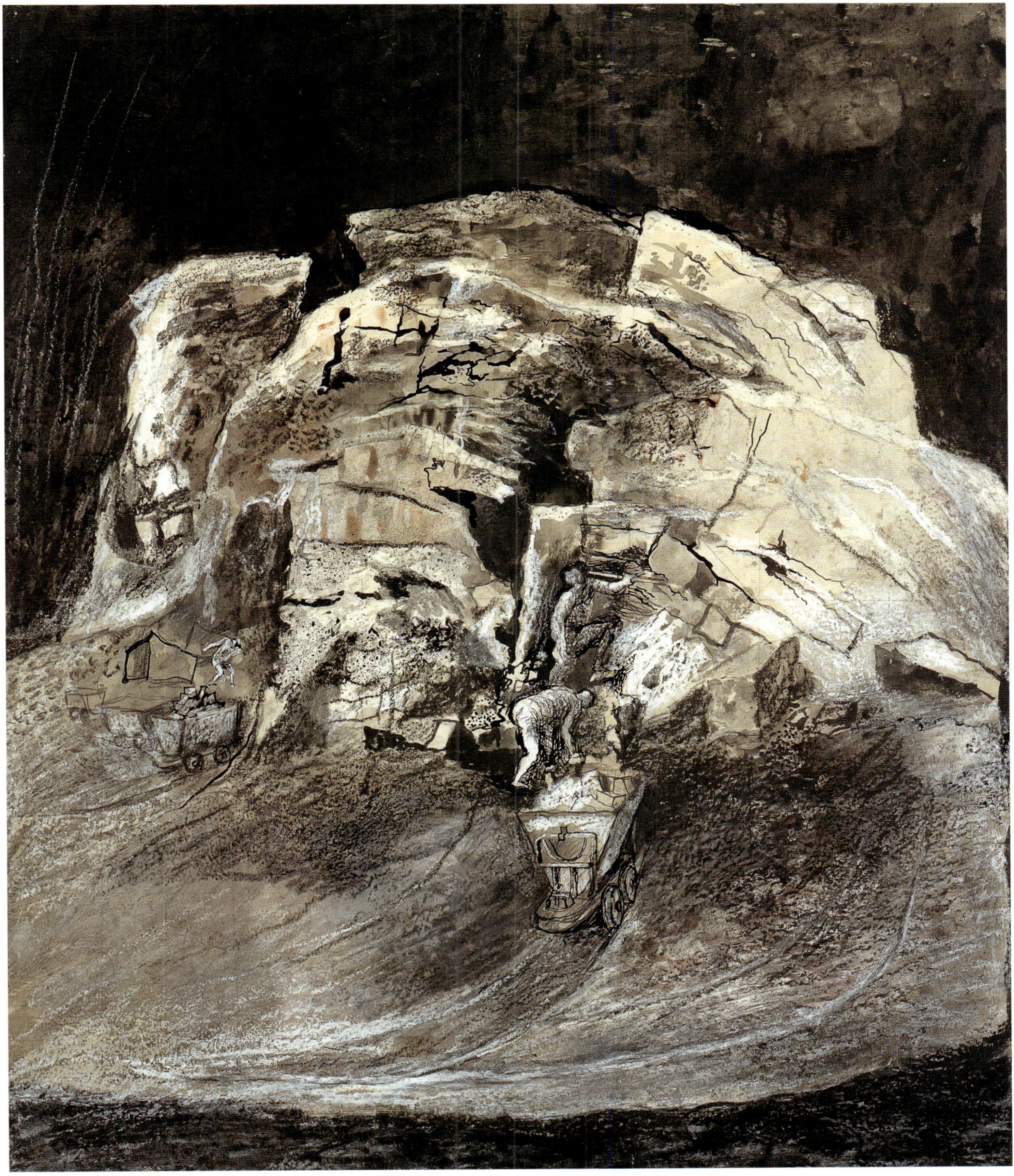

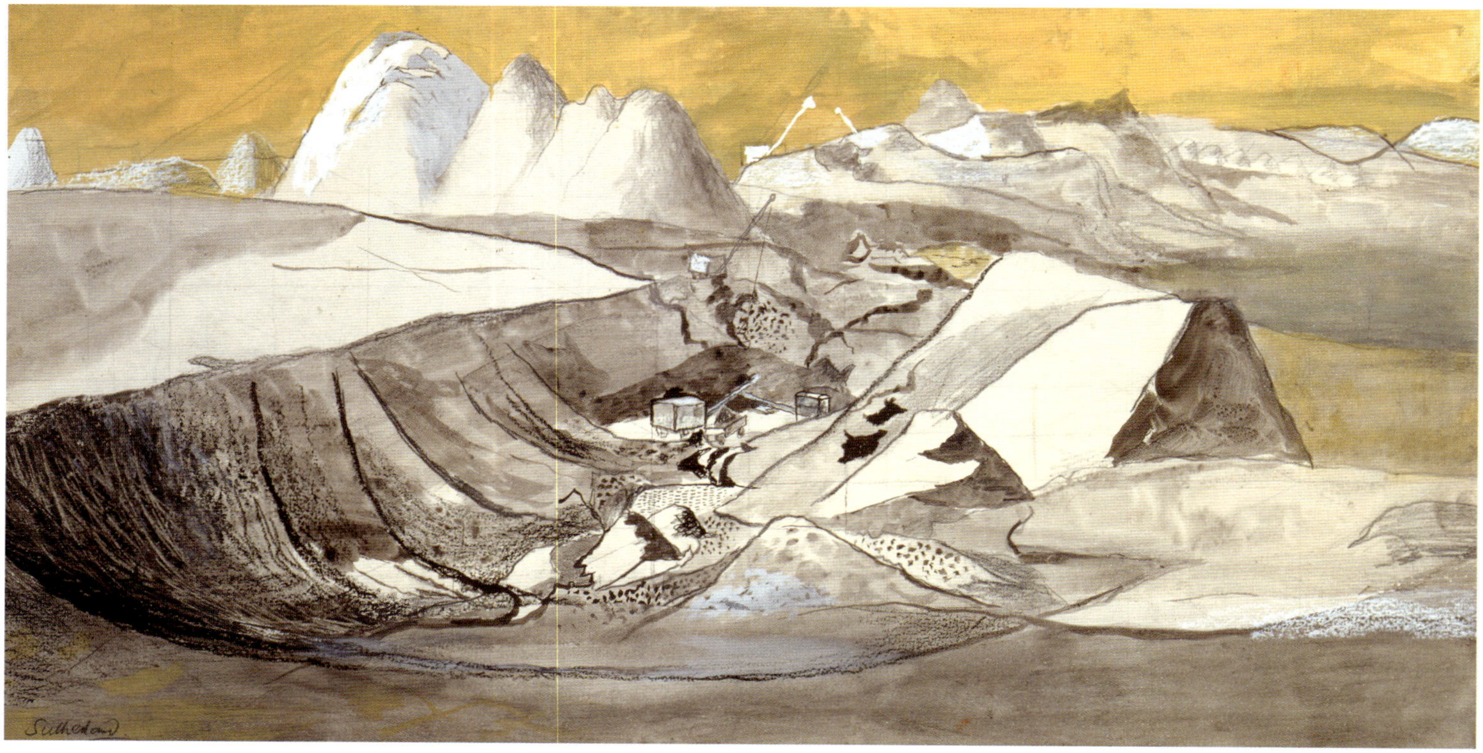

63.
Opencast Coal Production: Excavators
1943
Pencil, gouache and watercolour on paper
445 x 865 mm
Leeds Museums and Galleries (City Art Gallery)
28.12/47.

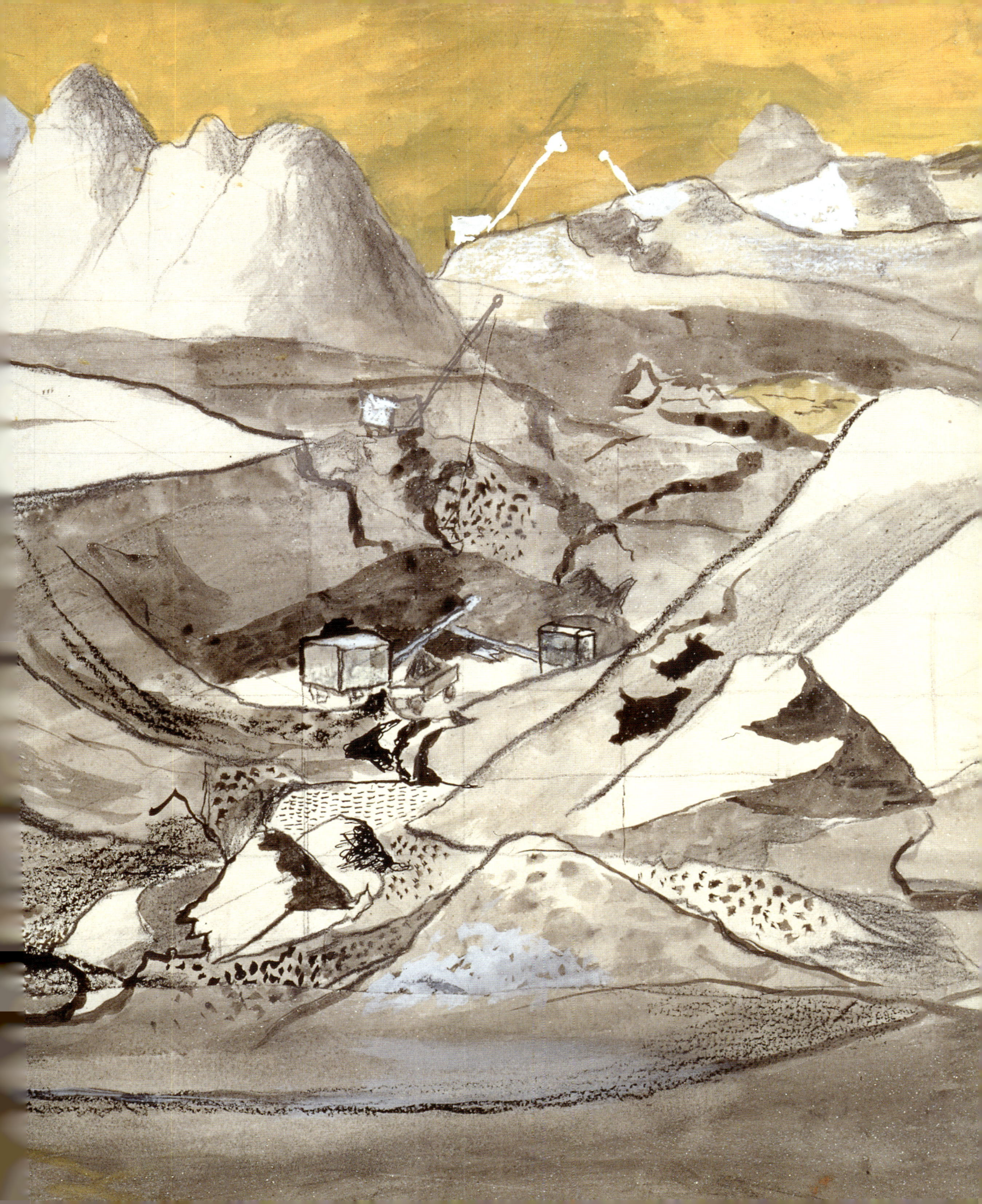

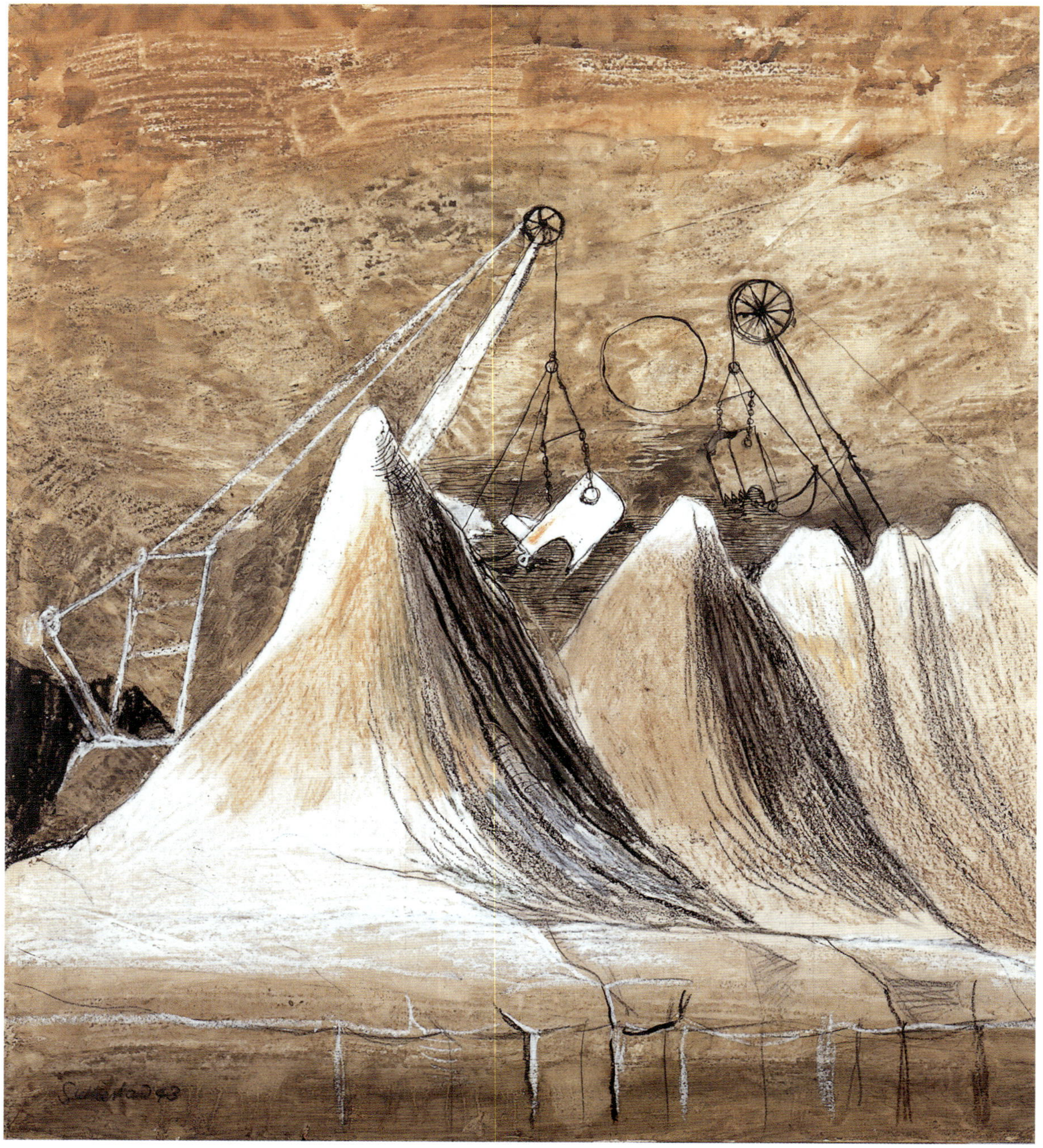

64.
Opencast Coal Production: Dragline
1943
Gouache and chalk on paper mounted on board
695 x 665 mm
Leeds Museums and Galleries (City Art Gallery)
28.8/47.

65.
Limestone Quarries – General View II
1942
Bodycolour, crayon and watercolour on board
575 x 497 mm
Laing Art Gallery, Newcastle upon Tyne (Tyne and Wear Museums)
F3424.

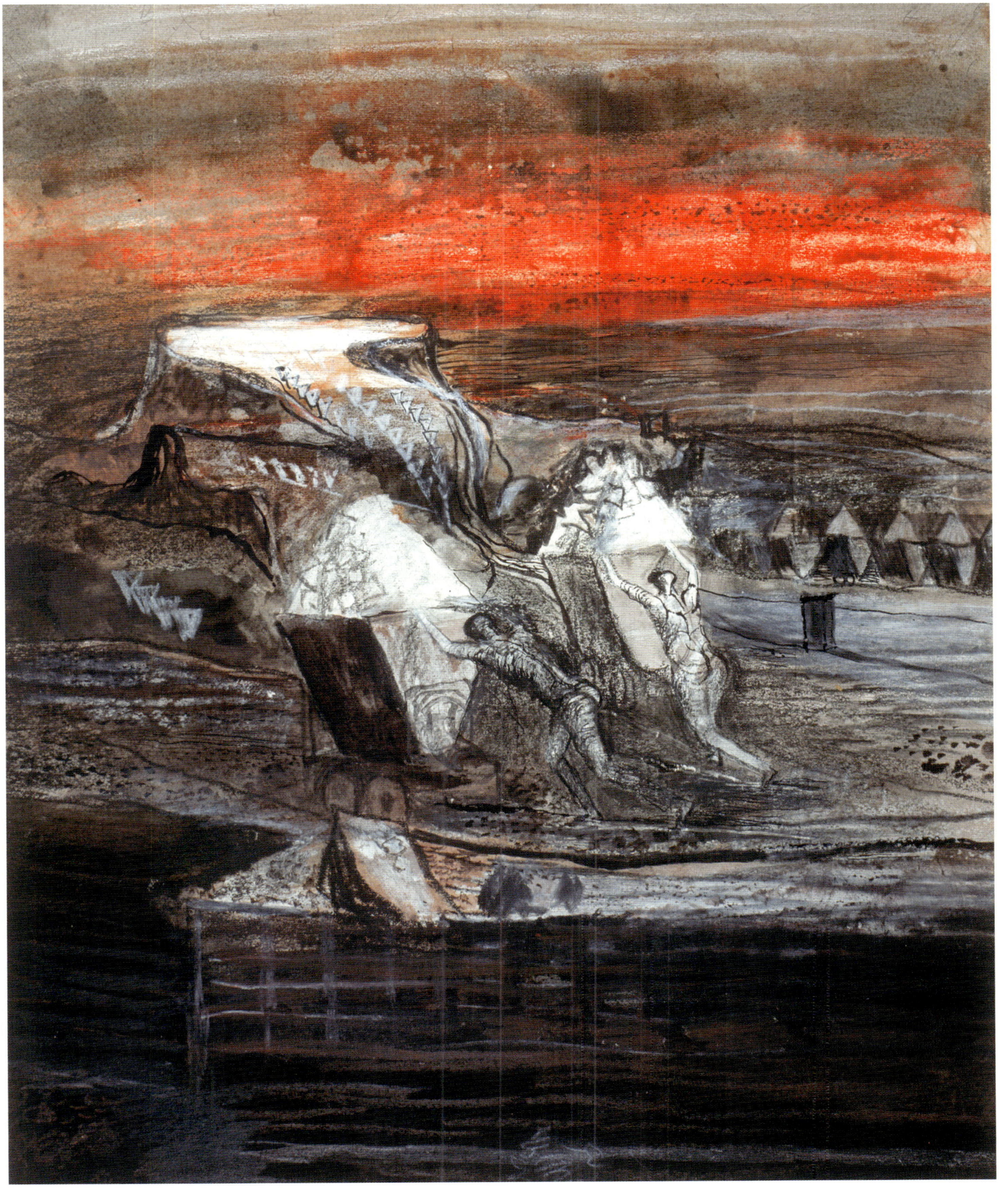

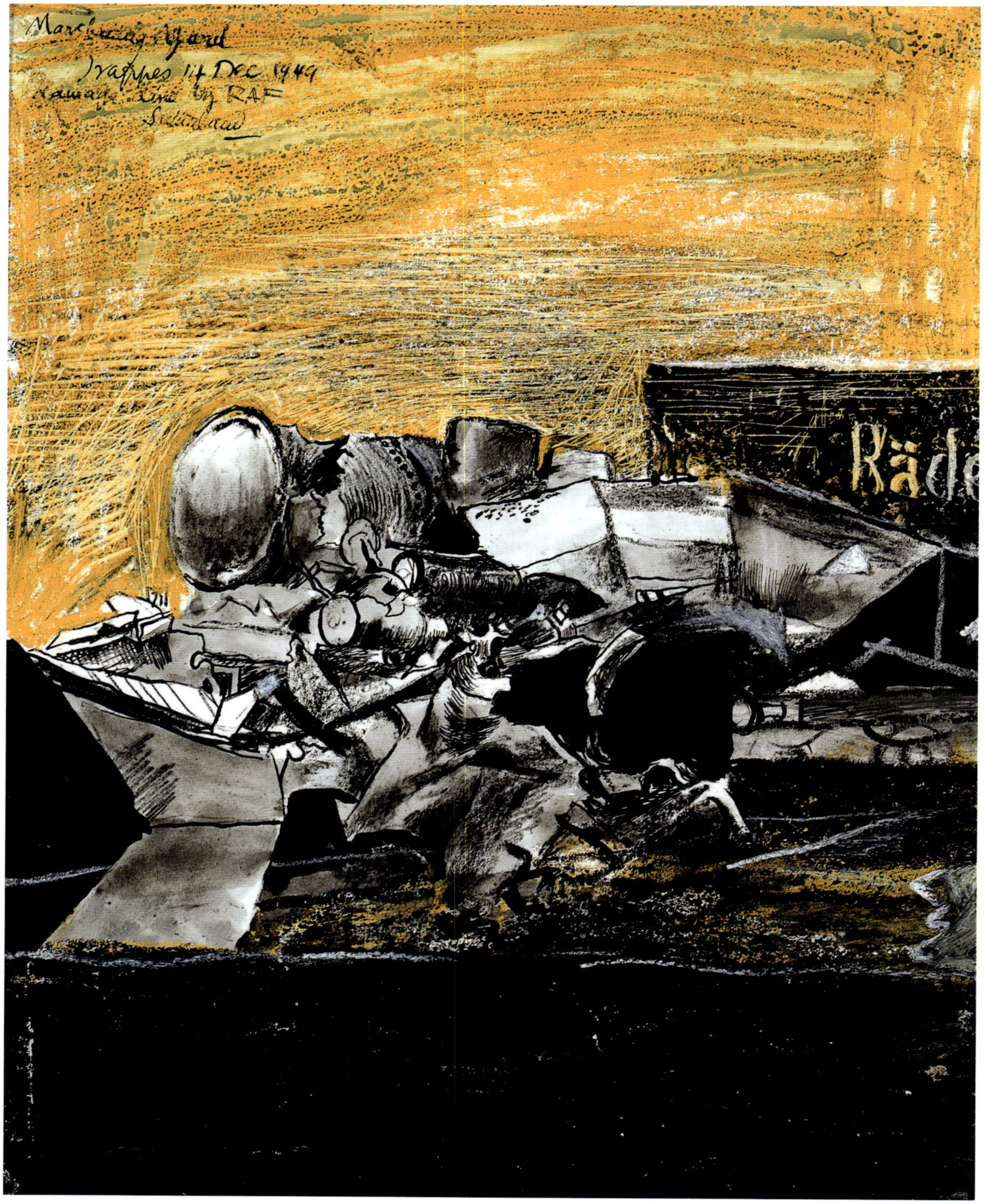

66.
Marshalling Yards, Trappes
1944
Gouache on board
425 x 350 mm
Leeds Museums and Galleries
(City Art Gallery)
28.10/47.

67.
Marshalling Yards, Trappes
1944
Oil on board
1282 x 1047 mm
Leeds Museums and Galleries
(City Art Gallery)
28.5/47.

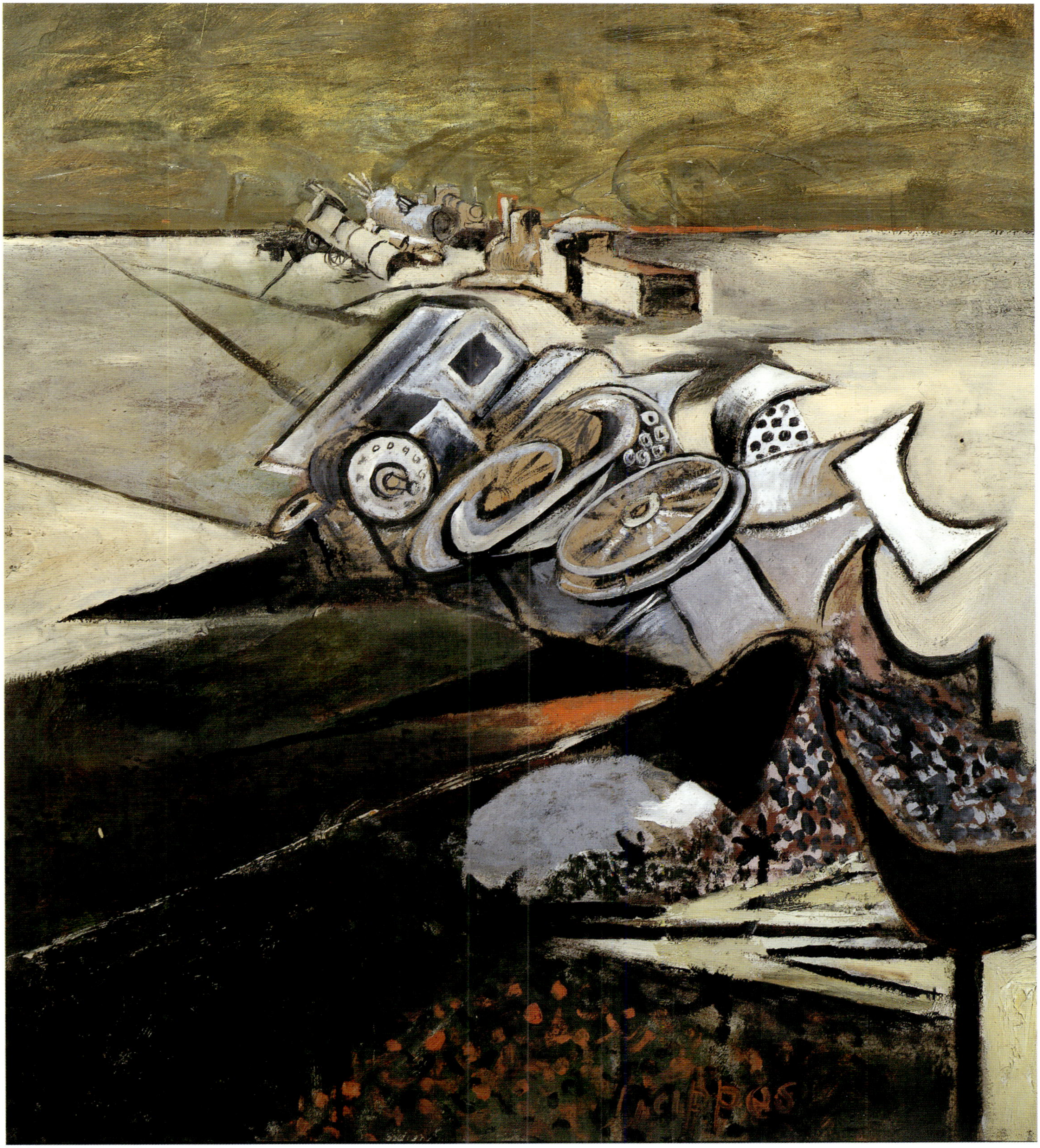

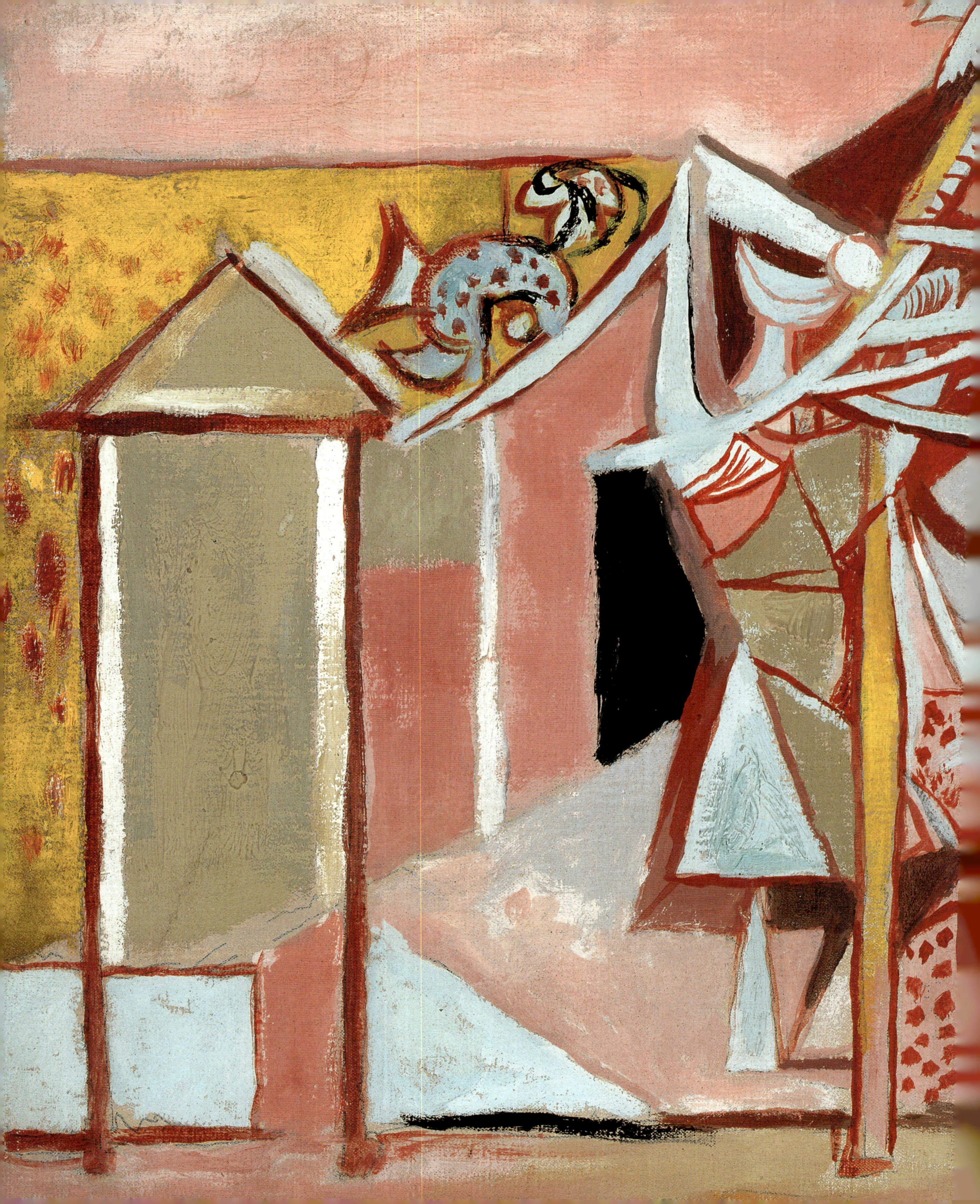

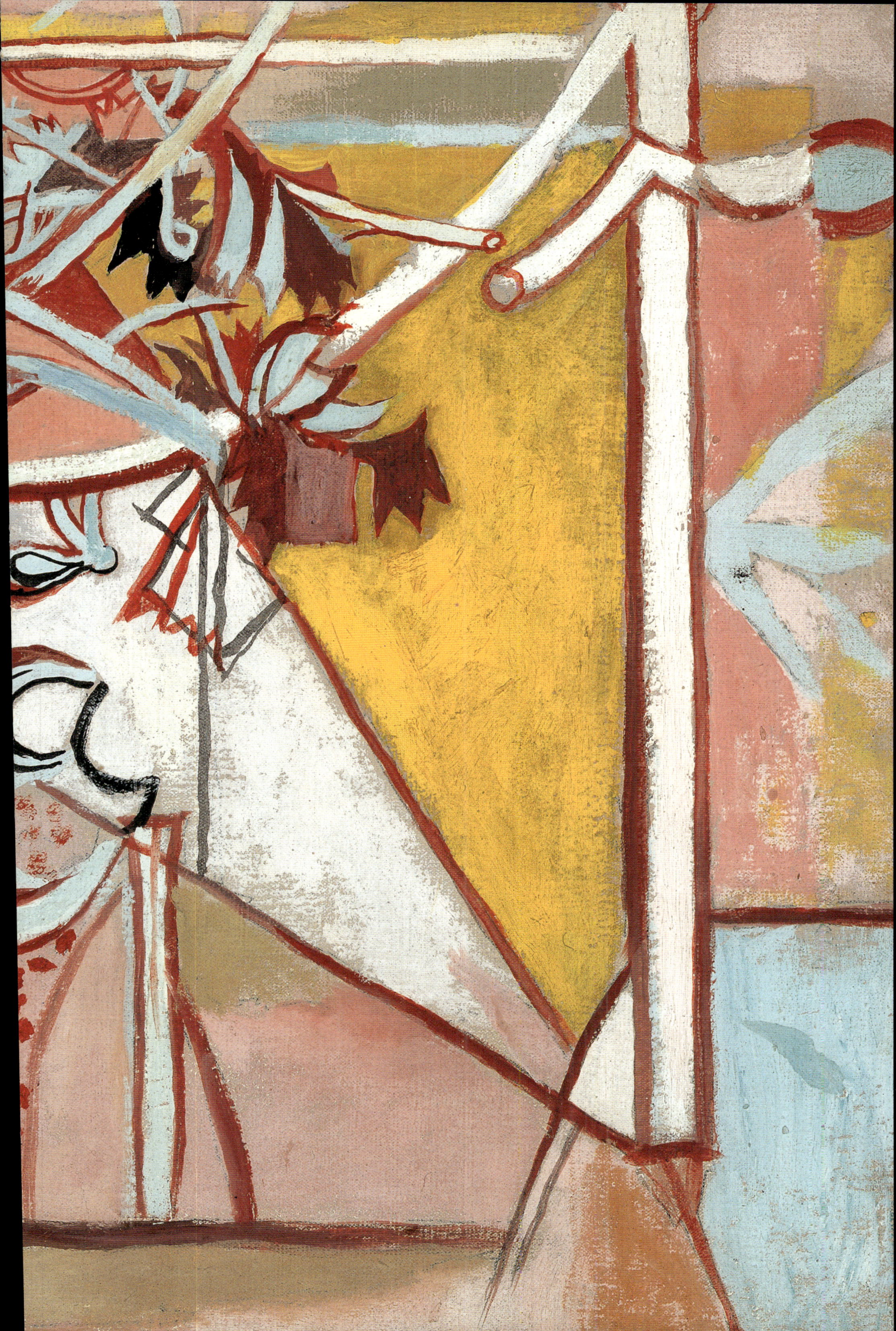

4

New Departures
1943–1950

Pink Vine Pergola
1947
(Cat. 80, detail).

Thoughts on Painting

Graham Sutherland

I think it is bad for a painter to try to explain his work. He is using up energy which could be better employed in painting, or he is tempted to rationalise the intuitive workings of his mind. Yet there are times when he can, profitably perhaps, give a clue; and this is all he can do.

Painting, of course, should explain itself; but for reasons which I will mention later, the particular qualities of life of certain kinds of contemporary painting are not immediately apprehended. Perhaps ways of approach may be found through other arts – though to explain one art in terms of another can be disastrous, if exact parallels are attempted. But the intention in certain kinds of poetry may help to clarify the direction of the kind of painting I am thinking of. One often hears people speak of poetical painting, of painters with a genuine poetical feeling, of painters with a lyric gift, and so on. Painting, it is true, can often be the equivalent of lyric poetry. But I am not talking about poetry in these senses: often what is meant by poetical painting shows itself variously in, say, a love of the ideal, a transfiguring and melancholy light, an ominous overtone, or a forced atmosphere of fantasy.

No, I mean poetry in another and greater sense – poetry which enlightens the significance and nature of things. Poetry also which makes things hold more than their original meaning, and which defines their essence. When Aeschylus tells us that "Dust is mud's thirsty sister", we immediately know something about the nature of dust. By personifying dust and mud, we apprehend, through words of the utmost economy, the essence of both. So, too, in painting, Picasso, in his "Weeping Woman", by a deliberate method – a kind of seeing inside and outside – underlines and embodies in his material the very essence of grief. Both Aeschylus and Picasso, therefore, in their various special ways of putting things, have shed a succinct light on the nature of things and emotions. It may be interesting in this respect, when one regards Picasso's gnashing woman to recall that Aeschylus tells us that "grief bites".

I am considering certain kinds of contemporary painting only. Not strictly abstract painting, which is concerned with the display of pure and absolute forms and colours in space; but painting, which, though it seems abstract or partially so, is essentially bound to reality, and concerned with seeing reality in a new way. By what process, it may be asked, does a painter concerned in this way arrive at his image? The process of transfusion is so mysterious that it is difficult to be precise. One can, I think, only hint at it.

The first reaction, of course, is through the eye. Perhaps one goes for a walk. There is everything around one; but one reacts to certain things only, as if in response to some internal need of the nerves. The things one reacts to vary. I have myself sometimes noticed a juxtaposition of forms at the side of a road, and on passing the same place next week they are gone. It was only at the original moment of seeing that they had significance for me.

I sometimes make notes. However brief these may be, this practice is useful to me; I can take my subject home with me as it were. If I react fully – with no preconceptions – it is as if I had never seen my subject before. In the studio, I remember; it may be an hour ago or years, and I react afresh. The images dissolve; objects may lose their normal environment and relationship. Then things seem to be drawn together and redefined in the mind's eye in a new life and a new mould – there has been a substitution, a change. But I feel this to be valid only in so far as the process of digestion has preserved in the substance of my material – paint and canvas – the sensation of the original presence, in its new and permanent form.

I cannot get much closer than that as to the process. Otherwise one risks that danger to which I have referred before of rationalising the workings of the mind, which are often irrational and certainly mysterious. But something of the kind does, I think, happen; to generalise about just what starts one off is impossible. My thorn pictures came into being in a curious way. I had been asked by the Vicar of St Matthew's, Northampton, to paint a Crucifixion. In the autumn of that year I had been thinking of the form the work was to take; in the spring of the following year the subject was still very much in my mind. So far I had made no drawings – and I went into the country. For the first time I started to notice thorn bushes, and the structure of thorns as they pierced the air. I made some drawings, and as I made them, a curious change developed. As the thorns rearranged themselves, they became, whilst still retaining their own pricking, space-encompassing life, something else – a kind of "stand-in" for a Crucifixion and a crucified head.

One question which people always pursue is that of obscurity. Why is so much contemporary art obscure? Of course, modern painting *is* more obscure than most art of the past. But if one duty of painting is to explain the essence of things and emotions, may not it also be a duty, sometimes, not to explain – but to accept? Do we need an explanation of the flight of a bird, or a flash of lightning? Do we need to be told why a rose is shaped thus? Coleridge said that poetry gives most pleasure when generally and not perfectly understood. These lines of Blake are possibly obscure:

> My Spectre round me night and day
> Like a wild beast guards my way;
> My Emanation far within
> Weeps incessantly for my sin.

but it may be argued that their mysterious music is actually enhanced by that obscurity. So in painting it might be argued that its very obscurity preserves a magical and mysterious purpose.

It could be said, on the other hand, that much contemporary work, which is thought to be obscure, may be merely suffering the time-lag in appreciation which has so often operated against painters in their life-time.

Today, too, we are faced with new problems of interpretation of phenomena and ideas, previously ignored. What, then, you will ask, happens to the belief that art is communication? Does a painter cease to communicate if people cannot identify what he has depicted? Does a form have to be nameable before it can affect? Again I say, is not the contrary also true? If we come across a new experience or a new taste, should we turn from them in disdain because they are unlike the experiences and tastes we do know? Might we not, in fact be *stimulated* because of their very newness and difference? Familiarity, I am afraid, is preferred, and breeds not contempt but approbation. The old dish is more palatable than the new and unfamiliar one. In "The Marriage of Heaven and Hell" Blake writes:

> "Then I asked: 'Does a firm persuasion that a
> thing is so make it so?'"
> "He replied: 'All poets believe that it does and in
> the ages of imagination this firm belief moved
> mountains; but many are not capable of a firm
> belief in anything'."

For myself I believe that a new vision must grow out of reality – that the mysteriously intangible must be made immediate and tangible.

People ask about my "Standing Forms". What do they mean? They do not of course *mean* anything. The forms are based on the principles of organic growth, with which I have always been preoccupied. To me they are monuments and presences. But why use these forms instead of human figures? Because, at the moment, I find it necessary to catch the taste – the quality – the essence of the presence of the human figure: the mysterious immediacy of a figure standing in a room or against a hedge in its shadow, its awareness, its regard, as if one had never seen it before – by a substitution. I find at the moment that I can make these qualities more real to myself in this way. It happens that I find these organic forms best for my purpose. They themselves are emotionally modified from their natural prototype. They give me a sense of the shock of surprise which direct evocation could not possibly do. Also, in these pictures, I am trying to return these forms after drastic rearrangement and emotional and formal modification to the field of purely visual response – to throw them back, as it were, into the original cradle of impact. Seurat did this in his "Baignade" and the "Study for the Grande Jatte" in the late S. Lewisohn's collection; today one must use other methods and other ways.

I think that today the time has come to do more than to be content to put a line round our reactions. By that I mean that the tendency has been to modify the forms of reality emotionally and intellectually, and to keep them in fact non-optical – or rather optical only in the sense that observation and reaction have produced a kind of visual shorthand, which intellectually and sensibly refers one back to their prototype in life, as in Picasso's "Guernica". I feel that now we can perhaps enlarge the field of painting by setting our emotional paraphrases of reality – they themselves have been conceived more optically – within the ambience of optical reality. Perhaps one of the reasons why I have recently tried to do portraits is that it is possible that I feel the need to narrow the gap between my "stand in" monuments and the real human animal. I cannot say for certain. It is difficult to say where the things with which one is involved at the moment are likely to lead one.

The Northampton Crucifixion

Portraiture has, of course, its own harsh limitations. The actual lay-out is so dependent on the idiosyncrasies of movement and pose, which the subject naturally assumes. If you alter those positions at the dictate of composition, you run the certain risk that in falsifying physical truth you falsify psychological truth. A portrait, I believe, must be like. By that I do not mean the so-called "speaking likeness" of attempted imitation, but the likeness which is the result of an attempt to fuse all the characteristic directions, movements, and tension of the head and body into terms of paint. People sometimes say: What do you feel about doing commissioned work? My answer is that one finds it no different from that which is not commissioned. But if, for instance, I was not interested in the head and character of a portrait subject, I would not accept the commission; because I should know that I could not make anything of it. Similarly there is the case of the Northampton Crucifixion. In the first place I was asked to paint an "Agony in the Garden". I did not feel at that time that I wanted to do that subject, and as I had wanted for some time to attempt a Vision of the Crucifixion I suggested that I should do this, and this was agreed. I did in fact find that there were other, self-imposed restrictions to reckon with and there was the setting to take into account, only moderately sympathetic. Also, today, we have got out of the habit of working for a specific place, and for a patron, and this gives rise to complexes and psychological inhibitions. In the main, however, I think we would get used to this. It has been asked if I felt the desire to continue in this field rather than to continue my personal experiments? If I want to make my imagery reflect my feelings about religion or the state of society? I cannot say that I think one can decide one's interest in such an arbitrary way.

The Crucifixion idea interested me because it has a duality which has always fascinated me. It is the most tragic of all themes yet inherent in it is the promise of salvation. It is the symbol of the precarious balanced moment, the hair's breadth between black and white. It is that moment when the sky seems superbly blue – and, when one feels it *is* only blue in that superb way because at any moment it could be black – there is the other side of the mirror – and on that point of balance one may fall into great gloom or rise to great happiness. You will, perhaps, have noticed that my thorn heads have blue backgrounds.

I would have liked to paint the Crucifixion against a blue sky – a blue background. The thorns sprang from the idea of potential cruelty – to me they *were* the cruelty; and I attempted to give the idea a double twist, as it were, by setting them in benign circumstances: blue skies, green grass, Crucifixion under warmth – and blue skies are, in a sense, more powerfully horrifying. The colour which in fact I did use – a bluish royal purple, traditionally a death colour – was partly dictated by certain factors already in the church.

In my earlier work I used colour very sparingly: often blacks and greys and one colour. Then my colour began to lighten in key and I used quite a variety of colours. Critics have said that my colour became light (and acid!) after I started to work in France! It is a prime example of the laziness of some of them; if they had bothered to enquire, I could have shown them pictures painted in 1944 which were very bright and light in colour. When I did start working in France, in 1947, I must confess that I did wonder how I had come to anticipate, by this lightening of key, the clarity of the steady southern light. Colour has two major functions. It is form and mood. That is to say that by its warmth or coldness it can create form; it can also create a mood; it is fascinating to make complete changes of colour in the background of a painting and see how the whole atmosphere changes. Colour can suggest depth and shallowness, heat and cold – it can even suggest sound. There is the story of the blind man who, when his companion described the effect of scarlet on the eye, exclaimed "It must be like the sound of a trumpet".

In talking about my painting in France I have been asked: Is it necessary to live within the landscapes one paints? From a purely physical point of view it is a convenience. One has longer time to find the things one likes, a longer time to react and for voluptuous awareness: one has calm, no hurry, time to notice how an infinitely small form at the foot of a tree is reproducing, in miniature, the whole structure of the surrounding landscape. In fact, though staying long in one place does not necessarily help me, one must stay in a place a fair time before one starts to work. But I do not think it makes very much difference where one is. I happen to work better and more easily in the sun. The historical emergence of landscape as a main, self-contained form of painting is fascinating and has given the painter greater freedom, but a curious thing about it is this: that unless one can reduce the object of a landscape to such a size as one can hold in one's hand – landscape without the imprint of man, that is to say landscapes which are not gardens or tilled fields – grand landscape can be awfully boring. Can you imagine anything more boring than mountain gorges? If you were to take a piece of lichen from a rock in one of these gorges, or pick up a shaped stone, a drawing of these would seem to be more interesting, because man, after all, could have plucked the lichen off the rock and picked up the stone. Landscape has loosened certain old ties. That is to say it has opened out a new field of form. But too much freedom may be bad. Fortunately art makes its own ties and laws. The kite flies only when attached to the string.

People have said that my most typical images express a dark and pessimistic outlook. That is outside my feeling. In the sense which I have previously mentioned, the precarious tension of opposites – happiness and unhappiness, beauty and ugliness, so near the point of balance – are capable of being interpreted according to the predilections and needs of the beholder – with enthusiasm and delight, or abhorrence, as with the taste of bitter-sweet fruit.

In any case the painter is a kind of blotting paper; he soaks up impressions – goes through "periods of fullness and evacuation" as Picasso has said; and is very much part of the world. He cannot therefore avoid soaking up the implications of the outer chaos of twentieth century civilisation. By that token tragic pictures will be painted – subconsciously perhaps, and without necessarily having a tragic subject. Picasso himself during the war painted tragic "still lives". Maybe one can only "mutter in darkness – spirit sore". But one has in one's hand the instruments of transformation and redemption.

(*The Listener,* 6 September 1951, pp. 376–78)

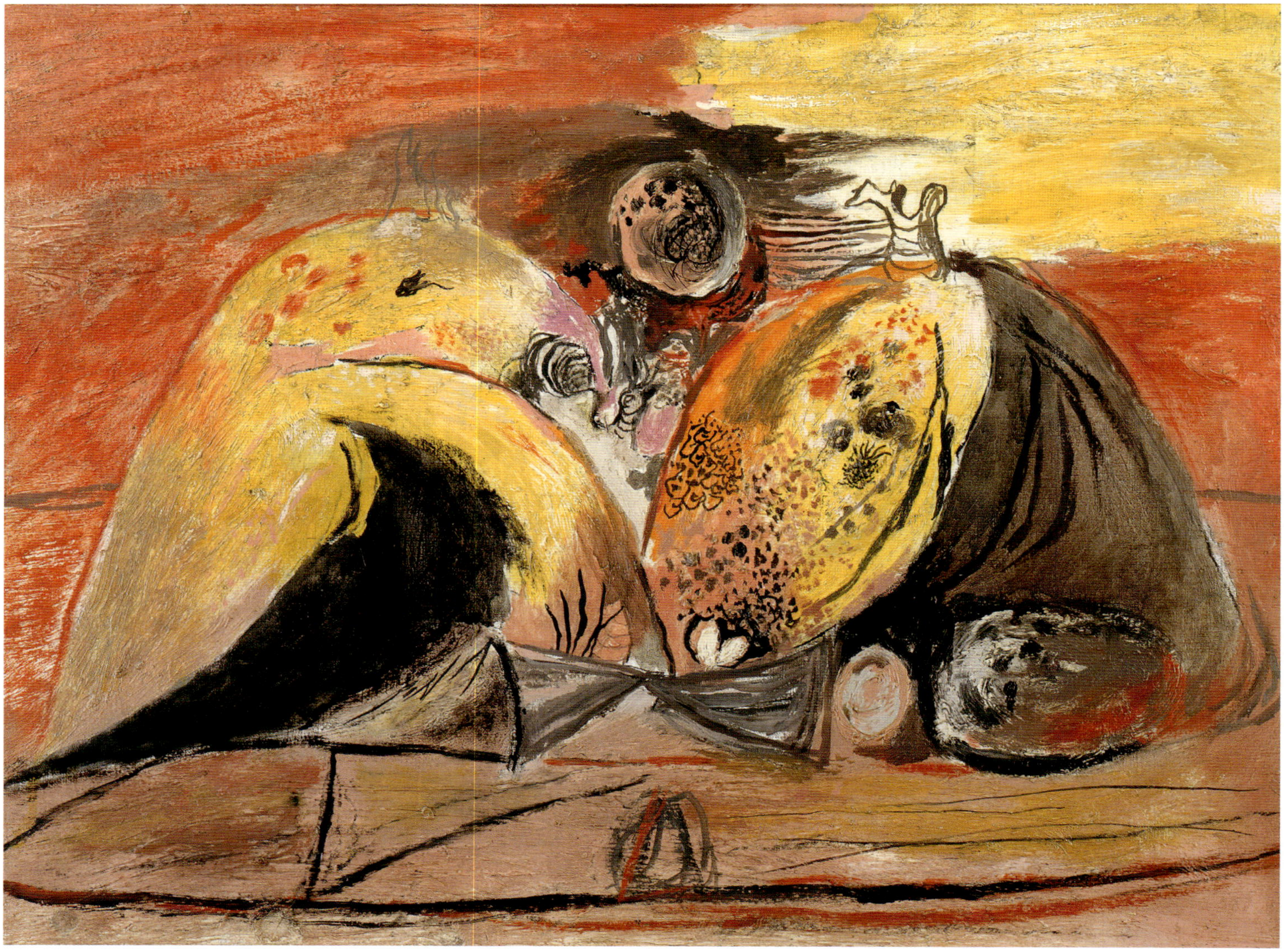

68.
Folded Hills
1943
Oil on canvas
496 x 676 mm
Private Collection

69. (not illustrated)
The Setting Sun
1944
Gouache and watercolour on paper
230 x 283 mm
British Council
P94.

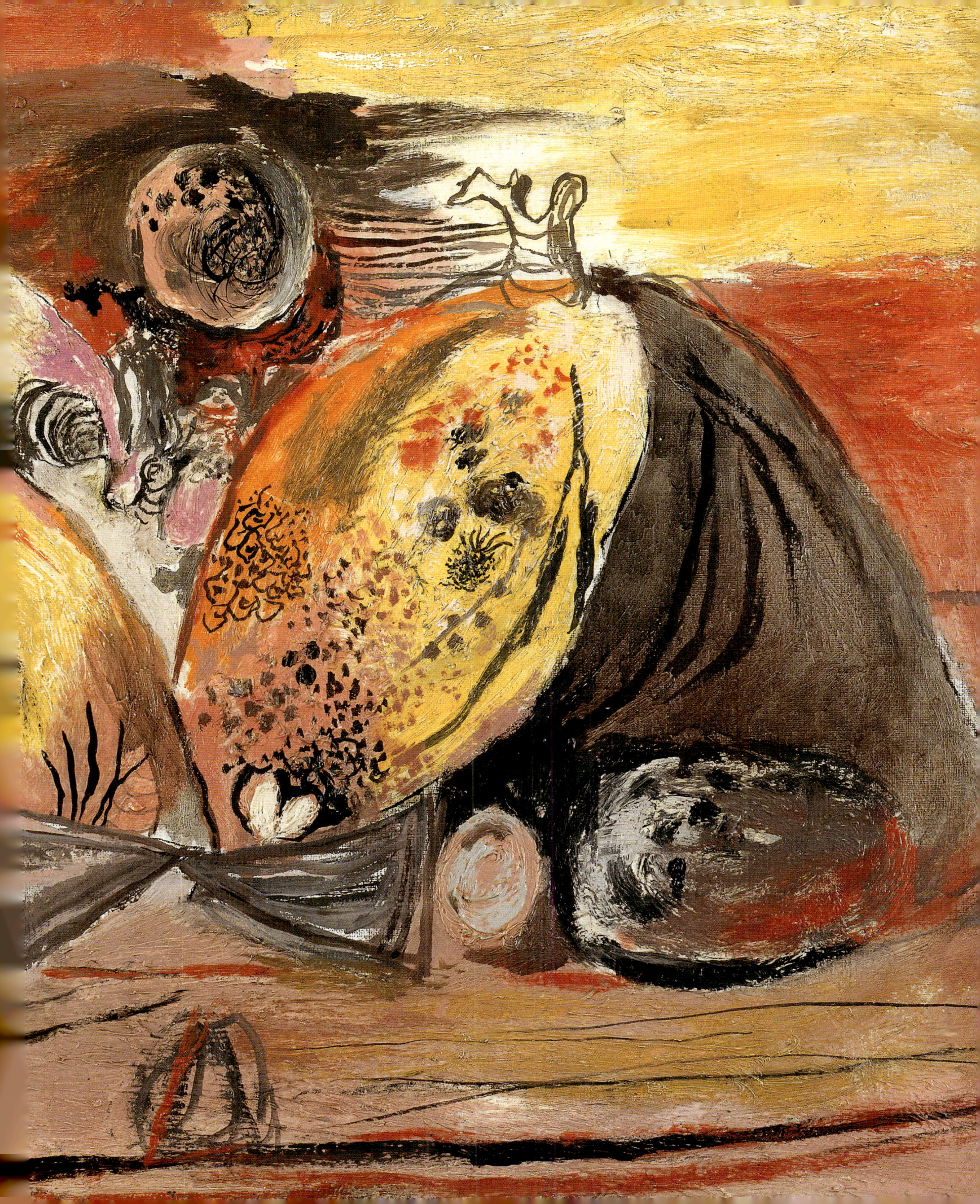

70.
Cornstook in Landscape
1945–46
Pencil, bodycolour,
brush and ink
603 x 426 mm
The Whitworth Art Gallery,
The University of Manchester
D.1953.7.

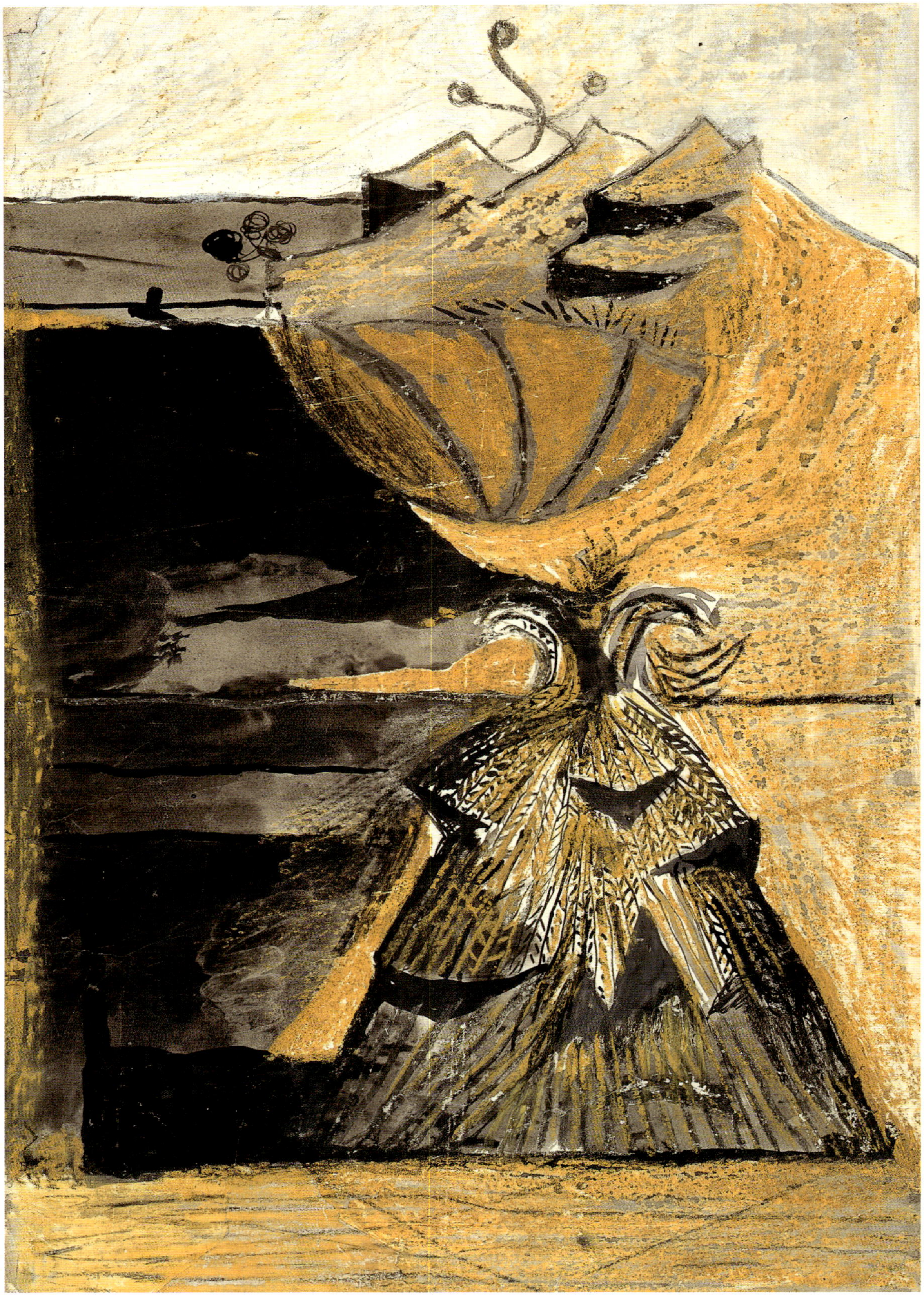

71.
Thistles and Sun
1945
Gouache, black and coloured
crayons on paper
450 x 404 mm
The Scottish National Gallery
of Modern Art, Edinburgh
GMA 763.

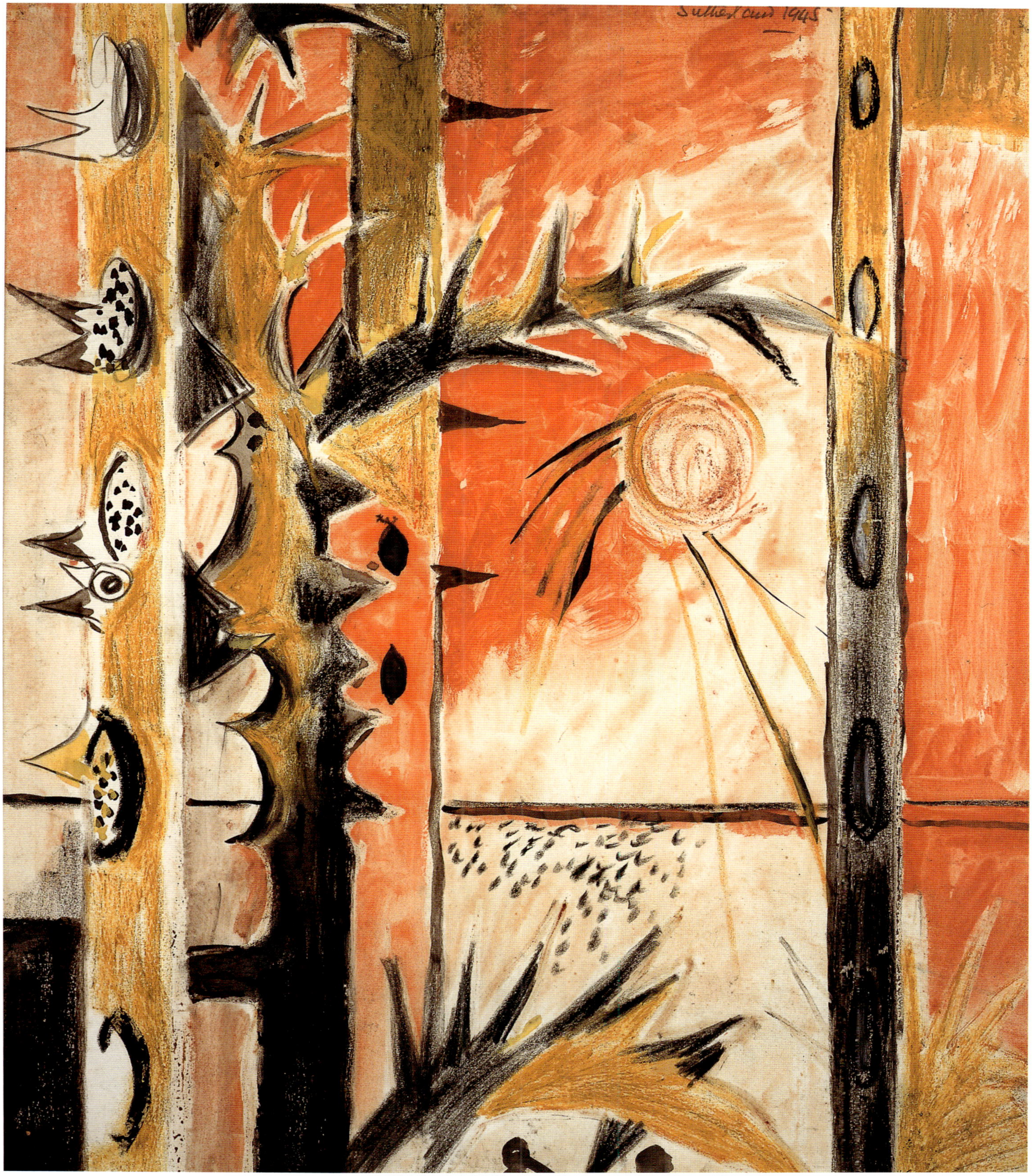
Sutherland 1945

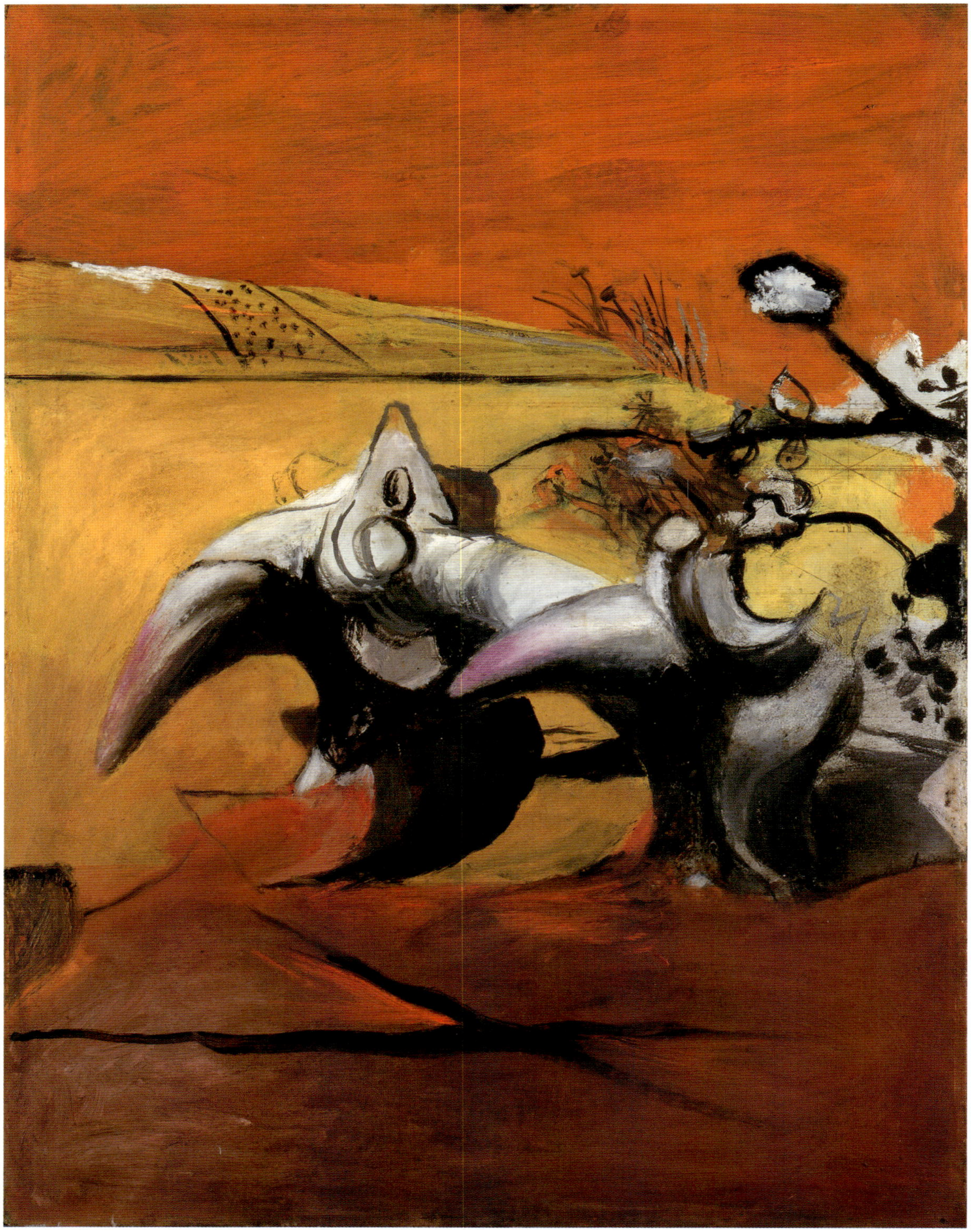

72.
Horned Forms
1944
Oil on board
813 x 641 mm
Tate. Presented by the Friends of the Tate Gallery 1966
T00834.

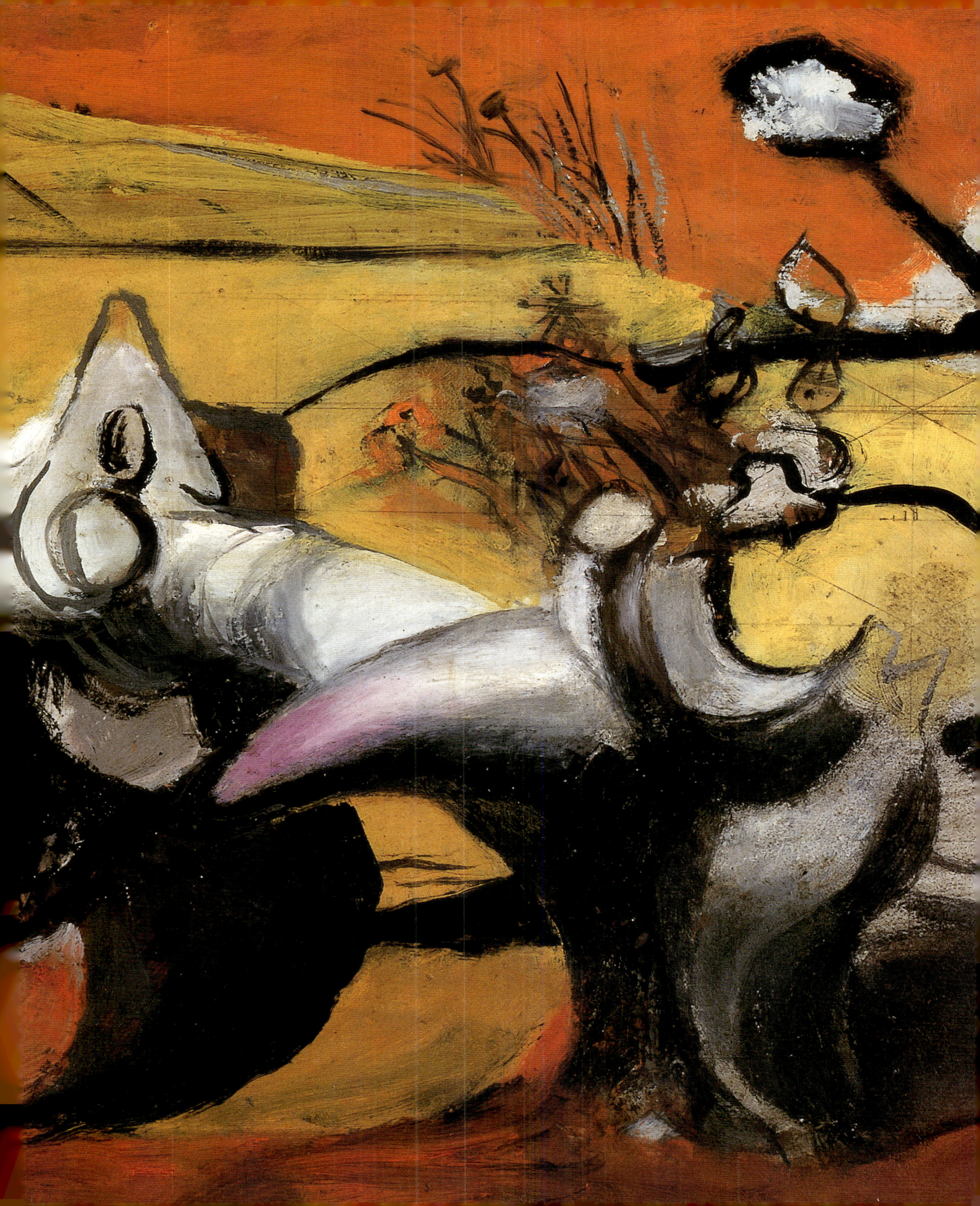

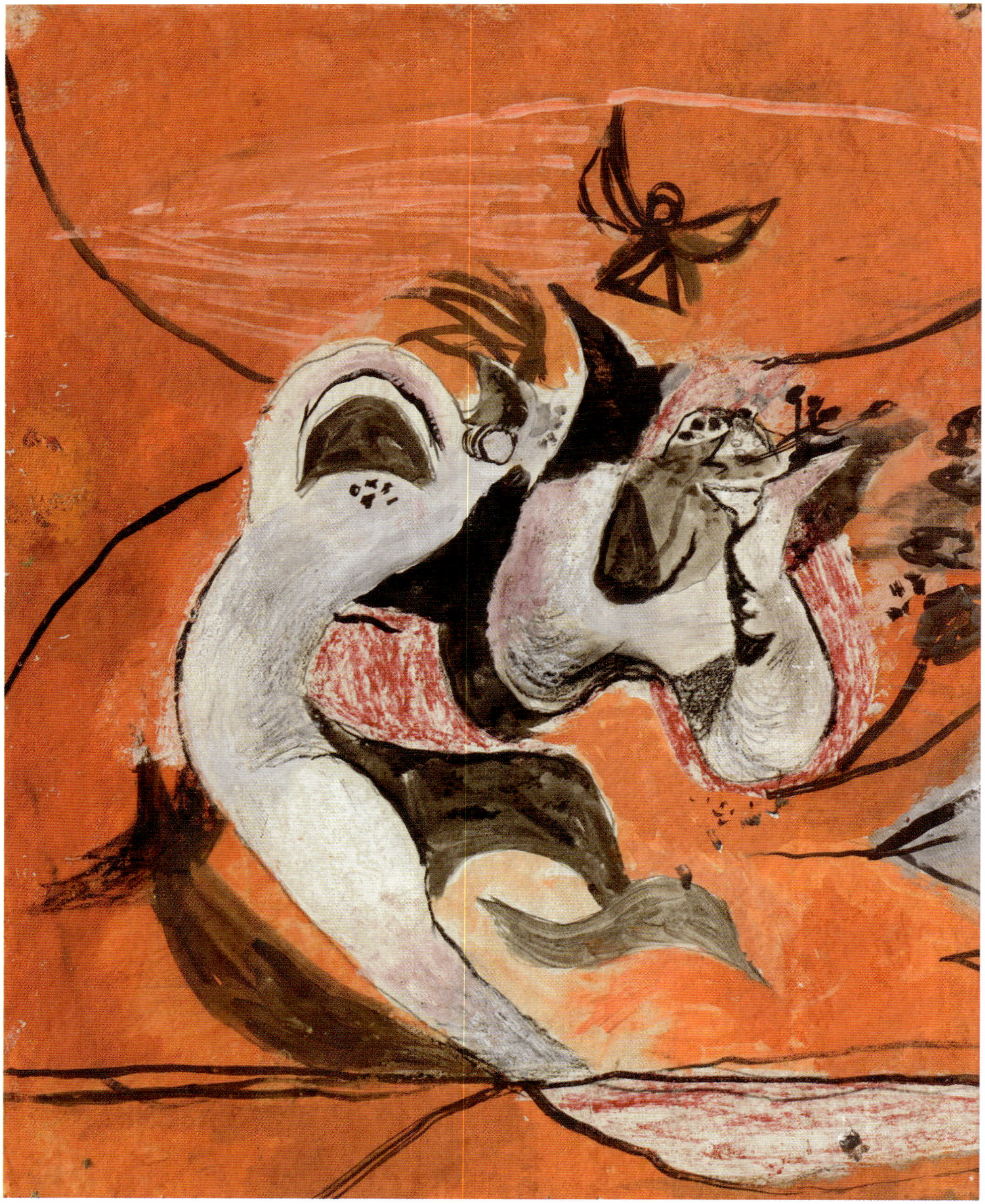

73.
Twisted Tree Form
1944
Pencil, bodycolour and watercolour on board
581 x 482 mm
Laing Art Gallery, Newcastle upon Tyne (Tyne and Wear Museums)
E5265.

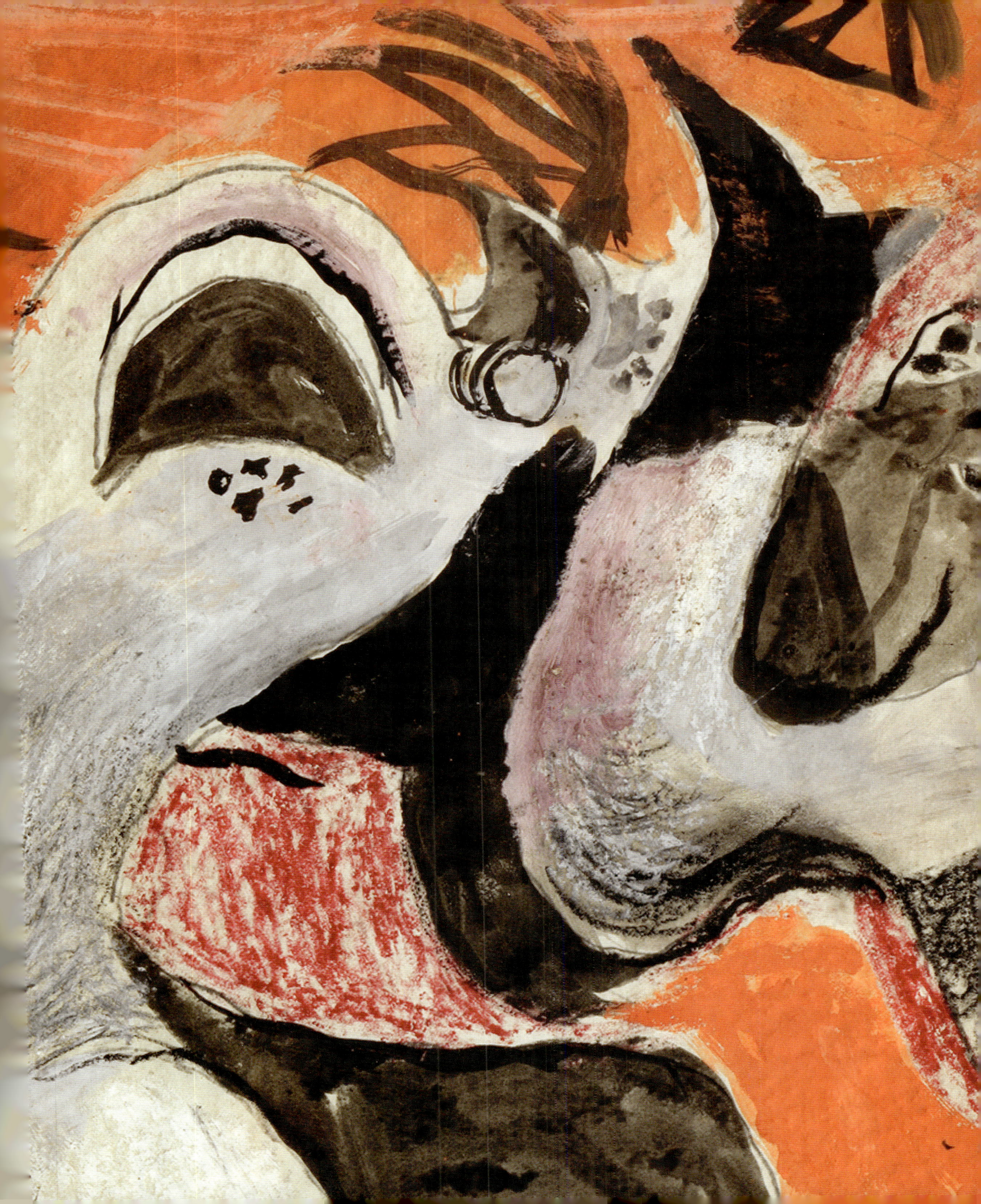

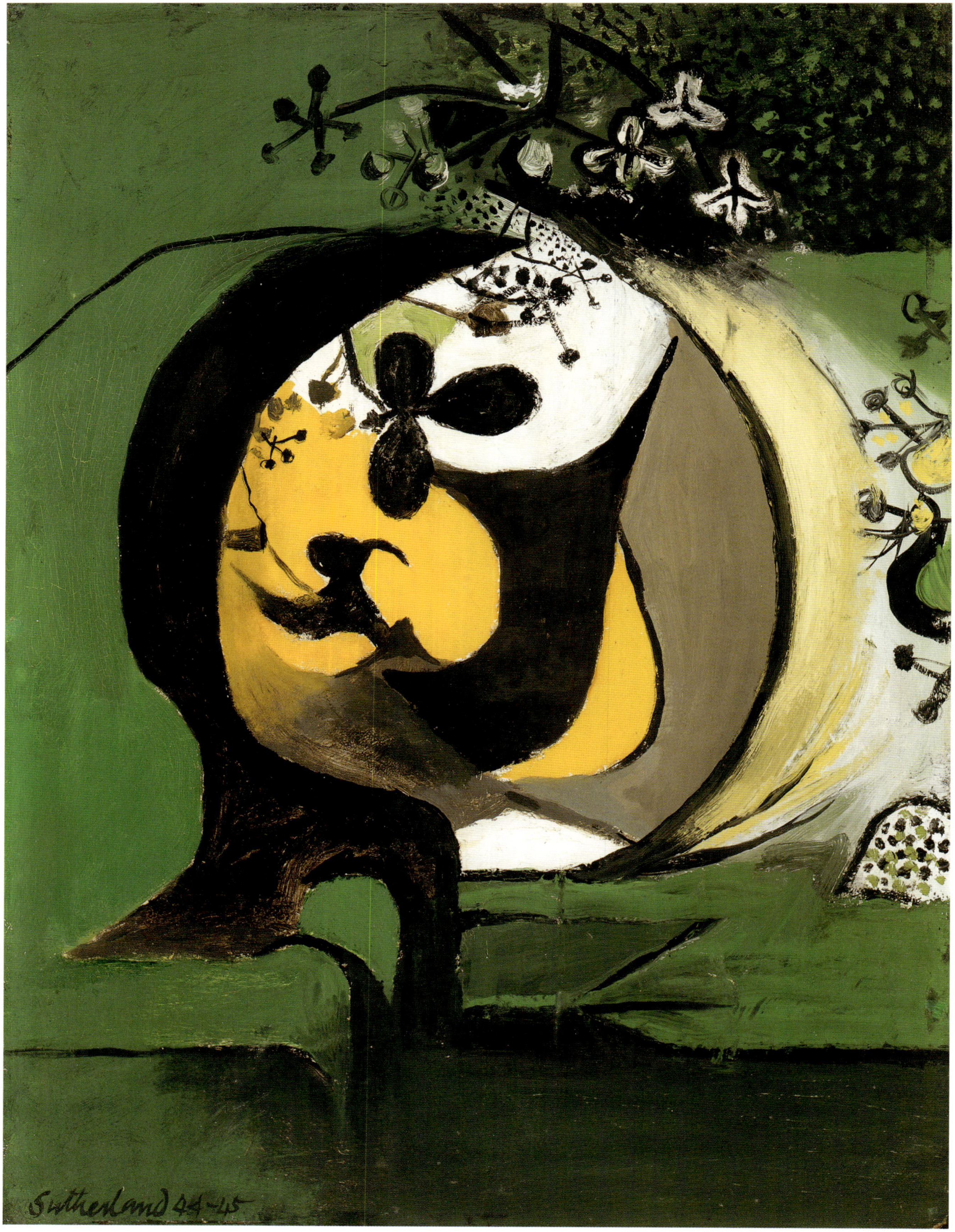

74.
Lane Opening
1944–45
Oil on board
941 x 711 mm
Private Collection.

Cats 74 and 75 belong to a series of variants on a motif previously explored in *Entrance to a Lane*, 1939 (Tate N06190 – not exhibited).

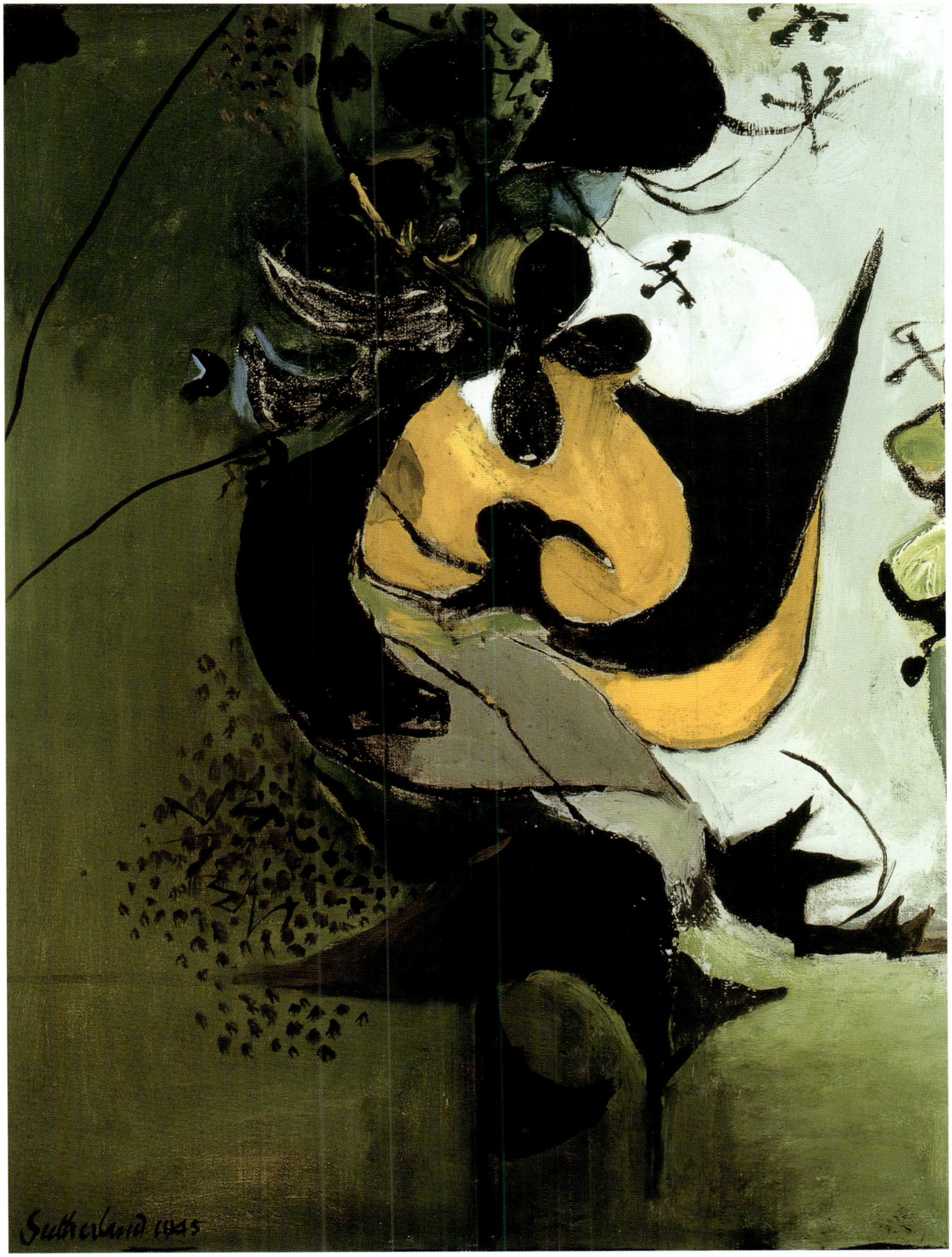

75.
Green Lane
1945
Oil on canvas
660 x 507 mm
Southampton City Art Gallery
1290.

About My Thorn Pictures

Graham Sutherland

Dear Curt Valentin,

About my thorn pictures; I can only give a clue, since the process of becoming involved with one's subject is always mysterious and not easy to explain. One reacts to the reality of tension in a subject, physical and spiritual or psychological; and that tension paraphrased and ordered should become immediate and intensified in one's painting.

I had been thinking of the Crucifixion (as you know I hope to attempt this subject for St Matthew, Northampton) my mind became preoccupied with the idea of thorns (the crown of thorns) and wounds made by thorns.

Then on going into the country I began to notice thorn trees and bushes. Especially against the sky, the thorns on the branches established a limit of aerial space. They were like dividers pricking out points in space in all directions, encompassing the air, as it were solid and tangible. I'd never noticed this before: but all kinds of ideas for pictures started to come into my mind. Apart from the large ""Thorn Trees" I had several ideas for "Thorn Heads." A sort of 'pricking' and demarcation of a hollow headshaped space enclosed by the points. All the paintings I have done started off with drawings and sketches direct from nature.

Yours,
Graham Sutherland 1-24-1946

(*Graham Sutherland*, exhibition catalogue, Buchholz Gallery, New York, 26 February – 23 March 1946)

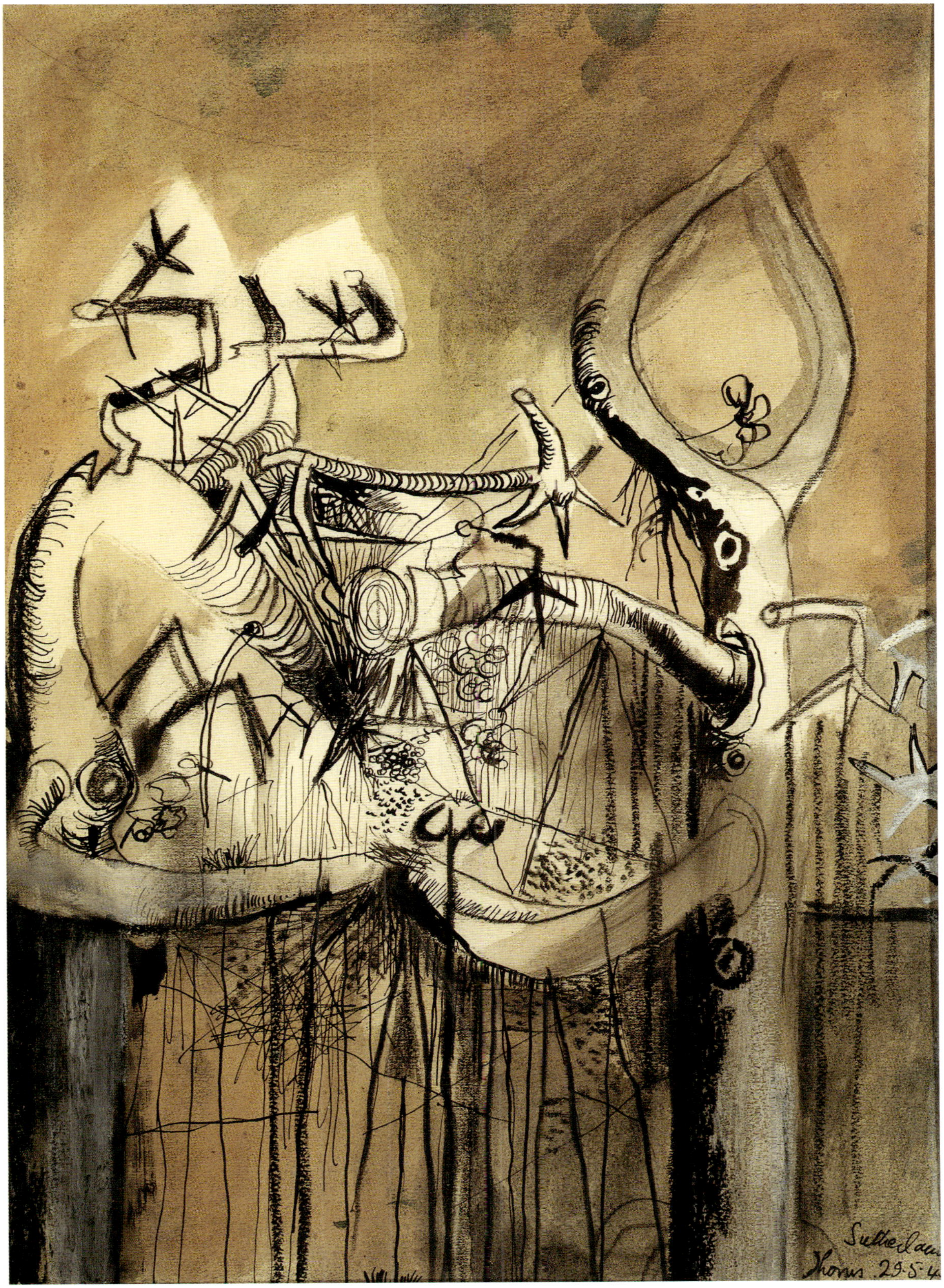

76.
Thorns
1945
Watercolour, chalk and ink on paper
410 x 315 mm
British Council
P2722.

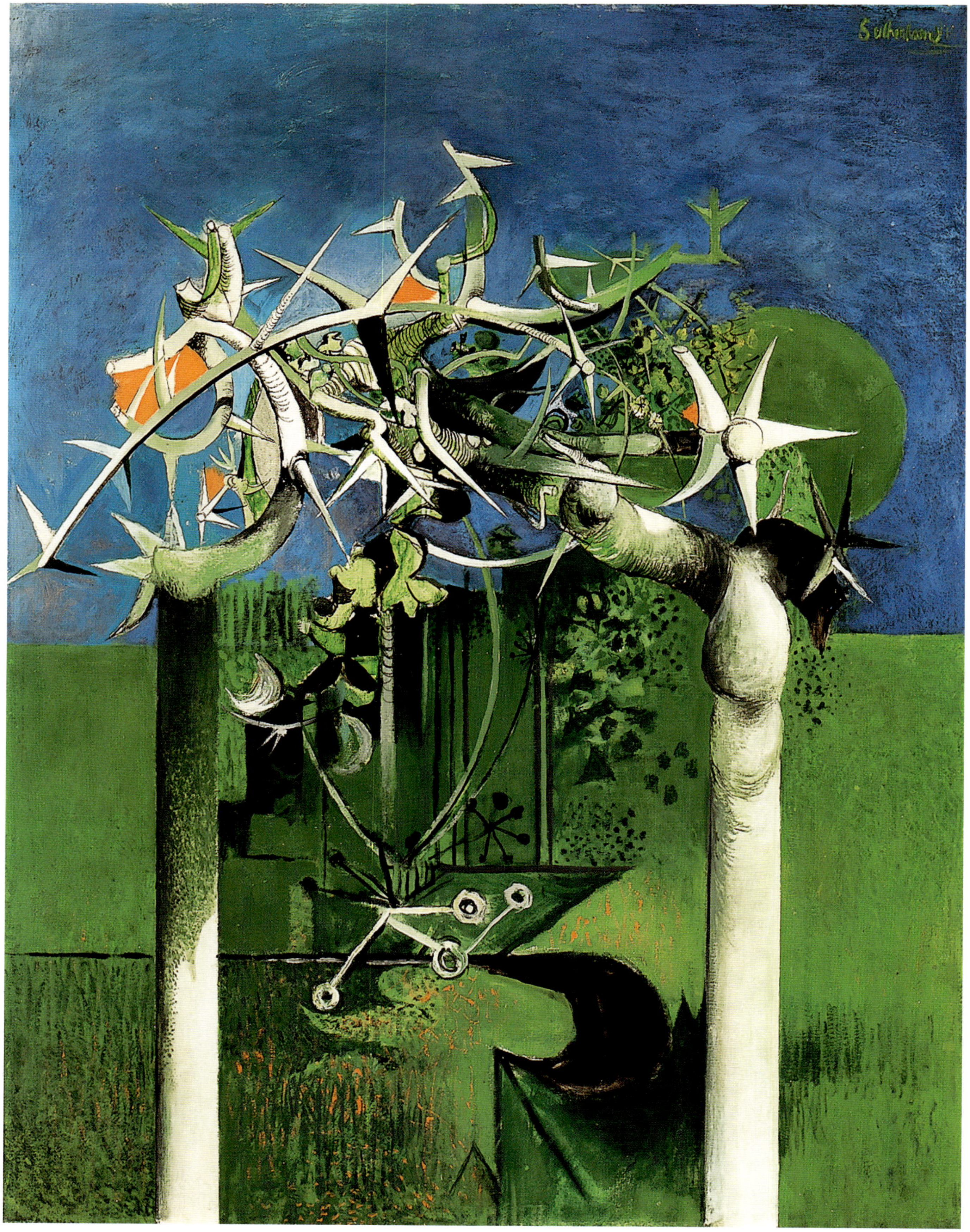

77.
Thorn Tree
1945–46
Oil on canvas
1270 x 1015 mm
British Council
P74.

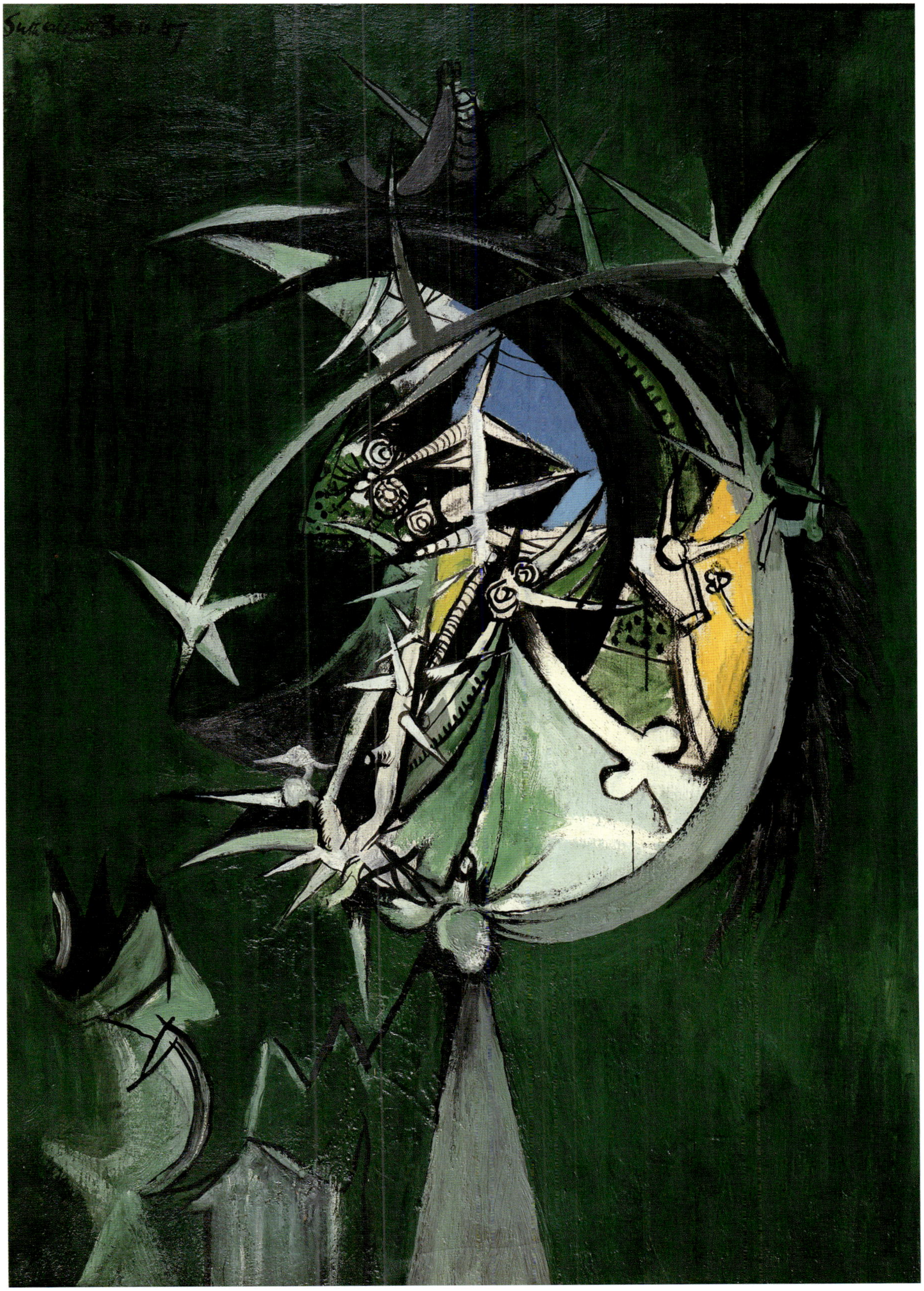

78.
Thorn Head
1947
Oil on canvas
1098 x 775 mm
Private Collection.

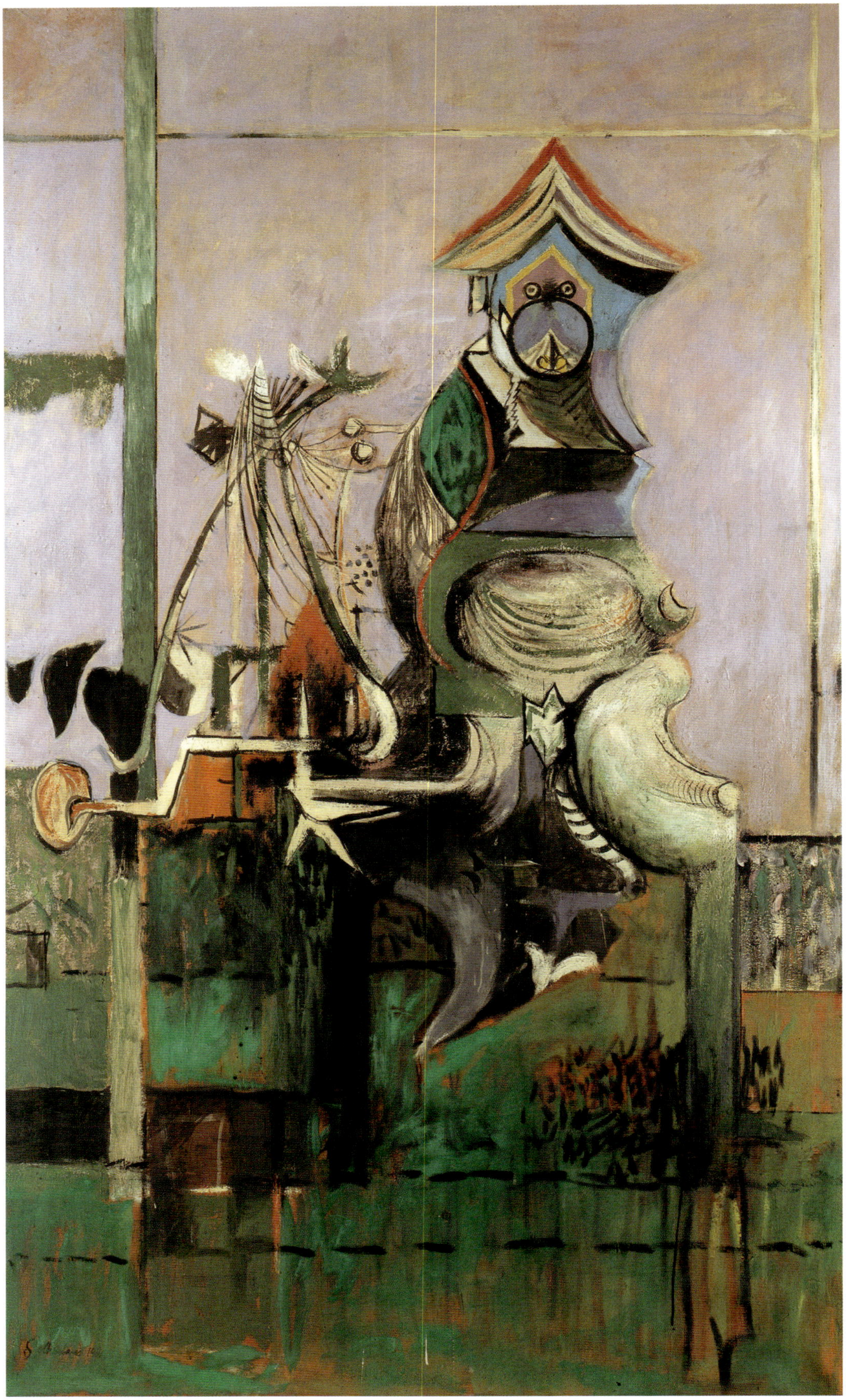

79.
Chimère I
1946
Oil on canvas
1970 x 1200 mm
Private Collection.

English Painting

Graham Sutherland

Sir,

In your issue of December 21st Mr Benedict Nicolson outlines the changes which have taken place during the last thirty years in the evaluation and development of English painting.

During the course of his argument – that English painting has gained by the enforced insularity of the war – Mr Nicolson writes of myself (and others) as having *turned their backs on Paris to seek inspiration in the English romantic movement of the early nineteenth century.*

I cannot let this pass. Current art criticism is peculiarly absolutist; and here is yet another example of the habit of art historians to over-simplify – to label, and to pigeonhole.

I do not deny that I received great adolescent stimulus from Palmer and Blake; but that does not mean that I turn my back on Paris. The question of influences is not as easy as that, and is surely a more complex and subtle matter than can be covered by such snap judgments.

Painters are affected by things which come to them from all over the place; from many kinds of painting and from many things.

One absorbs what one needs at a given time.

On the matter of insularity. Mr Nicolson affirms the impossibility of generalising about the virtue or vice of its effect on individuals.

Surely if English painting is to gain strength, in the long run it will do so in the open, where the eyes and mind are exposed to the widest variety of impressions; and not behind the sheltered wall.

Graham Sutherland

(*The New Statesman and Nation*, 25 January 1947, p. 74)

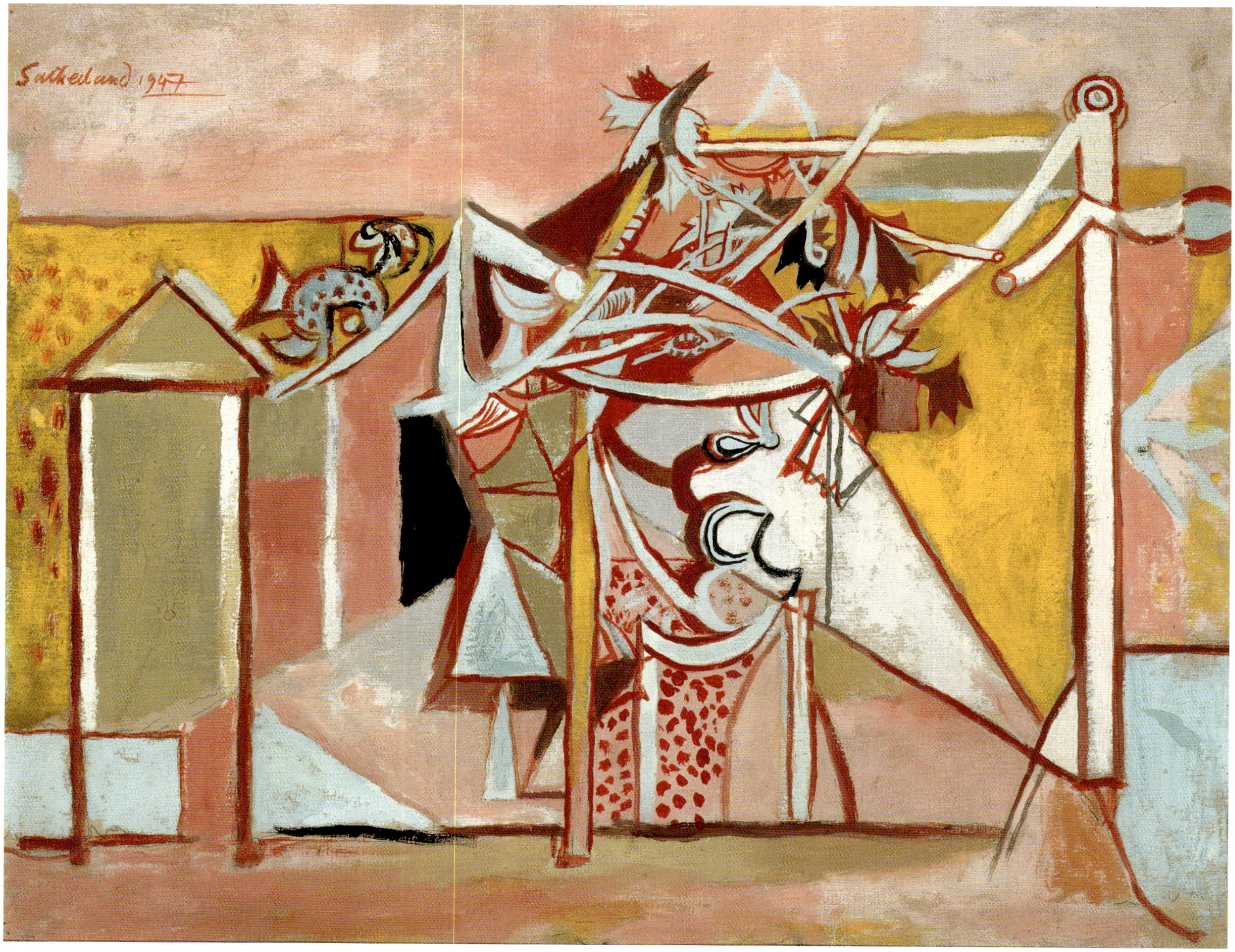

80.
Pink Vine Pergola
1947
Oil on canvas
508 x 648 mm
British Council
P46.

81.
Cigale
1948
Oil on canvas
663 x 497 mm
Redfern Gallery, London.

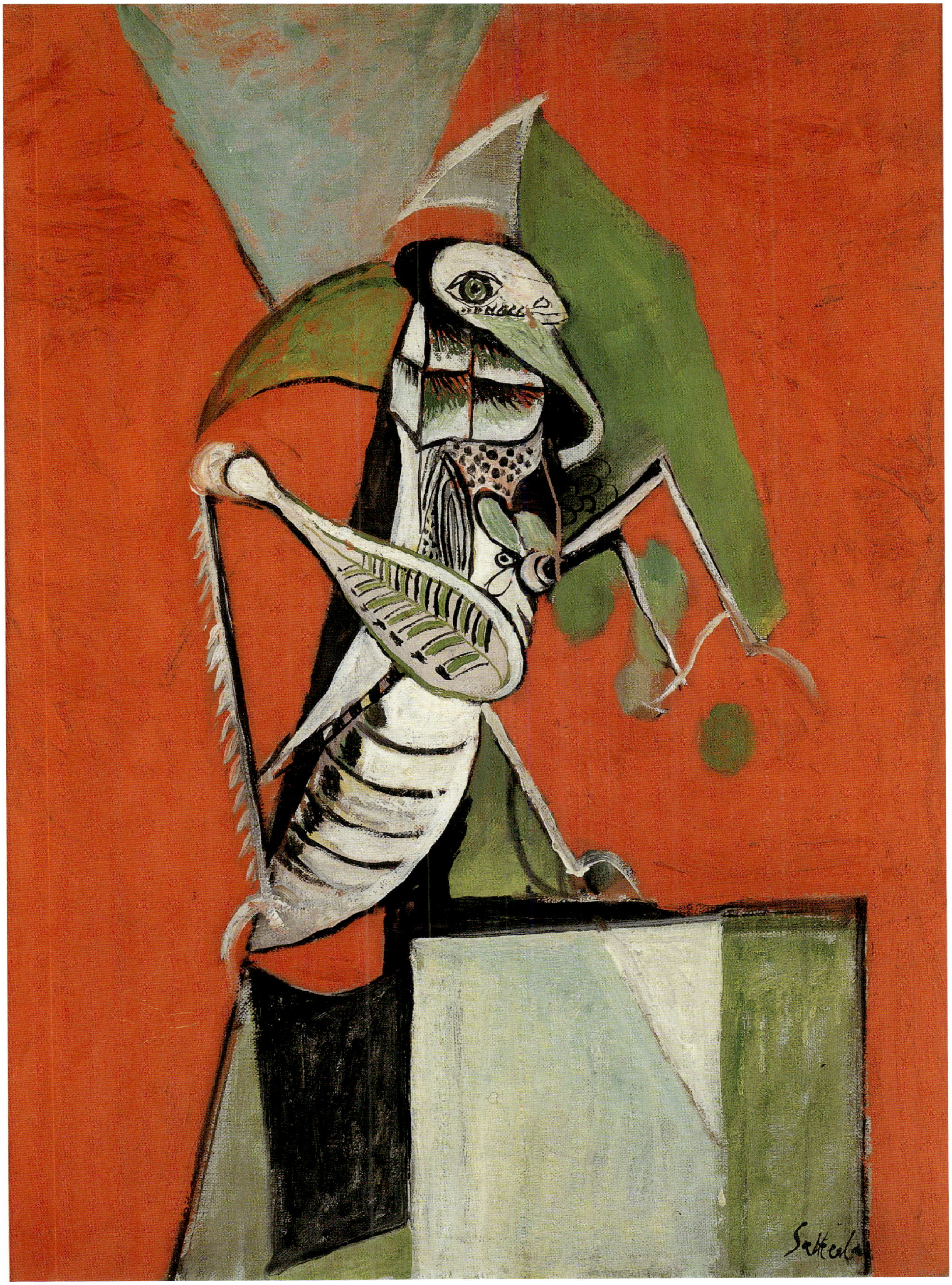

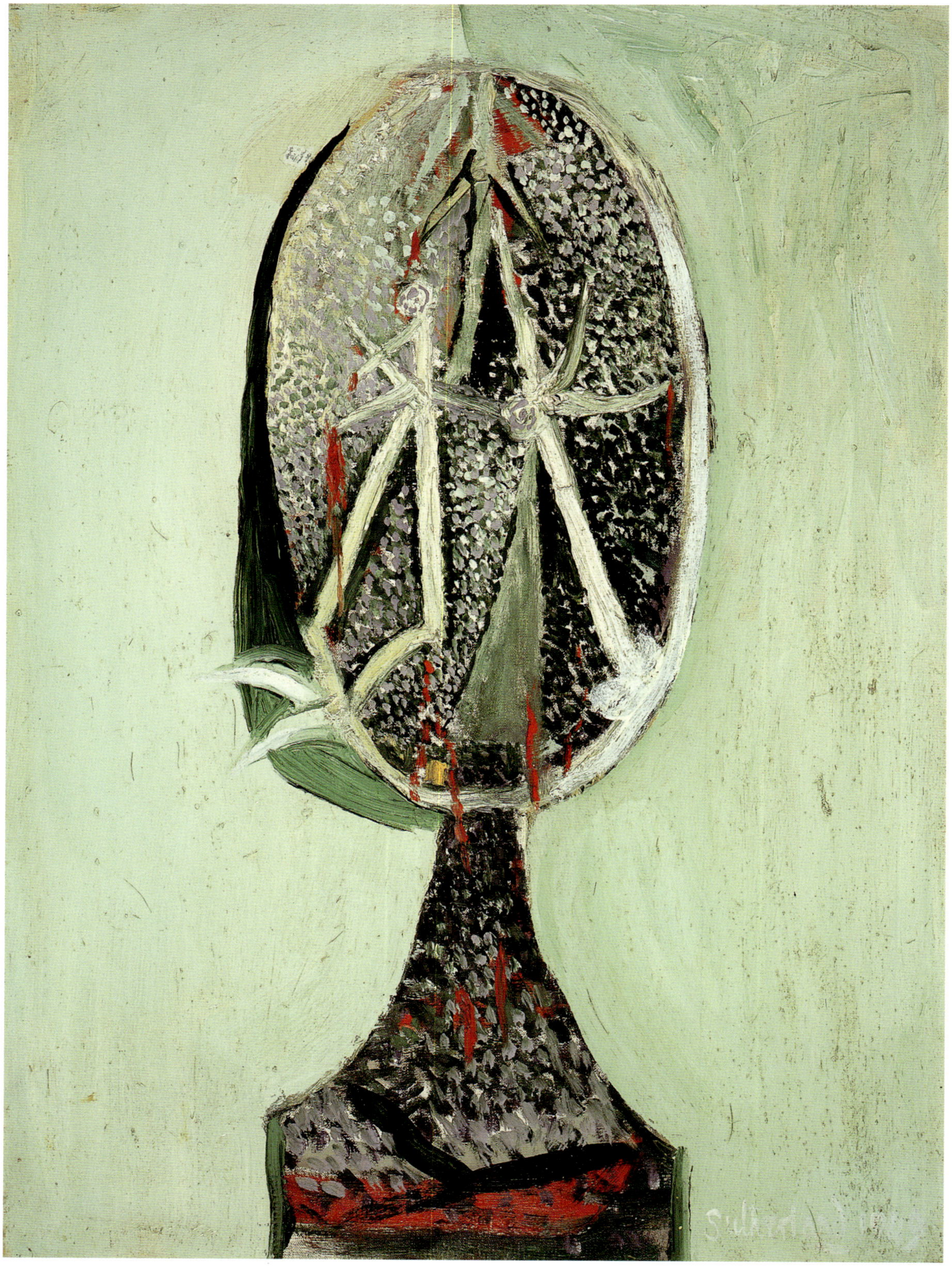

82.
Thorn Head
1949
Oil on canvas
607 x 460 mm
The Scottish National Gallery
of Modern Art, Edinburgh
GMA 1711.

83.
Standing Form
against a Hedge
1950
Oil on canvas
1346 x 1160 mm
Arts Council Collection,
Hayward Gallery, South Bank
Centre, London
AC188.

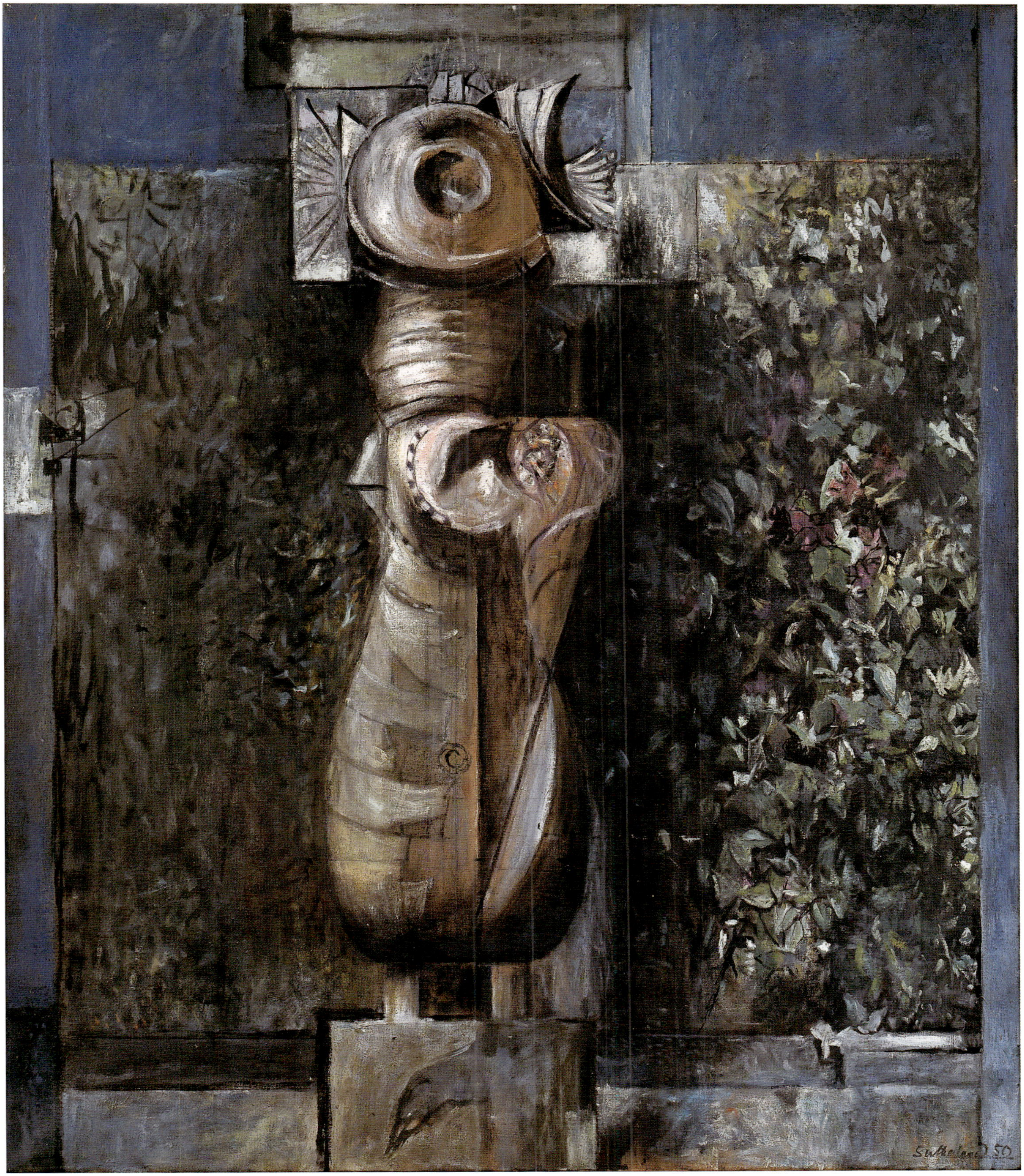

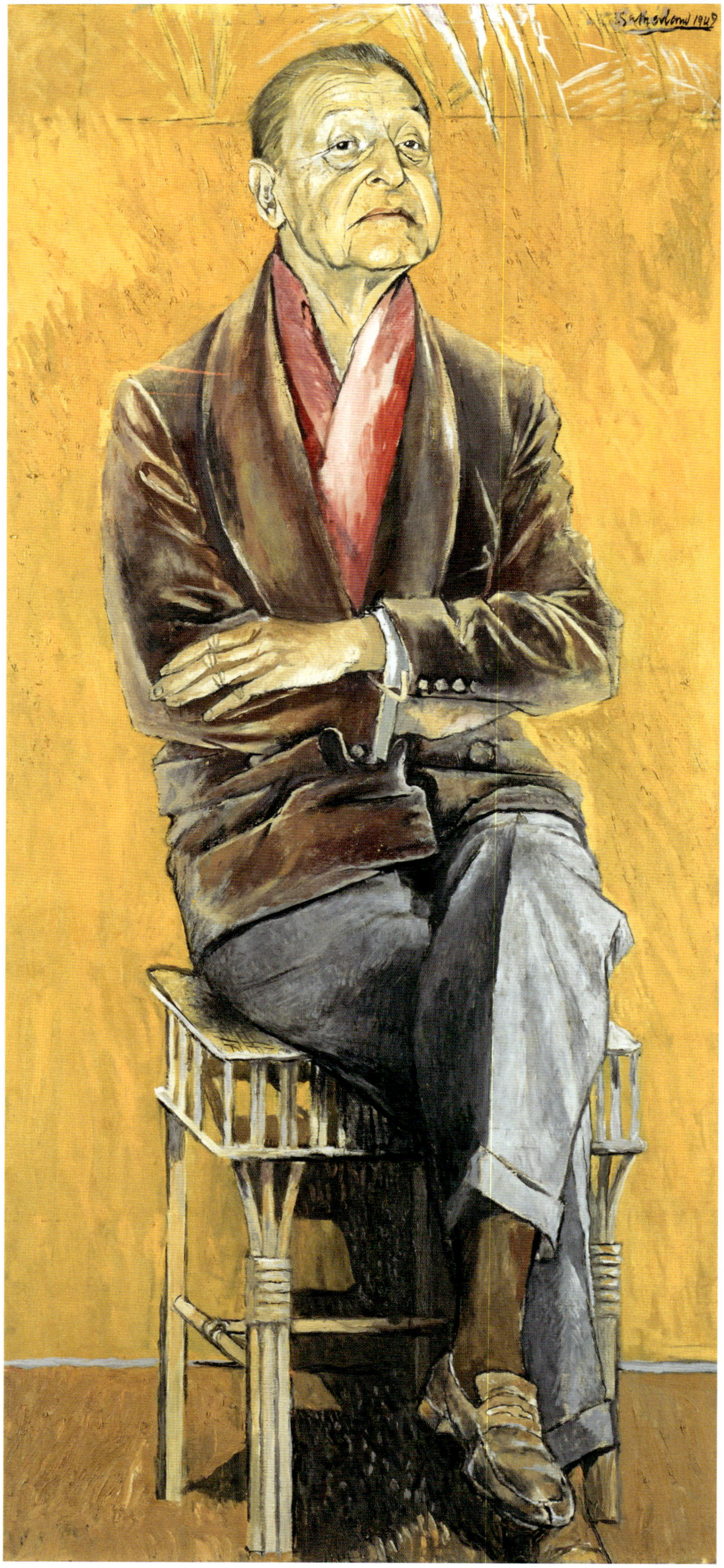

84.
Somerset Maugham
1949
Oil on canvas
1372 x 635 mm
Tate. Presented by
Lady John Hope 1951
N06034.

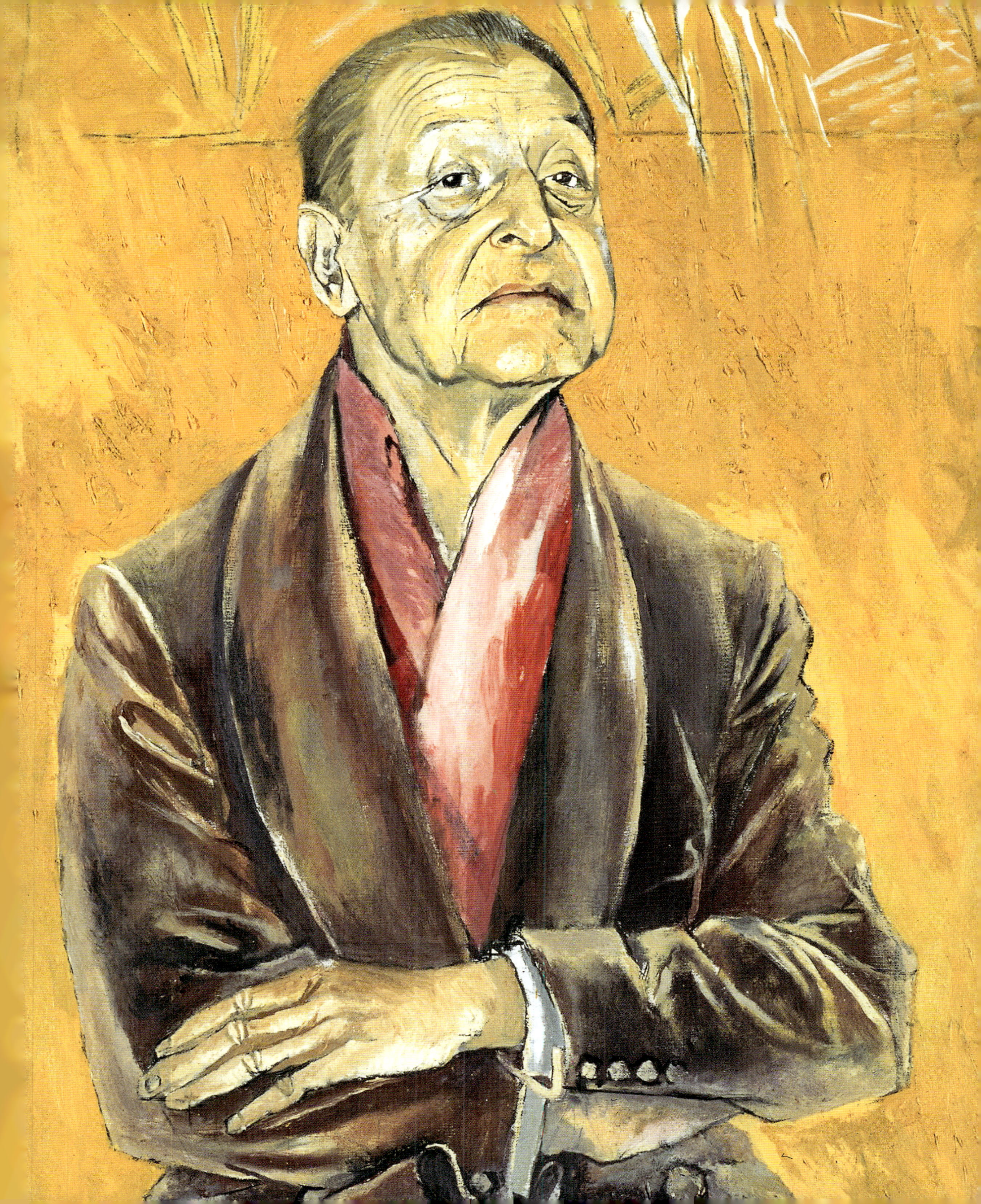

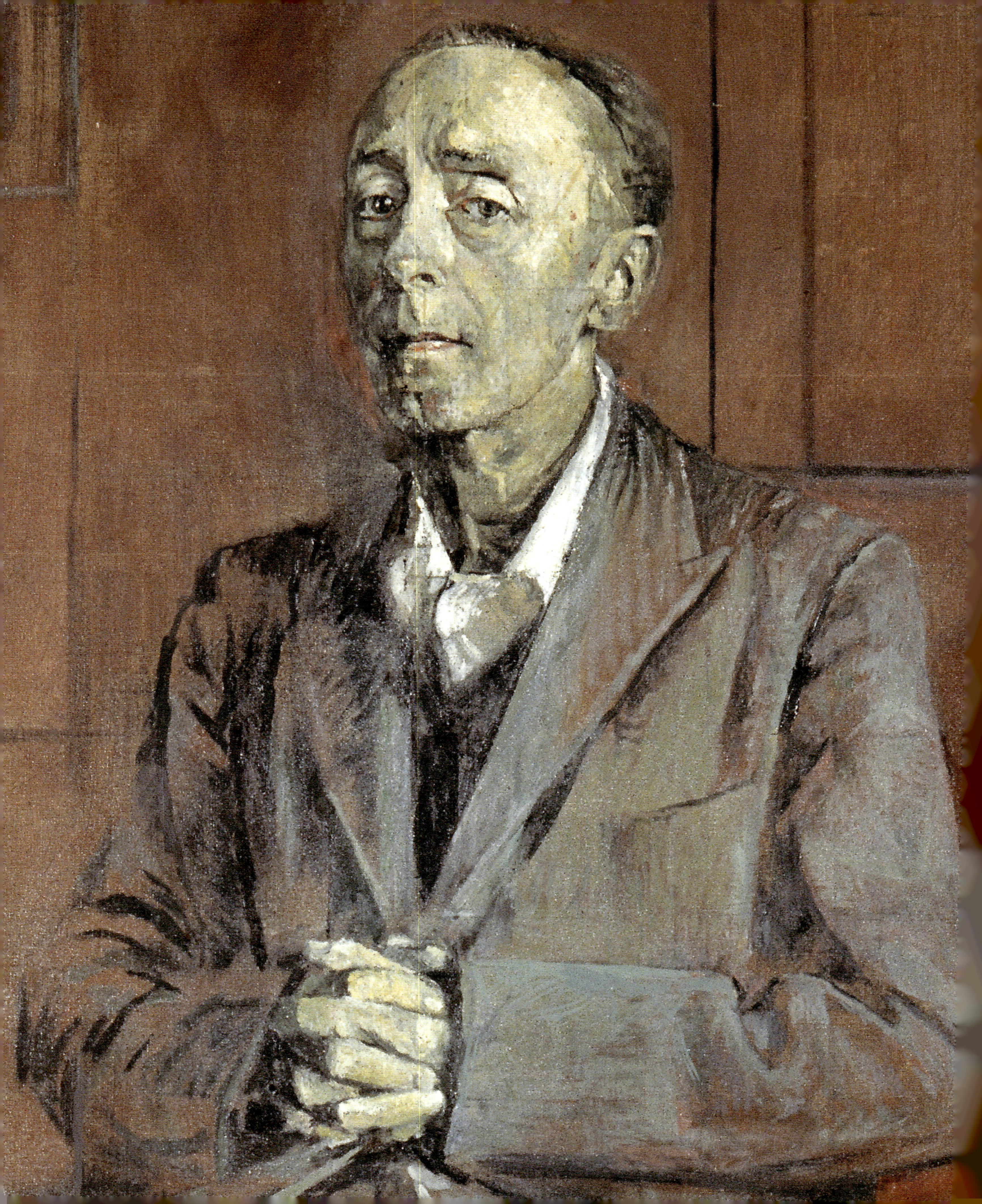

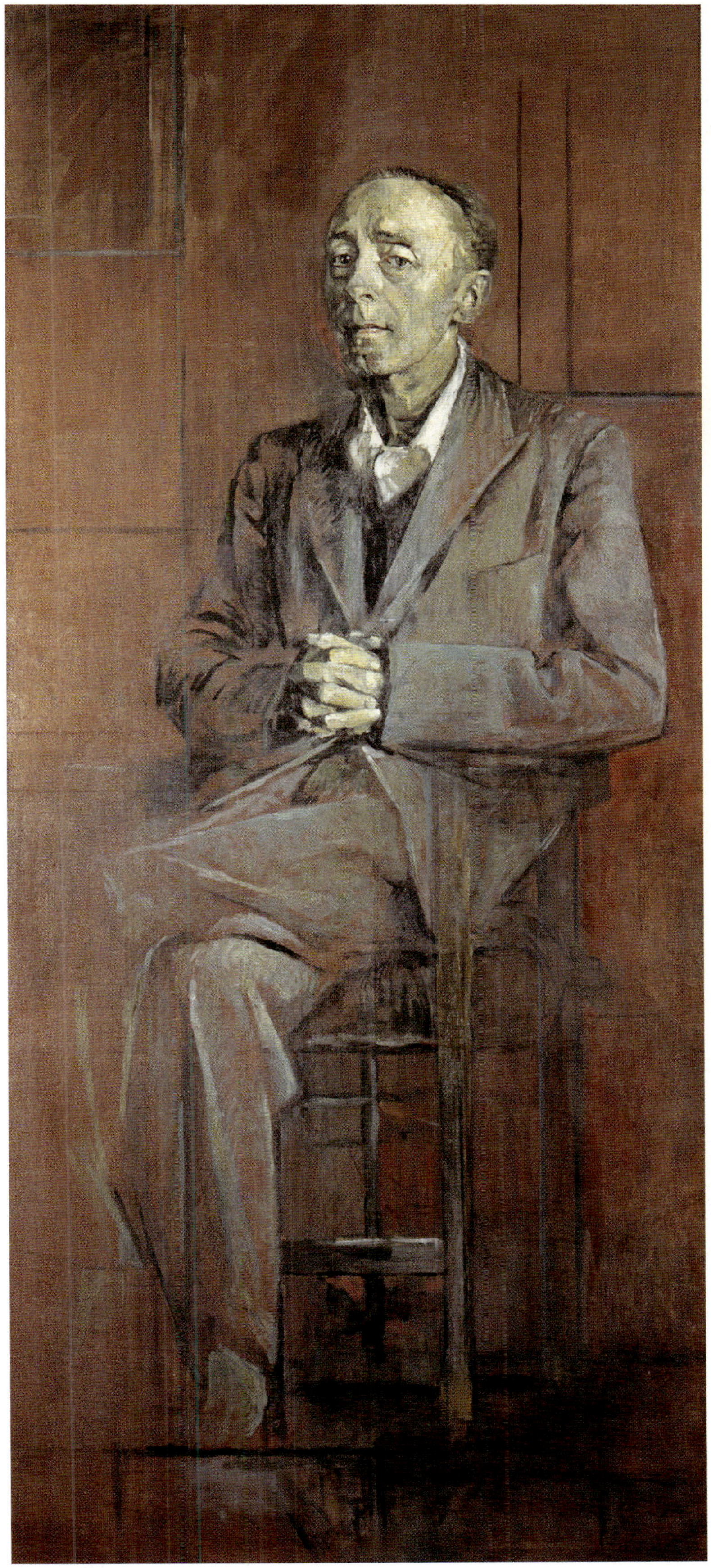

85.
The Hon. Edward Sackville-West
1953
Oil and gouache on canvas
1655 x 773 mm
Knole, The Sackville Collection, courtesy of the National Trust and Lord Sackville.

Graham Sutherland

Robert Melville

Sutherland's studio is a long, low room at the top of his house in the village of Trottiscliffe. It is lit by three windows, the largest of which overlooks the village green. It contains only essentials: easels, work-tables, a couple of chairs, a blackboard, a chest of drawers filled with a jumble of art books, sketch-books and paint rags, a roughly made cabinet with pull-out trays for drawings and water-colours. Two four-foot tubular lights stand up vertically from the floor and come into use when the daylight is bad or when he paints at night. (Sometimes he was painting until two o'clock in the morning when working on the Northampton Crucifixion.) There are no amenities: the floorboards are bare; the chairs not particularly comfortable. Everything is in sharp contrast with the comfort and elegance of the rooms downstairs. But the contrast with the studios of those painters of the past who achieved an equal fame in mid-career is greater still. The studio used to be a kind of salon; Sutherland's is a private place, and the people who have been privileged to see him working on a canvas could be numbered on the fingers of one hand.

As one enters, one has a back view of the easels and the blackboard; they are close to the door, and are stretched across the width of the room like a barricade. One has to get past them and turn round before one sees the life that animates this room.

There were two nearly completed oils on the easels, and twelve water-colours, all the same size, were pinned close together on the blackboard. The images on both the canvases were related to one of the water-colours.

For a while one doesn't really see the pictures; one is exposed to a force, to something analogous to concentrated heat or light. And if one snaps the eye's engagement to stare through the big window at the village green, one finds that some of the actuality of the scene has ebbed away; the cluster of cottages, the Inn with one of the Hanoverian kings on its signboard, and the road curving out of sight at the point where it meets two oast-houses turn into sentimental symbols; seem less real than the painted canvases. One's glance through the window discovers nothing, and simply records a typical rural scene, but the paintings confront one with the evidence of an intense concentration of all the artist's faculties upon the distinctiveness of things.

A small book bound in blue boards was lying on one of the work-tables. 'I wondered it you had read it,' Sutherland said. 'The commentary on personifying and synaesthetic images is absorbing. It's not unconnected with what I am attempting in my pictures.' It was *Aeschylus in his Style*, by Professor W. B. Stanford of Dublin University.

Several passages had been marked in red pencil. I started to read a verse quotation that was so marked, but was stopped by the phrase, *brightness from an ancient vine*, for it perfectly described the paintings of Vine Pergolas that were in Sutherland's last exhibition.

I said that I had heard that he was returning to the South of France soon, and asked him whether it has become essential to his painting to spend part of the year on the *côte d'azur*.

'It doesn't have to be the South of France,' he answered. 'I go away to find sunlight, and it doesn't particularly matter where I find it. The winter sun in England can be miraculous – can define objects with the utmost purity – but unfortunately one doesn't know beforehand the days on which it will break through. It isn't that I have to *paint* in sunlight, but objects are more alive, more thrilling, more mysteriously themselves when I find them in sunlight.'

We spoke of chance, then, as a factor in that process of 'finding'. 'The mystery of chance is fascinating,' he said. 'Why is it that sometimes one can be thrilled by a thing one day and find on the next that it seems to have no meaning? What causes that peculiar fusion and dovetailing of the senses at certain times? It's something of that kind that draws me to the Casino ... there are times when one makes all the right movements, and one's whole interior mechanism places the chips.'

'Downstairs,' I said, 'I noticed among your books Maritain's *Art and Scholasticism*, the novels of Mauriac, Graham Greene and Evelyn Waugh, and Claudel's *The Satin Slipper*; I suppose there's nothing particularly significant in that, except that the first and last are not read in this country nearly as much as one would expect them to be, considering their exceptional qualities ... I suspect that it's because the English translations are published by a rather narrowly Catholic firm. I expected to find them here because you are a Catholic ... Do you think that your Catholicism has any effect upon your work?'

I think he found this question rather naïve, but he answered me indulgently enough. 'I became a convert in 1928, a year before my marriage, and it was my wife who was the immediate instrument of my conversion. But I found it quite natural to become a Catholic – it was like coming home. The Church objectifies the mysterious and the unknown. It gave my aspirations towards certain ends a more clearly-defined direction than I could ever have found alone. It gave me a conception of a system whereby all things created, human and otherwise, down to the smallest atom – and its constituents – are integrated. It widened and superseded my vague pantheism. It also gave me a sense of tradition and of being a member of society. Even now I cannot go into a church on the Continent without feeling a curious thrill at being present at the enactment of mysteries which are enacted in precisely the same way in practically every country in the world, often at the same time. The sense of the canalisation of thoughts and energies on so vast a scale dumbfounds me. As to the effect on my work – who can say?'

My question was not really an attempt to find out something about his private life. It arose out of a strong feeling that his art does in fact express a religious attitude, although it rarely proclaims itself in symbols. And I can at least speak of the occasion that first gave me an inkling of it, although it really amounted to no more than an analogy between the general overtone of his last exhibition (held at the Hanover Gallery in June 1948) and a famous line from Marlowe that, so to speak, uttered the emotional impact of the pictures. The dominant colour in those pictures, as everyone who saw the show will remember – for it flamed out – was a hot, gong-like note, a luminous widening stain, of, I suppose, a kind of dark pink, and Marlowe's line came into my head through the din of a confused, unanalysable response: '*See how Christ's blood streams in the firmament.*' I was, I felt, simply the chance point of intersection where the meeting took place, and it could have occurred in anyone who knows Marlowe's line as a kind of reeling in the brain.

The end of my visit was approaching, and I took my last look at the two nearly completed canvases on the easels.

The canvases were tall and narrow; the images were portraits of heavy, massive root forms. One of them had particularly and uncannily the look of a portrait. It had two very short thick legs and stood on a kind of model's platform, with a piece of cloth pinned up casually behind it. It had many protrusions and a pitted surface, and could be called an Ubu of the plant world. It was not beautiful, but somehow wonderfully perfect in itself. It was not a caricature of the human, but so real a personality that one felt, in one's nerves, that the model came of its own accord for sittings. It had great monumentality but was very far from the calm idealistic forms conceived by the classical spirit; it expressed rather a sense of evolving tissue and inspired restlessness. The subtle use of a portrait schema – of a category of painting which is understood by everyone as a magical procedure for perpetuating a human presence – to define a vegetable form makes one sharply aware of being involved in that stream of creation where, after a short time, we all must drown. It could be the expression of a vague pantheism, yet I was certain that it was more than that, for I was aware of the presence of a personality within the structure of the forms that was not to be confused with the artist's characteristic moulding of his material: Sutherland had observed the root with an intensity that had transformed observation into insight.

Everything began to work out now and fall into place. In Stanford's book on Aeschylus, I found this passage marked in red: '*Aeschylus is outstanding in the boldness and vividness of his personifying metaphors. By them he creates a new kind of world in which grief can bite, fire and water are conspirators, the heart can wear a black robe ...*'. In another place he quotes an amazing line which is both a personifying and synaesthetic image; a line which Sutherland had already pointed out to me: '*The reek of human blood smiles out at me.*' Stanford speaks of a similar metaphorical usage in devotional poets like Herbert, Crashaw and Gerard Manley Hopkins, where it is a sign of a 'mystical sense of the unity of experience'.

Sutherland sometimes extends the range of an object by means of a pictorial parallel with a fully-developed Aeschylian metaphor, as when the Crown of Thorns, becoming a Thorn Head, assumes the attributes of a mocker, and its harmfulness laughs. But, in general, although he coins forms in much the same way as a poet coins words, he transforms the nature of an object without any marked alteration of its forms; he imbues an inanimate object with behaviour; it rises up or turns, it nudges or climbs upon another, it stares – but with all its being, it laughs, but not imitatively; its laughter is as mysterious as 'laughter in the eyes'. He is so conscious of the individuality of things that he comes to look upon a root or a leaf or a stone or even an entire landscape as a person. And I suddenly realised that these pictures which have broken down the categories of painting, and insist upon a still life or a landscape becoming at the same time a portrait, are what Gerard Manley Hopkins calls *inscapes*.

There is a passage in Hopkins' *Note-books* in which the act of perceiving an *inscape* is seen to be the reception of news of God: '*All things therefore are charged with love, are charged with God and if we know how to touch them give off sparks and take fire, yield drops and flow, ring and tell of him.*' It is in this sense that Sutherland's paintings can never be predicted and will always take us by surprise, for he perceives natural forms as individual utterances of God 'outside Himself'. It is in this sense, too, that we can speak of him not only as a great painter, but as a great Catholic painter.

In the art of extreme situations which dominates our time, Sutherland, 'looking upon the object as worthy of a personal love', creates works which are the pure antithesis of what Votan calls the 'concentration camp universe' of the Sartrean existentialists.

(*World Review*, February 1952, pp. 61–64)

Index of Works

Page numbers in **bold** refer to works illustrated.

Bacon, Francis
Painting, 1946 33, **34**, 38
Three Studies for Figures at the Base of a Crucifixion, 1944 **33**
Blake, William, The Blighted Corn from Thornton's *Pastorals of Virgil*, 1821/c. 1830 (Cat. 1) **51**

Karsh, Yousuf, *William Somerset Maugham* 40, **41**

MacQuitty, William:
Graham Vivian Sutherland; Lee Miller, 1943 **12**
Out of Chaos: photographs from the set **8**, **29**
Masson, Andre, *Ibdes in Aragon*, 1935 (Cat. 16) 16, **75**
Moore, Henry, *A Miner at Work*, 1942 (Cat. 54) **125**

Nash, Paul, *Landscape of the Megaliths*, 1934 (Cat. 15) 21, **74**

Palmer, Samuel:
A Cornfield by Moonlight, 1862–32 **23**, 24
The Herdsman's Cottage, or Sunset, 1850 (Cat. 3) **53**
Opening the Fold, or Early Morning, 1880 (Cat. 4) **54**
The Valley Farm, c. 1828 (Cat. 2) 13, **52**
Picasso, Pablo, *Guernica*, 1937 **18**, 20, 104, 144

Sutherland, Graham:
Association of Oaks, 1940 (Cat. 29) 18, **90**
Blast Furnace, 1942 (Cat. 61) **132**
Brimham Rock (published poster), 1937 **65**
Brimham Rock – study for the poster, 1937 (Cat. 12) 15, 21, **66–7**
Chimère I, 1946 (Cat. 79) 37, 38, **42**, **160**
Cigale, 1948 (Cat. 81) **163**
Clegyr-Boia, 1938 (Cat. 21) 15, **82**
Cornstook in a Landscape, 1945–46 (Cat. 70) **148**
Cray Fields, 1925 (Cat. 8) 11, 12, **58**
Crucifixion, 1946 33, **35**, 37, 44, 144–5
Dark Hill, 1940 (Cat. 28) **22**, **89**
Design for Poster, c. 1940 (Cat. 39) **106**
Devastation: City, Ruined Machinery, 1941 (Cat. 44) **112–13**
Devastation, City 1941: Fallen Lift Shaft, 1941 (Cat. 46) **115**
Devastation: House in Wales, 1940 (Cat. 40) **30**, **107**
Devastation 1941: An East End Street, 1941 (Cat. 42) 31, **109**
Devastation 1941: City, Twisted Girders, 1941 (Cat. 48) 28, **117**
Devastation 1941: East End, Burnt Paper Warehouse, 1941 (Cat. 43) **110–11**
Devastation 1941: East End, Factory Ventilation Shaft, 1941 (Cat. 45) **114**
Devastation 1941: East End, Wrecked Public House, 1941 (Cat. 41) **108**
Devastation in the City: Twisted Girders Against a Background of Fire, 1941 (Cat. 47) 28, **101**, **116**
Drawing of Tree Roots (with squaring), c. 1938 (Cat. 19) **79**
Dwarf Oaks, 1941 (Cat. 35) 26, **96**
Fallen Tree against Sunset, 1940 (Cat. 30) **91**
Feeding a Steel Furnace, 1941–42 (Cat. 59) 32, **130**
Folded Hills, 1943 (Cat. 68) 32, **146–7**
Foundry: Hot Metal has been Poured into a Mould and Inflammable Gas is Rising, 1941–42 (Cat. 58) **129**
Garden, The, 1931 (Cat. 11) 12, **61**
Gorse on a Sea Wall, 1939 (Cat. 24) **11**, 18, **19**, 20, 26, 28, 32, 70, **85**
Green Lane, 1945 (Cat. 75) **155**
Green Tree Form, 1940 (Cat. 33) 10, 24, **94**
Green Tree Form: Interior of Woods, 1940 (Cat. 34) 10, **17**, 18, 20, **95**
Hollow Tree Trunk, 1938 (Cat. 23) **84**
Horned Forms, 1944 (Cat. 72) 26, 33, **150–1**
Landscape with Rocks (Wolf's Castle), 1939 (Cat. 27) **88**
Lane Opening, 1945 (Cat. 74) **154**
Limestone Quarries – General View II, 1942 (Cat. 65) **137**
Limestone Quarry: Loosening Stone, 1942 (Cat. 62) **133**
Marshalling Yards, Trappes, 1944 (Cat. 66) **138**
Marshalling Yards, Trappes, 1944 (Cat. 67) **139**
Maugham, Somerset, 1949 (Cat. 84) **166–7**

Midsummer Landscape, 1940 (Cat. 32) 20, 26, 28, **93**
Miner Probing a Drill Hole, 1942 (Cat. 53) 28, **124**
Mountain Road with Boulder, 1940 (Cat. 37) 26, **98**
Number Forty-Nine (Cat. 6) 12, **56**
Opencast Coal Production: Dragline, 1943 (Cat. 64) **136**
Opencast Coal Production: Excavators, 1943 (Cat. 63) **134–5**
Pastoral, c. 1930 (Cat. 10) 46–7, **60**
Pecken Wood, 1925 (Cat. 5) **55**
Pembrokeshire Landscape – Valley above Porthclais, 1935 (Cat. 13) **71**
Pink Vine Pergola, 1947 (Cat. 80) **141**, **162**
Poems 1937–1942 (David Gascoyne), illustrations to **24**, 25, 37
Red Landscape, 1942 (Cat. 38) 26, **99**
Red Tree, (two versions), 1936 (Cats 17–18) 10, 13, 16, 26, 42, **76**, **77**
Sackville-West, The Hon. Edward, 1953 (Cat. 85) **168–9**
Slag Ladles, 1942 (Cat. 56) **127**
Standing Form against a Hedge, 1950 (Cat. 83) 12, 40, **165**
Studies for Midsummer Landscape, 1940 (Cat. 31) **92**
Study of Road Rising Between Hedges, 1940 (Cat. 26) **87**
Sunrise Between Hedges, 1939 (Cat. 25) **63**, **86**
Sunset in between Hills, 1938 (Cat. 20) **80–1**
Tapping a Blast Furnace, 1941–42 (Cat. 60) **131**
Tapping a Steel Furnace, 1943 (Cat. 55) **126**
Thistles and Sun, 1945 (Cat. 71) **149**
Thorn Head, 1949 (Cat. 82) **165**
Thorn Head, 1947 (Cat. 78) **36**, 37, **159**
Thorn Tree, 1945–46 (Cat. 77) **158**
Thorns, 1945 (Cat. 76) **157**
Tin Mine – A Declivity, 1942 (Cat. 49) 28, **118–19**
Tine Mine: Emerging Miner, 1942–43 (Cat. 51) 28, **122**
Tine Mine – Miner Approaching, 1942 (Cat. 50) 28, **120–1**
Tree Form, 1941 (Cat. 36) 25, **97**
Tree Forms in Estuary, 1939 (Cat. 22) **83**
Twin Ladles, 1941 (Cat. 57) **128**
Twisted Tree Form, 1944 (Cat. 73) 33, **152–3**
Two Miners Drilling, 1942–3 (Cat. 52) 28, **123**
Village, The, 1925 (Cat. 7) 11, 12, **57**
Welsh Landscape with Roads, 1936 (Cat. 14) 12, 13, 16, 21, **72–3**
Wood Interior (also known as *The Forest*), 1929–39 (Cat. 9) **59**

Further Reading

R. Alley, *Graham Sutherland*, exh. cat., London: Tate Gallery, 1982

J. Andrews (ed.), *Graham Sutherland. Correspondences. Selected Writings on Art*, Pembrokeshire: The Graham and Kathleen Sutherland Foundation, 1982 (collection of writings and interviews)

N. Barber, *Conversations with Painters*, London: Collins, 1964 (interview)

R. Berthoud, *Graham Sutherland*, London: Faber and Faber, 1982 (authorized biography)

R. Berthoud, 'Sutherland, Graham Vivian (1903–1980)', in *Oxford Dictionary of National Biography*, Oxford: Oxford University Press, 2004

Blast to Freeze: British Art in the 20th Century, exh. cat., Kunstmuseum, Wolfsburg/Hatje Cantz, 2003

G. Bruno (ed.), *Graham Sutherland: Storia Segreta 1922–1979*, Genova: Edizioni Colombo, 1991

D. Cooper, *The Work of Graham Sutherland*, London: Lund Humphries, 1961

D. Corbett, Y. Holt and F. Russell (eds), *The Geographies of Englishness: Landscape and the National Past 1880–1940*, New Haven and London: Yale University Press, 2002

P. Fuller, 'Nature and Raw Flesh: Sutherland and Bacon', in Boris Ford (ed.), *The Cambridge Guide to the Arts in Britain. Volume 9: Since the Second World War*, Cambridge: Cambridge University Press, 1988, pp. 119–30

M. Garlake, *New Art New World: British Art in Postwar Society*, New Haven and London: Yale University Press, 1998

D. Gascoyne, *Poems 1937–1942*, London: Nicholson and Watson, PL Editions, 1943 (illustrations by Sutherland)

D. Gascoyne, 'PL Editions and Graham Sutherland', in *David Gascoyne: Selected Prose 1934–1996*, London: Enitharmon, 1998

Graham Sutherland, London: Bernard Jacobson Ltd, 1993

Graham Sutherland: Early Etchings, London: Gordon Cooke, 1993

Graham Sutherland: The Early Years 1921–1940, exh. cat., London: Goldsmith's Gallery, 1986 (text by Nanette Aldred)

Graham Sutherland: Nature into Art, exh. cat., Swansea: Glynn Vivian Art Gallery, 2004 (text by David Alston)

Graham Sutherland O.M. (1903–1980): A Retrospective, exh. cat., London: Crane Kalman Gallery, 1999

M. Hammer, *Bacon and Sutherland*, New Haven and London: Yale University Press, 2005

M. and S. Harries, *The War Artists*, London: Michael Joseph, 1983

J. Hayes, *The Art of Graham Sutherland*, London: Phaidon, 1980

W. Hussey, *Patron of Art*, London: Weidenfield and Nicholson, 1985

J. Hyman, *The Battle for Realism*, New Haven and London: Yale University Press, 2001

F. Mann (ed.) *Eight European Artists*, London, Melbourne, Tokyo: William Heinemann Ltd, 1954

D. Mellor (ed.), *A Paradise Lost: The Neo-Romantic Imagination in Britain 1935–55*, exh. cat., London: Barbican Art Gallery, 1987

R. Melville, *Graham Sutherland*, London: Ambassador Editions, 1950

E. Newton, *In My View*, London: Longman Green & Co., 1950

Portraits by Graham Sutherland, exh. cat., London: National Portrait Gallery, 1977

R. Rosenblum, *Modern Painting and the Northern Romantic Tradition: Friedrich to Rothko*, London: Thames and Hudson, 1975

E. Sackville-West, *Graham Sutherland*, The Penguin Modern Painters (K. Clark, ed.), Harmondsworth: Penguin, 1944

G. Soavi, *The World of Graham Sutherland*, London: Zwemmer, 1973

J. T. Soby, *Contemporary Painters*, New York: Museum of Modern Art, 1948

P. Stansky and W. Abrahams, *London's Burning: Life, Death and Art in the Second World War*, London: Constable, 1994

Sutherland: Une Rétrospective, exh. cat., Antibes: Musée Picasso, 1998

Sutherland: The War Drawings, exh. cat., London: Imperial War Museum, 1982

R. Tassi, *Graham Sutherland: Complete Graphic Work*, London: Thames and Hudson, 1978

R. Thuillier, *Graham Sutherland Inspirations*, Guildford: Lutterworth Press, 1982

M. Yorke, *The Spirit of Place: Nine Neo-Romantic Artists and their Times*, London: Constable, 1988.

Credits

Photographic Credits

Figure illustrations

Figs 1 & 7: William MacQuitty International Photographic Collection, London.

Fig. 3: Courtesy of the National Portrait Gallery, London.

Figs 4 & 11: Bridgeman Art Library, London.

Fig. 5: British Museum, London.

Fig. 9: Tate, London 2005.

Fig. 10: DIGITAL IMAGE © 2005, The Museum of Modern Art / Scala Florence.

Fig. 12: Camera Press Ltd.

Fig. 13: Courtesy of the Shell Art Collection.

Catalogue illustrations

Cats 1, 8, 10, 14, 16, 22, 34, 41, 42, 43, 53, 58, 59, 60, 72 & 84: Tate, London 2005 (14, 16, 42, 53: Photography John Webb).

Cats 2, 3, 4 & 9: British Museum, London.

Cats 5, 6, 7, 27, 29, 71 & 82: The National Galleries of Scotland Picture Library / Photography: Antoina Reeve Photography.

Cats 11 & 57: Ashmolean Museum, Oxford.

Cat. 12: Courtesy of the Shell Art Collection.

Cat. 13: Leicester Galleries, London.

Cats 17, 19, 20, 26, 35, 37, 39, 68, 79: Matthew Hollow Photography.

Cats 18, 38, 40, 44, 48, 75: Bridgeman Art Library, London (www.bridgeman.co.uk).

Cat. 21: Doncaster Museum and Art Gallery M.B.C.

Cats 23, 52, 65 & 73: Laing Art Gallery, Newcastle upon Tyne (Tyne and Wear Museums).

Cat. 24: Photograph reproduced with the kind permission of the Trustees of the National Museums and Galleries of Northern Ireland.

Cats 25, 36, 49, 51, 63, 64, 66 & 67: Leeds Museums and Galleries / Bridgeman Art Library, London.

Cat. 28: Swindon Museum and Art Gallery / Photography: John Gibbons Studio.

Cat. 30: Darlington Arts Centre / Photography: Les Golding.

Cats 31, 32 & 61: Birmingham Museums and Art Gallery.

Cats 33, 50, 62, 76, 77 & 80: British Council / Photography: Rodney Todd White & Son, London.

Cat. 45: Bolton Museums, Art Gallery and Aquarium.

Cats 46 & 70: Whitworth Art Gallery, University of Manchester.

Cats 47, 54 & 56: Imperial War Museum.

Cat. 55: Private Collection / Photography: Rodney Todd-White & Son.

Cat. 74: Private Collection.

Cat. 78: Private Collection.

Cat. 81: Redfern Gallery, London.

Cat. 83: Arts Council Collection, Hayward Gallery, London / Photography: Mike Fear, 2005.

Cat. 85: The National Trust Photographic Library.

Further Copyright Credits

Images

Francis Bacon (Fig. 9): © Tate, London 2005.

Francis Bacon (Fig. 10): © Estate of Francis Bacon 2005. All rights reserved, DACS.

Yousuf Karsh: © Camera Press Ltd.

William MacQuitty (Figs 1, 3 & 7): © Estate of William MacQuitty.

Andre Masson (Cat. 16): © ADAGP, Paris and DACS, London 2005.

Henry Moore (Cat. 54) has been reproduced by kind permission of the Henry Moore Foundation.

Paul Nash (Cat. 15): © Tate, 2005.

Pablo Picasso (Fig. 4): © Succession Picasso/DACS 2005.

Text

Kenneth Clark © Estate of Kenneth Clark

Robert Melville © Estate of Robert Melville